The Technology Connection: Building a Successful Library Media Program

Kathleen Schrock, Editor

A Publication of THE BOOK REPORT & LIBRARY TALK
Professional Growth Series

Linworth Publishing, Inc.
Worthington, Ohio

Library of Congress Cataloging-in-Publication Data

The technology connection : building a successful library media program / [edited] by Kathleen Schrock.
    p. cm. -- (Professional growth series)
   Includes bibliographical references.
   ISBN 1-58683-008-2
1. School libraries--United States. 2. Instructional materials centers--United States. I. Schrock, Kathleen. II. Series.

Z675.S3 T247 2000
027.8--dc21

                                                                              00-044818

Published by Linworth Publishing, Inc.
480 East Wilson Bridge Road, Suite L
Worthington, Ohio 43085

Copyright © 2000 by Linworth Publishing, Inc.

Series Information:
      From The Professional Growth Series

All rights reserved. Reproduction of this book in whole or in part is prohibited without permission of the publisher.

ISBN 1-58683-008-2

5 4 3 2 1

Table of Contents

ABOUT THE EDITOR viii
INTRODUCTION ix

CHAPTER 1: DRAWING THE PLANS: LIBRARY MEDIA SPECIALIST AS ARCHITECT 1
   Overview 1
   From School Librarian to "Information TeAchnician" by Janet Murray ... 2
       An article to help LMS meet the challenges of the information age
   Taking the Internet Challenge: Using Technology in Context
      by Michael B. Eisenberg 6
       An argument for the concept of a unified print/nonprint library
   Managing a Constantly Changing Array of Machines, Programs
      and Processes by Edna M. Boardman 9
       Overview of daily life in an automated library media center
   The Sound of the Other Shoe Dropping by Doug Johnson 11
       Become the relevant information specialist in your school
   Information Power Prepares Library Media Programs for a New Age
      by Steve Baule 12
       A well thought-out discussion of the Information Power standards
   I Think I Can, I Think I Can by Alice H. Yucht 14
       Helpful tips for coping with change in the library media program
   Reflections on *Information Power: Building Partnerships for
   Learning.* What is a Librarian to Do? by Harry Willems 17
       A positive argument for the importance of LMS
   Help! Why Isn't the Smiley Face Smiling? By Steve Baule 18
       A simple plan for dealing with technology in your school
   5 Issues in Planning for Library Technology by Paul Rux 19
       A brief article that will make you think about your
         technological vision
   Integrating Technology Into Schools: Eight Ways to Promote Success
      by Bob Hoffman 20
       An overview of a successful technology use plan
   Implementing School Technology: Calling on Teachers
      by Anthony B. Maddox 22
       Involving teachers with the decision-making enhances
         the technology
   Copyright Laws & Software by Carol Mann Simpson 24
       An overview of what you can do to make sure the
         computers stay legal
   How Much, How Many and When? Copyright and Multimedia?
      By Carol Simpson 25
       An overview of the multimedia guidelines for fair use of 1996
   Technostress: What Is It? Can You Learn to Live with It?
      by Carol Smallwood 27
       Practical tips for making your daily job stress-free
   Technology & Stress: Are They Inseparable? by Becky Mather 29
       Proactive ideas for dealing with technology problems
         ahead of time

Table of Contents continued

A Fractured Technology Fairy Tale by Barbara Johnson 31
    A tongue-in-cheek story of inappropriate computer use

Building Arks for the New Technology by Judi Repman
and Teresa K. Blodgett.. 32
    Steps for renovations of library media centers

Organizing the Planning Team by Steve Baule 36
    Examples of effective long-range technology planning teams

Scheduling the Computer by Martin D. McKay 39
    Create a student management team to be responsible for
        computer access

Librarians Are From Venus, Technologists Are From Mars
by Doug Johnson 41
    Traits of the effective melding of LMS and technologist

A World of Change in 12 Short Years by Janet Hofstetter 43
    How many changes have you seen in your library media center?

Evaluating School Library Information Services in the Digital Age
by Nancy Everhart 45
    Research and evaluation processes in the library media center

Know-How to Help Kids Know Now by Lesley S. J. Farmer 47
    How to train your volunteers to assist with technology

105 Things Parent Volunteers Can Do–Other Than Raising Funds
by Andrea Troisi 50
    A great list of ideas for planning to use parents in the LMC

Braving the Waters, or How To Get Your Computing "Feet" Wet
by Pat Miller 53
    Practical tips on how to become a techno-wiz in no time

Crystal Ball Gazing into Library Land by Lesley Farmer 55
    A look into the future of school library media centers

The Right Filter for the Wrong Addresses: Regulating Net Access
by Carol Simpson 57
    A well thought-out article dealing with filtering of Net sites

Caveat Emptor: Looking the Internet Gift Horse in the Mouth
(Searching) by Sharon McCaslin 60
    Thoughts dealing with open access to the Internet

Another Look at Acceptable Use Policies By Carol Williamson 62
    An overview of the parts of a student AUP

CHAPTER 2: GATHERING THE TOOLS: LIBRARY MEDIA SPECIALIST AS GENERAL CONTRACTOR 65
  Overview 65
  Ergonomics: The Forgotten Variable by L. Jeffrey Fitterman 67
    Important considerations for the physical access to computers

  Educational Applications for Digital Cameras by Terence Cavanaugh
  and Catherine Cavanaugh 70
    Detailed analysis of digital cameras and their options

  Author! Author! Implications for Collection Development
  by Lesley S. J. Farmer.. 73
    Options for multimedia authoring programs at different grade levels

Table of Contents continued

Selecting and Evaluating Software by Carol Mann Simpson 75
    A series of questions to assist in evaluating software in some detail

How to Write a Winning Grant Proposal by Madeline Buchanan............ 76
    A simple, down-to-earth article with suggestions for writing grants

Proposal Writing for Technology Money: Part I
    by Richard Alan Smith 78
    In-depth information for writing RFPs

Proposal Writing for Technology Money: Part II
    by Richard Alan Smith 81
    Additional tips and pointers for writing grants for your LMC

Think Money in the Bank for Your School by Mary R. Hofmann 83
    Author shares successful grant-writing ideas

Moving Beyond Sneaker Net by Lesley S. J. Farmer 85
    A comprehensive overview of the planning of a network

How to Choose the Network Layout That's Right for You
    by Lesley S. J. Farmer.. 88
    An easy-to-understand description of network topologies

Growing Your LAN Piece by Piece by Lesley S. J. Farmer 90
    Well-done descriptions of routers, repeaters, bridges and switches

Now that You Have the Technology, How Do You Keep
    It Up and Running? by Becky R. Mather 92
    Priority-setting and teaming to help the technology keep working

Networkese: Jargon You Need to Know by Joe Huber 94
    A dictionary of terms to help you talk to maintenance
        specialists and vendors

Hardware Troubleshooting by Carol Simpson..................................... 96
    A reproducible checklist to allow computer users to
        diagnose a problem

How to Minimize the Dangers of Macro Viruses
    by Paul A. Ekhaml and Leticia Ekhaml 97
    Explanations of what triggers to look for when identifying
        virus problems

CHAPTER 3: SOUND FOOTINGS: THE LIBRARY MEDIA SPECIALIST BUILDS THE FOUNDATION 99

Overview 99

Fantasy and Fact in Computer Training by Lesley S. J. Farmer 101
    An argument for point-of-need training of teachers

Teacher Training Is Key by Paula Yohe 102
    A TechQuest model for training teachers to use technology

Ten Tips for Attracting Teachers to Technology Workshops
    by Robert Kirsch and David Miller 102
    Strategies for training workshops that work

Stage a Well-Designed Saturday Session and They Will Come!
    by Miguel Guhlin.. 104
    Tips for the design of a technology training program for teachers

Singing the Praises of On-site Training by Sandy Pope 106
    How to create tailor-made training sessions for your teachers

Table of Contents continued

A Model for Teacher-Directed Technology Training
  by Barbara Siegel 108
    The use of mentor teachers to build technology expertise

Integrating Technology from the Classroom Up
  by Miguel Guhlin 111
    How to empower teachers to use the technology effectively

Boolean Burritos: How the Faculty Ate Up Keyword
  Searching by Sherry York 113
    A super idea for a successful search training session

Web Page Evaluation: Views from the Field
  by Nancy Everhart 115
    A useful checklist for teachers to use for evaluation of Web sites

The CODE 77 Rubrics: Part 1 by Doug Johnson 118
    Graduated performance indicators for teachers' use of technology

Rubrics for Restructuring (Continuation of the CODE 77 Rubrics)
  by Doug Johnson 121
    Higher level performance indicators for teachers' use of technology

Workshops for Teacher Partners in Technology Integration
  by Lesley S. J. Farmer 124
    Characteristics of a comprehensive staff development program

Partnering with Teachers for Internet Incorporation
  by Lesley S. J. Farmer 127
    Concrete ways to work with teachers on Internet use
      in the classroom

The Upgrade: Easing Into Technology Integration
  by Doug Johnson 130
    Ten common classroom activities that can be "Internetized"

Professional Development They Will Cheer For!
  By Linda Skeele 131
    Practical, useful ideas for successful staff development

Philadelphia Library Power: Collaboration Form
  by Debra Gniewek 134
    A useful form for planning lessons with the classroom teacher

Ten Terrific Tips for Elementary Teachers by M. Gale Lyons 136
    Practical ideas for the integration of technology in the lower grades

What's in a Name? By Joe Miller 137
    The basics of creating, viewing, and sharing computer files

Matching Teaching and Learning Styles by Gil Caudill 140
    Helping teachers use technology for addressing the
      multiple intelligences

Teaching Ethical Technology Behaviors by Doug Johnson 143
    The importance of modeling ethical technology use for students

CHAPTER 4: BUILDING THE STRUCTURE: THE LIBRARY MEDIA SPECIALIST AS CARPENTER 145
  Overview 145
  How to Teach the 'Net by Lesley S. J. Farmer 146
    Modeling the process of effective Internet use for students

Table of Contents continued

Perfect Partners: Technology and Integrated Instruction
    by Nadine K. Hinton and Linda Orlich 148
        The benefits of incorporating technology across the curriculum

Harnessing Internet Resources for the Student Researcher
    by Carol Simpson 150
        An overview of how best to integrate Internet resources

Turn on to Reading Through Technology
    by Lesley S. J. Farmer 152
        Targeting the teaching of reading using the new tools

The Purpose of Information and Technology Assignments:
    Process or Product? By Betty Dawn Hamilton 154
        Ideas to help library media specialist measure the product/process
          of a research report

Putting Computer Skills in Their Place by Doug Johnson 156
        Technology and information literacy skills standards for students

A Research Project Filled with Real World Technology
    by Sharron L. McElmeel 157
        Great ideas for real-world research projects

The Changing Face of Student Research by Doug Johnson 160
        Performance-based assessment and primary sources

Empowering Young Women Through Technology
    by Lesley S. J. Farmer 161
        Methods and suggestions for narrowing the technology
          "gender gap"

Why Students Should Use Multimedia by Katherine Bucher 165
        Sample multimedia projects for research activities by students

Guidelines for Effective Multimedia Design
    by Elizabeth Downs and Kenneth Clark 167
        Practical design examples for teaching and using multimedia

Authentic Assessment of Information Literacy Through
    Electronic Products by Lesley S. J. Farmer 169
        The concept and tenets of authentic assessment

Yes, They Put on Quite a Show, but What Did They Learn?
    By Joanne Troutner 172
        Ideas and rubrics for effective assessment practices

Getting What You Ask For by Doug Johnson 175
        The library media specialist's role in designing
          performance-based assessments

Tailoring the Internet to Primary Classrooms by Kathy Tobiason 176
        Ideas and practical technology suggestions for the
          early learning years

Quick! May I Go on the Internet? by Barbara D. Stahl 178
        Rationale for teaching students to make the correct choice
          on the Web

Traveling Down the Highway: Stations on the Way to Information
    Literacy by Margaret Kernan 179
        A model for information literacy stations in the LMC

Table of Contents continued

What Do They Really Need to Know? Adventures in Curriculum
  Writing by Amy Pritzl 181
    A super list of skills for students in technology and
      information literacy
Making the Most of E-Mail by Leticia Ekhaml 185
    Netiquette practices for successful e-mail communications
Adventures In E-Mail Land by Joyce Kasman Valenza 187
    Sample projects and lessons learned from the use of e-mail

Chapter 5: Inspections: The Library Media Specialist as Building Inspector 189
Overview 189
The ABC's of Web Site Evaluation by Kathy Schrock 190
    A checklist of 26 critical evaluation criteria
6 Steps to Simplifying Student Searches by Joyce Valenza 192
    A model for introducing searching to grade nine students
Boning Up on Boolean Searching by Linda Turrell 194
    A concise explanation of Boolean searching and the Net
The Honeymoon is Over: Leading the Way to Lasting Search Habits
  by Melissa Pierson 195
    Explanation and tips for teaching the differences between
      search engines and subject directories
It Must Be True. I Found It on the Internet! by Kathleen Schrock 198
    A sample lesson to teach students to validate information
      found on the Web
Easy to Find but Not Necessarily True by Steve Baule 201
    Evaluation of Web sites and the need to include print sources
Seduced and Abandoned on the Web by Mark Williams 202
    Helping students look past the "glitz" to evaluate the information
Producing Information Consumers: Critical Evaluation and
  Critical Thinking by Kathleen Schrock 206
    Overview of the importance of teaching critical thinking skills
How to Use Soda Pop, The Blair Witch Project, and Other Methods
  to Help Students Learn to Evaluate Web Information Critically
  by Kathleen L. Spitzer 208
    A lesson model for teaching critical evaluation strategies
Webliographies: Much More Than Just a Bibliography
  by Nancy Robinson Marino 210
    Teaching students to evaluate information critically by giving
      them a place to start

Chapter 6: The Open House: Library Media Specialist as Host/Hostess 213
Overview 213
Getting the Year off to a Good Start! By Jacqueline Seewald 215
    Practical ideas for getting ready for the new school year
Don't Forget PR! By Katherine T. Bucher 217
    Ways to publicize positive technology use in the LMC
Technology: A Goldmine for Positive PR by Rocco Staino 218
    More ideas about using technology to promote technology

Table of Contents continued

Library Home Pages: A New Knowledge Environment
by Lesley S. J. Farmer 219
    Simple suggestions for creating and maintaining a library
        Web page

Parent Internet Driving School: Using Technology to Increase Parent
Involvement in Schools by Debbie Abilock 222
    A parent technology-training model to use as public relations
        and support

Techno-Parenting by Doug Johnson 224
    The use of e-mail communication to ensure parent support

Guerrilla Librarianship: Hold the Camouflage! By Joyce Valenza 225
    Tips and ideas for being assertive and keeping your program
        in the forefront

Making Friends in High Places by Cynthia K. Dobrez
and Lynn M. Rutan 227
    How to write a library media annual report that will be noticed

Successful Public Relations Efforts: Using the Departmental
Meeting as a Resource by Jacqueline Seewald 229
    Showcase library innovations at the smaller department meetings

Build Library Support With T.L.C. by Pat Miller 231
    Great ideas to publicize your library media offerings

Extra! Library Newsletters by Pat McAbee 232
    Ensure visibility for your LMC with a monthly newsletter

Two for the Road by Ann Dempsey 234
    Create a positive collaborative partnership with the teachers
        at your school

"Media" Starts With "Me": A Guide for Publicizing Library
and School Accomplishments by D. Jackson Maxwell 237
    Formal public relations ideas for promoting yourself and
        your program

Parent-Friendly Web Pages by Lesley S. J. Farmer 240
    Ideas for working with parent groups to become highly visible

Advocacy Building Influence at the Grass Roots Level:
Closing the School Year with Positive Public Relations
by Jacqueline Seewald 243
    Important and useful ideas to involve teachers with
        the LMC program

About the Editor

Kathleen Beck Schrock is the Technology Coordinator for the Dennis-Yarmouth School District on Cape Cod, Massachusetts. Kathy is the creator and maintainer of Kathy Schrock's Guide for Educators, an educational Web directory hosted by the Discovery Channel School. The Web site, a popular jumping-off place for teachers, may be found at <http://discoveryschool.com/schrockguide/>, and Kathy may be reached at kathy@kathyschrock.net.

Introduction

Building and maintaining a successful library media program in this day and age is an involved process. Whether you are considered a library media specialist, library manager, information specialist, technology coordinator, librarian, or instructional technology specialist, with the rapid growth of technology use in schools, your job responsibilities have most certainly shifted and changed. However, your goals to provide teachers and staff with information to support the curriculum and to prepare students to search, locate, and evaluate information have not changed. It does seem, at times, that the library media program and the role of the library media specialist have become unrecognizable as we worry about networks, acceptable use policies, filtering (or non-filtering), E-rate, and ink jet cartridges. It's time to step back and think about why we do what we do, why we do it successfully, and how we can continue to play an integral role in the information literacy arena in our schools.

The articles in this book have appeared in *Technology Connection, Library Talk,* and *The Book Report magazines* over the past five years. Although technology continues to evolve, all of the articles included have important tips, tricks, techniques, and suggestions that are useful as we think about our roles and programs. The title of this book, *The Technology Connection: Building a Successful Library Media Program,* is not meant to imply you do not already have a successful library media program in place. Instead, it is hoped that by reading the articles, you will learn of some successful practices that will help you "renovate" your program to be as successful as you know it can be.

The book is divided into six chapters, each dealing with a different aspect of the "building" process. Chapter One is titled *Drawing the Plans: The Library Media Specialist as Architect.* This chapter includes articles that inspire and validate the library media specialist's role in the school; tips for dealing with change and the inevitable stress accompanying it; and plans and ideas for Internet access, volunteer help, and much more. The articles were chosen to give you the background needed to set the "plans" in place for a model library media program.

Once the plans are in place, the next step in the building process is to hire a general contractor who brings the tools and subcontractors to the job. Chapter Two, *Gathering the Tools: Library Media Specialist as General Contractor,* includes articles dealing with the nitty-gritty details of setting up a technology-rich library media program. The topics cover everything from the correct height of a computer desk, to funding sources and grant writing, to technology maintenance and networking strategies.

The first step in the actual building process is to pour the foundation. Chapter Three, *Sound Footings: The Library Media Specialist Builds the Foundation*, deals with the library media specialist's role as teacher collaborator and as professional development provider for the staff in the areas of technology and information literacy. The articles present rationale, ideas, examples of successful practices, and checklists of skills needed both by teachers and library media specialists. Once the skills have been internalized, the footings have been poured. Now the foundation is in place to make teachers feel comfortable as they provide the level of technology and information literacy skills students need.

With the Internet accessible on virtually every desktop, students have access to a huge amount of information. Teaching them the research skills they need to survive in an information-rich world is the subject of Chapter Four, *Building the Structure: The Library Media Specialist as Carpenter*. The library media specialist deals with the processes of

- ▶ Identifying what information is needed (the reference interview),
- ▶ Teaching the skills necessary to find the information,
- ▶ Evaluating the information found in all sources, and
- ▶ Finding the alternative assessment strategies for presenting the information.

The library media specialist should be "building" upon the content framework created by the teachers to provide the life-long skills necessary to find and use information to solve a problem, prove a point, or find out more about a topic. The articles in Chapter Four include suggestions for teaching all of these skills, as well as ethical technology behavior, multimedia presentation skills, and much more.

Chapter Five, *Inspections: The Library Media Specialist as Building Inspector*, includes quite a few articles dealing with the singular skill of critical evaluation of Internet resources. The library media specialist's role is to teach students to look at all information with as critical an eye as the building inspector brings to a construction site. The articles in this chapter contain tips and checklists for helping students determine the authority, authenticity, and applicability of information they find.

Once the house is built, it is time to invite everyone over. Chapter Six, *The Open House: Library Media Specialist as Host/Hostess*, includes a multitude of articles dealing with library media centers and public relations. Publicizing successes in the library media program with student research reports and school-wide initiatives is another important part of the library media specialist's role. Traditional newsletters, invitations to visit, or use of a Web page to keep parents and community informed about the "new house" are good ways to ensure continued fiscal support, as well as creating a feeling of community.

Once the house is built, it requires constant upkeep. And once the successful library media program is up and running, keeping abreast of the newest research, continuing to read professional publications, and staying current with new technologies are the library media specialist's keys to ensuring that this new "home" does not fall into disrepair.

Kathleen Schrock
June 2000

Editor's note: Because many articles are reprints, some URL's mentioned may have changed. URL updates as of the date of publication of this book are located at the end of each chapter introduction.

CHAPTER 1

Drawing the Plans: Library Media Specialist as Architect

If you were starting to think about building a new house, you would peruse books of house plans, visit model homes, and consider all the options for the features you wanted. When starting to think about re-tooling, re-organizing, or re-evaluating a library media center program and facility, as a library media specialist you go through the same process.

The number of things a library media specialist is responsible for includes everything from selection of materials to teaching information literacy skills. With the advent of the Internet, the LM_NET newsgroup/listserv, and the abundance of professional journals available, it is very easy to learn about successful practices.

The amount of technology in the schools and in the library media center poses a potential new role for the library media specialist. Some of the articles that I have chosen deal with the new and exciting role of the library media specialist as instructional support specialist and how to deal with the stress this may entail. These articles contain ideas and thoughtful analyses to help you as you plan how to adopt this new role.

Another set of articles covers the types and amount of technology, the implications for library media center collection development, and the library media specialist's role in the instructional process—still other important considerations in this planning and gathering stage.

The ethics of copyright, acceptable use, filtering, and fair use are also important things to think about in the planning stage. Gaining familiarity with the legal issues involved will make it much easier to include information on these topics in both staff development and student instruction.

▶ URL UPDATE

From School Librarian to "Information TeAchnician" A Challenge for the Information Age by Janet Murray

Checklist for An Informational Web Page
http://www2.widener.edu/Wolfgram-Memorial Library/inform.htm

Research and Critical Thinking
http://www.crosswinds.net/~dboals/think.html

From School Librarian to "Information TeAchnician"
A Challenge for the Information Age

By Janet Murray

School librarians have a unique opportunity to adapt their professional skills to meet the challenges of the "Information Age." As electronic access to information proliferates in junior and senior high schools, librarians can model the adventure of lifelong learning by teaching faculty and students how to search the Internet for pertinent information, evaluate the reliability of information retrieved, analyze and synthesize the information to construct personal meaning, and apply it to informed decision-making. Library/media centers c an be transformed from static repositories of print and audiovisual materials into dynamic and evolving information technology centers.

Skeptics have noted that previous technological revolutions have failed to reform education, pointing to the intransigence of institutions or the resistance of teachers. In my experience, discussions of information technology too frequently focus on hardware, infrastructure, and data, as if these tools and resources alone will "automagically" reform educational practice to produce competent lifelong learners. Experienced educators know that we must add an "A" to "tech"; technology in isolation ignores the "a" in "teAch."

School librarians have the professional training and expertise to guide information-processing learning activities, so let's call ourselves "information teAchnicians."

School Librarians and the Electronic World of Information

Librarians at all levels have been exceptionally quick to recognize the potential of an electronic "library without walls." They also have been particularly proactive in identifying and analyzing issues pertaining to Internet use. The American Library Association and the American Association of School Librarians have made significant efforts to guide policy making and standards development.

In January 1996, The American Library Association adopted Access to Electronic Information, Services and Networks, an interpretation of the Library Bill of Rights. It draws upon previous interpretations to guide libraries in the development of policy, notably:

"Providing connections to global information, services, and networks is not the same as selecting and purchasing material for a library collection. Determining the accuracy or authenticity of electronic information may present special problems. Some information accessed electronically may not meet a library's selection or collection development policy. It is, therefore, left to each user to determine what is appropriate. Parents and legal guardians who are concerned about their children's use of electronic resources should provide guidance to their own children."

The new edition of *Information Power*, released in July 1998, incorporates Information Literacy Standards for Student Learning which have been included in "Indicators of Schools of Quality" by the National Study of School Evaluation. This powerful collection of nine standards and 29 indicators of proficiency in information literacy, independent learning, and socially responsible use of electronic information can provide the foundation for recognizing the school librarian's central role in a t echnology-enriched educational environment. The preface explicitly describes this connection:

"The learning process and the information search process mirror each other: Students actively seek to construct meaning from the sources they encounter and to create products that shape and communicate that meaning effectively. Developing expertise in accessing, evaluating, and using information is in fact the authentic learning that modern education seeks to promote."

ICONnect, a project sponsored by AASL, offers online courses in Internet applications. The Librarians Information Online Network (LION), maintained by the Philadelphia School District, is an exceptional resource for K-12 librarians. Peter Milbury's *School Librarian Web Pages* demonstrates the extent of school librarians' leadership in emerging electronic publication.

Introducing the Internet to Teachers

Successfully enticing teachers to use the Internet with their students may depend more on your teaching skills than your Internet skills. Create a comfortable, nonthreatening learning environment. Avoid overusing technical language. I use analogies to everyday experiences to emphasize that the Internet is not an impenetrable mystery, but merely a new research tool. Demonstrate patience and offer positive reinforcement. Model the adventure of lifelong learning by sharing your enthusiasm for this powerful information resource.

Use a well-designed tutorial to introduce teachers to online research. *Exploring the World Wide Web*, a workshop tutorial on Internet applications, combines text and exercises. Some teachers may prefer *The Internet Island*, a Web tutorial for teachers, because of its graphic replication of the Netscape screen. To learn about the Internet, explore *Hobbes' Internet Timeline*, by Robert H. Zakon, hosted by the Internet Society.

Locating Information

New and novice users frequently complain that finding pertinent and relevant information is like searching for Waldo in the popular children's books! In order for teachers and students to locate appropriate information pertinent to their research inquiries, they must first develop skills in searching electronic databases. Framing a question in terms which lend themselves to successful information retrieval is an important first step. Internet sites with hierarchically

Experienced educators know that we must add an "A" to "tech"; technology in isolation ignores t he "A" in "teAch."

organized subjects are useful to students who have not yet pinpointed their research topic. Students may also use concept mapping to refine their inquiry statements so they are neither too broad nor too narrow. They may learn to use synonyms or truncated forms of words to improve the accuracy of their searches. They need to understand the basic principles of Boolean logic in order to use Internet search engines efficiently. It is also important to recognize that different search engines yield different results because they use different methods to build their indexes. Students can benefit from an understanding of the different features of a variety of search engines.

Searching the 'Net is a series of interlinked, short Web pages with some introductory exercises to help students focus on electronic searching skills. Kathy Schrock's presentation at the 1998 National Educational Computing Conference ("Successful Web Search Strategies") provides a valuable overview of searching on the Internet.

Evaluating Information

Rapidly expanding access to the Internet compels school librarians to emphasize the importance of evaluating information retrieved. In an electronic publishing environment which allows anyone to create Web pages, it is imperative that students and teachers examine information sources with a critical eye. The standards which librarians have traditionally applied to print and audio-visual materials are also valid in an electronic setting. Students should consider the authority of the site, identifying the author and his or her qualifications, as well as the organization that

> *Librarians who find themselves propelled onto the information superhighway without adequate skills and preparation can use their Internet connectivity to guide their own professional growth. The map is in the glove compartment!*

Sites Cited

American Library Association
(<http://www.ala.org>)

American Association of School Librarians
(<http://www.ala.org/aasl>)

Access to Electronic Information, Services and Networks, an interpretation of the Library Bill of Rights (<http://www.ala.org/oitp/ebillrlts.html>)

Information Power
(<http://www.ala.org/aasl/ip_toc.html>)

Information Literacy Standards
(<http://www.ala.org/aasl/ip_nine.html>)

National Study of School Evaluation
(<http://www.nsse.org/>)

ICONnect (<http://www.ala.org/ICONN/>)

Librarians Information Online Network
(<http://www.libertynet.org/lion/lion.html>)

School Librarian Web Pages
(<http://wombat.cusd.chico.k12.ca.us/~pmilbury/lib.html>)

Exploring the World Wide Web
(<http://www.gactr.uga.edu/exploring/index.html>)

The Internet Island
(<http://www.miamisci.org/ii/ii0.html>)

Hobbes' Internet Timeline
(<http://info.isoc.org/guest/zakon/Internet/History/HIT.html>)

Searching the 'Net
(<http://www.teleport.com/~janetm/oii/search.html>)

Successful Web Search Strategies
(<http://discoveryschool.com/schrockguide/neccsrch/searchingnecc2/sld01.html>)

Thinking Critically about World Wide Web Resources
(<http://www.library.ucla.edu/libraries/college/instruct/web/critical.htm>)

Checklist for an Informational Web Page
(<http://www.science.widener.edu/~withers/inform.htm>)

Cyber Guides
(<http://www.cyberbee.com/guides.html>)

Web Quests
(<http://edweb.sdsu.edu/webquest/overview.htm>)

NASA's Classroom of the Future
(<http://www.cotf.edu/ete/modules/modules.html>)

The Big6 Skills (<http://www.big6.com>)

EdWeb (<http://edweb.gsn.org/>)

Child Safety on the Information Highway
(<http://www.4j.lane.edu/safety/>)

Acceptable Use Policies
(<http://www.netc.org/tech_plans/aup.html>)

sponsors the site. Assess the accuracy and objectivity of the information provided by distinguishing among facts, point of view, and opinion. Consider the currency of information by checking revision dates. Evaluate the relevance of the information; it is easy to lose track of one's original research question when confronted with an overwhelming profusion of resources.

Thinking Critically about World Wide Web Resources can help you apply traditional evaluation criteria to the Internet. *Checklist for an Informational Web Page* can help you structure your instruction in evaluation techniques. *CyberGuides* are useful checklists of Web elements which are important for schools.

Analyzing and Synthesizing Information

Once students have located information from a variety of sources, they need to selectively identify the pieces that are useful, and synthesize them to construct an original product that reflects their engagement in the process of critical thinking. Even in traditional research, prior to the Information Age, students often merely regurgitated facts without considering their significance. The current challenge is to provide students with authentic research tasks by posing fundamental interdisciplinary questions that do not have prescribed answers.

Research and Critical Thinking is a massively detailed site with sections on research skills and tools, search tools, and critical thinking on the Web. *Web Quests* and NASA's *Classroom of the Future* modules both provide models of Internet-based instruction. Michael Eisenberg and Robert Berkowitz's list of six information-processing skills (*Big6 Skills*) provides a useful framework for organizing instruction.

Applying Information Skills

The Information Literacy Standards developed by the AASL/AECT National Guidelines Vision Committee "describe the content and processes related to information that students must master to be considered well educated." The standards also define the information-literate high school graduate: one who has the ability to use information to acquire both core and advanced knowledge and to become an independent, lifelong learner who contributes responsibly and productively to the learning community.

Internet Implementation Issues

For librarians to successfully redefine themselves as "information teAchnicians," they must also keep informed about the larger issues pertaining to the use of Internet in schools. Andy Carvin's *EdWeb* is an excellent hypertext online "book" that explores technology and school reform. *Child Safety on the Information Highway* is another hypertext guide that is suitable for concerned parents. Defining appropriate acceptable use policies requires thoughtful consideration and experienced leadership.

Resources to guide the successful implementation of technology in schools abound on the Internet, although, ironically one must already have Internet access in order to benefit from them. Librarians who find themselves propelled onto the information superhighway without adequate skills and preparation can use their Internet connectivity to guide their own professional growth. The map is in the glove compartment!

Janet Murray is the Information Specialist at Kinnick High School in Yokosuka, Japan. She has been avidly adopting and promoting electronic access to information since she automated the first library in Portland (Oregon) Public Schools in 1985. Her new title, Information Specialist, reflects the Department of Defense Dependents Schools' commitment to redefining school librarians as instructional technology leaders. She can be reached via e-mail at janetm@surfline.ne.jp.

The content of this article grew from a workshop presentation to library media specialists at the Texas Computer Education Association annual conference in February 1997. A shorter version was previously published by the Well-Connected Educator <http://www.gsh.org/wce/archives/murray1.htm>.

FULL SPEED AHEAD ON THE INTERNET

Take the Internet Challenge: Using Technology in Context

By Michael B. Eisenberg

Picture this: A slick salesman-type person, broad smile on his face, open arms, extolling, "Technology is the answer, of course. Now what was the question?"

Technology for technology's sake. This is a common lament in education circles. And we aren't alone in this. Businesses and government agencies also suffer from the same concern: technology being touted as an end in itself, the answer to our prayers.

Technology out of context. What a mess, and what a waste. If that wasn't enough, now we have the same situation in relation to the Internet: "The Internet is the answer, of course. Now what was the question?"

Clearly, we must turn this around. The focus should be on the question—what do we want to accomplish in schools? Then, we must ask ourselves how can we use the Internet and other technologies in effective and efficient ways to reach our goals?

The Internet Challenge

For school library media programs the challenge is to use technology in general and the Internet specifically as a means to an end and not as an end in itself. Let's call this the "Internet Challenge." We want to focus on what we are trying to accomplish and how can the Internet help us to do so.

This Internet Challenge provides two tremendous opportunities for library media specialists. First, they are in an excellent position to meet this challenge within the library media program itself. Library media specialists can focus on their central functions of information services and information skills instruction and the use of the Internet meaningfully to meet those goals. Second, and even more importantly, library media specialists can play a key role in helping the entire school meet the Internet Challenge. Their experience with curriculum-focused information services and integrated information skills instruction places library media specialists in a direct and unique position to help classroom teachers integrate the Internet into everyday learning and teaching.

Meeting the Internet Challenge means continually focusing on the fundamentals of vision and purpose. The mission statement from *Information Power* (AASL/AECT, 1988) offers an energetic and essential vision for library media programs: "...the mission of the library media program is to ensure that students...are effective users of ideas and information."

In an information society, there is no mission more important. Library media specialists can accomplish this vital mission by providing essential information services (including access to collections, help and referral, and reading guidance) and teaching essential information literacy skills (as a full process, not just location and access to resources).

In terms of technology and the Internet, it's not "the library" and "technology," it's *the Library* including all information systems and resources used for learning and teaching. Students and teachers shouldn't be thinking about the search for information in terms of using "the library" and then "the Internet." We want them to think about using the Library, which includes the Internet. Today and in the future, the concept of Library should encompass the full range of information resources—electronic and print.

While this concept of a unified library is certainly not a new one, there is a tendency to lose sight of it among the complexities of new and emerging information systems and the ever-changing technological environment. In addition, our own library media systems sometimes work against the unified vision. For example, rather than a common access point and interface to *all* electronic resources, in too many situations we still have an online catalog separate from the full-text resources and separate again from access to the Internet. This doesn't necessarily require a common search system across all resources (although that might be nice), it simply requires that the system includes easy intellectual and physical access to all resources and networks that we would include under the concept of Library.

Commercial library systems should foster and encourage the concept by providing mechanisms for combining local and global systems along with site licensing agreements that allow us to offer Library on every workstation in the school and community.

But library media specialists aren't the only ones focusing on information resources and technology. Many teachers and administrators are getting involved with bringing the Internet and CD-ROM resources into their schools. We may say, "the unified Library should encompass all information systems and resources—including the Internet," but just saying it won't make it so.

This brings us back to our answer to the Internet Challenge. When library media specialists meet the Internet Challenge, they move to fulfill the concept of Library. Using the Internet in context addresses the needs of the library media program and the entire school. The Library is more than just the resources and the technology. The Library means library media specialists using the Internet within the program of information services and as part of information literacy skills instruction to ensure that students are effective users of information.

Here are some examples of how library media specialists can meet the Internet Challenge within each of these two functions—information services and information literacy skills instruction.

Information Services

Information services refers to the full range of services and activities available to students, teachers, administrators, and the community. Information services include

- resources provision
- reading guidance
- direct information
- curriculum consultation
- curriculum development.

Resources provision service refers to providing space, materials, and equipment to meet curricular and personal needs. Meeting the Internet Challenge for resources provision includes providing tools that help students and teachers to link Internet resources to curriculum needs, providing workstations and connections to the Internet, and sharing resources and building cooperative collections across regions.

Reading guidance service centers on promoting literacy and guiding in reading and materials selection. Meeting the Internet Challenge for reading guidance includes identifying and arranging for teachers and students to become involved in special collaborative Internet projects, such as *Live from Antarctica* and *MayaQuest*, and to interact with others globally through e-mail and discussion groups.

Direct information service involves providing assistance in locating and retrieving information. Meeting the Internet Challenge for direct information service includes providing students, teachers, and others direct help, referral, and question-answering service to put them in touch with the information they need.

Curriculum consultation service relates to providing advice on the use of information, resources, and technology in curriculum. Meeting the Internet Challenge for curriculum consultation includes using e-mail and electronic discussion groups to communicate with teachers and help teachers communicate with each other (locally and globally) on curriculum-related matters, professional issues, and decisions.

Curriculum development service refers to collaborating on the design, development, and evaluation of curriculum, particularly those units and lessons integrating information skills instruction. Meeting the Internet Challenge for curriculum development includes joint efforts to link curriculum and assignments and the plethora of resources,

Internet Applications in a Big Six Context

Big Six Skills	Internet Applications
Task Definition	e-mail, listservs, Internet Relay Chat, MOO, CU-SeeMe
Information Seeking Strategies	network navigation (World Wide Web, Netscape, Lynx, gophers), e-mail, listservs
Location & Access	Web navigation (Netscape) and search tools (Lycos, Webcrawler, Yahoo, Archie, Veronica)
Use of Information	download, upload, ftp
Synthesis	HTML and Web page creation
Evaluation	e-mail, listservs, Internet Relay Chat, MOO, CU-SeeMe

> ...the central question—how can we use the Internet in meaningful ways to help achieve educational goals—is often unanswered. Library media specialists are in a unique position to meet this Internet challenge.

projects, and services available through the Internet, and also to identify and develop relevant Internet-based curriculum projects.

Information Literacy Skills Instruction

Information literacy skills instruction offers another powerful opportunity to meet the Internet Challenge. Over the past 20 years, library media professionals have worked hard to move from teaching isolated library skills to teaching integrated information skills. The key word is "context," and effective integration of information skills requires two contexts:

(1) the skills must directly relate to the content area curriculum and to classroom assignments, and
(2) the skills themselves need to be tied together in a logical and systematic information process model.

Meeting the Internet Challenge also requires library media specialists to focus on both of these contexts. The first context is real need: curricular, life, or work. While it is certainly possible to learn skills in isolation, practice and research confirm that people learn best when the use and purpose are clear.

Students can learn to communicate via e-mail or to access a World Wide Web site, but they will eagerly internalize these skills if they see how the skills directly relate to their school assignments or personal interests. Electronic mail, for example, takes on meaning if students realize that it enables them to work with students from another state or country to complete a project for social studies. Accessing a Web site is more than a novelty when it relates directly to answering homework questions.

The second, and often overlooked, context is the information problem-solving process itself. Computer and telecommunications technologies are supposed to extend our abilities to solve problems. That sounds fine in the abstract, but what does it really mean? Again, practice and research tell us that when people understand how specific skills fit into an overall model or process, the power and usefulness of the specific skills are expanded. Yes, students recognize the value of using e-mail for communication, but this takes on new meaning when they realize that e-mail can help them to better define the task of an assignment by being able to interact with teachers and group members. Task definition is step one of Eisenberg and Berkowitz' Big Six information problem-solving model. (Eisenberg & Berkowitz, 1990)

How Internet capabilities can be placed in the Big Six information problem-solving context is shown in the chart on the left. The chart is easily modified as new Internet functions and resources are made available or as teachers and students find new ways to apply existing capabilities. The power of the Big Six model is in this ability to provide an adaptable context for learning and teaching Internet skills; in fact, for learning and teaching any electronic networking or information technology skills. (For a more detailed treatment of computer skills for information problem-solving see Eisenberg and Johnson, 1996).

Conclusion

In the mad rush to technology in general and the Internet in particular, the focus has centered primarily on the hardware and software and the commands and capabilities. Schools and businesses are already investing considerable amounts of money, time, and effort on getting connected to the Internet, but the central question—how can we use the Internet in meaningful ways to help achieve educational goals—is often unanswered. Library media specialists are in a unique position to meet this Internet Challenge. And if they do so, they not only establish a broad and encompassing concept of Library, they also go a long way to fulfilling their mission of ensuring that students are effective users of ideas and information.

Michael B. Eisenberg is the co-owner of LM_NET, Director of the ERIC Clearinghouse on Information & Technology, and a Professor in the School of Information Studies at Syracuse University, Syracuse, New York.

References

AASL/AECT (American Association of School Librarians and Association for Educational Communications and Technology) (1988). *Information Power: Guidelines for School Library Media Programs*. American Library Association.

Eisenberg, Michael B. and Johnson, Doug (1996). "Computer Skills for Information Problem-Solving: Learning and Teaching Technology in Context," ERIC Digest, EDO-IR-96-04, ERIC Clearinghouse on Information & Technology. Available on the Internet: gopher://ericir.syr.edu:70/00/Clearinghouses/16houses/CIT/IT_Digests/Computer Skills.

Eisenberg, Michael B. and Berkowitz, Robert E. (1988). *Curriculum Initiative: An Agenda and Strategy for School Library Media Programs*, Ablex Publishing.

Eisenberg, Michael B. and Berkowitz, Robert E. (1990). *Information Problem-Solving: The Big Six Skills Approach to Library & Information Skills Instruction*, Ablex Publishing.

MANAGING of/with TECHNOLOGY

MANAGING A CONSTANTLY CHANGING ARRAY OF MACHINES, PROGRAMS AND PROCESSES

by Edna M. Boardman

A student was waiting at the door when the library opened. "I've got a new computer at home, and I've been working on my term paper all weekend. Can you change it to Mac so I can work on it at school today?" We asked her what brand her new computer was and recognized the name of a common IBM clone. One of my aides took her disk and found an empty disk formatted to Macintosh. In a few minutes the student was happily clicking away on a Macintosh computer in our lab.

A glance at the open window on the computer screen said there was trouble. A student had created a hundred new untitled folders—and had put the hard drive icon into one of them.

A conference facilitator wanted to use a special program that would use our lab computers' entire memories. We would have to remove all our usual programs, install the new one, then later remove that and reinstall our programs. The nuisance factor was high. Should we have computers with more memory?

Computers have changed how we arrange our work. They shape our daily acts and considerations. Coping with technology demands vision and awareness and growing expertise in dealing with a plethora of technical matters. In the practical management of technology in the school library media center, it is necessary to assign jobs to individual persons. However, each of us must have enough general knowledge to cover for each other when we need to.

Vision, Overview, Decisions

Foresight is part of the library media professional's job. But with technology changing so rapidly, it is difficult to map and plan even a year ahead. Changes to hardware and software often grow out of the technical chores required to meet student and staff needs. In our library we expect everyone who deals with students and machines to consider better ways to do the job. This is an exhilarating way to push a staff. They use their good brains rather than wait for someone to tell them what to do next. Daily we hear comments such as, "The program with all the locks is more bother than it's worth." "We need more memory to run the math, art, and music theory programs."

Daily Life In An Automated Library

This is how we organize and manage day-to-day activity. The list of tasks is, by no means, exhaustive.

Circulation, Cataloging Systems

- Maintaining the online catalog, including keeping track of barcode numbers, entering new materials individually or in batches, deleting materials records, making changes as errors appear or new editions arrive, printing bar codes and spine labels, and printing out various categories of materials
- Maintaining backup tapes
- Starting the system in the morning; shutting it down at night

- Maintaining files of installation disks so that anything that is lost can be reinstalled, including the system disks
- Memorizing the 1-800 contact number and developing a first-name relationship with the customer service personnel of the software provider, especially in the first year or two
- Checking materials in and out
- Setting due dates (some daily), retrieving records, recording messages, printing out overdue notices, printing out an assortment of records, taking pictures of the screen
- Desensitizing and resensitizing materials to the theft detection system
- Entering and deleting from the computer the names of students and other categories of users

Teaching Library Skills

- Coaching a changing population of students as they learn to use the online catalog; helping them learn to interpret what they see on the screen; teaching them to select with specificity rather than waste a quarter ream of paper on unnecessary printouts
- Teaching students to search by author, title, keyword,

subject; to use Boolean options when the choices are too great
- Encouraging the teaching staff to be comfortable with online searching

Managing Computer Labs
- Setting reasonable, enforceable rules for use of the labs by students and teachers
- Learning the special quirks of a constantly changing bank of computers
- Installing and deleting computer programs
- Handling printer problems and maintenance
- Understanding enough about the workings of the network, the operation of the file server, and the daily problems with computers to minimize calls to the district technician
- Troubleshooting and answering never-ending questions; for example, knowing what to do when a computer freezes, how to make a graph, how to do a footnote, how to set margins and create columns
- Keeping each computer's hard drive and desktop clean
- Using special programs to retrieve accidentally deleted student projects
- Understanding the computers well enough so problems with memory, the system, and the control panel can be solved expeditiously
- Using anti-virus programs to clear student disks of viruses
- Explaining one more time why students cannot download programs to take home, or bring their own game programs to use when they are bored, or tie up the printer for half an hour to create a poster that says, "We love you, dude, and wish you an absolutely fabulous seventeenth birthday," or why they cannot bring soft drinks or candy into the lab or cross through it as a shortcut to the locker bay

Managing CD-ROM Disks
- Installing new programs and new versions of programs from services such as *NewsBank* and periodical indexes
- Keeping aware of permissions and limitations imposed by the contract the library has purchased
- Circulating CD-ROM disks purchased by the library, such as encyclopedias, atlases, and almanacs
- Assisting students to use these disks without getting into onscreen tangles
- Helping students decide what kinds of subjects or descriptors to use
- Thinking about better ways to make disk use more user-friendly

Managing Periodicals
- Printing out a daily overdue list and printing NCR overdue slips once a week
- Keeping track of problems, routines, orders, correspondence related to subscriptions
- Considering whether to replace an efficient paper system with a computer process

Managing the Internet
- Registering students on the Internet; validating them with our service
- Helping the teaching staff learn to use e-mail and locate Internet sites
- Dealing with the public's concern by enforcing district guidelines about use
- Considering how electronically-delivered materials can be used to enhance student learning

IN OUR LIBRARY WE EXPECT EVERYONE WHO DEALS WITH STUDENTS AND MACHINES TO CONSIDER BETTER WAYS TO DO THE JOB.

More Vision, Overview, Decisions

I am not the best technician on my staff, but I need to know the basic operation of our equipment and be aware of what is new. I get as many school technology magazines as I can. I go to classes, conferences, and meetings. Will our students soon be handing multimedia reports to their teachers? Will most of the information they use come to them over the Information Superhighway? Should we get a scanner? A special camera that registers images on a computer disk? (Others in the district have had one for several years.) I prowl the interactive television studio in my building.

I am keenly aware that we are making up the rules as we go along, that only a very few have been educated with this much electronic opportunity. We learn with the students. We would like to ponder more thoughtfully what we do with technology, but just now a lab full of students needs to know how to get their computers to put page numbers on their term papers. TC

Edna M. Boardman is Library Media Specialist for the Magic City Campus of the Minot, North Dakota, High School.

HEAD FOR THE EDGE

The Sound of the Other Shoe Dropping

By Doug Johnson

Where can I find answers to these reference questions while not leaving my desk?
- What is the atomic weight of boron or the size of the Andromeda galaxy?
- Are there any bookstores in Albuquerque, New Mexico, that carry a new book by Krol on computing?
- Last year Clinton proposed a new technology policy. Where can I find the text of this policy?
- What nights will the Denver Nuggets be playing home basketball games this season?
- What was the total amount of sales in liquor stores in the United States in September of this year? Was it more than last year?
- What's been written on the development of hiking trails for the handicapped?
- I've heard Clairol offers college scholarships. How do I qualify?
- Where can I get the monthly Consumer Price Index for the last decade as a computer file that can be imported into a spreadsheet?

Well, on the Internet, of course. Should this information source be of interest to librarians? It is more than interesting. It's critical to the survival of our profession!

Your answer to one question will tell if you'll be one of the survivors in the great print-information-to-digital-information shift: Why are you in the profession?

At the turn of the century, this country had lots of blacksmiths. Some stayed employed and some didn't. Why? If you asked the soon-to-be-unemployed blacksmiths why they were in the business, they'd have said, "Because I like horses." If you asked the other blacksmiths, those who stayed viable in their changing environment, the same question, they probably said, "Because I like helping people get from place to place."

When the horseless carriage came along, those with the transportation mission fixed wheels, banged out fenders, and even tinkered under the hood. They remained transportation specialists.

Ask yourself the same question: Why am I in the business? "Because I like books" is the wrong answer. I hope you said, "Because I like helping people find, use, and communicate the things they need to know."

Now as computers fill our schools, you're probably helping kids do Boolean searches, bang out reports with desktop publishers, and even travel the information highway. You've remained an information specialist.

Unfortunately, we as a profession have a history of dropping the ball when it comes to making new technologies our own. In how many schools is "AV" still separate from "library?" In how many schools is the librarian not seen as a computer expert, even though we all know that a tremendous amount of information is available to patrons in electronic format? In how many schools are keyboarding, word processing, database and spreadsheet use, and computer-assisted drawing no part of the media skills curriculum, even though two thirds of our mission is teach students to process and communicate information? How many of us are seen as teacher prep time babysitters rather than critical components of the total educational process, and thus expendable in tight economic times?

Our profession currently has a tremendous opportunity to stay (or become) relevant information experts. Pilot projects are being conducted throughout the United States to bring Internet access to K-12 teachers.

If you can't participate in one of these projects or your state doesn't have one, get on the Internet through a commercial online service. You will need access to a computer and modem (about $15 per month) and the ability to pay some long-distance charges if you aren't living in a larger community. Oh, and the willingness and determination to learning something challenging.

I recently read an Internet signature that taunted, "Libraries are for people who can't afford modems." Ouch. But if a critical mass of librarians don't become the online information specialists for teachers, students, and administrators, the next sound we hear won't be that of a ball being dropped, but the sound of the other shoe. TC

Doug Johnson, District Media Supervisor, Mankato Public Schools

NOTES

Information Power Prepares Library Media Programs for a New Age

By Steve Baule

IN RECENT YEARS, national, state, and local standards have become more important as both the general public and educators have looked for ways to gauge their schools' progress. One of the most fluid areas in education has been the library media program. In the past 15 years, school library media centers have tried to transform themselves from places where students go to use books into the information centers of schools, where information access is the first priority no matter what the format of the material. Much conversation has taken place between administrators, library media specialists, and other educators about the changing roles of the school library media specialists. The modern school library media specialist must not only be proficient with the wide range of information technologies available, but must still be able to work with teachers to instill in students information literacy skills. The American Association of School Librarians and the Association of Educational Communications and Technology have recently put this premise forward in a newly revised version of *Information Power: Building Partnerships for Learning*.

Information Power begins with the statement that information literacy is the keystone of lifelong learning. In our present society, complete with cellular phones, faxes, e-mail, Web sites, and online databases, it would be tough to argue against that statement. Library media specialists have built *Information Power* upon the concepts of information access, information literacy, and active and engaged student learning. In preparing the new standards, they have asked us to look at our schools as learning communities encompassing students, teachers, administrators, and parents. Though this is not a new concept in educational circles, it asks that administrators and classroom teachers expand their roles and involvement with library media centers. In order for administrators to participate more fully in the development and expansion of the library media programs within their schools, they should be familiar with the concepts and standards set forth in *Information Power*.

The book is divided into two sections: information literacy standards for student learning and building partnerships for learning. The first section does a good job of focusing on the needs of the student as a member of our information society. The second discusses how the library media specialist and library media program should support and complement the instructional programs of a school and the wider learning community. The information literacy standards will also be published as a separate companion volume so they may be easily distributed to greater learning communities without difficulty.

Though libraries have gone through a tremendous physical transformation in the past 10 years, their basic purpose as providers of information (in whatever form) has not changed. Likewise, the mission of the library media program remains unchanged from the original version of *Information Power*, published in 1988. It aims to "ensure that students and staff are effective users of ideas and information." The mission is accomplished by school library media programs that:

1. provide intellectual and physical access to materials in all formats
2. provide instruction to foster competence and stimulate interest in reading, viewing, and using information and ideas
3. work with educators to design learning strategies to meet the needs of individual students

Information Power outlines seven goals that help focus the library media program on the premise that the learning community must be focused on student needs and sustain a "creative, energetic library media program."

The information literacy skills a student needs to perform are presented as nine separate standards in three sections: information literacy, independent learning, and social responsibility. The standards in the first section focus on the ability of a student to access and evaluate the ever-expanding range of available information. The need of a student to be an independent learner who appreciates literature and strives for excellence is addressed in the second section of the standards. The last section recognizes the need for students to be taught how to use information in an ethical manner within the context of a diverse democratic society. *Information Power* does a good job of providing concrete examples of how each standard and the indicators under it can be accessed and integrated into curricular goals and objectives. This portion of the book would be helpful to anyone developing curriculum or course materials intended to address information literacy.

The second portion of *Information Power* addresses the issues of the school library media program's multiple roles. Under the recurring themes of collaboration, leadership, and technology, this section examines how the library media program must interface and intertwine with the broader instructional program. Collaboration is an obvious facet of the library media program, for nearly everything the program offers must be in conjunction with other instructional programs. Anything else would be library skills in isolation — sort of a modernized equivalent of the card catalog exercises in basal readers. Leadership may be a less-obvious facet of a library media program at first glance, but successful library media programs are based upon visionary leadership that moves its learning communities forward in addressing the complex issues of the

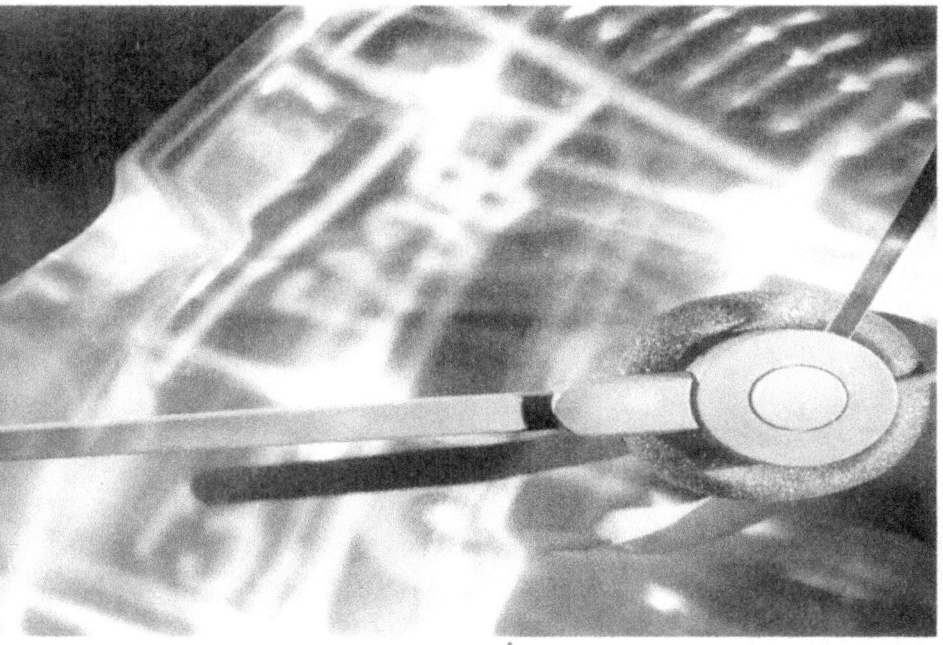

information age. Library media specialists who have embraced technology can be leaders in integrating technology into the instructional program of their schools.

The concept of leadership leads to the third facet, technology. Library programs need to continue to focus strongly on the integration of information technologies and electronic information access to be successful in the future. *Information Power* explains how the library media specialist can be involved in the effective integration of technology. The standards then review how these three themes run through the tripartite role of the school library media specialist as teacher, librarian, and program administrator. It is interesting to note that the program administration role has replaced the instructional designer/consultant role present in earlier documents. Since today nearly all teachers collaborate with more emphasis on team teaching, curricular integration, and general sharing of curricular information, the instructional consultant role has been subsumed as a section of the teaching role. In the same vein, the administration of networks, LANs, MANs, and WANs has become an important focus of many school library media specialists. As some library media specialists have become responsible for the supervision of technical staffs, the supervisory element of their positions has also been increased in many cases. The last chapter is devoted to the larger community of learners and how
the library media program can be connected into that community and used as a conduit for keeping diverse constituencies moving together toward common goals. Included as appendixes are a number of ALA and AECT policies, NSSE schoolwide goals for student learning, and an overview of
student performance assessment methods.

What the new version of *Information Power* cannot do is allow an administrator to use the standards to easily rate his or her library in relationship to other schools. The lists of equipment necessary for the program and the number of books a school should maintain in its collection are not in this new version. A few years ago, college accreditors and a law school went to court over whether the law school library had to have a certain number of volumes in its collection or simply have access to them electronically. The school won the case. *Information Power* is making a similar statement to school library media specialists and their administrators. It is not as important to have a large collection as it is that students and staff can access, evaluate, and use information effectively.

Overall, *Information Power* provides an excellent overview of how a school's library media program should effectively be integrated into the instructional program. AASL and AECT have taken a much wider view of the library media program in this version of the standards. The earlier version of *Information Power* was more focused on the equipment and facilities necessary to run the library media center. This version has taken a more global view of the library media program in light of the changes in the way our information society has changed. The focus of these standards has been rightly placed on student learning and information literacy.

Administrators at both the building and the district level will want to take time to review these new standards and discuss their implementation with the library media staff. Additionally, it is essential that the technology staff in a building or district be familiar with these standards and maintain an ongoing dialogue with the library media staff. In a society where, in many parts of the world, the electronic delivery of information is no longer considered a supplement for print but the default method, the technology and library media staffs must have an extremely close working relationship for either group to be successful. In the ever-increasing complexity of our information society, it would be hard to argue that anything will be more important to our students in the future than the ability to access and effectively use information.

Steve Baule is Director of Information Technologies at New Trier High School in Winnetka, Illinois.

Building Influence in the School Library

I THINK I CAN I TH[INK I CAN]

By Alice H. Yucht

Recently a former elementary school student, now doing graduate work in literary criticism, told me that she's writing a "deconstructionist" paper on the idea that the classic children's book *The Little Engine That Could*, by Watty Piper (Platt & Munk, 1930) is actually a radical feminist polemic. Once I stopped laughing, I began to think about that Little Engine, and about how she (yes, She, albeit blue in color!) symbolizes what's possible when someone is willing to make a change. Briefly, here's the story: When the red engine that normally pulls the train that carries playthings and good food to the children on the other side of the mountain can no longer make the trip, the dolls and toys try to find another engine to help them get the train to its destination. After being turned down by several other self-important big engines, the toys finally turn to the Little Blue Engine, who's only been used for switching trains in the train yard before. The LBE had never made this kind of trip before, but she understood why it was important, and so she changed her role to accept this new responsibility. "I think I can, I think I can," she just kept telling herself, and before she knew it, she HAD managed to get the train to the children in need.

Here are some strategies and guidelines to help you cope with change, using the word itself as a mnemonic:

C is for Cause and Choice.

There has to be a valid reason for any change to be necessary; not just a whim. And you'd better be prepared to defend the reasons for your choice, based on your perception of the need for the change! For example: My school district uses a rare (in the worst sense of the word) computerized circulation system, one which requires multiple operations for a simple checkout. Because I had a full-time aide who took care of all the circulation procedures, I never really bothered to master this particular program. Last spring the Board of Education, in its infinite wisdom, decided to eliminate my aide's position, leaving me with no clerical help in a busy middle school library. Cause/Choice: learn how to make this *&%$# program work, or change the procedure to something that will work more efficiently for me. Since (a) the whole district will be switching to a completely different circulation system in

next year or two; and (b) I don't want to be chained to the circulation desk when I should be working on resources with the kids; and (c) all the books do still have pockets and cards in them; and (d) all I really need is some way of knowing who's got what, and when it's due. . . I've chosen to go back to a very traditional, uncomputerized, self-service check-out system. There is now a 2-section box at the check-out station, with pre-stamped date-due cards in one section. Students sign the book card in the back of the book, put the signed card in the sign-out section of the box, then take a stamped date-due card from the box and put it into the book pocket. Voilá — checked-out book! At the end of the day I stamp, sort, and file the signed book cards. It ain't high-tech, but it does the job just fine, and until I get some clerical help again, that's the way it will have to be.

H is for Health and/or Humor.

Health: Is the proposed change meant to cure an existing problem, or prevent the problem from happening at all? Internet Filters are a prime example: Are they to be installed in order to ensure that our students will have access only to educationally appropriate sites, or because there have been complaints/problems because students have been surfing in strange places, or is the administration insisting on filters as a CYA public relations ploy, just in case something might happen? Humor: How many times have we said plaintively, "Someday we'll laugh about this"? What are we waiting for? Norman Cousins eloquently proved that laughter can be great medicine. As long as we're laughing *with*, and not *at*, maintaining a sense of humor can be one of the best coping mechanisms of all. My mother was a school secretary for many years. She taught me that one of the most important file folders to maintain was the one marked "Hah." Into this file go all those memos stating the obvious and then contradicting it a week later. Here's where you save cartoons, jokes, quotations (like Lily Tomlin's "No matter how cynical I become, it's never enough to keep up."), and other ephemera that makes you smile.

A is for Attitude and Ability and Action.

Attitude determines whether you see change as a possibility or a problem. Do you suffer from "PSYCHOSCLEROSIS"— A hardening of the attitudes? As in: If you make up your mind that you can do something, you're probably right. However, if you've made up your mind that you can't do something, you're probably right, there, too. When the Shiny New Passenger Engine couldn't be bothered, and the Big Strong Freight Engine thought the job was unimportant, and the Kind Old Engine didn't think it had the strength, it was the Little Blue Engine who saved the day by making the effort. It wasn't that the other engines were incapable; no, they were just unwilling or unable. And if you don't make the effort—put the gears into motion — get things moving — then there is no action, and change requires action.

N is for kNowledge (phonetic spelling) and Networks.

Eric Hoffer said: "In a time of drastic change it is the learners who inherit the future. The learned usually find themselves equipped to live in a world that no longer exists." Knowledge is information put to use, not just dead facts. Learn all you can about the proposed change, figure out the pros and cons, understand what's involved, and then make an informed decision. Think of it this way: A bend in the road is not the end of the road unless you fail to make the turn. When I first became a librarian, 30-something years ago, a self-advancing filmstrip projector was considered cutting-edge technology! Now elementary school students are doing PowerPoint presentations instead of oaktag posters. But no matter what kind of glue and glitter is used, it's still the content that's most important. Networks come in many forms: personal, professional, political, even physical. We all need these support systems to help us through the rough times. Think about how electric companies get and supply their power to their customers. They, and their competitors/neighboring electric companies, are all connected to a linked power grid, or network. This way each company can borrow power from another firm if their own supply is running low in an emergency. Everyone benefits and shares, for the greater good of all. And if one company has a unique problem, they can call on the combined resources and expertise of the entire network to help solve it.

G is for Growth.

Consider these statements:

"Everything that can be invented has been invented."
— *Charles H. Duell, Director of U.S. Patent Office, 1899.*

"Sensible and responsible women do not want to vote."
— *Grover Cleveland, 1905.*

"Who the hell wants to hear actors talk?"
— *Harry M. Warner, Warner Bros Pictures, 1927.*

"There is no likelihood man can ever tap the power of the atom."
— *Robert Miliham, Nobel Prize in Physics, 1923.*

"Heavier than air flying machines are impossible."
— *Lord Kelvin, President, Royal Society, 1895.*

"Babe Ruth made a big mistake when he gave up pitching."
— *Tris Speaker, 1921.*

"The horse is here today, but the automobile is only a novelty — a fad."
— *President of Michigan Savings Bank advising against investing in the Ford Motor Company.*

"Video won't be able to hold on to any market it captures after the first six months. People will soon get tired of staring at a plywood box every night."
— *Daryl F. Zanuck, 20th Century Fox, commenting on television in 1946.*

"What use could the company make of an electric toy?"
— *Western Union, when it turned down rights to the telephone in 1878.*

Gail Sheehy said it best: "If we don't change, we don't grow. If we don't grow, we aren't really living."

E is for Encouragement and Evaluation.

How many of us have started diets. . . . more than once? Quit smoking. . . . more than once? Without someone cheering us on, supporting and encouraging (and yes, monitoring) us, it's too easy to backslide into the old ways. Change needs a cheering section: someone to say, "Hey, you're doing good, it's really working." "I think I can, I think I can" does become "I thought I could, I knew I could" when you keep trying without giving up. Finally, Evaluation means taking time to assess whether the change is actually accomplishing its goal, and whether it's worthwhile to continue. . . .which brings us right back to looking at Cause and Choice all over again!

"I think I can, I think I can" has such a positive, forward-motion rhythm to it; who can resist?

Alice Yucht is a Librarian at Heritage Middle School in Livingston, New Jersey.

Another OPINION

By Harry Willems

Reflections on *Information Power: Building Partnerships for Learning.* What Is a Librarian to Do?

For an upcoming presentation, I've been reading and working through the national standards for school libraries prepared by the American Association of School Librarians (AASL) and the Association for Educational Communications and Technology (AECT). Nine standards are split into three sections: information literacy, independent learning and social responsibility.

The key to understanding the impact of the book is the diagram in Chapter 3. Denise Irwin, from Andover (Kansas) High School, uses an apple to illustrate the overlapping and concentric rings of the Information Power logo. The seeds are the nine information literacy standards for student learning. The core of the apple is the three themes of Information Power: leadership, technology, and collaboration. This core is the structure on which the library program is built.

The flesh of the apple is the library program, which is what librarians do, or should be doing, such as collaborating with colleagues and inservicing teachers on integration of technology and information literacy into curricula. The outer skin of the apple is the end product, the reason we planted the seeds—a community of lifelong learners.

Here are some of the lessons that I've learned:

Librarians must be leaders.

The school boards that employ the LMS (Library Media Specialist) can no longer afford to pay $18 to $25 an hour for the LMS to shelve books. Oh, do I need to duck? I feel the stares of grouchy librarians and my ears are ringing already. I know, I know, some of you don't even have library aides, much less a trained paraprofessional. This problem may be your first step in the leadership role. Identify the steps you need to take to move forward, and then take that first step. Find creative solutions.

Librarians must be collaborators.

Building influence begins with effective communications—written, spoken, and repeated many times. The librarian needs to know how to build bridges across the curriculum to weave information literacy into every aspect of the educational program. The librarian needs to volunteer for every committee that comes up, from technology to curriculum to textbook adoption to prom. Collaboration is building relationships.

Power is developed.

Pat Gaunce, the director of the West Wyandotte branch of the Kansas City (Kansas) Public Library (that has an effective school collaboration) has coined the phrase "Power is Not a Four Letter Word." Developing power and influence is a conscious act that begins with a plan developed specifically for your situation.

Schools need certified Library Media Specialists.

Librarians who take a leadership role and find constructive ways to do circulation and reshelving enhance the need for trained library media specialists. In the age of information, the beginning of the 21st century, it's ludicrous to think that untrained paraprofessionals, aides or others can be leaders in the science of information. In the same gasping breath, it's necessary to reiterate what was said in the beginning of this article. School boards cannot afford to pay professionals in the science of information to circulate and shelve books.

Whose problem is it? The librarian must become a leader in curriculum, technology, teaching and learning—a leader with vision and passion. The library system must provide leadership education. School boards must realize that the students from their district will compete for jobs and scholarships with students from districts that have integrated comprehensive information literacy skills honed by a visionary librarian.

Harry Willems is a Consultant and Assistant Director for the Southeast Kansas Library System in Iola, Kansas.

TECHNOLOGY PLANNING

Providing for Technological Support

HELP!

Why Isn't the Smiley Face Smiling?

When planning for technology, don't forget the support element.

by Steve Baule

Developing and implementing a plan to support new technology is often forgotten until the computers in the building start to cause problems. With a little foresight, you can avoid this pitfall.

First, find out what support services the classroom teachers and the administrator's secretary really need, instead of what you think they need. After you have gathered this information, you need to determine how to provide the most immediate support possible.

Second, train all these new users in basic trouble-shooting. Support this training with trouble-shooting lists—small laminated help sheets with answers to frequently asked questions. Be sure to include toll-free numbers for the software and hardware, if available.

Third, provide additional in-depth training to department secretaries or other staff so they can provide day-to-day user support. Train two to three people to this level of expertise so that no one individual is relied upon for all support. Teach them to perform preventive maintenance; solve all problems related to departmental software packages; glitches related to printers, CD-ROMs and other peripherals; and improper configurations of hardware. Schedule regular meetings with these support people so they can share information and air concerns.

Finally, assign a full-time technician to solve hardware problems and the more unusual software problems. Set up a response system for handling demands so that his time is not wasted on problems others could solve. Small buildings that cannot afford a full-time technician may need to share this position with other buildings in the district, or buy a service contract with a local vendor to provide support. Be sure that everyone knows who to contact for support and that the support person provides follow-up to make sure the problem has really been solved.

Putting together a responsive support plan is important to the overall success of technology within your school. Complement the plan with a cheerful attitude, a quick response to problems, and ongoing training—success is sure to follow! **TC**

Steve Baule is Coordinator of Instructional Resources, Glenbrook South High School, Glenview, New York.

TECHNOLOGY PLANNING

5 Issues in Planning for Library Technology

BY PAUL RUX

An understanding of these issues will help media professionals to analyze and guide planning for technology in libraries.

Recently, I evaluated several automation grant applications as an external consultant. This task turned out to be a learning experience for me in terms of learning about planning for library technology.

Five issues stood out in the applications: technological vision, systems thinking, job analysis, budget, and statistics. An understanding of these issues will help media professionals to analyze and guide planning for technology in libraries.

..1..

Technological vision means one has a grasp of what is possible with information technologies. Because of networking, such vision must transcend computing to include telecommunications. It must include connecting with multiple end users beyond libraries, other information providers, and partners. For maximum return from investment in library technology today, networking and information partnerships are prerequisite paradigms for cost-effective planning.

..2..

Systems thinking means we recognize the potential for technology to connect us with others. Connecting means sharing, which requires us to think in term of group cooperation and planning, not traditional stand-alone operations. This dynamic also upends the traditional local funding of library service, since networking transcends narrow geographic boundaries.

..3..

Job analysis means we need to look at the human interface with technology. This includes training in technology for patrons as well as staff. Such patron training represents a golden opportunity for libraries to become a critical public access point to new information technology, especially for the "information poor." Providing this access, in turn, will redefine our jobs.

..4..

Budget means we need to recognize computing and telecommunications as legitimate library costs, not incidentals to books and magazines. When such costs are formally recognized in budgets, technology will start to get the support it needs to keep libraries alive and vital.

..5..

Statistics means that more than ever before technology can help librarians measure what they do. This spells increased accuracy in reporting, marketing, and deployment of limited resources. The technological capability to collect hard numbers about what libraries do can result in greater efficiency and credibility in the eyes of funders.

The content of the grant applications revealed that librarians do indeed have technological vision, know how to think in terms of systems, have thoroughly analyzed their jobs, and are on the lookout for ways to make the case for more budget. Unfortunately, most planners wrestle with these issues in isolation. We need to develop ways to share our insights and discoveries about these facets of planning for technology. We can learn a lot from each other. **TC**

Paul Rux is founder and president of Information Consulting Services in Dodgeville, Wisconsin.

– Showcasing Technology –

INTEGRATING TECHNOLOGY INTO SCHOOLS—EIGHT WAYS TO PROMOTE SUCCESS

BY BOB HOFFMAN

When a technology use plan is needed to obtain a grant, whose input should be solicited to get a handle on what's needed in your school? And what—besides computers, software, and training—should the plan and the grant proposal include? School technology integration is not just a matter of buying some hardware and software and holding a couple workshops for teachers. If this is the extent of your plan, the computers will simply collect dust.

A review of the literature on implementing technology shows there are at least seven groups of "stakeholders" who should be consulted when planning a major technology initiative. District administrators and board members should be consulted about their "vision" for technology in the district as a whole. Curriculum directors want input about what kinds of instruction are going to be supported. The school site administrators also have their own set of goals and priorities. If a district technology committee or coordinator exists, you'll want to check there, too.

Classroom teachers will need to provide information about what they teach, how they teach it, and how technology might play a role. District or site maintenance supervisors should be consulted about infrastructure (power, telephone, networks, furniture, security) and maintenance. And teachers' union representatives will want input on how the new technology is going to change teachers' roles and relationships.

BEGIN BY GATHERING INFORMATION

Options range from a school- or district-wide "visioning" exercise to surveys and interviews with stakeholders. Many technology committees send out questionnaires to everyone, including parents, and then interview key representatives of each group. Once they've gathered everyone's initial input, they draft a plan. In the past, technology plans have focused on hardware and software, with a little staff development thrown in for good measure. Nowadays, that isn't enough.

ADMINISTRATIVE SUPPORT IS KEY

For technology integration to succeed on even a modest scale, it must have strong support from the school board and from district and school site administrators. Teachers begin using technology both because they choose to and because they feel their organization expects them to. Recognition, advancement, and financial rewards are among the incentives offered to teachers by many schools who tie technology implementation to school-wide or district-wide goals. Administrators and board members are the allocators of resources for getting technology up and running with funds and staff development opportunities.

TEACHERS MUST BE CONVINCED

No matter how you present it, technology complicates teaching. Teachers need adequate training and support if they are to accept

---

THE "BIG EIGHT" REQUIREMENTS FOR IMPLEMENTING NEW TECHNOLOGY:

1. Administrative support

2. Staff development and technical support

3. Availability of technology

4. Technology use plan

5. Technology coordinator

6. Facilities and maintenance

7. Assessment

8. Broad participation

it. This includes day-to-day help with problems of organizing time, space, supervision, operations, and access. Teachers will need to be given release time, or find time on their own, for self-study, inservice training, conferences, workshops, and classes. Topics covered should include specifics on buying, choosing, and using technology tools.

ONGOING EDUCATION IS ESSENTIAL

Experts agree that comprehensive and extended staff development is necessary for full integration to occur. Outside consultants, as well as technology mentor teachers and a school technology coordinator, will help smooth the learning process. Studies have shown that the influence of a coordinator leads to greater use of computers for promoting higher order thinking skills. The technology coordinator, who usually guides the technology plan, can also more easily pursue purposeful strategies to obtain funds for further implementing technology than can individual teachers.

Both teachers and students need many opportunities to examine and use computer programs that develop deductive-reasoning and problem-solving skills, create tests, use drill and practice exercises, and develop their own personal interests in researching, organizing, and reporting information through spreadsheets, databases, and word processing programs.

SUFFICIENT EQUIPMENT IS A MUST

All this planning and training is of no use unless sufficient hardware and software are available to meet demand and provide ready and convenient access to equipment and programs. Some schools favor computer labs; others distribute one or more computers into classrooms in addition to or in place of a centralized lab. The type and location of equipment and all other technology-related information should be integrated into a long-range (three- to five-year) technology plan.

Broken equipment, slow repairs, and inadequate facilities spell disaster for technology integration, so be sure to include maintenance and repair costs in your plan. Also be sure to address assessment and evaluation methods that reflect the effect of the new technology on students and teachers.

COLLABORATION IS RECOMMENDED

Research shows that individual teacher-level decision making results in greater use of computers for basic math and language arts skills. Schools with strong internal decision making also provide more staff development activities. Even the number of computers per student and the amount of daily computer use is greater in schools with strong internal collective decision making by groups that include teachers and administrators.

Others recommend collaboration with outside agencies—partnerships with companies or universities, for example, that may provide financial and material resources or technology training expertise. Choose the type of collaboration that will reap maximum benefits for your school. **TC**

Bob Hoffman is an Assistant Professor in the Department of Educational Technology at San Diego State University, California.

STAFF DEVELOPMENT: GETTING EVERYONE ON BOARD

IMPLEMENTING SCHOOL TECHNOLOGY
Calling on Teachers

By Anthony B. Maddox

Information technology (IT) remains an ominous specter in many elementary, middle and secondary schools. Without question, some teachers are using technology with varying degrees of success to create and discover curriculum materials, improve student learning and experiment with novel instruction practices. Many others, however, are simply not comfortable with technology and have few resources to invest in acquiring the substantial hardware, networks, software and services needed to use IT effectively.

The lack of teacher involvement with IT in schools may be due, in part, to conditions resulting in IT paradoxes, not dissimilar to those experienced in industry. An IT paradox is a situation where increasing expenditures on technology results in less-than-expected outcomes. In schools, improved learning, enhanced reading skills and better math performance are obviously desired student outcomes. For teachers, curriculum enhancement, improved instruction and better instructional resources are also highly desired outcomes. Strategies that foster teachers' technology awareness help increase their involvement in the planning, deployment and integration of IT initiatives, ultimately eliminating the conditions that could lead to IT paradoxes.

To illustrate this point, let's explore how IT paradoxes in schools can be exposed and eliminated while demystifying technology for classroom teachers. Begin with the premise that technology implementation is expensive. Many studies, primarily from industry, indicate that the real cost of computerization may run from two or three times the cost of hardware technology alone. Consequently, at least one half of an IT budget should be allocated for nonhardware expenses such as software, services, training and expertise.

If school officials view acquiring hardware as the initial challenge in developing an IT infrastructure, then they're unlikely to devote a large percentage of their resources for nonhardware "intangibles." However, if they don't invest in these essential intangibles, the software, services and expertise needed to integrate and use technology will lag far behind the hardware deployment.

Imagine computer boxes arriving at a school before the teachers know what to do with them. Arming teachers with the information to use technology before, during and after purchase will increase their role in technology integration.

The Usability Issue

Software is a critical element of IT implementation, but much existing educational software is teacher and student unfriendly, despite continued attempts for improvement. Some researchers have indicated that an increased emphasis on user-centered design could help make software easier for them to use.

As computers and networks become ubiquitous in schools, software evaluation practices specific to the education objectives of each school site and district will give teachers a better understanding of how they can integrate technology into their classrooms. Identifying the strengths and weaknesses of software will help schools adopt and reject software based on its potential to benefit educational practice.

There are quantitative, qualitative and heuristic usability techniques (some appropriate for use by students) that may be applied to software that can help in the software acquisition process. If this usability issue is addressed, teachers can view software through a new lens. Software designers may even wish to have teachers help develop educational software specifications from the conceptualization stage.

Services are also a fundamental part of any technology implementation. Fortunately, there is a growing realization among educators that successful technology outcomes require specialized management support services and expertise. Some of these services are technical (hardware maintenance, network administration, user training and software installation), while others are informational (libraries, databases, help desks and software hot lines). Alas, all cost money and compete for schools' limited funds.

The good news is that there are many different school service providers: consultants, students, teachers, technology coordinators, school districts, nonprofit partnerships and for-profit educational service agencies. The bad news is that there are potential side effects that may interfere with how these services are provided and performed. Correctly identifying IT experts and determining whether they should be full or part time, temporary or permanent, in-house or outsourced, voluntary or compensated is necessary to ensure their expertise matches schools' educational and technological objectives. Knowledge of expertise preconditions can alert teachers to the need to be questioning and critical of expert opinions while requesting that expertise be shared using a language that is familiar to educators.

The material above describes some preconditions for IT paradoxes but also the basis for defining a contextual "envelope" for regular, routine teacher participation in technology planning, deployment, integration and utilization.

Teachers as Knowledge Brokers

To develop effective processes and procedures, we must consider that teachers serve as knowledge brokers. We must be aware of the nature and amount of information for which they are responsible, the array of services they need or must create to achieve desired outcomes and the resources they need and the responsibilities they have as professionals. Given their professional duties and the increasing demands of educational restructuring, they will need assistance to see technology as friend and not foe.

Where will teachers get this assistance? Unfortunately, teachers are one of the few professional groups without a well-staffed, technology-enhanced, support infrastructure for their professional activities. Physicians rely extensively on nursing professionals, medical technicians and advanced biotechnology. Attorneys interface regularly with legal clerks, law enforcement and judicial professionals and massive case databases. Engineers need technicians, drafting professionals and sophisticated computational resources.

How likely is it that teachers, without help, could develop sufficient awareness of and interest in technology paradoxes that would lead to their trial, evaluation and adoption of technology in addition to other responsibilities? Does state-of-the-art technology easily allow teachers to develop their own educational products and services on demand and integrate them into core educational service activities? Rarely (although increasingly) do nonentrepreneurial professionals in other disciplines need to address similar questions or are they asked to assume such self-supporting roles.

Teachers could benefit from extensive, sophisticated on-site and remotely accessed IT support structures that enhance professional activity, preserve time, increase knowledge, focus attention, demand accountability and increase compensation. These are incentives and responsibilities shared with professionals in many fields and occupations. Yet K-12 teaching professionals are asked to proceed as though some invisible hand will ultimately orchestrate technological innovation at their school site.

Teachers are generally interested in practical ways to seek information and create exciting learning environments. Involving them at the conceptualization stage of IT planning, deployment, integration and utilization is a good way to support their personal curiosity for knowledge. Both novice and veteran teachers could work together on such tasks. Seasoned teachers can bring their experiences into the technology implementation process. Additionally, newer teachers can bring an awareness of technology that may allow things to be done that experienced teachers dismissed years ago. Technology presented through an intermediary that serves as a "critical friend" can bring these teachers together. Thus from a pool of nearly three million American teachers, there is a rich source of educational knowledge that could lead to viable information technology-based educational products and services.

Adopting IT implementation rules of engagement that combine bottom-up, event-based teacher knowledge with top-down, goal-driven technology objectives will send a signal to teachers that that are recognized as knowledge producers as well as technology users. A hidden benefit is the possibility of reducing the cost of IT implementation by avoiding IT paradoxes. TC

Anthony B. Maddox is with the Graduate School of Education & Information Studies, University of California, Los Angeles.

Reprinted from Upgrade *(February 1997) with permission of Kathleen Rakestraw, Director of Communications, Software Publishers Association.*

Copyright Laws & Software

By Carol Mann Simpson

Because computer software is not covered by exactly the same regulations as print and audiovisual resources, the use of computers in schools has opened a Pandora's box of concerns for librarians.

What are the definitive rules about software copyrights? Like written works, computer programs are protected under copyright laws. In addition, computer software is generally protected by a license agreement—a contract over and above copyright that further restricts what the purchaser may do with the product. Both copyright and license agreements specify how the software may used, including how it may be copied, loaned (circulated) or disposed of.

The law states that copying software may include making a duplicate of the diskette, copying the program onto a hard disk, or loading the program into a computer's RAM.

Copyright law allows the software's purchaser to make one archival copy of the diskettes in the package. These "backups" are not to be used unless the original diskettes are lost or damaged beyond recovery.

Since loading software into a computer's RAM does not destroy the copy on the hard disk or the diskette, some software packages grant the user permission to maintain two simultaneous copies of the software. This does not mean, however, that the software may be loaded onto two different computers at the same time. Doing so is a clear violation of copyright law, unless the user has written permission to the contrary.

Purchasers are bound by a signed license agreement that must be signed before sending in the product registration certificate. There are also "shrink wrap" licenses, which take effect the moment the purchaser unwraps the package. Some states have limited the power of such automatic licensing agreements, but be sure to read the fine print.

Is it enough that all software purchased by the library is properly licensed? Maybe not. If the library has computers equipped with hard disks, there's a good chance that students or teachers have installed copies of their personal software on school machines. Since this copy of the software duplicates—rather than replaces—the software on the owner's machine, it is likely to be in violation of copyright. This means you and your school could be liable for copyright infringement.

Don't have time to peruse all the hard disks in the building? The Software Publishers' Association offers a free program called SPAudit that will do the sleuthing for you. The program scours the hard disk for programs produced by SPA members and creates a list of all the programs on the hard disk. In addition to the SP Audit program, the Software Publishers' Association offers a kit of information about software copyright. To order either, call 1-800-388-7478 or write to the Software Publishers' Association at 1730 M St. NW #700 Washington, DC 20036. The SPA fax number is 202-223-8756.

Remember, it's to the benefit of their members for the SPA to conservatively explain software copyright regulations. **TC**

Carol Mann Simpson is Facilitator—Library Technology, Mesquite (Texas) School District.

WHY MULTIMEDIA?

feature

How Much, How Many and When? Copyright & Multimedia

By Carol Simpson

Multimedia is a copyright infringement nightmare! In creating a multimedia presentation, a student or teacher is likely to deal with copyrights on all aspects of the production that aren't actually originated by the author: video, graphics, music or other sound recording, and computer data. Thanks to the hard work of a group of media producers, publishers and media consumers, guidelines on the use of multimedia in education were approved late in 1996. These guidelines outline acceptable use of copyrighted materials in educational fair-use situations. The multimedia guidelines are not law, just as the fair-use guidelines are not law. They simply represent an agreement on limits of use between those who own the copyright and those who wish to use the copyrighted materials. Compliance under the guidelines doesn't mean the use is "legal." It means the copyright holder agrees not to sue someone who uses his or her materials within these limits.

The new agreement on Fair Use Guidelines for Educational Multimedia provides concrete limits on the types and amounts of material that may be included in works created by teachers and students. One must follow the four tests of fair use that apply to *all* uses of copyrighted materials in schools:

• The purpose and character of the use, including whether the use is for nonprofit educational purposes;

• The nature of the copyrighted work, for example, is it factual or creative;

• The amount of and substantiality of the portion used in relation to the copyrighted work as a whole; and

• The effect of the use upon the potential market for and value of the copyrighted work.

One of the first new guidelines calls for all materials used in multimedia works created by students and teachers to be properly cited as being taken from the works of others. The guidelines also state that multimedia works made from the copyrighted materials may be used only in support of the education of students in nonprofit educational institutions. Such specific wording is typical of this document. This prohibition removes any debate over whether there is a fair use of multimedia for businesses, churches and other non educational institutions.

THE TECHNOLOGY CONNECTION: BUILDING A SUCCESSFUL LIBRARY MEDIA PROGRAM

CHAPTER 1 DRAWING THE PLANS: LIBRARY MEDIA SPECIALIST AS ARCHITECT

Retention and Access

The new guidelines permit multimedia works made by students to be used in the class for which they were created, and retained by them in portfolios maintained for job interviews or college applications. Teachers may use the multimedia presentations they create in face-to-face instruction, and they may assign students to view the presentations on their own. Teachers may display their own multimedia programs at conferences and workshops, and they may retain the programs they create in portfolios for job interviews or evaluations. There is a limit to an educator's right to keep a work created from copyrighted material, however. While a student may keep a work indefinitely, a teacher may only keep a work for two years from the time of its first use with a class. Beyond the two-year window, permission to retain or use the material is required for *each* portion of copyrighted material used in the presentation.

Quantity Limits

The guidelines specify the amounts of different types of copyrighted materials from a single source that may be used in all multimedia projects created in the course of a year/term. In other words, from any one video, recording or database, a specific limit is assigned that a student or teacher may not exceed in a single year/term. Should a teacher reach this theoretical limit, any additional material in a presentation would require permission. Students, especially in grades K-8, are granted more leeway. An example would be the teacher who uses several images from a library book to create a multimedia presentation for his class. The number of images used reaches the limit assigned in the guidelines for this type of material. Before the year/term is finished, the teacher wishes to use additional materials from the same book for another multimedia presentation to his students. The teacher will need to request permission in advance before he may use the additional images.

The limits per year/term are:

Motion media (film, video, television) — up to 10% or 3 minutes, whichever is less, of an individual program.

Text (prose, poetry, play) — up to 10% or 1,000 words, whichever is less, of a novel, story, play or long poem. Short poems less than 250 words may be used in their entirety. Only three poems by one poet or five poems by different poets from an anthology may be used. For poems longer than 250 words, only three excerpts from one poet or five from works by different poets in an anthology are permitted.

Music, lyrics, and music video — up to 10% but not more than 30 seconds from a single work (or combined from separate extracts of a work). It makes no difference if the work is being used as a musical work on its own, or it is an incidental accompaniment to some visual material. If a video clip has music in the background and you can't separate the music from the visual material, you will be restricted by the 30-second limit for music. If the music is altered in any way, the fundamental melody must be maintained and the basic character of the work should be preserved.

Illustrations, cartoons and photographs. A work may be used in its entirety but only if no more than five images from a single artist or photographer are used in a multimedia work. In addition, if images are taken from a single collective work, no more than 10% or 16 images may be used.

Numerical data sets (computer databases or spreadsheets) — up to 10% or 2,500 fields or cells, whichever is less, may be used from a copyrighted database.

How Many Copies?

An educator may make only two copies (including the original) of the multimedia work. An additional copy may be made if one of the copies is lost, stolen or damaged. If more than one person co-authors the multimedia work, each may have one copy of the work and may keep it as long as allowed under the creator-type (student or teacher) guidelines.

Other Restrictions

The opening screen of the multimedia work and any accompanying printed materials must contain a notice that the work contains copyrighted materials that have been used under the fair-use exemption of the U.S. Copyright Law. While changes may be made to support specific educational goals, the author must clearly indicate that such alterations have been made.

The power of multimedia and the computer applications that support it also provide powerful liability for the users. While you have the capability to grab a frame from a film, extract a single face from a photograph, or isolate an instrument from the accompaniment of a popular song, you may not exceed the limits imposed in the multimedia guidelines without permission from whoever owns the rights to those items.

NOTE: All references made to "multimedia works" refer to productions including copyrighted materials. Obviously, any multimedia production the teacher or student creates in its entirety would be totally under the control of the creator.

Carol Simpson is the Editor of Technology Connection *and the author of* Copyright for Schools, Second Edition, *published by Linworth Publishing, Inc.*

Guidelines to remember when creating multimedia presentations:

- Students and teachers *may* use copyrighted material in multimedia presentations if quantity limits are observed.

- Students and teachers *may* use copyrighted material in multimedia presentations if they support direct instruction.

- Students and teachers *may* keep the multimedia presentations they create for class, though teachers face a two-year limit.

- Specific limits are established for the amount of material that may be used in multimedia presentations, based on the original medium.

MANAGING of/with TECHNOLOGY

Technostress
What Is It? How Can You Learn to Live with It?

by Carol Smallwood

If you find you are often "out of memory" like your hard drives, then indeed you have joined the vastly expanding Technostress Club. And, if we think it will all go away and we have adapted, note what software king Bill Gates predicts in his book *The Road Ahead*: "The revolution in communication is just beginning. It will take place over several decades, and will be driven by new applications, new tools, often meeting currently unforeseen needs."

Stress in itself isn't bad; it challenges and exercises our creativity. But when it gets to be too much, it hampers our performance and can have other serious consequences. Stress is often a result of increased responsibilities. Just trying to avoid becoming a technology has-been is stressful.

Dealing with increased access to information, changes in social values and increased needs of staff and students can make us feel out of control. Suddenly, technology isn't making the job easier; instead, it is producing unforeseen problems with no precedent for solving them.

At times we are faced with impossible tasks. Too often the budget for books and materials is sacrificed for CD towers, accessing the Internet, remedial software. We have no on-site technology support when things go wrong. And, too often they do go wrong. Software mastered this year requires us to learn updates the next. Students quickly learn to defeat a security system that took days to devise. Add personal stress from changes in family structure.

We recognize stress by lack of energy, a shortened temper, using self-destructive escape measures that have adverse results on those closest to us. We begin to question our choice of profession; job performance decreases; visits to the doctor increase. Days are filled with ordeals to get through rather than challenges to enjoy.

Stress isn't going away, so how do we deal with it? First, acknowledge that it exists, then fine-tune our senses to know when we have too much. In my case, I know I have had it when I can't remember things I've just done or the day of the week, and my left eye flutters.

Keep track of the times of the day, days of the week, or months of the year when you feel the most stress. You will begin to see a pattern. At these times of stress, do jobs that are the easiest. Cover books, file vertical file material, change display cases or bulletin boards. Take personal days offered to you in your employment contract.

When you are the most rested, plan realistically, on paper, yearly, monthly, weekly, daily activities. Keep plans simple. Your days will be less stressful because you don't have to keep so many things in mind. Crossing off completed tasks provides incentive.

When dealing with adults or students, remember that their behavior toward you is not usually personal. How they relate to the world has little to do with you. When people cause you stress, concentrate on others who are supportive. Draw on your inner reserve in times of crisis. Fix or find a "rest spot" in your workplace that relaxes you. Perhaps it is a picture, a wall hanging, a favorite book on the shelf, whatever works. Let it remind you that the present experience is only a small part of the whole. Many other important and lasting places and things are outside your media center, and soon this crisis will make little difference to you.

If you have a place out of sight, a periodical storage room for example, keep an old knotted bath towel handy to hit the floor with occasionally. Releasing hostile feelings this way sounds silly, but it works much better than having to take back words spoken in anger.

Become smarter in recognizing no-win situations. Stop beating your head against the wall trying to change what can't be changed. Accept some situations as fact, no matter how illogical. Leave it and go on. Deal with situations in which you can make a difference. This takes wisdom and courage.

Give yourself a fighting chance by getting eight hours of sleep every night. Keep those annual physical and dental appointments with your doctor and dentist. Eat a balanced diet. Exercise. Park your car in an inconvenient parking spot and walk a distance to get to your school building.

We are creatures of habit and it is much easier to keep doing the things we always have done. Observe your habits as if you were another person. Write down suggestions. Begin by changing one habit that isn't too difficult to change. Then select another and do the same. See how much better the new habits are for you.

Alternate mentally and physically difficult jobs. Know when you work best at each job. Don't tackle learning a new computer program at the end of the day when you are beat. Don't move dozens of bookshelves at one time. On the other hand, don't rotate jobs to create more work. For example, enter books in the database only when you have enough to warrant changing your computer screen. Be conscious of time and motion efficiency. Save vertical file materials until it is worthwhile to get out the master list, select and print subject headings.

Guard against perfectionism. How important is it that all the bar codes are in the exact spot on all magazines? If you discover that the title you have entered from your light pen or scanner doesn't match up with the material or has no bar code, what is the best action to follow when checking out material? Instead of making impatient students wait for you to enter a new bar code, release the material to reliable students and put a post-it-note under the circulation card to alert you to correct the material when it is returned. If some students are likely to deny having material on receiving an overdue notice, have them return for the book before they leave for the day.

Use free time to make your workplace run smoother. If you resent spending several hours after school working, revise your work habits or your resentment will taint your attitude overall.

If you do not have a library policy in force, making one will reduce stress. Read *School Library Journal's* November 1995 article, "ALA's Banned Books Week a 'Sham,' Says Colorado Ministry." Have a policy in place before you need to use it.

Before getting Internet access, see how others have managed student access. Arrange screens so they are easy to watch from the circulation desk, even if it takes some rewiring. Octagon or hexagon computer furniture saves floor space, but you cannot see all screens at once.

Anticipate busy times such as the beginning and ending of the school year. Do all jobs that can be done before these times. When a job looks too large, whittle it down by doing it in steps. When boxes of books are donated, get them ready in steps. First, decide which books are to become part of your collection and establish all call numbers and subject headings. Applying book jackets and plastic covers for paperbacks are the last step before entering each one into the database or typing cards for the card catalog. Limit the number of books you process this way and rely on book jobbers for full processing.

Look for shortcuts to make your job easier. Stamp date due cards ahead of time. Keep daily records so that end-of-the-year records are easy to compile. If entering several years of back issues of magazines, put bar codes in sequence and enter them in that sequence so you don't have to enter each bar code manually. Your cataloging software should have the option to provide bar codes in automatic correct sequence. This will work with other materials, too.

If you are in the process of buying computers, select all of them to run on the same platform. It is easier to work with only one type. Look into leasing agreements to avoid problems in disposing of obsolete equipment and managing large outlays of money for new. Have the computers wired so that one switch turns everything on or off at once. If you are just beginning to list books on computer, put bar codes on fronts of books to make checkout easier.

Consider joining local tech groups for peer support, information exchange, frustration venting. Network electronically with others in state and national professional organizations.

To save room on your CD-ROM tower, keep CDs that are not used every day in their bar-coded cases, ready for students to check out in the library. When you get a software update, sit down immediately and learn the changes so you can answer students' questions quickly. Be sure updates are really worth getting. I was recently disappointed when I updated a program. There were a few advantages, but the updates made the program more cumbersome.

Order paper, cartridges, ribbon and other supplies in advance. Buy in quantity for better prices. Know when funding becomes short to avoid running out. Use 20-pound paper for dot matrix printers to avoid jamming. Fifteen-pound is less expensive but it isn't worth the frustration.

Streamline your wardrobe. Color coordinate. If you are responsible for food preparation at home, prepare food in quantity to simplify meal preparation and provide inexpensive lunches and quick dinners. Use the time you save to relax and enjoy gardening, watching television, playing sports. Do not shortchange yourself by skipping this time.

Robert A. Gross and Christine L. Borgman note in "The Incredible Vanishing Library," *American Libraries,* October 1995: "At its heart, the library is devoted to scholarship." I am saving my fine money to buy a small, bronze bust of William Shakespeare. It helps me feel that the task of collecting nickels and dimes is going to some good purpose, and it makes a statement about the library—that good things endure. I will put it in a place I can see easily. When I look at it, I will know my current turmoil is not so important.

Always there will be those who show little consideration for your job. There will always be students who hate school, parents who cannot see the harm they are doing their children, administrators that place media centers at the low end of the totem pole, voters that bash schools, colleagues that drive you up the wall. We cannot change everything and everyone nor can we eliminate stress. But we can manage to live with what we find on our plates—no small task, no matter what the profession. **TC**

Carol Smallwood is Media Director at Pellston (Michigan) Public Schools and a frequent contributor to professional magazines. Previously she was a Title I public library consultant and has taught various grade levels and subjects. Her latest book, Recycling Tips for Librarians and Teachers, *was recently published by McFarland & Company.*

THE HUMAN SIDE OF TECHNOLOGY

Technology & Stress

Are They Inseparable?

By Becky Mather

Does technology add stress to the media specialist's life? I did not know what true stress was until I acquired a lab of 35 networked computers. Even during a normal day when everything is working almost perfectly, there are constant interruptions because a printer has jammed or because a student or teacher has forgotten a password. Perhaps a student typed a crucial research paper at home using an obscure word processing program, and your software will not open the document from his floppy disk. The list of minor situations goes on and on. Chances are good that you, the media specialist, are perceived as the person who is the most knowledgeable about computers. Suddenly you are the school's technology troubleshooter—not an enviable position.

And it gets worse. Recently our network file server was scheduled for replacement with a newer, more powerful model. Even though the timing was inconvenient, we decided to go ahead with the work because we were experiencing so many problems. The work that was expected to be completed in one week actually took almost five weeks. Fortunately two of those weeks were winter break, but the other three were a nightmare. Our server runs four labs, one of which is in the media center. Another lab is in the business department, where classes were unable to do much of anything for three weeks. Students were much more understanding and patient than teachers. Many teachers found it difficult to be flexible and vented their frustrations on the media center staff. I dreaded going to school each morning during those weeks until I learned to shrug my shoulders and smile. After all, I was also relying on the network specialist. I had a storeroom full of books I could not check in and pages of handwritten check-outs to unscramble. The only card catalog available was the one in my head. The lesson here is that eventually we will have to function temporarily without the machines that we have become dependent upon. To be able to carry on without computers, we must have a plan before the need arises.

Media specialists are not the only people coping with technostress. Students can experience frustration that may not be readily apparent. The students we see most often are those who feel comfortable working with computers. In a large school, it is easy to miss the kids who are uneasy around computers and, therefore, avoid using them. When those students are forced by a class assignment to use a computer, they may be too embarrassed to ask for help. It is this type of student who labors over a 10-page paper only to lose it through an error in the saving process. When that happens, it is difficult to convince the student that a computer really is a labor-saving, user-friendly device.

If my school is fairly representative, there also are many teachers who are uncomfortable around computers. They can be quite defensive and vocal about their discomfort, often disguising it as disdain. Computers break down, they say, but books never do. However, once their own children enter college, they will eagerly put aside their misgivings to learn the joys of e-mail. Maybe that shows that people can be taught new tricks if convinced there is a good reason to learn them. At the other extreme are the teachers who believe that the Internet is the best source for any and all types of information. However, it is still quicker and easier to find the winners of the last Olympics in an almanac than it is to locate the information on the Web, especially when the user has to log in to the network and use a painfully slow Internet connection. Technology for the sake of technology is a difficult concept to overcome because its supporters are fervent in their beliefs. But why use a computer if there is a faster, easier, better way to find information? Sooner or later administration will want to assess the effectiveness of all the technology being used to enhance student learning. Undoubtedly the media specialist will be part of that process in the development or implementation of a technology assessment tool.

There is no question that technology completely changes the nature of the media specialist's job. Before computers, students writing four-letter words on the study carrels were a concern. Now computer abuse drives me wild. I have to glue the covers on the mice so students cannot remove the balls. The determined students keep inventing new ways to get into DOS and explore, and Internet abuse is a constant source of frustration for our media center staff. In spite of having signed an acceptable use policy, students still attempt to chat, play games, and visit inappropriate Web sites. Some even cut classes to surf the Net. One student underwent a police investigation for the alleged use of fake credit cards through the Internet. Another used his home computer to establish a Web site maligning our high school. Although these two examples are the extreme, Internet abuse in our school has led to the development of yet another, more stringent discipline policy.

I honestly do not remember how I spent my time BC (before computers). Now 95% of my day is devoted to technology-related tasks for which I had no prior training. And while this is not a negative change, any change is stressful.

There is no denying that technology adds stress to a media specialist's life. The key to minimizing stress is to be proactive from the beginning. Try to anticipate problem areas and plan to deal with them in advance. In spite of the hassles, however, I would not choose to return to life as it was BC. For me, technology is both a joy and a welcomed challenge. I have grown personally and professionally because of my involvement with computers, and my students have become better researchers and skilled computer users. The learning curve is steep at first, but it eventually eases. However, it never becomes completely flat because in the world of technology, change is constant. TC

Becky Mather is a Media Specialist at Muscatine (Iowa) High School.

Separating Technology and Stress

Here are some strategies I recommend for minimizing the amount of frustration and stress associated with the integration of technology into our media centers.

Set reasonable expectations for yourself; publicize them, and stick to them. You cannot possibly know everything or do everything. You might choose to discontinue some of the tasks you performed BC or, if possible, assign them to someone else. Make sure your staff knows your areas of expertise as well as your limitations. Learn all you can about the areas in which you want to be competent. Read books, take classes, and join listservs and user groups. You do not need to become a systems engineer, but you should learn enough to handle the day-to-day operation of your network. Train another person as a network administrator so you can share responsibilities. When a trained professional works on your machines, ask questions and take notes. Develop lots of patience, a sense of humor, and a thick skin.

Campaign for adequate technical support. Ideally, employ a trained network person at the building or district level. Outsource the network jobs that are too complex for in-house personnel. Train student helpers to do some tasks and to assist other students. Recruit parent volunteers, especially those with computer training. It is frustrating when no one is available to install new software or hardware or to repair a minor problem. Expensive equipment is wasted when it cannot be used.

Educate your staff and students. Do not assume that everyone will come to you eagerly seeking training. You will have to advertise and recruit, especially among the faculty. Make instruction practical and hands-on. People do not fear what they understand, so help them understand what your media center has to offer. Go slowly and be patient with those less experienced. The technology-related stress felt by these folks eventually can trickle down to add to your stress, so do all you can to minimize their discomfort.

Establish and maintain open, active communication with students, teachers, administrators, school board members, and parents. These people do not know what is happening in your media center unless you tell them. Let others know in advance, whenever possible, when something is not or will not be working, so they can plan accordingly. Tell them what needs to happen to remedy the problem and the expected time line. The more these groups understand your purpose and needs, the more likely they are to be supportive.

A Fractured Technology Fairy Tale

Barbara Johnson

Once upon a time there was an elementary school that had very little technology. Although the teachers and students managed with what they had, life was not good. All of the teachers knew it could be better, and most of them hoped that someday it would be. The word spread that the students and teachers needed more technology, and suddenly their wish was granted with bond issue money.

Days went by with committees studying this and that until finally the assistant superintendent said, "Let's move on this." And so they did. They ordered tons of stuff—so much, in fact, that it took extra time to deliver it. Days and weeks went by. Nearly everyone had given up on the delivery when one brisk fall day the computers appeared at the school, and all was wonderful because every classroom got some.

But then the teachers turned on the computers and found only Windows 95 plus three software applications. One teacher discovered that with a single click on the desktop icon he could locate the old software. But several teachers found that they still did not have enough, so they proceeded to solve that problem.

The first teacher said, "I have lots of software at home. I'll just bring it in." And so she did.

The second teacher said, "I'll just use some of this software that a student brought to school. That'll fix me up." And it did.

The third teacher said, "I'll just install some of each of yours. That'll work for me." And it did.

The busy teachers set out to add their software. They huffed and puffed until it was all loaded. Then they stopped to see what they had done.

The word spread that the students and teachers needed more technology, and suddenly their wish was granted with bond issue money.

The first teacher's computer could no longer find the network because she had reconfigured her files. The second teacher's computer had software loaded illegally. She was using pirated and single-user software. The third teacher's computer had a virus that was spreading by leaps and bounds. She had even infected her home computer.

The assistant superintendent said, "I told you so. Remember, we talked about these problems earlier in the year." He also told them that they were going to need to find help for their problems on their own. He calmly produced the signature pages they had signed at the beginning of school. They read:

"I am aware that my classroom computer is not virus-protected on the hard drive; therefore, I will not insert diskettes that have not been virus-checked by the media center.

"I am aware that I am not to install software on my classroom computer unless it has been approved by the media director. If approved, and the installation process asks me to overwrite files or reconfigure my hard drive, I will seek immediate help and Just Say No!

"I am aware that I am not to install software that is not school property, whether by purchase or by donation, and that the original copy of the software will be kept with the computer. Only one installation will be made on one computer unless authorization has been given by the company by such licensing."

Unfortunately, this technology story did not have a happy ending. May all the stories you write this year end happily ever after.

Barbara Johnson, Mustang Trails, Mustang, Oklahoma.

TECHNOLOGY PLANS THAT WORK

feature

BUILDING ARKS FOR THE NEW TECHNOLOGY

By Judi Repman and Teresa K. Blodgett

My interest is in the future because I am going to spend the rest of my life there.

—Charles F. Kettering
(from Quotations Home Page: http://www.lexmark.com/data/quote.html)

A recent U.S. General Accounting Office (GAO) report titled "School Facilities: America's Schools Not Designed or Equipped for 21st Century" (available online at http://www.gpo.ucop.edu; select GAO Reports database and search by title) presents a disturbing picture of American public school facilities and their suitability for supporting the technological future. Data gathered for this report indicate that many American schools lack the wiring necessary for computers and communications and that more than half have insufficient

capability in modems, phone lines for modems, phone lines for instruction, conduits/raceways, and fiber optics. If school library media centers hope to realize the vision presented in *Information Power* and other calls for educational reform, renovating our facilities for the functional use of technology must be a top priority. While it is impossible to offer a "recipe for renovating" that everyone can follow, we hope to offer some useful suggestions here.

Begin at the Beginning

The first step in considering any renovation of a school library to incorporate technology is to decide what purpose the technology will serve. Every school library media center should be moving toward the use of technology for reference services and information gathering (which may include CD-ROMs, laser discs, the Internet and the World Wide Web). Students also will become producers of materials in a variety of technology formats—perhaps publishing their works on the Web or creating multimedia presentations. More and more technology will be used in the administration of the school library, from automated circulation and inventory to book ordering and interlibrary loan. If you don't consider these possibilities *before* your renovation project begins, it is likely that you will end up with facilities that still do not meet the needs of students or faculty.

Evaluating your current facilities and completing an inventory of your existing equipment is an important aspect of this process. You should consider the following items:

Electrical Outlets: How many? Where are they located? How much wattage is available per circuit/outlet? (A crucial piece of information—the UL wattage for the equipment should not exceed the wattage of the outlet.)

Lighting: Natural light is excellent for many library activities like reading, but glare from windows and the inability to darken a room for use with LCD projection systems can be a problem. Skylights in areas where monitors or projection panels will be used are especially difficult, so you might want to consider rearranging your furniture to use areas with skylights for casual seating or ranges of shelving.

Security: Considering the cost of library technology, and the potential for students to engage in non-educational activities with that technology, security concerns are a fact of life. Students using technology should be visible to the school library media specialist, even if that means moving the library offices or replacing existing walls with window/walls. An additional security consideration is related to the confidentiality of library records and the use of automated circulation systems. Glass-topped computer desks where the monitor sits below the desk surface are one solution to this issue. You should also investigate the technical requirements of any security system that is installed in your library to see if computer terminals need to be located a specific distance away from the security gates.

Individual vs. clustered workstations: If security is your only consideration, clustered workstations are probably the best approach since this arrangement allows you to see more students at once. However, in many cases congested workspace is a more serious problem, which may lead you to utilize individual workstations. The individual approach also allows the technology to be placed closer to the point of need, that is, you may be able to put OPAC terminals in your stacks or CD-ROM periodical databases in the periodicals area. Remember that if you do choose to have individual workstations, you will lose some of the natural collaboration that seems to occur when a group works with technology. The level of noise is also an issue to be considered.

Sitting vs. standing: This is a decision that must be made based on the kinds of activities that you

If you don't consider these possibilities before your renovation project begins, it is likely that you will end up with facilities that still do not meet the needs of students or faculty.

expect to be involved in. While it is not a major hardship to stand at a terminal to complete a 10-minute database search, it is difficult to create a multimedia presentation while standing at a computer with no additional workspace. Providing the kinds of access to technology required by the Americans with Disabilities Act should also be a factor. The two items listed in the additional resources section below provide excellent guidelines for furniture and adaptive technologies that should be included in any technology renovation plan.

Printing: Printer quality has improved over the past few years but we also have higher expectations for the product. Students searching the World Wide Web or a CD-ROM atlas might want to print out a color copy of a map or picture. The three most common printer types are dot matrix, laser, and ink jet. Dot matrix is probably the least satisfactory in terms of speed and quality of the printed product, but it is usually the least expensive to purchase and to maintain. Ink jet printers produce a high quality product at a high rate of speed, but cost and replacement of cartridges can be a problem. Laser printers are fast, quiet, and produce excellent results, but their initial cost is high as is the cost of toner. For high quality color printing you might consider an ink jet printer with separate cartridges for each color (as opposed to a color cartridge unit). Some combination of printers might be the most cost-effective solution. For example, low-cost dot matrix printers could be used for printing at OPAC stations while color ink jets could be used in multimedia production areas.

Computer Hardware: Selecting computer hardware is certainly a challenging task. The positive aspect is that as the speed and power of the technology has

> *The technology we will need to support the students who will be in our schools in 10 years may not even have been invented, so it is important that we don't make these important decisions based on what has worked in the past or on the outdated equipment we currently use.*

greatly increased, costs have decreased. This does not make reading and interpreting system requirements any easier! As you consider whether or not to go with a single platform or multiple platforms, you must again consider other technologies available in your school and your school district and the software available for the system. Even if you only select a single platform, you must still consider compatibility among different models of computers. CPU (Central Processing Unit) speed, RAM (Random Access Memory), and hard disk size are critical aspects, and while it might be tempting to save several hundred dollars by choosing a slower computer with less RAM, you may be selecting equipment that will be obsolete before it is even unboxed. The requirements for processing speed, graphics and audio capabilities and storage will increase as new generations of software are developed and as Internet and World Wide Web access become more common in school libraries. While upgrades are available, we have found that it is usually better to begin with the best equipment that you can afford.

Networking: Networking of computers within a school, across a school district, throughout a state, and in global networks is a trend frequently addressed in the pages of TECHNOLOGY CONNECTION. The GAO report cited above notes that "this technology infrastructure, although initially more costly than the basic computer/printer, may have substantially more value. Educationally, it can link even the most remote or poor school with vast resources, including the finest libraries and the best teachers, for a wide range of courses or course enhancements." You may choose to have an in-library network for your OPAC and CD-ROM tower in addition to a gateway to a district- or state-wide network for Internet access. Different networks may require high speed modems or specialized ISDN or T-1 lines. Specialized wiring requirements may force you to create columns throughout your facilities for electrical outlets or you may have to drop conduit from the ceiling to bring in cables. To realize the benefits of participating in any of these network initiatives, school libraries need to consider the physical requirements. Cabling and rewiring are activities that require coordination with other departments and outside service providers. Keep in mind that their priorities are going to be different from yours—expect delays and plan accordingly.

A Few Special Considerations

As you begin to think about the kinds of technology that are already in your school library media center and how your facilities should be renovated and remodeled to make their use more efficient and effective, you also should consider some technologies that may be coming to your media center, such as CD-ROM, Internet access, and distance learning.

CD-ROM. Renovation requirements for CD-ROM may seem to be similar to those of renovating for any computer setup. However, if you will be networking CD-ROMs using a CD-ROM tower, you may need to purchase special furniture to house the tower and give some extra thought to access and security. If you will need to change discs frequently, the tower needs to be easily accessible, without forcing you to lie on the floor or climb over computer desks. If you will be doing small or large group instruction for CD-ROM use and need to be able to project what is on the computer screen, you may need easy access to the computer to be able to connect it to an LCD panel. If students are going to be using CD-ROMs for lengthy periods of time, you need to provide adequate workspace and comfortable seating.

Internet Access. Even though we have emphasized the benefits of networking, we realize that many school libraries will be able to provide Internet access only through the use of a modem and telephone line. While it is theoretically possible to place a telephone line anywhere, practically you may be limited to an outside wall. As with CD-ROM technology, students may spend extended periods of time "surfing the Net," which means they need additional workspace. If Internet access is limited to a small number of computer stations, you need to make sure that each workspace can accommodate students working collaboratively.

Distance Learning. Will students at your school be able to study Japanese by satellite? Will your faculty be participating in professional development activities through the Internet? Distance learning may necessitate any or all of the kinds of technology, hardware and networking capabilities already described, and it may also require you to provide additional spaces for small and large group instruction. It is difficult to know what kinds of physical spaces will be needed for distance learning in most schools, but it is apparent that individuals and groups of students will need spaces where they can participate in interactive, high-tech learning experiences.

Renovating school library media centers to incorporate the technology to meet the needs of today's students is both a challenge and an opportunity. While in many cases we can "make do," when we want to add Internet access, distance learning, or a CD-ROM network, we have to make some changes. It is important to maintain a sense of humor and a vision. The technology we will need to support the students who will be in our schools in 10 years may not even have been invented, so it is important that we don't make these important decisions based on what has worked in the past or on the outdated equipment we currently use. Here is another quotation (this one credited to Anonymous) from *The Quotations Home Page*: "No more prizes for predicting rain. Prizes only for building arks." Technology is the rain in today's school library media center. Now it is time to focus on building good "arks" to support its use!

Additional Resources

Three resources that are especially helpful in dealing with the whole process of renovating a school library media center are Mary Lankford's article, "Design for Change: How to Plan the School Library You Really Need" (*School Library Journal*, February, 1994, pp. 20-24); *Designing and Renovating School Library Media Centers* by June Klasing (published in 1991 by the American Library Association); and *Planning the Library Media Center Facility for the 1990s and Beyond* (a 1991 publication available from the Texas Education Agency, 1701 North Congress, Austin, Texas 78701). All cover issues about the importance of planning for renovation, working with architects and other school personnel, and general space and furnishings considerations. If you are involved in a school-wide renovation project, you may want to consult *Designing Places for Learning* (Association for Supervision and Curriculum Development, 1995), which presents a broader picture of the impact of school facilities on learning. Finally, while there are a number of sources that discuss access issues, two that seem most helpful in school library settings are "Granting Each Equal Access" by Linda Lucas Walling (*School Library Media Quarterly*, Summer, 1992, pp. 216-222) and *The Americans with Disabilities Act: Its Impact on Libraries* (American Library Association, 1993). TC

Judi Repman is an Associate Professor of Instructional Technology in the College of Education at Texas Tech University, Lubbock, Texas. Teresa K. Blodgett is an Education Specialist/Technology at Region 17 Education Service Center in Lubbock, Texas.

TECHNOLOGY PLANS THAT WORK

feature

Organizing the Planning Team

By Steve Baule

Organizing the strategic or long-range planning team is one of the most important tasks to ensure the long-term success of educational technology planning within your school. The planning team must provide curricular and pedagogical expertise, technology expertise, and administrative support, and must develop support among all stakeholders.

Expertise Needed on the Planning Team
Curricular and Pedagogical Expertise
Technology Expertise
Administrative Experience
Support from All Stakeholders

Because the planning efforts must focus on how educational technologies can support the instructional process, heavy emphasis should be placed on curricular expertise. The team must have an understanding of the school's overall curriculum plan and the long-term goals for curricular improvement as well as a firm understanding of the instructional or pedagogical methods presently being used and any new instructional methodologies being brought into the curriculum through other planning or improvement efforts. The team also should represent the whole spectrum of subject disciplines and or grade levels represented within the planning unit. Those selected to provide the primary curricular expertise on the team should be those most respected for subject area knowledge within their departments or grade levels. Relying only on teachers who are the prominent technology users within the building will not necessarily provide the depth of curriculum expertise necessary to ensure the development of a successful technology plan. Including a nonuser of technology within the planning team often can keep the plan realistic.

In providing for technology expertise on the team, focus on those individuals who can provide the user's point of view in addition to those who can bring more in-depth hardware, software, and networking knowledge to the team. It is important that the team include individuals who use technology with students in classroom or library media center settings. Including only library media specialists, technology coordinators, or technology support people removes the "technology experts" from the instructional process. Teachers who use technology successfully in the instructional process are essential to the success of the planning team. The team's technology expertise needs to be able to cover what is manageable within a classroom and what is possible. The first area is related to the expertise of teachers who have used technology successfully. The second area is most appropriately addressed by instructional technologists or other technology support staff members who understand both hardware and software.

Since administrative support is essential in ultimately seeing if the planning efforts are to bear fruit, the planning team must include representation from the administration at all levels. Administrators provide a constant communication channel between the administration as a whole and the technology planning team. Additionally, administrative representation can generally provide the expertise and authority necessary to develop budgets, grant proposals, and staffing requests.

It is important that all the stakeholders be represented in the team's makeup, so all departments, grade levels, and functional areas of the building or district feel that their interests are represented in the planning process. Failure to do this can cause the entire effort to be hamstrung by those departments or individuals who feel that their needs have not been considered. Individual stakeholders or departments not represented on the planning team can be included within the process in a number of ways. Involving all of the building leaders in the selection process is one of the most effective ways to provide these stakeholders some ownership of the process from the outset. The methods and rationale for selecting team members should be communicated to the entire staff so that all of the stakeholders will feel that they have had a voice in the selection process.

Care also must be taken to keep the team to a manageable number of members so the team can have effective dialog about the issues before them, with the active participation of all the members. Additionally, the team must be able to meet regularly—often difficult with a larger group.

Since successful technology planning requires the careful study of curricular, support service, and administrative needs, it is usually necessary for each building to have its own planning team in place to offer assistance to the district-level team as well as to plan for the unique needs of an individual school. In many cases, a district plan will focus more on infrastructure and overall guiding principles, while the school teams will elaborate on how technology will interact with students and teachers in the library media center and the classroom.

The Successful Building-Level Team

Developing a technology planning team at the building level requires representation from the administration, the library media center, the classrooms, and the clerical and support staff. If at all possible, the building principal or an assistant principal needs to be involved directly in the process, possibly as committee chair. In buildings with several administrators, the administrator responsible for curricular issues should chair the committee.

In those cases where it is not possible for the administration to fully participate on the planning team, the principal should designate the library media specialist to head the planning team since the library media specialist is most likely to have an overview of technology and curricular programs throughout the building and most likely is used to developing and managing a budget. In those schools that have an administrator assigned to instructional technology issues, that administrator should lead the planning team.

The school's library media specialist also must be a member of the planning team. In many schools, educational technology has entered the school through the library media center, and the library media specialist is often viewed as the technology expert in the school. Even in schools where the library has yet to embrace technology, the library media specialist needs to be included on the planning team, and if the school has a computer teacher, that person should also be included.

A representative sample of classroom teachers will form the major portion of the planning team. Teacher members selected for the team should be regarded by their peers as good instructors and should represent a range of technology skill levels.

It is important to have teachers who represent each of the skill levels present among the building staff. Teachers who are occasional technology users represent a large portion of most building staffs and should not be neglected when forming the planning team. If the building staff includes a large number of non-users, that group should also be represented. It is also important to make sure that some of the more educationally conservative or traditional teachers are included to help anchor the team. Including only teachers who are openly enthusiastic about educational technology deprives the planning team of the broader perspective necessary to be successful.

The classroom teachers also need to span the range of grade levels and subjects represented in the building. In large comprehensive high schools, it is important to provide representation from the core curricular areas as well as the elective areas. If possible, large high schools that have strong departmental organizations should include department chairs.

The educational support personnel of the school also should be represented on the planning team. Often, the clerical and secretarial staffs have computer and technology needs that are otherwise overlooked. These staff members also often have some of the strongest computer skills within the building. Including community members and parents on the planning team is another option to be considered especially in areas where PTAs and other community organizations are a major avenue of obtaining technology for the school.

Following this formula should result in a team of six to ten members, which is easy to manage and is not too large to encourage free discussion.

The Effective District Planning Team

Like the building team, it is important to provide broad representation of the entire district on the planning team, balancing inclusiveness against the need to keep the team to a manageable size. The district team should

---

Example of a K-6 elementary school technology planning team
Principal
Library media specialist
5th grade teacher
4th grade teacher
1st grade teacher
Art teacher
Teacher's aide

Example of a large high school technology planning team
Technology coordinator
Library media specialist
Math department chair
Business education
   department chair
Chemistry teacher
English teacher
Foreign language teacher
Social studies teacher
Guidance secretary

parallel the makeup of a building team. Central office representation is necessary in order to provide district-level leadership and the broad perspective that central office administrators can provide. The district business office should be represented in order to assist in developing budgets and to provide input into the administrative computing needs of the district. If the business manager is included in the planning process from the start, he or she is more likely to be supportive in finding internal funding sources and grant funding. The administrator leading the planning team should be from the assistant superintendent level if at all possible. If the district has a technology coordinator who is not at the assistant superintendent level, he or she should co-chair the team with an assistant superintendent.

The team should include a representative sample of classroom teachers, library media specialists, support personnel, and building-level administrators in the same manner classroom teachers were selected to serve on the building-level team. It is important to make sure these team members are among the most respected in the district. Choosing only those who are extremely supportive of technology deprives the team of the broadest possible view of district needs.

Some districts try to include students, parents, or other community members on the planning team. In general, if the team follows the guiding principle that technology planning should answer curricular and administrative needs, the need to include these groups is no greater than on any other district committee. Often, business people who deal with technology but who have little knowledge of educational technology or of instructional methods are brought into planning teams. It is important to gather input from these groups, but not always appropriate to include these groups on the planning team.

Another group often considered for inclusion on the planning team is consultants. In districts without internal educational technology expertise, consultants can be a valuable resource. In many cases, staff members of neighboring districts that have moved faster in the area of educational technology can serve as inexpensive consultants, helping the district avoid mistakes made in their own district. Occasionally, if approached properly, a superintendent will release technology staff to consult with another district at no cost as a good-will gesture.

Always obtain references from other educational institutions before employing a consultant. Since schools often use technology very differently from business and industry, avoid consultants without experience working with schools.

Community members who work in technology-related areas are often willing to donate their services to the school or district in order to assist the planning process. Community members involved in the telecommunications and cable industries are especially valuable in the determination of infrastructure needs and the various options a school or district has in developing a telecommunications infrastructure.

The other potential group to draw members from is the school board itself. This can be done in several ways: the school board may appoint one or two interested board members to participate in the planning team's activities; the board may form its own technology subcommittee that could serve as a link between the leadership of the planning team and the school board as a whole; or interested board members might simply attend the planning team's meeting as they wished in order to gain an understanding of the process, but without a formal relationship. Including board members is important; it helps them to understand the entire process and prepare for the eventual staff, training, and equipment requests that will land before them. School boards are almost always more receptive to items that they see as part of a larger plan and not simply as a patchwork of unrelated and costly requests.

Including all of the stakeholders in the makeup of the planning team is an essential step. Curricular expertise is as important if not more important than technical expertise. The administrative decision makers need to be included or they must be supportive of the team's leadership. Classroom teachers, school library media specialists, and support staff should all be represented. Adding community representation, parents, students, and board members will depend upon the political state of your district. Whatever you do, do not shortchange the organization of the planning team. A well balanced planning team can make the difference between getting the plan approved the first time through or going back to the drawing board. **TC**

Steve Baule is Coordinator of Instructional Resources, Glenbrook South High School, Glenview, Illinois, and an Editorial Consultant for TECHNOLOGY CONNECTION. *He is also the author of* Technology Planning, *published by Linworth Publishing, Inc.*

Example of a district planning team

Assistant superintendent—curriculum
District business manager
High School technology coordinator
Elementary principal
Middle School library media specialist
Elementary library media specialist
High School science teacher
High school art teacher
7th grade math teacher
Middle school allied arts teacher
Computer/keyboarding teacher
5th grade teacher
1st grade teacher
Personnel office secretary

TECHNOLOGY ORGANIZATION AND STAFFING

Scheduling THE Computer

By Martin D. McKay

Scheduling student time on computers can be a problem whether you have one or multiple computers in a classroom. The first response usually involves cutting the day into neat blocks and establishing "computer time." This seldom works since available time rarely matches individual or class needs or interests. Another frequent response involves using the computer as a reward for completed work, which gives gifted or more advanced students almost exclusive use. And this response frequently leads even gifted students to careless, hurried tasks, working to finish rather than to learn. However, both of these responses are better than the other popular choice: Since there is no way to schedule use fairly, don't let anyone use it.

Even a single computer can provide a variety of independent, small group, or diversified full-class experiences. You can begin eliminating your scheduling problems by having the students schedule themselves. Select a computer management team from within the class that embodies the scope of your class in both social and academic terms. All students must feel that they are represented and have access.

The Teacher's Role

The function of the management team is to recommend a working schedule for computer usage. You should establish the initial scheduling criteria, such as "Try to be sure everyone has a turn." And you may also wish to establish rules relating to "game time" and fun vs. work. Remember, however, that both represent computer usage, and both are important.

Students submit their usage requests to the management team. The management team then prioritizes these requests and creates a recommendation for the schedule, which is submitted for your approval. This step provides a safety valve and allows you to retain control. It may be necessary to go back to the management team to revise a schedule, particularly in the early stages of the project. As a rule, however, management team students take their task seriously. As soon as the students realize that you have given them a genuine role, they will identify what is appropriate and will apply it.

Keep communication open and monitor development. Your scheduling problem should be solved. Now you can employ the usage request procedure to extend student projects, expand computer usage, and diversify your classroom management procedures through the management team structure.

You have established some initial criteria to prioritize scheduling and to be sure that the group was accountable. Now, allow the management team to develop its own criteria and make decisions to expand usage. They may think the number of students involved should be a factor. Do projects submitted by groups of students have priority over projects by individual students? What about timeliness? Should they give priority to projects involving current topics or to long-term projects? Is recreational use appropriate? Games, in fact, are an issue in themselves. What about games that are based on teaching or learning? As things are resolved and the program develops, your management team and the class as a whole can slowly take over ownership of computer time, projects, and ultimately their own learning.

Student Role Definition

Over time the role of the management team must be expanded. You can let them provide evaluative feedback. Which programs are working? Which aren't? What software or device might we add to help more students get more things done? The management team can help generate new levels of use or achievement. How can we get Johnny or Susie to do more things to help their grades? What should we do to help the class get better spelling scores? Students can help with support or training. "Betty is having trouble preparing her presentation. Would you help her set up her slides?" "Could you please schedule some time for one of you to help Charlie learn how to use this program?"

When you reach this stage, it is appropriate to assign areas of responsibility. Someone is responsible for knowing graphics and how to get them into various presentation or word processing programs. Another student helps set up graphs or move information between various programs. Assistants can be established and students can be rotated on and off the management team so that others have the opportunity for responsibility and leadership training.

As usage expands the need for advancement, technology will also expand. Each step above that initial device—multiple computers, networking, and online access—allows even greater flexibility and can provide the impetus for more independent, small-group, and full-class learning experiences. It is much easier to schedule projects with two computers than with one. When you get to three or more classroom machines, the whole paradigm changes and scheduling problems become negligible. Network and online access open broader areas for communication and learning. All the resources feed upon one another and all grow together. TC

Martin D. McKay is the Technology Consultant for the Bridgeport (Ohio) Schools. He is also a member of Ohio's SchoolNet faculty, supervising 78 school districts in 19 counties.

NOTES

HEAD FOR THE EDGE

By Doug Johnson

Librarians Are From Venus; Technologists Are From Mars

While it has not quite reached the proportions of the famous feuds between the cattle ranchers and sheepherders, there is definitely tension in many schools between the librarians and the technologists. In case you need help, I've developed a short field guide to help you tell the difference between the species.

Job Title	Librarians	Technologists
Primary gender	Female	Male
Background	Frustrated English teacher	Frustrated math or science teacher
Reason for entering field	Likes books and quiet places	Likes gadgets and quiet places
Hairstyle	Hair in bun	Hair in ponytail
Eyewear	Cat's-eye glasses (neck chain optional)	Horn-rimmed glasses (tape optional)
Accessories	Pins and scarves with book motif	Pocket protector, which holds small screwdriver
When asked for help	Hovers	Hides
When opposed	Whines	Sulks
When presented with technology problem	Always blames the equipment	Always blames the user
Most often seen by others	Cataloging, reshelving, stamping, "shush"-ing	Fixing, carrying, wiring, muttering
Seen by administrators	Replaceable by clerk	Replaceable by technician

I expect you can add to this brief, facetious list. The folks I've known who fit these descriptions are rapidly disappearing from schools. In some schools, their positions aren't being refilled. Classroom teachers, clerks, technicians, or contracted services are doing the daily work that they once did just to keep libraries open and computers working. These are usually places where small children sit in still straight lines, waiting in quiet desperation for the next set of worksheets or computer drills. There is little progress being made toward making these schools places where more children are being taught more important skills in more effective ways.

But in other more enlightened schools, a new professional has arisen. Education has not yet established a commonly agreed upon name for this hybrid breed that has taken the best, most professional tasks from the practices of library science and technology. But I've seen these folks in action. For purposes of this short article, let's use the name "Educator X." A field guide for this rare bird might read like the one on page 42.

These folks bring to the educational table critical knowledge of the issues of copyright, intellectual freedom, and information literacy. They contribute an understanding of the use and potential uses of networks, educational software, and computerized productivity tools. Educator X has a whole school view and works to see that information technologies are integrated into all curricular areas.

But these individuals don't just magically appear. They are produced in or migrate to habitats that have certain characteristics.
1. The institutions in which they work have a desire for change.
2. These institutions provide Educators X with time to work and learn. That means they do not provide teacher prep time or babysit study halls. It means they do not teach six classes

and have an extra prep time to do technology or library work. Integrating information technologies into the school is their full-time job.

3. Educator X environments provide clerical and technical support. Books must be reshelved, software must be loaded, and equipment must be checked out if the school's daily activities are to continue. If paid support staff is not available, the professional usually ends up doing those tasks instead of the planning, teaching and supervising ones.

4. These schools understand that Educator X needs staff development opportunities beyond those offered to classroom teachers. Their schools find resources to send them to conferences, workshops, and planning meetings dealing not just with technology or libraries, but also with assessment, graduation standards, and other areas of curricular reform with which libraries and technology might assist. Educator X then becomes the in-house support person for broad reform initiatives.

5. When hiring for such positions, the people who do the hiring of all school personnel look at people skills first and at technical skills second. Little things like the ability to write and speak clearly, respond to others with empathy, handle conflict, and supervise others are viewed as more important than being able to catalog a videotape or install a network card.

6. Schools in which Educator X thrives have high expectations of all their staff, but especially of their leaders. Their governing boards expect plans, goals, time lines, and reports. They expect clear and regular communication with parents and the public. They expect responsible, visionary leadership.

The names don't really matter. I have known Educators X who are called librarians, technology directors, media specialists, information specialists, computer coordinators, information literacy teachers, and teacher librarians. Those of you who fill the Educator X role know who you are. Those of you who want to become an Educator X or want to hire one know the habitats in which they thrive. **TC**

Doug Johnson is the District Media Supervisor for the Mankato (Minnesota) Public Schools.

Job Title	Educator X
Primary gender	Equally divided between males and females
Background	Librarian, technologist, or classroom teacher who has had the confidence and commitment to grow and learn
Reasons for entering field	Wanting to help students and teachers by improving education; fascination with information and its uses in all formats
Accessories	Professional journals, professional network, and competence in technology use
When asked for help	Teaches
When opposed	Asks questions, builds consensus, and adheres to principles
When presented with technology problem	Looks for root cause and long-term solutions
Most often seen by others	Teaching teachers or team-teaching in the classroom
Seen by administrators	As leader and indispensable ally in educational restructuring
Important tasks not always seen by others	Constantly familiarizing oneself with new books, audiovisual materials, software, and online resources; trying new educational strategies; working with curriculum committees
Finds time to get important tasks done by...	Delegating duties to an adequate clerical and technical support staff

A World of Change in 12 Short Years

By Janet Hofstetter

This librarian looks back over 12 years of innovations in the school library.

IF YOU CAN REMEMBER libraries without computers, you may not be all that new to the profession. I vividly remember the day about 12 years ago when I requested a computer for the library. The response was, "What do you need a computer in the library for?"

At the time, the only thing I really wanted was word processing and a printer for overdue notices. A few months after my first request was denied, a Tandy Model IV, then state-of-the-art equipment, appeared in the library with no software and no instructions. I felt doomed.

Fortunately, the agricultural education teacher had a computer and was willing to recommended software to get me started. He is now our full-time district technology coordinator, managing all classroom and lab computers, including our networks.

My daily routine has changed drastically since the first computer arrived in the library. Through a Missouri Incentives Grant in 1987, I automated the catalog with only a server and two computers. Suddenly my priorities changed from manually checking items in and out to teaching students how to use the online catalog. Power outages, low voltage on an ancient electrical system, and troubleshooting equipment created a new kind of stress.

Even with all the stress that technology has created, I certainly would not return to the old ways of running a library. Gone are the accession books, handwritten overdue notices, files of checkout cards, and hand-tallied statistics. We kept the old card catalog intact, just in case our system goes down. When we moved into a new high school building four years ago, the network was down for six weeks. At least students could find some items from the collection even though we have discontinued adding cards. During those weeks, students gained a new appreciation for the online catalog.

Accessioning new books takes less than half the time I spent manually processing them. Even so, I may spend more time than other librarians because I enter MARC records myself. This may seem like a waste of time, but I find that I have a better handle on what is in the collection when I have spent some time with the books. I make sure each record contains keywords students might use to find the book.

I still have a shelf list although it is hand written. I use the clean side of an old catalog card to catalog each new item and then, as time permits, I enter the information into the circulation system. Rather than throwing away the cards after entering the data, I file them for spot checking shelves or comparing barcode numbers when something seems wrong with an entry. Old habits die hard.

If I am weeding books, I pull the shelf cards as I weed and box the books for immediate disposal. As time allows, I can work from the shelf cards to delete entries. Recently I weeded about 500 fiction books because some were duplicate titles. There was no question which one had been discarded because I had the barcode number on each card for verification as I deleted records.

Statistics in Minutes

I have always believed that we should keep statistics on facility and collection use. Automation cuts down on the paperwork of statistics and is definitely more accurate. However, automation can skewer some statistics unless we take the effects into account.

Because the online catalog gives students quick access to the information they need, they are more likely to take notes in the library than check out books for an assignment. A side effect was lower circulation statistics, which could lead administrators to believe the library books were used less often. Now I ask students not to reshelve books they have used in the library. I scan the barcodes in the "reshelve" mode (with Follett *Unison* software) before the books are returned. This not only keeps a record of what books are used most often but also gives me an excuse to keep students from misshelving the books.

In our school, library-use statistics are so readily available that the superintendent does not hesitate to request them when he is working on a report or a grant. The principal also knows from my quarterly reports that library materials are well used. I should add that reference books are used more often but show less wear because students are more likely to use them in the library rather than checking them out.

For students and teachers, finding books is far more efficient. From networked classroom computers they can determine if a book they want is currently available in the library.

The Internet & Other Outside Resources

Computer technology has made it possible for us to meet the diverse needs of our students even though the library collection is small. I have gained both time and library space by eliminating many of the magazines we used to store because they were indexed in the *Readers' Guide to Periodical Literature*. Now, students find and print magazine articles from full-text databases such as *SIRS Researcher*, EBSCOhost, and Infonautics' Electric Library, using library or classroom computers.

A code of ethics, or acceptable use policy, for students using the Internet is yet another feature that is new to the 1990s school library. At our high school, both the student and his parent or guardian are required to sign the code before the student can use the Internet. A copy must be on file with the librarian or teacher in charge of the computer. I keep the original signed codes in a notebook and make copies when students need them for classroom teachers.

On the circulation system, I place two asterisks after the student's first name before I file the signed code. Students must present their I.D. card at the desk to get permission to use the Internet in the library media center. When we scan the I.D., we can see the two asterisks. We check out a barcoded permission card to the student. He may use the Internet for up to one hour. The cards are returned to a basket at the desk along with a log of sites visited. We keep the logs for about 10 weeks so we can track how the Internet is being used.

Time to Learn

Everyone needs time to learn how to use sophisticated computer programs. In the late 1980s, when Dialog online services were an innovation, we had to learn specialized search techniques to reach a few hundred databases. That experience has made it easier for me to learn how to use the search engines on the Internet. The transition for me is somewhat like learning to diagram sentences; I often think about how the search would have been constructed for Dialog and this makes my use of terms with search engines more precise.

> **Computer technology has made it possible for us to meet the diverse needs of our students even though the library collection is small.**

One of the hardest things for me to do was to move from DOS to Microsoft Windows. I suspect my unwillingness to learn the new system is influenced by memories of the amount of time it took me to learn how to manipulate the old system. I realize that this transition from one operating system to another is far easier than the transition from manual circulation to an online catalog. The difference may lie in the fact that I desperately wanted the automated system. This helps me understand how teachers feel about giving up their old techniques that worked so comfortably for so many years.

Fax machines, copy machines, teleconferencing, computer presentations, e-mail pen pals, video tape editing equipment, color printers, and distance learning are just a part of what has now become common in most schools. None of that was mentioned in my certification classes 20-plus years ago.

A recent experience in a music store made me realize how rapidly technology has made information accessible. My husband knew the name of a song but not the performer. We used a kiosk to search for the title, found several artists, browsed the titles of other songs on the albums, and found out how many of the CDs the store had in stock. Just as with the online library catalog, we got the "address" of the album and decided to buy it, all within less than 10 minutes. I wasn't at all impressed until my husband voiced his amazement at how easily we found the album with only one tiny piece of information. Such experiences are common in today's high school library.

Janet Hofstetter has been the high school librarian in California, Missouri, for 19 years. She has previously shared her original puzzles for National Library Week use, tips, and articles on one-person management, grant writing, and budget stretching in The Book Report. *Her article on introducing mentally disadvantaged students to computer use appeared in the April 1996 issue of* Technology Connection. *She is a reviewer for both magazines.*

A Modern Learner's Riddle

When she talks to community groups, Janet Hofstetter recites this verse to show how homework has changed for students. To review the definitions of keyboard terminology, she has also formatted the riddle as a crossword puzzle for students.

I am not playing baseball,
But my HITS are more than two;
My pencil lies there idle
While I MARK a phrase or clue.
I may DELETE my errors,
Or INSERT things I forgot,
And even keep a FILE of stuff
I think I'll use a lot.

I ENTER from a KEYBOARD
Instead of through a door,
I SAVE some quotes on a FLOPPY DISK
As over words I pore.
I PRINT reports on paper,
And make copies as I please;
And then to EXIT from a SCREEN,
I press ESCAPE with ease.

KEY WORDS unlock ideas
When I SEARCH a DATABASE,
And spelling is important
As I type a name or place.
What is it that I'm doing
That results in info fast?
I'm using a COMPUTER
And my homework's fun at last!

—*Janet Hofstetter, 1994*

Evaluating School Library Information Services in the Digital Age

By Nancy Everhart

This paper was first presented at the ISIS '99 (Information Services in Schools) Online Conference (www.csu.edu.au/research/cstl/isis/).

A new graduate of our program recently called me in a panic about a job interview. She was being considered for a position as a school librarian in a progressive Upper East Side Manhattan elementary school. The school had no library. Instead, there were rich classroom collections supported by electronic resources via a school LAN. I must admit my first reaction was a negative, albeit traditional, one: No library? But on further reflection, I began to imagine the possibilities—high levels of collaboration between the librarian and the teachers along with an opportunity to redefine the whole concept of school library information services. Even under traditional circumstances, evaluating these services is a challenge unto itself, but one that all school libraries are facing as we move to a digital environment.

Numbers and Types of Services

Evaluating school library information services takes the same two basic forms as all evaluation—quantitative and qualitative. Many State Departments of Education or professional associations provide checklists for types and numbers of services they expect their school librarians to render. Hawaii is typical. In their guidelines, 14 services are listed. Programs are evaluated as being in "Phase 1" if they provide at least 75% of those services, "Phase 2" if they provide 85%, and "Phase 3" for 95%. School librarians can use these tools internally to not only develop an awareness of types of services that might be offered, but also how they rank in providing them. The American Association of School Libraries (AASL) also will be releasing a national evaluative rubric, covering a wide range of school library media services, that can be used by school library media specialists and administrators.

A large quantity of services may be offered, but are the users responsive to them? Surveys and interviews of students and faculty will furnish data on the users' awareness of, and satisfaction with, services. These qualitative measures also can function as a device for users to suggest new services. Surveys are especially useful for measuring attitudes and gathering data from a large number of people in a short time that can be easily analyzed and summarized.

Interviews work well with children who are too young to respond to a survey. A popular interview method for evaluation purposes is the focus group interview. A focus group consists of a small, representative sampling of those people whose opinions you are interested in obtaining. Responses from focus group interviews can also be utilized as a basis for developing surveys.

Facilities

Even in the encroaching digital age, in most schools today provision of information services still takes place within a physical facility called the school library media center. The physical facility itself has a profound impact on the types of services that can be offered. At the most basic level is the location of the library. Is it in a place where it is easily accessible? Does the location make it convenient to offer services before and after school? What is the feeling you get when you walk in the door?

Quantitative guidelines as to the overall size of the library, as well as recommendations for the provision of specific areas within it, are available from Washington and Louisiana. Qualitative issues are also addressed.

Usage

Usage is another quantitative measure of service. Some traditional measures are usage of the facility (attendance) and the materials (circulation). Compiling circulation statistics and keeping track of attendance are prevalent, and sometimes rote, activities, without much thought going into how to use the results for comparisons, trend analysis, and achievement of goals. When the data are translated into output measures, it can be interpreted for beneficial school library evaluation.

These reports can be valuable in determining the impact of either introducing or eliminating services via calculating attendance and/or circulation statistics pre- and post-service. Circulation and attendance figures are meaningless, however, when a school library is run on a fixed schedule with students exchanging the same number of materials each week. When evaluating usage on a flexible schedule, it is not necessary to continually evaluate for the entire year. You can choose a "typical" week or month and make predictions based on that data.

Attendance counts can be gathered quite easily if the library has a turnstile. If not, there are alternative methods, such as having students sign an attendance sheet, collecting passes, or counting heads. Rather than simply totaling attendance figures, a succinct and indicative measure is the Visits Per Student to the library during the year. This is calculated: visits per student = attendance per year/student population.

Circulation

Circulation is the most common method of measuring usage. More valuable than total circulation might be the following statistics for a school library:

Circulation Per Student
annual circulation/number of students in school
Turnover Rate (average time each item has been circulated)
annual circulation/total library holdings

Sophisticated analyses of circulation can be performed with an automated

> Many State Departments of Education or professional associations provide checklists for types and numbers of services they expect their school librarians to render.

system. One example is to calculate the Relative Use Factor:

$$\frac{\% \text{ of circulation}}{\% \text{ of collection responsible for that circulation}}$$

A relative use of "1" means that area of the collection is being used in direct proportion to the number of items available. Areas of the collection with high relative use factors can be strengthened, and those with low factors more heavily promoted.

It is also meaningful to monitor in-house use because there are materials that are used in the library but are not recorded with normal circulation methods. In-house use can be calculated by examining materials left on tables and desks, interviewing patrons, observing, leaving survey forms in books, and scanning the materials with a portable bar-code scanner.

Changes Due to Technology

As students increase their use of electronic sources it becomes ultimately more important to evaluate how well the "library" (whatever that definition might entail) meets particular needs rather than how many items reside on the shelves in a particular subject. Because electronic sources won't be checked out, service measures, observation, computer reporting options, and examination of student work are needed in place of circulation statistics.

Fill Rate

One of the major problems with circulation statistics is that there is no way of knowing whether or not the materials taken out actually reflect what the user wanted or if electronic sources are being used to satisfy a need. In order to ascertain this, users must interviewed to see if they found what they wanted. The resulting statistic, called the "fill rate," is defined as the percentage of successful searches for library materials in any part of the library collection and is calculated by dividing the number of successful searches by all searches. Users need to be interviewed as they leave the library in order to determine the fill rate.

OPAC/Network Reports

Automated systems for school libraries generate a wide variety of reports for evaluative purposes and, if studied, can be used to make planning and administrative decisions. The types of reports vary according to the type of automated system. For example, OPACs commonly report on patron searching and can generate statistics on the number of searches, how many were successful or unsuccessful, and searches matching certain parameters. The data can be used for a variety of evaluative purposes, such as measuring the effects of instruction or publicity.

Software for networked terminals offers additional reports. For example, it is possible to monitor searches per terminal, per location, by database used, or by Web site accessed. When students are assigned individual passwords, reporting software is capable of generating statistics on individuals as to where, when, what, and how they used network programs. With this additional information school librarians can evaluate the impact of location and student demographics on usage. Analyzing these types of reports and communicating findings to administrators are becoming increasingly important as students gain access to information resources via the school library but not within its walls.

Observation

Observation will often clarify what automated reporting systems don't reflect. Student behaviors at computer terminals might involve asking others for help, using printed guides, revealing body language, and verbal comments. Often these behaviors will provide clues for areas of information skills instruction. When using observation as an evaluation technique, one needs to define the behavior to be studied and standardize the process used to observe. Designing a data collection form or checklist is imperative.

Examining Student Work

Examining student work may be employed to determine the number, types, and currency of sources; use of other libraries; and the search process itself. Methods for examination include checking bibliographies, assigning logs to keep track of the research process, and developing incremental rubrics to assess information literacy skills.

School libraries can choose from a wide array of service evaluation techniques. It is important to match the correct evaluative method to the problem you are trying to solve, use the data obtained to make short- and-long range plans, and report the results to the appropriate people.

Nancy Everhart, Ph.D., is Assistant Professor in School Library Media at St. John's University, Division of Library and Information Science, Jamaica, New York, and the author of Evaluating the School Library Media Center *(Libraries Unlimited, 1998).*

For further information:

<www.infotoday.com/MMSchools/MarMMS/gonzalez3.html>
"Virtual School Libraries: A Dream or Reality?" by Brenda S. Gonzalez

<www.voicenet.com/~bertland/libsf/stlibs.html#usa>
"State Pages Relating to School Library/Media Services," by Linda Bertland

<home.ptd.net/~everhart/statedocument.html>
Nancy Everhart's School Library Media Evaluation Instruments on the Internet

<www.dese.state.mo.us/divinstr/curriculum/library/appendixf.pdf>
Evaluation survey forms for the school library media center—provided by the Missouri Department of Elementary and Secondary Education

<jura2.eee.rgu.ac.uk/dsk5/research/material/resmeth/rmeth6_1.htm>
"Observational Research Methods" by Elaine Sinclair and Lisa Dickson, The Robert Gordon University, Aberdeen, Scotland

<discoveryschool.com/schrockguide/assess.html>
"Kathy Schrock's Guide for Educators: Assessment Rubrics"

KNOW-HOW TO HELP KIDS KNOW NOW

By Lesley S. J. Farmer

retired businessman; a part-time secretary; a young mother using co-op daycare; a college student. What do these people have in common?

They all share an interest in helping as school library volunteers, particularly in helping with technology. Because they come with a variety of skills and expectations, each needs special assistance and training. Here are some pointers to maximize their contribution —and make the library a more savvy technology place for kids.

> While most volunteer training is small-scale, considered thinking and planning will pay off in higher volunteer contribution. If training is done in a convincing and engaging manner, volunteers will respect the librarian and carry out the needed task with more conviction and efficiency.

INTRODUCTION

Volunteers are an important part of making the library a meaningful experience for all students. While volunteers cannot substitute for professional expertise, they can reflect and help implement the school's vision. By sharing time, skills and knowledge, volunteers make a productive contribution to a child's education, as well as provide much-needed support to library media teachers. Some possible technology functions that volunteers can assume include:

- Tutor: computer and other technology skills
- Supervisor: lab use, production techniques
- Programmer: planning and implementing library events and training for parents
- Communicator: making displays and posters, designing flyers and newsletters
- Producer: desktop publishing, videos, slide shows, displays, Web pages
- Technician: operating, maintaining, troubleshooting, training others
- Office assistant: inputting, installing, circulation work
- Fund-raiser

INTERVIEWING

The first encounter with a new volunteer is the most important, for it establishes the relationship between the two persons. Moreover, it paves the way for effective school volunteer utilization. The first meeting should include the basics: the school's mission, an overview of the library's functions within the school, the role of the volunteer, the roles of the library staff and their relationship to the volunteer, and the specific contributions of the individual volunteer. The volunteer coordinator or librarian needs to ask volunteers about their interests, abilities and time commitments. The volunteer's library duties can be matched to his or her personal profiles: the job assignment may consider the volunteer's preference for one steady job versus a variety of tasks. Ideally, each volunteer function should include a job description. After the librarian or volunteer coordinator identifies policies, clear expectations and performance standards, the volunteer training can begin.

TRAINING

Effective training is the main factor in making good use of volunteers. When volunteers learn to do a task well and contribute to the library through their service, they become positive ambassadors to the community. Time spent in explaining how to work in the library becomes a valuable investment. Training is usually an ongoing activity paralleling the needs and interests of volunteers as they grow in their roles in the library. Typically, the library media teacher gives an overview of the job and trains the volunteer to give basic assistance. Additional training depends on the librarian's needs, volunteer capability and interests, and available time. Small group and individual training programs will benefit greatly from flexibility and good documentation (e.g., manuals and reference sheets). In general, on-the-job training consists of these steps:

- The librarian explains and models a correct procedure.
- The librarian guides the volunteer step-by-step in performing the specific procedure.
- The librarian supervises the volunteer's work and corrects actions as needed.
- The volunteer carries out the process correctly and independently. Sometimes the best training is not a formal presentation by the librarian, but a demonstration by a practicing volunteer or a clear guide sheet that a volunteer can use independently.

Since most volunteers are adults, librarians need to take into account their learning characteristics and needs. For example:

- Adults are experienced learners. Librarians should build on such expertise, going from the known to the unknown. Librarian and volunteer should have a reciprocal relationship.
- Adults have limited time. Training must be well-prepared and immediately useful.
- Adults learn in response to their own interests and needs. Librarians should foster self-improvement. The trainer should also consider physical needs: breaks and food.
- Adults have strong habits. They need to feel safe in order to take learning risks.
- Adults need to see results. They need to practice new skills, preferably with coaching.

What are the implications for training? Make it useful and meaningful, make it hands-on. Deal with mixed abilities and a variety of learning styles. Let volunteers share experiences. Make it fun!

While most volunteer training is small-scale, considered thinking and planning will pay off in higher volunteer contribution. If training is done in a convincing and engaging manner, volunteers will respect the librarian and carry out the necessary task with conviction and efficiency. Librarians should ask each volunteer to record personal training sessions. A central training spreadsheet can be maintained, with session names and the volunteers' experiences recorded.

TECHNOLOGY ISSUES

Technology poses special challenges for volunteer training. The spectrum of potential expertise varies tremendously among volunteers. An expert COBOL programmer may be available, as may be a Royal typewriter enthusiast. The library media teacher may need to help a volunteer unlearn prior technology practices. While the librarian needs to respect and honor the volunteer's skill, she or he must be firm in delineating the procedures and practices to be followed in the library. This may be difficult for some volunteers who have been managers or technology experts in their own work worlds. Or, the volunteer may know a better way to do something; the librarian can ask the volunteer to demonstrate it for evaluation.

Some volunteers may want to help in technology because they want to learn those skills for personal growth. While this is a commendable action—lifelong learning—it is the librarian's job to remind volunteers that the first priority has to be educating the students. For techno-neophytes, the best approach is to build on present skills. For example, if the person can type, show him or her how to do simple word processing. The person who has supervisory or reception skills might be able to act as a lab aide to keep students "on track." Eager learners also can pair with more experienced volunteers, which frees the library staff and promotes other volunteers' expertise.

Regardless of the volunteers' skills, they should have basic orientation of the library and its resources and services. They should all learn a core set of skills so that the library staff can count on them as back-up. Sample tasks include: basic lab routines, circulation check-out, network login and logoff, Internet navigation, and basic CD-ROM operation. It is best if volunteers do not know security codes so that they won't be tempted to use them—or be asked by others to invoke them.

DEVELOPMENT

Effective supervision is an art, and it is especially crucial in handling volunteers' services. The library staff must maintain a delicate balance between following a volunteer's every movement and abandoning the person. Since each volunteer has a different response to supervision, the librarian needs to be sensitive to each volunteer's needs and comfort zone. As the volunteer learns a new skill, closer supervision is necessary in order to clarify details about the particular function. When the volunteer demonstrates competency, supervision can assume a lighter touch. Volunteers recognize degrees of supervision, and value autonomy because of the trust that it implies. Of course, the most positive situation occurs when the librarian and volunteer work side by side. The immediate supervisor should also oversee volunteer scheduling, evaluation and problem-solving; the volunteer coordinator takes a school-wide perspective on these matters.

Sometimes a mentality may exist that volunteers are second-rate, that they cannot be dependable or accountable. Neither is true. Volunteers need to know that their contributions are meaningful, respected, and appreciated and that their performance levels are important. A name tag with the school logo is one symbol of a significant contribution. Most people want to do their best and may need help in knowing how to improve their performance. The sooner problems can be recognized and solved in cooperation with the volunteer, the more successful the experience will be for both parties.

Equally important is recognizing good work. Particularly when persons are not paid for their work, they need to know that they are valued, especially for specific tasks that are well done. Volunteers not only give valuable service hours, they serve as supporters to get out the word in the community that the library deserves strong financial and moral support.

Lesley S. J. Farmer is the Library Director at Redwood High School in Larkspur, California.

NOTES

Volunteers: Parents and Students as Managers of School Technology

105 THINGS PARENT VOLUNTEERS CAN DO – OTHER THAN RAISING FUNDS

By Andrea Troisi

Parents can volunteer in your library program in ways that reflect their own interests and skills—without having to bake cookies, sell candy bars, or conduct magazine drives. Avoid stereotypes when requesting help from parents. A mother may do an excellent job of adjusting shelves, mounting televisions on walls, and routing computer cables. A father may be a natural at designing bookmarks, decorating the library for the holidays, or setting up displays of new books. Ignore gender and take advantage of each parent's special talents.

COMPUTERS

1. Participate in task forces developing plans for new technologies.
2. Serve on a committee to develop an acceptable use policy for the use of the Internet.
3. Form a Technology Coach program to help teachers and students with minor computer hardware and software problems.
4. Train other parents on the use of instructional technology.
5. Install new computer software on classroom computers.
6. Help with wiring for Internet access.
7. Install network software.
8. Engrave the school name and the serial number on computers and audiovisual software.
9. Install computer and audiovisual security kits.
10. Change ribbons and ink cartridges on printers.
11. Use digital cameras to take pictures of events and download them into the computer.
12. Scan materials, such as student portfolios, into the computer.
13. Design, update, and maintain web pages.
14. Teach parents, teachers, and students how to use the Internet.
15. Help monitor student use of the Internet.
16. Conduct Internet searches for teachers.
17. Locate alternate funding opportunities.
18. Conduct ERIC searches.
19. Help write grant proposals.

AUDIOVISUALS

20. Train students, teachers, and other parents to operate 15mm movie projectors, reel-to-reel tape recorders, video cameras, videocassette recorders, digital cameras, and other instructional technology equipment.
21. Transfer 8mm movies of school events to videotape.
22. Make overhead transparencies.
23. Use a splicer to repair videotapes, films, filmstrips, and audiocassettes.
24. Train student as audiovisual helpers.
25. Help students use microfilm and microfiche readers.
26. Use a microfiche camera to take pictures of rare books, documents, and archival materials.
27. Mount, mask, clean, treat, and store slides and transparencies.
28. Organize slide trays for slide projectors.
29. Videotape school events and student performances.
30. Videotape television programs with school year duplication rights for classroom use.

31. Duplicate audiocassettes and videotapes when copyright regulations permit.
32. Use a digital camera to take pictures that can be imported into reports, web pages, and student portfolios.

READING PROGRAM

33. Form a support group for the parents of reluctant readers. Hold regular meetings and supply them with materials and suggestions on how to help students become better readers.
34. Help maintain classroom reading logs.
35. Conduct an after-school reading club.
36. Give book talks about favorite books.
37. Help students with book selection.
38. Participate in a Parents-as-Partners Reading Program.
39. Sponsor students in Readathons.
40. Help students check out and return books.

STUDENTS

41. Share information about careers, hobbies, or special interests with students.
42. Organize a hobby day when students can learn about new hobbies or share their own.
43. Create hands-on learning centers.
44. Edit sloppy copies of student work.
45. Hold conference with student authors during writing workshops.
46. Laminate student-produced books that will be included in the library collection.
47. Help students with their entries in essay and poster contests.
48. Chaperone field trips.
49. Organize parent patrols to monitor hallways, bathrooms, and school grounds.

SPECIAL NEEDS

50. Tutor students with a one-on-one approach.
51. For the visually impaired and the learning disabled, tape record books, textbooks, and classroom notes.
52. Obtain Braille and audio books from the library for the visually impaired.
53. Help teachers modify testing conditions for handicapped students.
54. Assist with hands-on performance assessment tasks.
55. Photocopy materials for learning-disabled students and highlight important information.
56. Compile research materials for students who are on home teaching because of an illness or accident.

CLERICAL

57. Bar code print and non-print media for library automation projects.
58. Attach security tags to library materials.
59. Obtain and return interlibrary loan materials from other libraries.
60. Use deacidification spray to neutralize the acid paper in books, newspapers, and archival documents.
61. Apply non-skid shelf tape to shelves.
62. Install wire book supports.
63. Put periodicals and pamphlets in magazine protectors.
64. Put book covers on books.

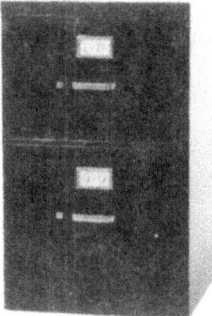

65. Use clear tape to reinforce book covers.
66. Organize and maintain vertical files.
67. Bind documents.
68. Comparison-shop for the best prices for library materials.
69. Identify sources of free materials and send for the materials.
70. Compile reviews of print and non-print materials.
71. Input data for automated library automation systems.
72. Assemble boxes and rare book enclosures for thick pamphlets, paperback books, damaged books, and special or fragile books.
73. Conduct inventories.

ARTS AND CRAFTS

74. Help with arts and crafts projects.
75. Make puppets, manipulatives, and flannel board figures.
76. Transfer book-related themes to T-shirts, using either transfer paper or the Hanes T-Shirt software.
77. Make book displays.
78. Make murals for library walls.
79. Put pictures in albums.
80. Laminate student work or vertical file material.
81. Mat, frame, and display student artwork.
82. Make banners and wall hangings.
83. Design bookplates and put them in books to acknowledge patron gifts and memorial donations.
84. Make shelf markers or book dummies to indicate materials in circulation.
85. Make storage cubes, floor level browser tables, reading terraces, display shelving, and child-sized furniture.
86. Sew beanbag chairs.

PARENT REPRESENTATION

87. Represent parents as stakeholders in the development of school library policy.
88. Serve as a parent representative on site-based curriculum and school management committees.
89. Mentor the parents of new students, especially those who are language minority students. Provide them with the telephone number of a parent who can help them adjust to the new school.
90. Sponsor an orientation program for parents at the transitional periods, such as kindergarten or the first year of middle school.
91. Offer homework assistance, providing tips on how to help their children with their homework.
92. Staff a homework hotline.

COMMUNITY

93. Write a letter to the editor in support of library programs.
94. Conduct petition drives in support of library issues.
95. Address the board of education members, asking them to promote school library programs.
96. Write to elected officials to encourage public spending for school libraries.
97. Work in the campaigns of school board candidates who back school library programs.
98. Conduct voter registration drives to increase the number of library supporters who vote in school board elections.
99. Recruit Adopt-A-School partners.
100. Photograph events and send the photographs to the parent newsletter, the district-wide newsletter, or the local newspaper.
101. Write articles about library activities for the local media.
102. Maintain a clipping file of newspaper articles about the school library.
103. Help parents and students obtain public library cards by inviting public librarians to register new patrons at school events, such as Open House, Parent/Teacher Conference Day, and Sports Night.
104. Develop and maintain a resource file of guest speakers.
105. Arrange author visits.

Andrea Troisi is a School Library Media Specialist at LaSalle Middle School, Niagara Falls, New York.

NOTES

Braving The Waters, or How To Get Your Computing "Feet" Wet

By Pat Miller

Like it or not, technology is pervading our lives. We are expected to use and promote technology, and to teach its uses to others. For some of us, the impetus for becoming computer literate was like standing on the edge of a a frigid swimming pool, watching our friends each jump in ahead of us. Although they call back to us that the water's great, we know full well it will be shockingly uncomfortable. The worst part is knowing we must make the jump. It's an apt analogy, because taking the plunge is the first step toward becoming computer comfortable.

Just Jump In

The water will always be cold, but as we all know, once you've been in it a while, it doesn't seem so frigid. Stop making excuses. Stop waiting until you have more time, more funds, more expertise, more need for technology. Begin now. Carefully reading this magazine is a good start.

Admit You Don't Know

What I dislike most about the so-called learning curve is that I feel stupid for most of the incline. Computers made me feel inept, and I was reluctant to admit that in professional company. But I've found that most technology users are not computer experts. Instead, they are eager to learn and experiment, and are able to live with not knowing, or knowing just a bit more than their students. We have all known young computer enthusiasts. They aren't always smarter than we are, just more comfortable with the unknown. Confessing computer confusion usually brings forth compassion and assistance from both young and adult computer wizards.

Be Patient With Yourself

I began to think of learning with computers as similar to learning French. I never expected to learn another language in a few weeks, or even a few months. After more than a year of instruction, I often made mistakes as I learned to think and speak in French. The computer connection is a foreign one, and we need to give ourselves time and allow for frustration. We also need to have confidence that we *will* become computer-able. After all, we learned our *first* sophisticated language before the age of three!

Read, Read, Read

Read magazines, books, newspaper articles. Read when it makes no sense, and when it all makes sense. Just as we began to speak by imitating what we heard, we will begin to understand computerese by frequently encountering the same terms, the same jargon, the same procedures. As Malcolm Gladwell noted in "The Tipping Point" (*New Yorker*, June 3, 1996), change comes about when a critical mass is reached. For example, no matter how often I read about Internet procedures, I kept getting confused about the terms Archie and Veronica. Mnemonics failed me, and I began to despair of ever mastering this seemingly impossible language. Yet the day came when I *knew* how the Internet works, how to send e-mail, and how to get a program to load and run. Months of reading brought on a seemingly overnight competence and confidence.

Get a Computer

If you have only begun to "play around" with a school computer, it's imperative that you get a computer for home. Check your computer suppliers for rebuilt or refurbished machines. My refurbished Pentium came with 12 programs loaded, a CD-ROM drive, and a huge memory for less than $700 without monitor. In the privacy of my home, I have more uninterrupted time, and I can experiment and ask questions of my knowledgeable teenagers. I get lots of encouragement from online fellow learners.

Attend Training

In my area, courses are offered by computer stores and a community college, at library and reading conferences, and through a regional education service center. In their latest course offerings, the service center offered more than 40 one- or two-day classes in everything from e-mail and Internet procedures to advanced uses of technology. In these classes, my experience has been that there is *always* someone who knows even less than I do. It's a perfect arena to ask questions and get personal help.

Try Things

Don't wait until you are an "expert." I've discovered through trial and lots of errors that it is difficult to break hardware or software. It is also rare to get so thoroughly lost that you cannot be rescued. There's an incredible elation when you install your first program or figure how to get out of a tight spot by yourself.

Ask Lots of Questions

Help is plentifully available. I've discovered that most of those who are further down the technology road than I are most delighted to pause and give assistance. Ask your students, your friends, your children, and the salespersons at computer stores. Go online and ask questions on a listserv like LM_NET, ask vendors and speakers at conferences, even write letters to editors of computer magazines like this one. Use technical support services for programs you use. There is usually a phone number with all major brands of hardware and software. I've found the majority of these telephones are manned by incredibly patient humans.

Make Allies

Talk with others about what they are doing and what works for them. A sympathetic ear and some trusted advice is often more helpful than all the well-written prose in a computer manual.

Continue With All of the Above

You are never finished learning about computer uses. You just progress to another stage, another program, another application. The exciting thing about technology is the way it continues to progress and move forward. As you teach technology applications, you will find yourself learning alongside and from your students. and you will discover that your friends were right—the water's fine! **TC**

Pat Miller is a Library Media Specialist at Walker Station Elementary, a K-5 school of 1,200 students in Sugar Land, Texas. She has been swimming at the shallow end of the technology pool for about two years, and welcomes responses from fellow dog-paddlers

---

References and Suggested Readings

These are a few of the books and magazines I have read and used in my technology odyssey.

Benson, Allen C. and Linda M. Fodemski, *Connecting Kids and the Internet: A Handbook for Librarians, Teachers and Parents*. Neal-Schuman. From Net safety to curriculum integration, these 377+ pages cover all the basics.

Classroom Connect: The K-12 Educator's Practical Guide to Using the Internet and Commercial Online Services. Wentworth Worldwide Media (1866 Colonial Village Lane, P.O. Box 10488, Lancaster, PA 17605). Short, easily understood and applied articles, and numerous useful Web sites.

The Complete Idiot's Guide to... Works for Windows, for example. Explanations are clear and terms are carefully defined. True to the subtitle, *For People With Better Things to Do*, each chapter is sprinkled with sections called "The Least You Need to Know." Alpha Books/Prentice Hall Computer Publishing.

Easy PowerPoint 4 or *Easy Microsoft Office* are two of a series of QUE books I found especially helpful. They include lots of screen shots. QUE (201 West 103rd Street, Indianapolis, IN 46290).

Handler, Marianne G., Ann S. Dana, and Jane Peters Moore, *Hypermedia as a Student Tool: A Guide for Teachers*, Libraries Unlimited.

PC Novice Guide to the Internet. One of a number of guides in magazine format, this comes with easy instructions on e-mail, Web pages, newsgroups, and selecting appropriate software. PC Novice Guide Series, P.O. Box 82511, Lincoln, NE 68501, 1-800-367-7333. Other titles include guides to Windows applications, going online, selecting software, and computing basics.

Rathbone, Andy, *Multimedia & CD-ROMs for Dummies*. IDG Books. Part of a seemingly endless series of "references for the rest of us!," these guides rely on humor to make the learning curve less steep. Sidebars include tips and highlighted "technical stuff," which you can skip as desired.

Technology Connection: The Magazine for School Media and Technology Specialists. Linworth Publishing (480 E. Wilson Bridge Road, Suite L, Worthington, OH 43085). Issues are themed and contain reviews.

Crystal Ball Gazing into Library Land

By Lesley Farmer

The high school library of the near future can be a community learning center according to our author's crystal ball.

I'M NOT INTO CRYSTAL BALL gazing. I do read palms on an elementary level, and I like near-future science fiction. But my growing collection of "libraries in the future" articles attests to my cynical take on extrapolating current trends into the future. So why am I writing this article? My inspiration lies in a 1996 publication by the California State Library and a private organization called the Institute for the Future. The title of their endeavor is *Entering the 21st Century: California Public Libraries Face the Future.*

It has been said that "as California goes, so goes the nation." That statement comes from the observation that demographics emerging in California come to other states soon afterwards. Or think of the rising businesses and industries in California: technology, service, entertainment. They forecast the trends for the rest of the country.

California may even be said to be on the bleeding edge as it confronts state welfare reforms and political budgets. Proposition 13, which slaughtered California public and school library budgets in the 1970s, is now being emulated in other states, such as Oregon, that are trying to balance their budgets. Fortunately, California seems to be on the upswing of that dismal nadir of money politics and is legislating other funding, particularly for technology in libraries. Other states should take note.

This is to say that, all things being equal, school libraries might well see themselves in the following scenarios in the near future, say by 2007.

Form Follows Function

Probably the most obvious change in school libraries will be in function-based space allocation. For example, computers and reference materials will be housed together because students will use both in their research assignments. However, students will access CD-ROMs from networked computers (the library being a node in the school's LAN). Students will each have an account so they can upload the information they find to their own hard-drive space.

Computers and other means of media production will be kept together so students can share research findings and other works. Videotaping will continue to be an important part of reporting and student presentations. Most likely, the school will have a video conferencing center, with the ability to upload to a central video distribution center. Students will then download information to both the reference and the production center, depending on their informational task.

Students will be expected to work competently with all of means of production. Even slides will be used when a still picture is considered the best way to capture a piece of information.

In fact, the production center will include magazines and other print items that may be scanned for inclusion in presentations.

The Old Times

There will continue to be a demand for the traditional aspects of the library. With all of the stimuli bombarding young people, and the apparent sense of displacement, the library can continue to serve as a safe and neutral haven for students. The collection should remain balanced, so students can get a variety of opinions from which to form their own stances. Libraries will continue to be a place where students can browse the shelves, seek information privately and at their own pace, and read reflectively.

There is a growing awareness that collaborative reading and reflection improve reading and interpretation; there's also a simple social need to get together for food and talk. Taking the coffee-house model of 90s bookstores (and acknowledging the fact that many teenagers are coffee drinkers), the near-future library will include a reading-socializing wing where students can discuss their latest reading (book, article or Web site) while sipping a *latte.* This will be a site where students form study groups to probe English texts or math problems, and a place where chess and dominoes are tolerated.

With the push for information literacy, the library's space will also have to accommodate lecture/presentation areas. These areas will include projection screens for videos, computer screen amplifications, and live Internet sessions. Multimedia stations with projection systems will be the norm as librarians and teachers demonstrate research strategies to students.

School libraries of the near future will create spaces for students to interact with their reading: comfortable stuffed chairs and cozy corners that facilitate escape reading. Students will value private spaces that foster individuality. The library will also legitimize student "lobbyists" by identifying areas for specialized interests: a girls' computer center, a lesbian-gay collection, a multilingual section. These interest groups can customize their areas and invite other students to delve into the subject areas in a meaningful way.

Student Support

More libraries will have a learning lab section, which facilitates student learning through tutors and special resources. Those resources will include books and magazines for new readers and audiocassettes and videotapes related to curriculum units. Tutors will store their materials in the library and will be able to use library equipment that will help their students, such as text scanner/readers, audiocassette players, and camcorders. The lab will also make room for student read-alouds and other shared reading that engages reluctant readers.

Tutors can be adults or students. Cross-generational opportunities will abound as baby-boomers reach retirement age and want to be involved with education. Peer tutoring will be part of the required social service component of school graduation within the next 10 years. In an effort to develop articulated programs across grade levels, more cross-age tutoring will occur, such as high schoolers acting as research guides or Internet navigators for younger students.

Community Support

School libraries will routinely be open in the evening, staffed by paraprofessionals or credentialed librarians. These hours will encourage parents and other community members to access the library. Evening and summer programs will bloom, including literacy courses, parent education sessions, and tutoring. The school library may well become the neutral town hall forum, where discussions of issues can be videotaped for community-wide dialogue. The librarian can take advantage of these opportunities by developing book lists on issues and publishing the lists on the Net.

Publications

Librarians' writings will be focused on a wider audience. For instance, book lists and Web pages will be created to meet specific unit needs, such as local environmental issues or time-sensitive political causes. Librarians can broaden their media expertise to produce video conferences, interactive multimedia presentations, and information

> **The school library may well become the neutral town hall forum, where discussions of issues can be videotaped for community-wide dialogue.**

computer kiosks.

As students sit down at their workstations, they will be greeted with library information and guided on information literacy "tours." It may well be that, since students will have individual accounts, they will have to pass an information literacy test or run through a computerized course before they will be able to log on to library services. In fact, before they can access the simplest program, students may have to agree to a computer policy statement, which will appear on the monitor screen. This may become necessary in the nation's increasingly litigious society.

Planning Space

If the librarian has an office, it will include a planning table, preferably wired to computers and audiovisual equipment, so that she or he can work with classroom teachers as they design lessons. A professional reading collection should be maintained. To collaborate in teaching and planning, teachers need access to professional books and journals. The library will be the place where teachers can collaborate informally and work hand-in-hand with the librarian as they examine the available resources and ways to make learning meaningful for their students.

Working With Other Agencies

"It takes a village to raise a child." This will be the assumption over the next five years. School libraries will work with health agencies to provide information for the personal needs of students. Businesses will come to the library to talk about school-to-work competencies. Governmental entities will routinely ask student options about political issues and have students hold mock votes to identify youth concerns.

Obviously, school and public librarians will work together to provide resources and services for students—and lobby for library support. Professional librarians will regularly collaborate so students will experience a seamless service continuum between the two types of libraries. This kind of collaboration will grow among all types of libraries.

From Gaze to Reality

What is described here is a vibrant community learning center. When teachers and students, as well as parents and other community members, realize that the library is the most cost-effective means to provide information research and sharing, then the library can become "the right resource at the right time to the right person." Of course, none of these advances may happen. It is up to school librarians to exercise their authority and collaborative spirit to make these scenarios realities. The crystal ball is in your hands.

Lesley S.J. Farmer is the Library Media Teacher at Redwood High School in Larkspur, California. She is also the consulting editor for the Professional Growth Series published by Linworth and an editorial consultant to the magazine Technology Connection. *She is the author of a number of books, including* Workshops for Teachers: Becoming Partners for Information Literacy *(Linworth).*

THE INTERNET: CONNECTING WITH THE CURRICULUM

The Right Filter for the Wrong Addresses: Regulating Net Access

Electronic resources have broadened the number of things librarians must evaluate and select. Now you might be called on to select a filtering program to restrict access to inappropriate sites on the Internet.

By Carol Simpson

Turning students loose on the Internet brings shudders of apprehension from the most liberal educators. Media coverage of the bizarre, erroneous and downright dangerous sites has raised public concern over the appropriateness of allowing students to freely explore the Internet. Parents of a conservative bent demand that access be withheld from minor children. At the same time, the American Library Association has endorsed a policy of unrestricted access to electronic resources in the same way that equal access to print materials has been supported in the past.

Balancing the fears of parents with the pressures from professional groups requires a fine tightrope indeed. With one group advocating no or very limited access, and another group supporting total access, what is the school to do?

A solution popular with administrators seeking a "pat" approach is filtering. Internet filtering programs such as *SurfWatch*, *CyberSitter*, *Net Nanny*, or *Cyber Patrol* restrict access to some sites. Once installed on a computer, the filter is automatically invoked if the user attempts to access a World Wide Web site identified as inappropriate for student access.

Many filters only work on graphic browsers, such as *Netscape* or *Mosaic*. Many filtering programs notify the user of the restriction when he types in the address. Some programs also filter newsgroups and electronic mail. Other filters use proprietary formulas to identify potentially "dangerous" sites. One program has identified the tilde (~) in an address as a dangerous sign. The tilde is often used to indicate a personal page—including pages created by students. Using a package that filters on this character would prevent students from seeing their own Web pages!

Who Decides What Is Filtered?

Many of the filter vendors will not reveal their selection criteria, citing "proprietary" information. If you don't know how the software company decides what it will filter, how can you be certain it will do what you want?

Some programs come to the purchaser with names of blocked sites already entered. On a few of these programs, you can enter the names of sites to be blocked. For example, the software might be configured to block graphic pornography, but you also wish to restrict access to hate groups. If you know the addresses or URLs (universal resource locators) of the hate groups' pages, you can enter them into the database of restricted sites. The problem is you may not be aware of every inappropriate site.

Some software will allow you to select different types of sites for blocking: graphic pornography, sexually explicit but not pornographic material, information about bomb-making and guns, personal pages, games, job opportunities, or bizarre information.

Other filtering software might restrict all sites except those you enter into an "approved" list. This is sometimes called "reverse filtering" or "positive filtering." Some proponents of this type of software liken it to book selection in libraries. Find the good sites and allow students access only to those sites. However, the Internet is so large and changes so rapidly that this becomes impractical. How can one claim to have found all the good, educational sites? What about new sites? What happens when a "good" site links to a site that might have both useful and potentially harmful information? Do you block access to the useful information because it sits next to less-accepted material?

Some filtering software "reads" the page to be displayed, looking for words or phrases on a list of prohibited items. If the software finds something potentially offensive, it replaces the problematic string of letters with some ASCII character, such as an asterisk. You might see something like this: Satan rules over ****. Other programs simply will not load any page or document that contains words from the hot list.

Reverse filtering software may come with a pre-loaded list of prohibited words or allow you to add or delete your own choices. While you might not have to worry about students being exposed to words such as "sex" or "breast," be certain that the software doesn't also filter words such as "sextant" or phrases like "breast cancer."

Filtering software can wield lots of power. Some goes beyond policing the World Wide Web. They also scrutinize e-mail, gopher and file transfers. Other packages monitor or restrict access to files on the local hard disk. This is useful where students tamper with or attempt to disable files.

Some of these programs can monitor and record every single transaction a user initiates while on the Web. While this might make it easier to track down potential vandals, it also puts the teacher or librarian in the position of being the Internet police. Librarians, in particular, might have some ethical problems with this type of usage tracking, especially in light of position statements of the American Library Association regarding free access to library materials.

State and federal laws regarding privacy of library transactions might also make tracking of usage problematic for libraries. Automation software generally deletes checkout records once a transaction has cleared so that libraries cannot violate federal privacy statutes by maintaining a history of users' transactions. Filtering software that keeps records of every site a student visits might also violate those same statutes.

In addition, since many sites are poorly identified in their titles, a student might retrieve a listing of an inappropriate site when doing a

---

Some Questions to Ask Vendors

1. Who decides what will be filtered? Some packages are sold with a pre-selected set of blocked addresses. Who selected them? Can you add or delete addresses?

2. Does the filtering package do more than filter addresses? Does it monitor or restrict files on the school's hard drives? Does it police teachers' and students' use of the Internet?

3. How often will the filter software be updated to reflect changes in Web addresses? How are updates installed?

Web search, and only discover the error when he clicks on that link. Should he be disciplined for simply investigating a "hit" brought back from a search engine? Most of us have had the experience of getting sites in a Web search that made us ask "How on earth did that show up in this search?"

Filtering software that marks certain users as "problems" or locks students out of further searches simply because they click on a poorly identified link will be difficult to administer. Monitoring and clearing the audit trails will take time. Maintaining student search histories can potentially impact student willingness to investigate areas of personal need.

Wandering Sites
One unresolved problem with Internet filtering involves the frequent changes of Internet site addresses, both good and bad. The Internet's shady citizens are smart enough to know that if they stick around in one place for any length of time they will be found out and probably put out of business. To avoid that happening, they move their addresses frequently. That is what makes filter lists a less-than-complete method of restricting access to inappropriate sites.

The undesirable addresses documented in the list of restricted sites may become obsolete in short order, and the new site will not yet be listed, making the new address perfectly accessible. This is also a problem for the positive filters. A useful and appropriate site may appear but cannot be accessed because the necessary modification hasn't yet been made to the list of approved sites. If filters are used for teachers as well as students, the teachers cannot help locate new and appropriate sites because they aren't allowed to "surf" to locate them.

What Are the Real Costs?
Vendors will provide generous incentives and site licensing deals to entice you to sign up. What does that cost really entail? Many of these products charge per computer. While $25 per computer sounds inexpensive, multiply that by the number of computers at your building or in your district. You might be surprised by the real cost!
What do you get for that price? The software and documentation? What about updates? The Net changes daily. Updates are a necessity if the filter is to be up to the task of restricting access to inappropriate sites. How often can you get an update? Are they issued weekly? Monthly? Yearly? Consider that students will be able to access the sites that will be blocked until the next update is installed.

How will you install updates? Must you assign a technician to that task? Will he be required to visit every computer every time an update arrives? Can teachers install their own updates? Will they?

What if the vendor could configure the software to check the vendor's Web site every time the computer is turned on to check for new sites to block? Would that satisfy your maintenance requirements? Consider the impact on the network of 500+ computers all being turned on at 8 a.m. and logging on to the same Internet site to check for updates. Would that amount of network traffic swamp your connection? If you access the Internet via modem, would you be able to support that many connections every time your users turned on their computers?

As with most complex problems, the problem of keeping students away from inappropriate Internet sites will require a complex solution. Education about school policies and appropriate use of the Internet is a key ingredient. Students and teachers must know what to look for and how to find it. Acceptable use policies and student (and teacher!) codes of conduct provide guidance about what Internet activities may be tolerated and which will bring down a series of consequences. Monitoring and supervision of Internet-capable computers, plus keeping students on task, will eliminate some of the too-much-idle-time problems that can arise.

Nothing short of unplugging the computer will guarantee that a student can never access inappropriate material on the Internet. Don't live with a sense of false security, and don't put yourself in a position of potential liability by assuming that a filtering program will do all the work. **TC**

Carol Simpson is the Library Technology Facilitator for the Mesquite, Texas, Schools. She is also the Editor of TECHNOLOGY CONNECTION.

NOTES

SEARCHING

Caveat Emptor: Looking the Internet Gift Horse in the Mouth

by Sharon McCaslin

For librarians, access to the Internet is like annexing a large, constantly changing and growing bookstore. As we joyously run up and down the aisles saying, "Oh, yes, we can use this!" or "I know just the student who will want that!" we tend to forget that this "bookstore" comes with an all-or-nothing clause. While we focus on the beneficial items, this source also contains subversive politics, exhortations to violence, bomb-building instructions, and pornography. In fact, since this "bookstore" is being constantly restocked, we have no way of knowing just what is in it at any given time. Given many communities' reaction to controversial materials in the schools, librarians need to develop a rational policy for access to the Internet.

The penalties for ignoring this problem can be severe, nor is it likely to resolve itself. The Internet is an international medium, and, as such, it is not regulated by any one state or country's laws. In the United States, there have been attempts to sue people in another state for what they put on the Internet, in effect trying to apply local censorship bans to other jurisdictions. So far these attempts have been unsuccessful, although anyone who has accidentally dipped into the alternative lifestyles bulletin boards can understand the impulse. However, none of us would like to see other cultures impose restrictions on our own tradition of free speech.

There are several ways school systems try to control this uncontrollable medium. Some have resisted access entirely. Others have set up a controlled menu, and provide access only to selected resources. But, one of the reasons we want our students to use the Internet is so that they can learn to "surf the net" themselves. The only possible way to attempt control in that environment is the unpalatable option of monitoring each student's activities, much like reading over a student's shoulder in the library. This takes far too much staff time and still doesn't permit the student to explore and learn on his own. In fact, just as teachers try to encourage judgment and discrimination in reading, we also hope to teach students to evaluate and select Internet resources. This sort of education is possible only if the students have free access to cyberspace.

School systems that intend to give their students open access to the Internet should set up policies which explain and affirm the principles of freedom of speech, freedom to read, and free access to information. Given the revolutionary nature of the Internet (we are not talking basic book selection anymore), it would be appropriate to have a specific policy relating to Internet use. Any such policy must take into account the probability that students may encounter controversial material on the Internet and that students, teachers, and school officials will be shouldering new responsibilities along with their new freedom on the Internet.

Regardless of what amount of control or freedom a school board

Access to the Internet raises a new set of questions about the right to read, the responsibilities of access providers, and the right to privacy. The book selection policy won't answer all of them.

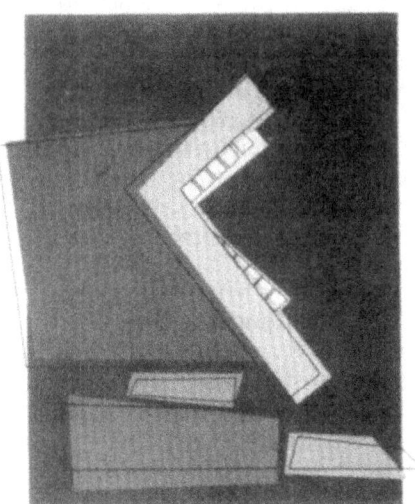

How will you install updates? Must you assign a technician to that task? Will he be required to visit every computer every time an update arrives? Can teachers install their own updates? Will they?

What if the vendor could configure the software to check the vendor's Web site every time the computer is turned on to check for new sites to block? Would that satisfy your maintenance requirements? Consider the impact on the network of 500+ computers all being turned on at 8 a.m. and logging on to the same Internet site to check for updates. Would that amount of network traffic swamp your connection? If you access the Internet via modem, would you be able to support that many connections every time your users turned on their computers?

As with most complex problems, the problem of keeping students away from inappropriate Internet sites will require a complex solution. Education about school policies and appropriate use of the Internet is a key ingredient. Students and teachers must know what to look for and how to find it. Acceptable use policies and student (and teacher!) codes of conduct provide guidance about what Internet activities may be tolerated and which will bring down a series of consequences. Monitoring and supervision of Internet-capable computers, plus keeping students on task, will eliminate some of the too-much-idle-time problems that can arise.

Nothing short of unplugging the computer will guarantee that a student can never access inappropriate material on the Internet. Don't live with a sense of false security, and don't put yourself in a position of potential liability by assuming that a filtering program will do all the work. **TC**

Carol Simpson is the Library Technology Facilitator for the Mesquite, Texas, Schools. She is also the Editor of TECHNOLOGY CONNECTION.

NOTES

Another Look At Acceptable Use Policies

BY CAROL WILLIAMSON

A well-written policy protects everyone in the school from bumps and potholes on the information superhighway.

Generally, schools' acceptable use policies (AUPs) focus on two concerns: how to deal with the accessing and transmitting of information inappropriate to the school setting, and how to maintain the efficient operation of the network. Most K–12 policies include the following:

- A brief explanation as to why the school district is offering Internet access to its students and staff, often with a short description of what the Internet is and what it has to offer.
- A warning concerning the availability of adult-oriented or sexually explicit information available on the Net that can be accessed either purposely or accidentally.
- A reminder that Internet access should be treated as a privilege with responsibilities for the user.
- A description of what constitutes acceptable and unacceptable use.
- The consequences of violating the Acceptable Use Policy, which may include revoking privileges, school disciplinary action and even legal action, if appropriate.
- A disclaimer absolving the school district from responsibility in a number of areas.

Many schools also include warnings in their policies stating that students may not use the Internet for illegal, commercial, or political purposes, gain access using someone else's account number, or disrupt network operation in any way. Other AUPs warn about violating copyright laws, vandalizing data, invading the privacy of others, posting anonymous messages, posting personal communication without the author's consent, posting hate mail or mail with harassment and/or discriminatory remarks, exhibiting antisocial

> **System administrators, media specialists, and teachers must be sure that student users understand each part of the AUP before they are given accounts.**

behaviors, and accessing or transmitting information containing profanity, vulgarities, obscenities, or any other inappropriate language.

Other guidelines relate to the smooth operation of the network, with emphasis on the fact that the Internet is not an unlimited resource as some might think. In contrast to all these warnings, some schools frame their AUPs in very general terms, perhaps to afford them leeway in interpretation or to avoid criticism by anti-censorship groups.

Disclaimers, Disclaimers and More Disclaimers

The following disclaimers are found in some AUPs:
- The school district retains the right to monitor file server space and review materials on user accounts. That is, the privacy of e-mail is not guaranteed. An account holder uses the Internet at his or her own risk.
- The school district assumes no responsibility for costs caused by the way the account holder chooses to use his or her network access. There is no guarantee of the dependability of the system or of the information accessed on the system. Conditions and services will change from time to time.

Users are warned to protect their accounts by not giving out personal information such as last name, address or phone number, and to safeguard their passwords by keeping them private and changing them frequently. Finally, school districts emphasize that from time to time the system administrators can make determinations on whether special uses of the network are consistent with the AUP, and they can deem what is inappropriate use with their decisions being final.

Acceptable use policies generally conclude with a place for the student and parent (if the student is under 18) to sign. Forms are then kept on file at the school. It is rather obvious that an acceptable use policy can become a fairly long document if a school district chooses to include very specific information. For this reason, it would be wise for school officials to provide a means for parents and students to ask questions. Furthermore, system administrators, media specialists, and teachers, must be sure that student users understand each part of the AUP before they are given accounts. It would be a good idea to remind students with Internet access at home that the district's acceptable use policy might differ from the rules set down by their parents. Stress that while using the Internet at school they must follow the guidelines in the school district's AUP.

Finally, all staff should understand the ramifications of the guidelines. They should discuss with each other any areas that might be misinterpreted and come to a common agreement about enforcing guidelines. Cooperation and consistency are essential.

It is hoped that school districts will understand the importance of including a discussion of their acceptable use policies in any Internet training sessions they offer to staff. This information will go a long way toward ensuring that the Internet will be used as a valuable tool for information retrieval. **TC**

Carol Williamson is a Library Media Specialist at Parkway Schools, Rockford, Ohio.

NOTES

Gathering the Tools: Library Media Specialist as General Contractor

How do you know what to buy? How do you know where to find it? With so many vendors calling you, how do you know which one to pick? When it comes to choosing the tools needed to effectively run both your library and school networks, it is best first to call other library media specialists who are in similar circumstances, but about six months ahead of you. They can fill you in on the trials, tribulations, and costs to avoid when putting in a network.

The articles in this chapter deal with hardware, software, and networking issues for keeping a successful library media program up and running.

Networking, whether it is Novell, NT, or AppleTalk, is not rocket science. However, it is important to understand the terminology and requirements for an effective networked environment. The most integral part to the planning of any network is the ability to look ahead to potential uses of the bandwidth and network capacity.

- Are you putting six drops in every room, but hooking up only two computers right now? Perhaps you can get away with a smaller digital lease line.
- Are videoconferencing and distance learning going to be part of the high school curriculum in a few years? Perhaps you should plan to segment that part of the network or give that area an additional link to the Internet.
- Who is going to maintain the network and what is the chain of command for work orders?

All of these issues and more are discussed in the articles in this chapter.

It is impossible to know what the future will hold in the area of technological advances. Already wireless is as speedy as some 10BaseT connections and is a good fit for some schools. Personal portable devices are becoming commonplace, and the impact of attaching hundreds of these devices to a network has not yet been fully realized. The "last mile" of Internet access, the connection from your Internet service provider to your school, is now made up of bigger bandwidth, such as DSL, T1, and cable modems. With the increased use of high bandwidth applications in schools, the amount of bandwidth will never be sufficient.

Your job as library media specialist should allow you to sit on the committees that set the guidelines for Internet uses and abuses. These articles provide you with the rationale and vocabulary needed to help you make the best decisions.

The building process may include writing grant proposals to obtain money for technology. Information, tips, and tricks for writing winning grant proposals are also included in this chapter. There is even an article dealing with the creation of a multimedia publishing center made from "scrap" technology items found around your school.

One of the ISTE Recommended Foundations in Technology for All Teachers is knowing the correct technology terminology. By learning how networks work and the correct terms to use for the description of the parts and pieces, you will soon be a valued member of your school or district technology committee. Once you internalize an understanding of the network make-up, you can concentrate on the best use of the network to enhance teaching and learning.

▶ URL UPDATE

Ergonomics: The Forgotten Variable
by L. Jeffrey Fitterman

National Institute for Occupational Safety and Health
http://www.cdc.gov/niosh/homepage.html

Proposal Writing for Technology Money: Part 2
by Richard Alan Smith

Yahoo Education: Grants
http://dir.yahoo.com/Education/Financial_Aid/Grants/

Grants Web Homepage
http://www.srainternational.org/cws/sra/sra.htm

How to Minimize the Dangers of Macro Viruses
by Paul A. Ekhaml and Leticia Ekhaml

McAfee AntiVirus Center
http://www.mcafee.com

Ergonomics: The Forgotten Variable

By L. Jeffrey Fitterman

In 1981, a relative sent me two informative articles from a Florida newspaper. The first article dealt with computer programming instruction at a vocational institute, and the second article dealt with computer literacy instruction at an elementary school. The photos showed students at both schools trying to access the technology in a laboratory setting.

At the elementary school, the tables were adult size, and the monitors and keyboards were placed so high that students were viewing monitors at a 45-degree angle and using keyboards they couldn't even see.

At the vocational institute, I noticed that one student in a wheelchair was not using the computer terminals. I was so interested in knowing why that I contacted the school and spoke to the student. He relayed a story that curled my already-curly hair. The student could not access the computer terminals unless he was switched from his custom contoured wheelchair to a standard hospital wheelchair. This transfer was necessary because the table was too low and a cross brace prevented the custom wheelchair from getting close to the table. Both wheelchair transfers took approximately 30 minutes out of the three-hour class and produced undue physical stress on the student.

Both of these situations could have been easily remedied with a basic knowledge of ergonomics.

What is Ergonomics?

Ergonomics, or human factor engineering, involves developing systems with dimensions that can be adapted to the variety of people expected to use them. It is essential for all of us to have a general understanding of ergonomics.

The President's Committee on Employment estimates that one out of every 10 persons in the United States has or will have limited mobility due to temporary or permanent physical or sensory disability. Many technology users have been accessing these technologies incorrectly for so many years that physical conditions requiring treatment are now surfacing.

We need to think of everyone who uses technology, especially those with physical or sensory impairments. Whether we are using a computer, a hammer, or a pencil, correct seating and positioning should be of primary concern to all those interested in higher productivity and environmental safety.

How should we start designing an appropriate setup?

- Be empathetic to the needs of the individual user.

- Interview users about their specific needs. Assess their abilities, not their disabilities. Determine if users needs any special accommodations. Do they wear bifocals? Are they prone to back or neck discomforts? Are they distracted by noise or glare? Are they left-handed?

- Learn about the latest ergonomic design characteristics by reviewing Web sites, ergonomic publications, and federal guidelines and by attending training.
- Discover the latest technological advancements in this area by subscribing to relevant technological publications and attending related training and conferences.

Design Considerations

Assess the needs of individual users. I do not know any users who will access their environments as depicted by an ergonomic design figure found in new computer installation booklets (see figure 1). This figure is meant only as a reference point. Users will never sit as straight or hold their hands and arms as robotically as the figure depicts. Users have different torso shapes, leg and arm lengths, and eyesight.

Examine the following six areas when considering a design for a user.

1. Physical and sensory abilities of the individual
2. Posture of individual user
3. Arm and hand placement
4. Backrest and lumbar support
5. Keyboard type, elevation, sensitivity, and placement
6. Monitor placement, size, and resolution

Whether we are using a computer, a hammer, or a pencil, correct seating and positioning should be of primary concern to all those interested in higher productivity and environmental safety.

Environmental Considerations

The surrounding environment is commonly overlooked when designing a work area. We tend to spend time looking only at our immediate work environment. Equally important environmental factors, such as illumination, space and time should be considered. Contrast, intensity, tone, color, brightness, hue, and saturation are environmental factors that can set the tone of our work site. While dark colors reduce reflective light and cause the work site to need additional lighting, bright colors (super white) can cause reflective and annoying glare. A happy medium between the wall and ceiling paints, furniture, and flooring is essential.

Have you ever tried to give directions or position equipment when a wall is curved or a labyrinth design is applied to traffic areas? Space factors pertain to traffic areas, work area, and clearance. Movement and safety of people and equipment is compromised if angles less than 90 degrees are used in a work site design.

The following is a list of suggested space requirements for work sites:

Tables
- 5 to 6 feet desktop space (width) per machine.
- Minimum desktop depth of 27 to 30 inches. Extra depth is needed to allow access to rear connectors if components are bolted down.
- 2 feet (width) of desktop space on one side of components for user work area. Allow space for lefthanded users.
- Sturdy construction without

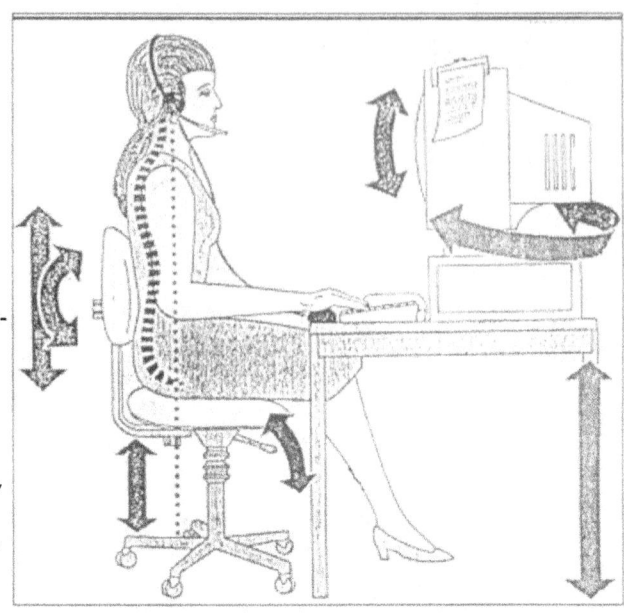

Figure 1.

cross braces to obstruct chair from fitting completely under desktop.
- Fixed table base to allow for permanent wiring, stability, and security.
- Adjustable desktops to allow adjustments for adults and students of all sizes and physical impairments.
- Non-conductive table construction to curtail the possibility of electric shocks from frayed and poorly grounded electronics.

Chairs
- No one chair design works with each user. Users should pick a chair that best fits their individual needs.
- Chairs may need wheels, lumbar support, or height and tilt adjustments.

Monitor Height

The optimal height is four inches from keyboard level to bottom of monitor screen for touch typists and one to three inches from keyboard level to bottom of monitor screen for beginning typists (see figure 2). Beginning typists frequently look at their fingers and key locations while intermediate and advanced typists do not. By reducing the need for movement of the head and neck, these measurements reduce fatigue.

Additionally, users tend to use the top half of the monitor for word processing, database, and spreadsheet applications. Proficient programmers of commercial and educational software use the top half of the screen for data changes and the bottom half for status and control changes.

Ambient Noise and Light

Try to reduce noise from printers, fans, and air conditioning, system cooling, and power supply units. Place an insulated pad between the device and the surface area, such as the floor or desktop. Purchase printers that switch into sleep mode when not in use. Make sure that air conditioning filters are clean and air flow is not restricted.

Try to reduce glare from outside sunlight and overhead general lighting. Use monitor screen shades and hoods to reduce glare. Turn monitor screens away from light sources, such as windows, reading lamps, and overhead track lighting.

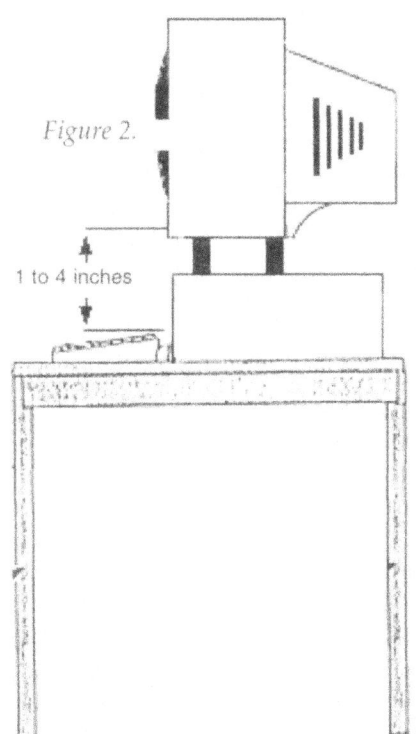

Figure 2.

1 to 4 inches

Electricity

- Static electricity occurs in dry winter months. To reduce static electricity, do not use thick pile carpet. Ground yourself to a metal appliance before operating delicate electronic devices.

- Keep the temperature and humidity at a comfortable level. Recommended levels are 72-78 degrees with 60-75% humidity. A humidifier may be necessary during dry and cold winter months. Air conditioners usually are adequate dehumidifiers.

- Four grounded outlets per work station is recommended, with a minimum of 20 amps of current per station. General current use: monitors 1-3 amps; computers 1-2 amps; printers 1-8 amps; scanners 1-3 amps.

- Surge protectors, voltage regulators, UPS (un-interruptable power supply), and lightning arrestors are recommended. In most cases, surge protectors will not protect against lightning strikes, but they will protect your technology from severe drops and spikes in electrical current. To protect against lightning strikes, call your local power company for assistance with lightning arrestors. A master power switch should be included as a safety cut off to insure that all equipment is quickly turned off in case of an emergency.

Hazards

Pesticide oxidation is caused when pest control services are used in your work site. Pesticides can build up over a period of time when inadvertently sprayed onto and into electronic components. When equipment is turned on, the equipment heats up and releases the pesticide in the form of a gas. Another chemical consideration is ozone. Ozone emission is released from laser printers when printing. Both pesticide oxidation and ozone emission can produce mild to severe irritants, such as dry throat and nose, headache, sore eyes, nausea, vomiting, and pulmonary congestion.

Additional Information Sources

For information on topics related to ergonomic design, contact:
- American Conference of Governmental Industrial Hygienists (www.acgih.org)
- National Institute for Occupational Safety and Health (www.cdc.gov/niosh)
- Occupational Safety and Health Administration (www.osha.gov)
- Underwriters Laboratory (www.ul.com)

Every user has a right to a safe environment to work, learn, and play. When designing a work site or classroom setting for the use of technology, ask yourself these questions:

Are work conditions keeping users from working to their highest potential?

Are users safe from physical, chemical, and electrical hazards?

If not, where can I go for additional assistance? **TC**

L. Jeffrey Fitterman is Coordinator of Technical Services, Florida Department of Education, Florida Instructional Materials Center in Tampa, Florida.

Educational Applications for Digital Cameras

By Terence Cavanaugh and Catherine Cavanaugh

A middle school science teacher watching a lunar eclipse takes out a digital camera and snaps a few shots of the eclipse through a telescope. Next the teacher pulls up the images on her personal computer. Using simple imaging software she creates a short animation of the eclipse and then enlarges one of the images to make a moon mapping worksheet. The next morning in class, she distributes copies of the worksheet; then using her computer with an overhead projector and LCD panel, she shows her classes the eclipse.

While this scenario may seem like science fiction to some, it can easily be done with today's digital cameras, electronic devices that digitize images. Digital cameras have come a long way in affordability and ease of use, and students and teachers at all levels now are using them in just about every curriculum area. These cameras provide opportunities for uses not only in curriculum but also in support and assessment.

Advantages and Disadvantages

Advantages of digital cameras over film cameras include higher turnaround speed for production of useable images and instant availability of images for output to print, videotape, or an image file. A digital image can be used in printed documents and presentations such as *HyperStudio* or *PowerPoint*. It is also easy to duplicate a digital photograph; prints and computer files can be copied indefinitely at almost no cost. In addition, you can realize major savings since you won't need to buy film or pay for developing. Storage space is saved because images are stored in digital form. You can create photographic images using standard computer and printer hardware with no other special equipment, and image appearance and quality can be easily controlled or adjusted using software included with cameras.

However, using digital cameras has its negatives. Compared to prints and slides, digital image quality is usually lower. In general, higher-quality cameras cost more, with standard photograph-quality cameras running into the thousands of dollars. Overall consumer models range anywhere from $100 to $3,000 and you must do all your own processing work.

Educational Uses of Digital Photography

Digital photography can assist in many areas of education. Identification photos or badges can easily be printed and updated, and photos can be produced for updating students' files and for school events. Photos of school property for record keeping, documenting crime or vandalism, and insurance inventory can be kept efficiently. Teachers and students can display digital photos in a variety of ways, including posters, multimedia displays, and presentations of student projects. Displays for open house, awards night, and fairs also can be created digitally. Anyone can take pictures for school newspapers and local broadcasts or even a digital yearbook.

For curriculum, digital photography allows for electronic field trips, using stored images shown in the classroom, recorded onto a videotape, or uploaded to a World Wide Web page. In advance of a field trip, classes can preview images of a site, and after the field trip, teachers can review with pictures taken during the trip.

You can create assignments with pictures to illustrate the items and processes that are used in the class. Digital photos also are useful for sharing information with absent students, or e-mailing the images from the classes they missed. Examples of classroom applications of digital imaging include photographing measurements, instruments, sports equipment or positions, recipe ingredients, and pictures for vocabulary or reading lessons; supplement worksheets with pictures specific to the course. Most digital cameras may be used with lenses or other optical instruments like microscopes and telescopes to make special images available to the entire class or to create animations or a time lapse photo series of processes, such as butterfly metamorphosis. Customize displays and bulletin boards with photos from school, lab, classroom, or student performances. Classes can include pictures in their correspondence with donors, volunteers, business partners, guests, and parents.

In assessing learning, digital photography is effective in both traditional test construction and in production of alternative assessments. Including students' photos and images of their 3-D and performance work in portfolios allows documentation of a greater variety of work than would otherwise be included; creating more authentic evaluations including images of items or processes from class experience.

Using the Digital Camera

Taking pictures with most digital cameras is like taking pictures with a regular camera—point the camera at the subject and push the shutter button. Most digital cameras have viewfinders, but some have LCD (liquid crystal display) screens that display the image before recording. An advantage to the LCD is the ease of viewing or deleting stored images from camera memory without the need to connect the camera to a computer. Unlike standard cameras, which store pictures on film, the digital camera's storage memory may be in the form of flash chips, PCM-CIA cards, disks, or even hard drives. Memory limits on digital cameras vary and may be supplemented with memory cards or special storage disks. Adding a memory card usually costs more than $200. All cameras have a delete feature, which may allow you to delete selected images or may require you to delete the entire memory. Some cameras allow images from a computer to be saved as photos in the camera for use in print or video applications.

Digital cameras usually connect and download to a computer running a camera/imaging program. Most cameras use the computer's serial or parallel ports. Some require an additional computer hardware card to be installed in the computer while others download through infrared, and some connect directly into a computer slot. A few digital cameras have video output that allows the cameras to send a video signal directly through to a television or videocassette recorder.

All digital cameras save pictures in a digital file format, which may be camera-specific, or a standardized format such as TIF, JPEG, or BMP. The format used to save the pictures will determine the amount of disk space needed. Picture storage formats can be easily converted using a graphics program. If the camera has the ability to output a video signal, videotape can be used to show or archive pictures. Stored images can be printed using specialized photo printers or standard black-and-white or color printers.

Students and teachers at all levels now are using digital cameras in just about every curriculum area.

Applications for Digital Images

After digital images have been transferred from the camera to a computer, they can be e-mailed as attachments or sent to any fax machine using the computer's fax/modem. Images can be incorporated into print, such as posters, signs, reports, banners, certificates, and any other publishable print document. Iron-on transfers allow images to be printed on items such as T-shirts, aprons, banners, and flags. Depending on the features of the camera, images can be recorded directly onto video for presentation without a computer. Images also can be added to word-processing documents and presentations and can be included on home pages for the World Wide Web after they have been converted in a browser supported format such as GIF or JPEG.

Accessory Equipment

Almost any printer can print digital images, but for the best quality, a high-resolution inkjet or laser printer is recommended. New photo printers that use glossy photo paper are now available. Most cameras include their own cables for connection to either a PC or Mac platform computer, and some cameras include the cables for direct video output. Most cameras also include an image-handling software program. Depending on the software, the options may be as simple as view and save, or may have numerous picture editing capabilities. Pictures can be used with popular graphics and imaging software programs, such as *PhotoShop* or *Corel Graphics*. Since images often are large files, and saving them can use lots of disk space, it is possible to save the images in more compressed formats like JPEG or GIF to conserve your disk space. For saving many images, an external drive is recommended.

Comparing Digital Cameras and Other Digitizers

A flatbed or hand-held scanner is an alternative to a digital camera, but it is not portable and often involves more steps in getting a digital image. For anyone who digitizes few images and has access to a scanner, it is a reasonable option. Cameras such as the *QuickCam* must be physically connected to a computer to work. When taking pictures within sight of a computer, these cameras work well. Cameras tethered to com puters are also useful for com puter videoconferencing and can make short digital video files. Inexpensive video digitizers, such as the *Snappy*, can convert a signal from a video recorder or video camera and then digitize the images as stills or motion video. For converting standard slides and photos to digital format, a *Photo CD* can be produced commercially. However, the processing costs for *Photo CDs* can be more than a dollar an image. Some photo labs will develop film and send out digital copies on floppies or by e-mail with paper prints.

Smile and Say, "Digital!"

For anyone who uses a camera, the adjustment to digital cameras will be easy, and the rewards will be a richer educational experience with a fun and flexible tool. Now is an ideal time to learn to use a digital camera. Costs are on the decline, and the selection of features is on the rise. Some camera manufacturers provide extensive support though their help lines and World Wide Web sites. Certain manufacturers have responded to their popularity in education by investing in online libraries of digital camera lessons and classroom ideas. These lists, often contributed by educators, are accessible free on the Web. Picture your future with a digital camera, and you'll be inventing your own uses in no time at all. **TC**

Terence Cavanaugh is a Physics Teacher at Lely High School in Naples, Florida. Catherine Cavanaugh is a Coordinator at the Whitaker Center for Math, Science, and Technology in Naples.

NOTES

MULTIMEDIA

Author! Author! Implications for Collection Development

by Lesley S.J. Farmer

Information literacy includes the *processing* of information as much as access to worthwhile sources. More and more, educators realize that students need to interpret, synthesize, organize, and make information *their own*—and that they must share their findings with others. This need brings an additional consideration to collection development: acquiring authoring tools.

Definitions

The following definitions will be used in this article:

Authoring tool: computer software that enables the user to manipulate information so it may be shared with others, especially for instruction. Examples include word processing, desktop publishing, databases, spreadsheets, multimedia programs, hypermedia programs, and programming languages (including mark-up languages for producing Web pages).

Multimedia program: computer software that allows users to incorporate two or more media, such as text and graphics; often multimedia also includes audio, and increasingly it encompasses motion (video) as well. Sample programs include *Kid Pix*, *Avid VideoShop*, and *Director*.

Presentation program: computer software that enables a user to create a sequential series of screens into a slide show on computer. Sample programs include *ClarisWorks Slide Show*, *Persuasion*, and *PowerPoint*.

Hypermedia program: computer software that combines the qualities of a multimedia program and a presentation program, but also permits linking of screens or blocks of information in a nonsequential manner. Hypermedia programs allow the greatest amount of interactivity. Sample programs include *HyperCard*, *HyperStudio*, *Digital Chisel*, *SuperLink*, and *LinkWay Live!*

Authoring system: a dedicated computer program that allows users to design a course-long set of interactive computer-based instruction, usually incorporating testing and record-keeping features. Sample programs include *Authorware Professional*, *TenCORE*, and *Plato*.

Performance Goals

Although librarians typically base collection development policies on user and institutional needs and interests, the current focus on student performance goals drives the requirement for collections that support desired student competencies. As an example, several school districts in Marin County, California, have adopted the student performance goal: "Use technology as a tool to access information, analyze and solve programs, and communicate ideas." The accompanying descriptor states: "The student demonstrates competence in the use of authoring tools, graphic applications, and telecommunications...Creates products using technologies."

What do these products look like at various levels?

• At second grade, "students, either individually or in small groups, utilize technology to communicate their understanding of a topic or create an expressive work."

• At fifth grade, "[a] cross-curricular project presented by a small group, utilizing at least two authoring tools plus two other technologies."

• At eighth grade: "[a] cross-curricular solo project utilizing at least three authoring tools plus three other technologies."

• At twelfth grade: "Within a curricular context the student will produce a solo project which exhibits mastery of the following technologies: authoring tools, graphics, telecommunications, plus items from at least two different technology categories; or, the student will develop a portfolio that incorporates the use of three or more technology categories with sample works from at least four subject areas."

Because the library is the information center and provides extensive access to resources, *including production tools*, the librarian must examine and acquire authoring tools that reflect student performance goals.

In some cases, the decision is simple: acquire the authoring tool that has been adopted as standard throughout the school or district. Although it shows that the library responds to student needs, this approach reflects a reactionary role rather than a pro-active one. Authoring tools can constitute a sizeable commitment of money and instruction; therefore, it behooves the librarian to take part in the original acquisition decision and help to influence it.

Selecting Multimedia Authoring Programs

Multimedia authoring programs represent a relatively new arena for many librarians. It may feel daunting to evaluate and compare these tools. In their book *Interactive Multimedia Instruction*, Schwier and Masanchuk provide a good list of factors to consider:

• Portability: Does the program exist on both computer platforms? Does the library have the computer systems to support the program? Can the program be used at several sites? Can a product created by the program be shown on different systems? In some cases, the presentation station needs to have the entire software; in other cases, it needs only a stripped-down "player" software program; in still other cases, the product is self-sufficient. Does the product look the same on different machines; for example, how well do screen size, fonts, and special effects translate among computers?

• Copyright: What is the licensing agreement? Can the program be transported to another station? Can the program be duplicated within the site? Is the program networkable? In some cases, the school has to buy a separate license for each station; in other cases, especially networked systems, up to a certain number of stations may load the program simultaneously.

• Incorporating peripherals: How easily can the program access CD-ROMs, laser discs, videos, and other computer programs? Does the program copy the external source material, or does it provide an active link to other equipment that must be attached when doing the multimedia presentation? Is additional hardware needed to accomplish these tasks, such as video or sound cards? How sophisticated are the connections with peripherals: Is random access possible, can special effects be generated, can multiple sources be linked or merged?

• Ease of operation: How intuitive is the interface? Can the user create a product without inordinate instruction? Are directions clear? Is the program robust (i.e., doesn't crash easily)? Is onscreen help available? Does an onscreen tutorial or tour exist? How helpful is the accompanying written documentation, if available?

• Flexibility: Can the user create a variety of "looks," or is the program rigid in its structure? Can the user approach the program from different angles: screen by screen or through flowcharts or using outlines? Does the user have the option to incorporate programming techniques or macro scripts? Does the program allow for different user levels of sophistication (for example, can a novice youngster create a satisfying product while the expert hacker stretches the program's capabilities)? Can the user import elements from other programs such as graphics, sounds, and *QuickTime* movies?

• Interactivity: How much control does the user have in developing and viewing the product? Is branching available at the user's discretion? Can the developer create a test option? Is it possible to incorporate feedback information? Can the program record and maintain user interactions?

• Text: What variations exist in type fonts and styles? Can a single *field* or screen incorporate type variations? Does the type feature work like a word processing program or is it limited to a graphics approach (that is, does it have no word wrapping and editing capabilities)?

• Graphics: What drawing and editing tools are available? Is color supported and, if so, to what degree? Can images be imported? Can images be animated?

• Audio: Can sounds be edited? What imported kinds of sources are accepted: analog, digital, MIDI?

• Video: Can the program accept various video import sources? Does it support full-screen motion video? What compression and decompression capabilities does it have? To what extent can video be edited?

Next Steps

Student performance expectations can help the librarian determine what authoring programs to consider to support that learning. Then, after evaluating the existing computer system capabilities and possible peripheral tie-ins, the librarian can decide which program is the best fit for the library and the rest of the school.

As with other collection development, acquisition is only the first process. The next step is use of the software. The librarian, teachers, and students will need instruction not only in technically operating an authoring program, but also on information manipulation and presentation if authoring is to be an educationally sound activity. But that is another article. Stay tuned! **TC**

Lesley S.J. Farmer is the Library Director of Redwood High School in Larkspur, California. She is the author of the forthcoming book, Training Student Library Staff, *to be published by Linworth Publishing.*

Further Reading

Barron, Ann E. and Gary W. Orwig. *Multimedia Technologies for Training.* Libraries Unlimited, 1995.

Gayeski, Diane M. *Multimedia for Learning.* Educational Technology Publications, 1993.

Handler, Marianne G., Ann S. Dana and Jane Peters Moore. *Hypermedia as a Student Tool.* Libraries Unlimited, 1995.

Robinette, Michelle. *Mac Multimedia for Teachers.* IDG, 1995.

Schwier, Richard A. and Earl R. Misanchuk. *Interactive Multimedia Instruction.* Educational Technology Publications, 1993.

SELECTION AND EVALUATION

Selecting and Evaluating Software

By Carol Mann Simpson

Beyond the usual questions about operating systems and hardware requirements (will this program run on our computers?), there are a number of other points to consider when evaluating programs for purchase. Among the questions we should ask are:

Who will use this software? If the program will be used by students, would a student be able to use the program *before* he reads the manual? Students, and many teachers, aren't likely to read lengthy print directions before entering a program. A program that is self-explanatory is preferable to one that forces the user to read printed materials.

Are "help" functions built into the software, and if so, how do they work? (The F1 key is reserved for "help" menus in many programs. Students may expect this to be true of all programs.) Will the user have to resort to a printed manual to find answers to his "help" questions?

Where will the software be installed? Will the user take this software home to operate? If so, are the installation instructions simple enough for a novice computer user?

What instructional methods are employed? If the program is designed for drill and practice, does it take advantage of the power of the computer? Is true remediation offered to those who don't pick up on the concepts, or does the program simply repeat the original instructional sequence or replay missed questions? What responses are offered to correct and incorrect answers? Some research has shown that students get bored with repetitive rewards for correct answers and will knowingly give an incorrect answer to see what type of response the computer will provide. Is an incorrect answer rewarded more creatively than a correct one?

If the program offers direct instruction, does it provide appropriate levels of instruction for the subject matter? Is the program broken down into appropriately small steps for the intended audience?

What records does the program keep and where does it keep them? If this is an instructional program, what types of records does it keep? Are these records sufficient for a teacher to assess student progress, or is it simply a list of scores? Are student scores available to students, or is a special password or program required to access student progress reports?

Can I customize this program? Is it possible to select which features will be visible to student users? If students use the program, will they be directed into certain channels, or may they select program options freely? May print limits be set so users cannot print excessively long reports? Can search results be limited?

Is there a screen saver to eliminate monitor "burn in?" Are timeout limits user-definable? Is the customizing option available to all users, or may it be locked out via password or secret keystroke? If the program is network compatible, may the supervisor specify the subdirectories for program files, data, temporary files, and user output? Can the program be updated if data within the program changes?

If the program will be used for reference in the library, what type of "search engine" is employed? Are search options apparent from the main menu, or does the user have to figure out a complex path to discover the desirable features? Is there a Boolean search capability?

If the program is intended as a research tool, is the data in the form of citations, abstracts, or full-text? Does the program include graphics, charts, video clips, or sounds? How current is the data? Is output always directed to the printer? Is it simple (or even possible!) to specify the printer so you can take advantage of your printer's capabilities? Can program output be directed to floppy disk or hard disk so the student can take the information directly to a word processing program without retyping.

What other programs perform similar functions? Is this program the best buy for the money? How does it compare to other programs with similar functions? Is a single feature worth a significant additional cost, especially if the function of the program is similar to another, less expensive program? What type of technical support is offered by the producer? Is it free? Is it available via toll-free number?

These questions will help, but don't rely only on the answers to these questions. Not enough is said about the "seat-of-the-pants" method of software evaluation. Your gut feeling is probably a valid means of determining the usefulness of a particular program, provided that practical and financial considerations enter into the picture. When two packages have similar features and capabilities, you, as someone familiar with your students and faculty, can make an intuitive decision about what program will be best received and used. TC

Carol Mann Simpson is Facilitator— Library Technology Mesquite (Texas) School District.

NOTES

GRANTS, CAR WASHES, AND BAKE SALES: FINANCING TECHNOLOGY

feature

How to Write a Winning Grant Proposal

THE PROPOSAL SHOULD DETAIL THE PLAN FOR RESOLVING THE PROBLEM. READERS MUST UNDERSTAND THE NEED FOR THE GRANT, THE TANGIBLE SOLUTION IT WILL GIVE TO STUDENTS, AND THE DIFFERENCE IT WILL MAKE IN STUDENTS' LIVES.

by Madeline Buchanan

It seems that just as new technologies become available to us, school funding decreases. Many schools are turning to grants to provide funding for technology. As they do so, the competition for grant moneys grows greater each day. Grant committees now receive five to six times more applications than the number of grants they plan to provide. How can you make sure your proposal stands out from the rest?

Several points will help you prepare your proposals. First, remember that the length of the grant proposal does not make it better. Readers may have gone through hundreds of grants before reading yours. A long, drawn-out proposal may turn them off. Use as little educational jargon as possible. Remember that a grant proposal should specify not only the requested equipment, software, or materials but also the underlying reason for acquiring the technology. The grant writer should present a specific learning objective in sharp, clear focus.

An appealing grant title will catch the eye of the grant reader. Grant readers may not be educators—they may be business people, bankers, lawyers, and even blue-collar workers. The grant description should be short and to the point, no more than 50 to 75 words, and should outline the substance of the proposal. You might ask a neighbor, friend, or someone who is not an educator to read the description. If he or she doesn't understand it, you should rewrite it. The description should state the compelling argument clearly and concisely, and it should also indicate the expected results—or what students should learn from having the equipment or software.

Readers need to know *why* they should consider your request. You should describe the present situation, the magnitude of the problem you want to correct, and the danger in not correcting it. The proposal should also detail the plan for resolving the problem. Readers must understand the need for the grant, the tangible solution it will give to students, and the difference it will make in students' lives.

While the goal of a grant should be general and broad, each objective should list possible and measurable skills the students will learn.

A list of activities should also be included in the grant proposal. These may include daily classroom activities such as assigned reading, projects, journal writing, or field trips, that should culminate in an evaluation, either on paper or through observations. A means should be indicated for measuring each student's gain in knowledge or ability through the project activities. This will give the company awarding the grant a way to know that goals and objectives are met.

The budget is an important part of the grant proposal. It lists materials and supplies to be used in student activities and should include anything necessary to achieve the goals and objectives of the project. Be sure to explain special items that appear expensive and unnecessary so that the readers will not misunderstand them. Two areas that are usually omitted from grant budgets include miscellaneous and staff development. Miscellaneous items include such necessities as postage for shipping or paper and diskettes for computers. Staff development includes time and manpower for training teachers to use new equipment or programs so that the grant activities will run smoothly. Individuals who are involved in the grant should be paid for their time in staff development activities. A good means of determining proposed staff development charges is to use your school board's hourly rate for staff development activities. In your request, you may mention ways that school, community leaders, and parent-teacher organizations will help to achieve the purpose of the grant.

Finally, remember that if you don't apply, you don't win. If you do apply and win, your students will have a chance to participate in a project that will help them prepare for their futures. **TC**

Madeline Buchanan is the Media Specialist at W.J. Christian School in Birmingham, Alabama.

> *Remember that a grant proposal should specify not only the requested equipment, software, or materials, but also the underlying reason for acquiring the technology.*

PART 1
Proposal Writing for Technology Money

The guiding principles for proposal writing are to get to the point quickly, to be organized and relevant, to document what you are saying, and to provide everything that is called for in the RFP.

By Richard Alan Smith

Much of successful proposal writing, whether for instructional technology or any other purpose, is dependent upon the writers' ability to convey to the proposal evaluators what the proposal is all about and why the writers should get the money. Thus, successful proposal writing hinges as much on salesmanship as on the actual project being proposed.

Proposals are not written out of thin air. You will usually start with what is called a "Request For Proposal" (RFP) that is issued by a funding agency. Funding agencies vary from organizations as large as the National Science Foundation, offering a million or more dollars, to a local department store that offers funds for several computers.

Most RFPs contain requests for information or variations on these requests that are listed below. The requests will usually fall into separate sections and each section requires a response. Even if a funding agency only asks for a general proposal, leaving the form up to you, it is a good idea to frame your proposal with the following basic categories:

Introduction

Statement of Need

Goals and Objectives

Plan of Operation

Evaluation Plan

Budget

Supporting Documents

Make certain each time you start a category or sub-category called for in the proposal that you label them exactly as they are named in the RFP.

The guiding principles for proposal writing are to get to the point quickly, to be organized and relevant, to document what you are saying, and to provide everything that is called for in the RFP. In general, an RFP explains what is required for each section. Here is what is usually included.

Introduction

This is usually a one- or two-page overview of the goals of your project, what you plan to do if you get funded, why your project target population was selected, and why the target population needs the project. This short synopsis is what the evaluators will read first. It serves as an advertisement for your proposal and must be written in a way that will motivate the evaluators to read your entire proposal with a bias towards funding it. Remember to get to the point

Editor's note: This is the first of two articles on technology grant writing.

quickly and to write in a manner that projects your excitement for the project.

Hence, introductions that begin with sentences such as, "Reading, the quintessential element of socio-economic, environmental, macrobiotic interrelationships between mind, forest pulp matter and crafters of text-based delivery systems" should be replaced with something like, "Our reading project builds upon the results of four other successful reading projects by combining them with advances in educational technology as well as with new information gained from research in the field of reading education." You will elaborate on what you have written in the sections that follow.

Statement of Need

Make certain that you state the need in the first sentence of the first paragraph. Elaborate by explaining the need and then go on to provide the supporting evidence that documents the need. Evidence that deals directly with the need for your specific project is far more convincing than evidence that simply states that there is a need for whatever it is you plan to do. Thus, a sentence such as, "The reading scores of our fourth graders, as measured by the MAT 7, indicate that 80% of them are illiterate" will carry far more weight than a sentence such as, "Tests, too many to list, indicate that the reading ability of children in the United States is not acceptable."

Goals and Objectives

Keep in mind that goals are global statements of what you want to

Above all, keep the evaluation plan simple. You will have enough to worry about if you get funded, without having to worry about an intricate evaluation plan.

happen, such as "Our goal is to improve the ability of our students to read." On the other hand, objectives refer to specific results such as "Our objective is to have 80% of our fourth graders reading on grade level." In essence, the objectives form a kind of contract between you and the funding agency. The key here is that the goals and objectives must derive from the "Needs" section.

The goals and objectives must be easily understandable. Accordingly, do not confuse the goals and objectives with additional statements that indicate how you are going to achieve them. Do not add unnecessary descriptive material.

Plan of Operation

The plan of operation explains how you will operate your project. Include an overview of what you are trying to implement as well as how you will implement it. It is very important to organize this section carefully. If you do not present a good written plan for the project, it will be an indication to the proposal evaluators that you will not be able to implement the project effectively.

Start by briefly describing the philosophy underlying the plan of operation. Explain what will result from the plan. Then describe, step-by-step, how you will get those results, using such techniques as time lines and charts. This is the place to explain, for example, details of the innovative way you will use instructional technology and how that process will improve the ability of students to learn to read.

It is in this section that you will discuss the staffing and management for your project. Make certain to include staff responsibilities, linking them to specific project assignments. Then explain how the project will fit into the larger organization of which it is a part. Even if the RFP does not require it, attaching descriptions of the capabilities of personnel in the form of brief biographies or resumes is helpful. These are usually placed in appendices. Remember to include a statement of capabilities that explains why the organization backing your proposal is more than capable of implementing it, upon obtaining funding.

Evaluation Plan

Always key evaluations to the goals and objectives of the project. Thus, if your goal is to teach children to read, evaluate what percentage of the children learned to read and whether that percentage is educationally significant. Don't attempt to evaluate the level of reading enjoyment reached by the children taught to read by the project.

Remember to document the events of the project as they take place. Keep track of the numbers to allow for their analysis later.

You will need to decide whether to use an external evaluator, someone who is not part of the project staff. If you do so, budget for the evaluator. Above all, keep the evaluation plan simple. You will have enough to worry about if you get funded, without having to worry about an intricate evaluation plan.

Budget

Anybody who reads your budget should have a good idea of what the project is trying to accomplish and the process it will use to obtain its goals. In essence, the budget describes your project in financial terms. Thus, it is important that the budget reflects all aspects of the project. Readers of the budget will note whether enough funds have been included to cover the personnel, supplies, and expensive (for example over $500) permanent items such as desks and computers. Sometimes funding agencies will only fund part of a proposal, such as the hardware. If that is the case, the budget should reflect contributions from your school or school district that will provide the other necessary items.

Be careful in this section. If your project is funded, the person or persons in charge can be held accountable for providing the items and personnel you said would support the project. In any event, make certain that you ask for enough money to carry out the project. Keep in mind that if you don't, the proposal evaluators will question whether the project is planned well enough for a successful implementation. Each RFP

Make certain that you ask for enough money to carry out the project. Keep in mind that if you don't, the proposal evaluators will question whether the project is planned well enough for a successful implementation.

will usually include budget guidelines for allowable costs. Within the guidelines, include money for personnel, benefits, supplies, contracted services, equipment rental, postage, printing and travel.

Appendix—Supporting Documents

An Appendix is usually the final section of an RFP. The Capabilities Statement of the organization submitting the proposal can be placed here, if it hasn't been called for in a previous section, such as the proposal's introduction. The Capabilities Statement simply states why your organization (school, district, or team, such as your school and a local college or business) would be able to successfully implement the project when funded.

This section usually contains the letters of support from representatives of every organization that has been identified as having a role in the project. This would include letters from your school principal, the district's superintendent, any professors you have involved, and the heads of any businesses that will work with the project. The letters should say how pleased the participants are with the wonderful project described in the proposal, and that they are fully committed to providing the time or materials that the proposal indicates.

Anything else you would like the evaluators to see that has not been described in the main body of the proposal may be placed in the Appendix. Be careful about the page limit of the proposal. If the RFP limits the total number of pages, inclusive of the Appendix, then stay within that limit. If not, you are only limited by common sense, bearing in mind that proposal evaluators will probably not review an extra 50 pages that are not required by the RFP. However, they might be tempted to look at a few extra pages, if they are well written and attractively presented.

In closing, keep in mind that a grant proposal is a package that will be judged not only on the concept being presented, but also on your ability to package and sell that concept. A proposal that makes the evaluators work to understand its basic elements, that does not get to the point quickly in each section, that does not look attractive on printed paper, or that does not follow the proposal writing outline provided by the funding agency, is a proposal with a very poor chance of getting funded and a very good chance of getting set aside, only partially read. **TC**

Richard Alan Smith is Director of Instructional Technology for the Houston (Texas) Independent School District.

PART 2
Proposal Writing for Technology Money

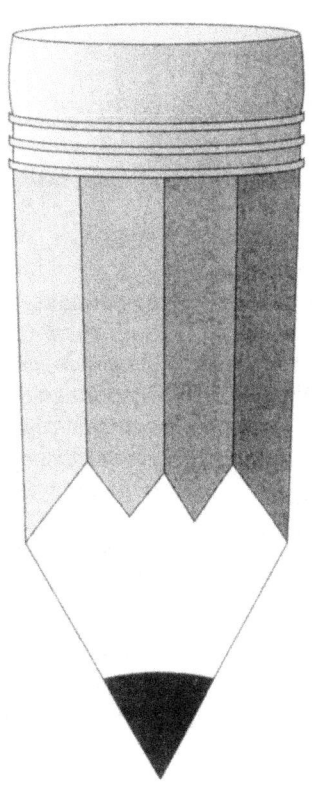

The way your proposal looks on the printed page, its spacing and layout, will suggest a lot about your ability to manage the proposed project.

By Richard Alan Smith

Editor's Note: See the April 1997 issue of TECHNOLOGY CONNECTION *for the first article in this series.*

Get to the point quickly in the first sentences of each section of your proposal. People who evaluate proposals have taken on a thankless task, many times without pay. They may be faced with a stack of proposals, and after the first two, their patience usually begins to wear thin. Don't make them search for the first mention of your response to the section under consideration. For example, beginning the needs section with a sentence such as, "In a survey of 200 parents, we discovered that only 5% had ever used a computer, and none had a computer in the home to assist their children with school assignments," would probably gain favor with proposal evaluators.

However, a needs section that began, "Computers have long been used in schools as an aide to the educational process and can be found in many different configurations within classrooms. Teacher training has progressed from a haphazard occurrence to one that can be depended upon to take place with some degree of regularity. It is also known that computers can also be used effectively at home although..," would win few points with evaluators.

Follow the guidelines of the funding source. Proposal writing is not an exercise in free expression. Evaluators usually follow a checklist to decide how many points should be awarded to each section of your proposal. Your ideas need to be presented clearly and in correct order. Label each section of your response to match the same section in the Request for Proposal (RFP).

Frequently, if the evaluator cannot easily find the section, no points will be awarded or the proposal can be barred from further consideration. Also, if the RFP says the proposal can be no more than 15 pages and you submit 18 pages, the proposal evaluators may simply stop reading after page 15.

Write clearly and simply. Remember to be specific and concrete in your explanations and descriptions. Write in the active voice stating outcomes in what *will* happen not in what *should* happen. For instance, a statement such as "By the end of this project we hope there will be at least some improvement in reading scores" should be replaced by a statement that reads, "By the end of this project reading scores of a majority of the students will improve as indicated by..." Or a statement such as "We believe we can establish a management plan that will be cooperative in nature" should be replaced by, "The management plan that follows describes a cooperative system that will improve the day-to-day project operations."

Image is very important in proposal writing. The way your proposal looks on the printed page, its spacing and layout, will suggest a lot about your ability to manage the proposed project. If your proposal looks like a mess, the evaluators are likely to think that any project you attempt will also resemble a mess. On the other hand, adding superfluous packaging such as ribbons or pretty boxes will not help. Of course, neatness, spelling, and grammar all count. This makes even more sense since your proposal most likely describes a project that you believe will improve the education of children. Ask several qualified people to read and edit your proposal before you send it to the funding agency.

Stretch your writing resources. If your proposal is a group writing effort, or particularly if your group plans to write many proposals, consider buying portable word processors, which usually cost between $300 and $500 each, to extend the writing time per person.

Do not reinvent the wheel. Instructional technology is a field of study with its own theories and collection of projects and methods. Your best bet is to build on projects already implemented by others and described in detail in research journals. These projects can be modified and extended to meet your proposal's needs.

You are already reading TECHNOLOGY CONNECTION, so you are off to an excellent start. Other sources for general project and instructional technology policy information include *Learning and Leading With Technology* (formerly *The Computing Teacher*), *Electronic Learning*, *Technology and Learning*, and *T.H.E. Journal*.

To get an idea of what research has been done or is current in instructional technology try *Journal of Research on Computing in Education*, *Journal of Educational Multimedia and Hypermedia*, *Computer Assisted English Language Learning Journal (CAELL)*, *Journal of Computing In Childhood Education*, and *Journal of Computers in Mathematics and Science Teaching*.

Establish a track record. Your proposal stands a better chance of being funded if the readers of the proposal know who you are. You can become known in the field of educational technology if you write articles for magazines, make presentations at conferences, and become active in professional organizations.

Ideas for articles can come directly from what you are doing in your classroom. You need only to become familiar with the writing style and content of the educational technology magazine to which you are submitting your article. Upon request, each magazine can send guidelines for writers to help you shape your article to its requirements.

Making presentations at conferences is another way to become known in your field. You can present at a conference the same type of material that you would submit for an article. The important point is that you make the effort to meet as many of the other conference presenters as possible since conference presenters have a high probability of being selected as proposal evaluators. Engage them in conversation about what they presented so they will remember you.

There are educational technology organizations in every state, such as the Texas Computer Education Association and the Florida Association of Computer Educators. These organizations usually are involved with local conferences and publications.

Know where the money is located. Your school district may already have someone responsible for finding grant opportunities. You can ask that person to watch for educational technology RFPs.

You also should check grant sites on the World Wide Web. Yahoo! - Education:Grants (http://www.yahoo.com/Education/Grants/) focuses on education. Grants WebWWW Homepage (http:9/12/96/infoserv.rttonet.psu.edu/gweb.htm) provides general information on grants-related Internet sites and resources and includes funding opportunities for federal and nonfederal money, grants databases, and proposal development tools.

Writing a proposal takes time. Allow enough time to complete the proposal before the deadline. If you are asked to write a proposal, make an estimate of the time you think is necessary. If you can't be given the time you think is necessary, don't accept the responsibility. **TC**

Richard Alan Smith is the Director of Instructional Technology for the Houston Independent School District in Houston, Texas.

> *Your ideas need to be presented clearly and in correct order.*

> *Remember to be specific and concrete in your explanations and descriptions.*

Think Money in the Bank for Your School

By Mary R. Hofmann

From both sides of the fence, as a grant proposal writer and a reader of others' proposals, the author gives us some guidelines.

SIX YEARS AGO, district officials "encouraged" our middle schools to write grant proposals for a share of the state's pot of school restructuring funds. Having little or no choice, a task force formed at my school and charged in blindly. None of us believed we had a prayer, but somewhere midway through the process we became true believers in our mandated project. To our utter amazement, our proposal not only brought us a million dollars but was also selected as the example for judging other proposals. Since then I've been involved in writing several other smaller grants (from $25,000 to $90,000—not exactly peanuts) and have so far batted 1000. I've also read and scored other schools' proposals.

I've learned many lessons along the way, not the least of which is that grant writing isn't for the meek. There aren't any quick and easy tricks; every grant is different. On the other hand, some patterns do exist, providing a bit of consistency, and some elements of style have worked more successfully than others. I'm happy to share these tidbits if you promise two things: write only proposals you believe in, and write them only with a group of believers. (One voice is best, but it should represent a team). Grant readers can tell.

Pieces & Parts

Lots of people take the bull by the horns and go out hunting for grant money, which I'm told is available aplenty from innumerable public and

> To our utter amazement, our proposal not only brought us a million dollars but was also selected as the example for judging other proposals.

private sources. Since my experience has been with responses to RFPs (requests for proposals) from regional, state, or federal sources, I'll limit myself to them. These government proposals are so structured and have such stiff requirements that they are probably excellent models to use for writing the less-rigid private funds proposals.

While every RFP has its own peculiarities, most have fairly standard sections. Typical are:

PROGRAM ABSTRACT or EXECUTIVE SUMMARY. This is the whole ball of wax on one page. I know I'll either hook the proposal readers or lose them here, so I usually do this page last, and with care and flair. The abstract must include the problem (in a paragraph or so), the solution (a synopsis of the proposed project), the funding requirements (a paragraph on where the money will go and how the project will continue without it), and whatever the RFP says the funding source needs to know about your school.

STATEMENT OF NEED. In a page or two, I try to address the reasons for the proposal; that is, the problems we need to solve with the help of the grant money. In my writing, I answer questions such as:

What do we want our students to be able to accomplish? A need isn't, for example, computers. Instead, our kids need to learn to become proficient users of technology and the solution to that need might require additional computers. (Remember, it's all about kids, not about books or equipment or stuff, except insofar as stuff helps kids.)

How do we know students have a need? Here's where we trot out test scores, demographics, information about parent involvement, and any other documented evidence of need, buttressed by lots of research evidence.

How will the grant make a difference? Here's where I wax optimistic, building toward the Goals and Objectives section. But I'm also careful to show my readers we aren't pathetic. Our kids and staff are terrific—they just need a boost!

The statement of need is about people and their needs: *Think who and why.*

III. GOALS AND OBJECTIVES.
Teachers must write goals and objectives for their classrooms, and this isn't much different. A goal is huge and general (e.g., our kids need to become information literate), while an objective is, well, objective and measurable (e.g., students will learn to use a networked computer to access information on the World Wide Web). The goals and objectives need to tie nicely back to the needs.

This section is about fulfilling the needs: *Think what.*

IV. METHOD/DESCRIPTION OF PLAN.
Whatever it's called, this section is about implementation. I meticulously, but colorfully, describe what we're going to do, tell how we justify what we're doing with research and expertise, explain exactly how we're going to go about doing it, and show how our actions will address the needs we identified. Here's where either we make the reader a believer or we don't.

Closely related is STAFF DEVELOPMENT, which is sometimes a separate section. The best of plans will fall on their faces if nobody is willing and able to implement them. Here we put forth a plan to train the staff to make the plan work. Staff development is expensive, so we make how it's going to be paid for clear. Grant readers will quickly "deep six" any proposal missing a detailed staff development plan—almost a proposal within the proposal—to ensure that every human contingency is covered.

This section details the plan: *Think how.*

V. EVALUATION.
Evaluation should be an integral part of any plan, from a lesson plan to a grant proposal. How can we tell—throughout the project and at the end of it—that we've fulfilled our end of the deal and had the desired impact on the kids? We look for ways of tracking our progress, such as logs, reflections, surveys, as well as students' progress, like benchmarks proficiencies. And we propose a culminating evaluation that the grant source can use as its assessment.

This section is the test: *Think so?*

VI. BUDGET.
When filling out the budget forms, I am careful to work with district requirements, making sure we can do what we say we'll do, and that what we do fits what our plan says we'll do. I actually laughed out loud once in reading a grant proposal when, after poring through a warm, fuzzy, student-centered narrative, I encountered a budget in which the lion's share went toward a huge piece of hardware for the school office. I searched diligently for a rationale, found none, and killed the proposal.

The rubber hits the road in the budget. Grant readers can see right through deceptions: *Think oh, really?*

VII. CONCLUSION/FUTURE ISSUES.
While we might consider a grant a windfall, funding sources like to think of grants as seed money. One of the first questions we ask ourselves in the planning stages is, How can we continue this plan when the grant money ends? I make sure that the grant sources know their money will benefit students long into the future.

This section is about the future: *Think, what then?*

VIII. CONCLUSION/FUTURE SUPPORT DOCUMENTS.
Grant sources are specific in what kinds of support materials they require. I give them exactly what they ask for.

Standing Out from the Crowd

Most RFPs come with gruesomely detailed instructions, which the wise grant writer follows to the letter. Grant readers look at scores of proposals and have rubrics to follow in scoring them. They will literally cut off excess pages, gag at cutesy creativeness, and knock points off for wordiness. The proposals that jump out and make grant readers want to cheer do two things: They follow the instructions and rubrics precisely and the writing makes the project come alive on the page. How do you accomplish this?

I start by making a "frame," or outline, literally copying the headings and pertinent instructions from the RFP onto my computer. I can then fill in holes and delete the fluff. This outline keeps me firmly on task and aligned with the rubric that the grant readers will be using.

Since I want the readers to "see" my vision as clearly as I do (and I do my best to know what kind of readers they will be), it's important that I keep my writing personal and vivid. I want to show them what the grant money will accomplish, so I draw word pictures, rather than list colorless jargon.

If I write a list, I list with flair. In one grant, for example, I spent a whole page contrasting what exists now with how it will look in the future. As a device, I began each line with "From . . . (describing an element existing in our school)" and drew the contrast, indented, on the next line with "To . . . (showing how the same element would be transformed)." I'm told the readers loved it. They could see what I saw.

I believe visual impact is vital. One way grant readers know we're capable, talented, and able to pull this thing off is by reading a proposal that reflects competence, but not glitz. It should have no errors, should look clean and professional, and should have an occasional graph or chart to add clarity and break the monotony of text.

Last, I always have several people read the proposal, both fellow planners and others who haven't been involved. I make sure they're all people who will have no qualms about criticizing the proposal. Money's at stake here and I don't need a cheering section. I promise them I won't whine or get defensive, and I don't. Invariably, they find problems, and invariably (well, almost invariably), I fix them.

Mary R. Hofmann is the Library Media Teacher at Rivera Middle School in Merced, California.

NETWORKING: MOVING BEYOND SNEAKER NET

Lesley S.J. Farmer

From the days of sneaker net (carrying disks from computer to computer) to the era of wide-area, electronic networks has been only a few short years. The author recounts her experiences along the way.

Remember when networking referred to shmoozing with the powers that be, or conjured up images of the Old Boys? Now its usual first connotation is electronic connecting, either locally (LANs) or widely (WANs). This article is the first in a series on electronic networking as it applies to school library environments. It has the distinction of being a work in progress—it will be documenting a real-life networking installation and implementation in my library. Besides explaining network jargon and dealing with general concepts, I will cover specifics such as hardware and peripherals, modem use and other telecommunications issues, security, and trends. Now you can have all the vicarious experience without the first-hand hair pulling—and can build on my practical, hard-won knowledge. Even if you learn just a bit of vocabulary (such as sneaker net, which means moving data by taking a diskette and literally walking it from one computer to another), you can impress the cocktail party crowd. Enjoy!

WHY DO YOU WANT TO GET FROM HERE TO THERE?

The ultimate reason to network is to communicate: to move data and other information between you and others, and to send and receive messages among individuals and groups. It's a lot faster and cheaper to send a series of announcements electronically to a predefined group than to type and mail them individually. Electronic messaging also cuts down on telephone tag. Data also constitutes a major aspect of networking: creating, modifying, exchanging, storing, and retrieving information from local or remote sites. Databases may be centralized or decentralized; with networking, the locale becomes less significant, while database management becomes more important. Resource sharing is also facilitated through networking, be it equipment such as printers, or collections of data. Network groupware enables people to coordinate activities through use of shared calendars and scheduling.

If networking seems like such a good idea, why aren't more libraries networked? Usually the reasons include time, money, and knowledge. So what else is new?

Hopefully, the knowledge you gain here will help you move along the path to networking.

PRIOR NETWORKING LIVES

I have participated in several networking ventures over the years. My college computing included hooking dumb terminals to a central mainframe computer to do statistical analysis. I remember touch-screen OPACs (public-access catalogs); I would invariably hit the wrong part of the screen and be sent to a wildly inappropriate part of the catalog. (It gave browsing a whole new meaning.) I played with Dialog, fearing that I was racking up terrible phone bills while I tried different terms and combinations. I explored remote sites through EcoNet, and learned the joys and frustrations of sending database information over the lines. Each time I received valuable information, but at the cost of some frustrating learning.

My first LAN (Local Area Network) installation used a now-defunct piece of software recommended by a chipper computer salesperson who never did give me full training on macro commands and other installation details, but who still managed to get $100 an hour for consulting. **Lesson 1:** Check reviews and other users before purchasing software. **Lesson 2:** Observe the entire installation, and ask lots of questions until you are perfectly clear about the process—get trained! By default, I learned about delays in spooling (the process by which computer tasks are ordered to do in turn). I discovered that remote printing of cardstock could be a disaster when I wasn't near to unjam the paper. I also learned that moving furniture could result in cutting cable lines, thus necessitating expensive rewiring. **Lesson 3:** Put wires under the carpet or under some kind of shielding.

WHERE TWO OR MORE MACHINES ARE GATHERED: PEER-TO-PEER NETWORKING

My next foray into networking was peer-to-peer networking, actually a rather ersatz connection where all machines are created equal and have equal computing status. I remember wanting to relocate a computer from a classroom lab to the library, and being told that I couldn't because all the machines were networked. In this case, the computers were connected through built-in LocalTalk software (part of Apple's System 7) and simple connectors with telephone wire between machines to share a printer. No programs (also known as applications) were being uploaded or downloaded. It took some convincing, and a simple demonstration, to prove that taking one computer out of the loop did not affect the so-called network's integrity.

In peer-to-peer, also called interpersonal, networking, users can also exchange electronic mail and can share datafiles. Typically, information is distributed throughout the system so management and security are flexible—and often loose. Peer-to-peer networks are relatively inexpensive, but they are also slow and can handle only a limited number of machines. In addition, one "creative" student can damage a number of computers simultaneously. Where I have eight Macintoshes linked to a single printer, students often think that their document will never get printed, so they tend to push the print button several times, backing up the spooling that much more. **Lesson 4:** If a computer has a scanner, have a separate printer for that machine; otherwise, a scanned image can entail a 15-minute holdup for other documents spooled after it.

Ethernet is not vaporware. For the lucky few who have not experienced it, vaporware is a product that theoretically exists, but somehow never appears—or at least not when it's supposed to. It is like vapor: invisible. Vaporware may be considered the product of (usually) good intentions.

I was blessed with Ethernet at my present school when I received an account (i.e., login name and password) to the district's server, so I correspond by e-mail with my colleagues (interestingly, most other users were (are?) administrators) and have access to student records for inputting overdue book bills.

Ethernet, I found out, is a specific technology used to transport data from computer to computer, and requires special cards and cabling. A central computer acts as the server, controlling the data traffic, and the computers linked to it are called clients. Ethernet is typically used to link DOS machines, although it has gained acceptance in Mac environments, especially for large systems that require fast throughput.

Basically, a client-server network offers fast and sophisticated performance. Security is tighter; the systems manager can configure the network to allow for different levels of access to different applications. Client computers can even be diskless, booted from the server, thus eliminating the possibility of student manipulation. Localized problems can be diagnosed and solved more easily. The network can also be expanded to meet increasing needs. Moreover, networking makes it possible to connect different computer platforms, usually Macintosh and DOS, so anyone can use any application in a transparent manner (although it's still easier for a Mac to read a DOS application than vice versa). As more CD-ROMs are incorporated in the library and a vaster array of computer library services becomes available, client-server networks become a cost-effective way to go.

Still, networking the library with a file server was a scary thought for me because I knew of too many cases where one computer breakdown brought the others to a screeching halt. I found out that with the appropriate topology (i.e., linking) of computers and good management (i.e., knowing what's happening throughout the network), such crashes wouldn't happen. Of course, if the server is down, the whole network crashes except for the applications that reside in each machine. On a more general note, networks are not easy to install or maintain; I would need outside, expert help.

A WORD ABOUT NETWORK APPLICATIONS

Before I even thought about cables and cards, though, I had to examine the existing software applications to see if they were truly networkable. Some CD-ROMs were single-use only, so I kept CD-ROM drives in the library computers so those applications could still run on an individual workstation. I also found that I could put on their own drives some unit-specific CD-ROMs having marginal use and change them as needed for different assignments; in that way I could keep the flexibility of stand-alone equipment and take advantage of network-wide access to applications such as the library catalog and magazine indexes.

Unfortunately, compatibility is not a clear-cut issue. I remember checking a particular DOS-compatible machine and asking the salesperson how compatible it was. "Very." What did that mean? What percentage? "80%." Which 80%? I did not buy the computer. Network applications possess the same kind of fuzziness. An application that is truly network incompatible won't run—usually. Or it may corrupt a file on the network, or just show incompatibility in some areas, or freeze without warning, or just not print. Network-compatible applications can share files with other applications at some level; desktop programs can fall into this definition. Network-centric applications take advantage of the network's capabilities to connect with needed peripherals or other applications and operating systems; library circulation programs often fit into this category. Finally, a network-specific application typically works with just one network protocol, such as Novell's NetWare; applications producers may develop their product in light of the network programming.

If you're lucky, the library application will indicate in the manual or on the package whether it is network compatible. However, you may need to call the software producer, and sometimes even they do not know for sure if the product will work correctly. Fortunately, as more libraries network, producers are becoming more aware of the issue. Unfortunately, different producers do not handle network issues in the same way. For example, the application you used on a single station may suddenly cost more because you need to pay a network fee. Some products come in single- and multi-use versions. Some products stop working once two or more users try to access them simultaneously. **Lesson 5:** Software network compatibility must be dealt with case by case.

DEFINITIONS

Client-server: a network scheme in which one computer (server) acts as a traffic cop, sending program files and data to other computers (clients).

Dumb terminal: a computer, monitor, and keyboard whose only capability is to connect to a large computer and interact with the programs running there.

LAN (Local Area Network): two or more computers linked together to share information.

Mainframe computer: a large, relatively expensive computer capable of interacting with many types of computers and terminals.

Peer to Peer: linking computers in a way such that each has access to information stored on the other.

WAN (Wide Area Network): Computers linked via various means, across a city, state, or greater distance.

HOW TO GET FROM HERE TO THERE

Even with the basic computers in place, and the applications in line, and the network software chosen, the real networking lies ahead. Basic issues include the following:

- *Designing the network topology:* How should you structure the connections?
- *Planning the server:* What functions does it serve? What capabilities does it need?
- *Equipping each client computer:* How much memory will you need? What cards? What software must you install?
- *Configuring the network software:* How should it be managed? What security measures will you need? What is the access?
- *Cabling:* How is the server linked to the library? How does cabling link from the wall to the machine? What kind of cabling do you need?
- *Dealing with data transport:* How will machines talk with each other? How will you keep signals from being distorted? How will messages and tasks be prioritized?

Lesson 6: Networking is never finished. Sitting with an open 486, Ethernet card in hand, I will provide answers to the above questions in the next issue. Stay tuned! TC

Lesley S.J. Farmer is the Library Director of Redwood High School in Larkspur, California. She is the author of Creative Partnerships: Librarians and Teachers Working Together, *and* Workshops for Teachers: Becoming Partners for Information Literacy

NETWORKING

How to Choose the Network Layout That's Right for You

by Lesley S.J. Farmer

Networking *is a new ongoing column for* TECHNOLOGY CONNECTION, *and we welcome Lesley S. J. Farmer as our regular contributor. Lesley is a library media teacher in Larkspur, California, and has extensive experience as a school librarian, as a young adult and children's specialist in public libraries, and as a library science instructor. She is also the author of a number of articles and books on librarianship, including* Workshops for Teachers: Becoming Partners for Information Literacy *and* Leadership within the School Library and Beyond, *both part of Linworth's Professional Growth Series.*

One of my favorite topics in mathematics is topology: the properties of figures in elastic space. I am intrigued by the idea of a one-dimensional strip of paper and a bottle whose inside is outside.

Sometimes I feel as if *I'm* being turned inside out when figuring out how to structure network lines. It's not as much fun as theoretical math, but then maybe it's the practicality that strips away the fantasy of it all.

The reality is that the way computers are connected makes a decided difference in how the network operates. This article examines major structures and provides criterion to use when choosing the best layout for your needs.

A Couple of Old-Timers

A **daisy-chain** topology lines computers up in a row, with a cable between each one. (See figure A.)

It's the easiest way to connect computers, but is not very efficient. The classic use of this layout is for sharing one printer among several terminals. The disadvantage is that any break between computers results in two networks. In the instance of a printer, computers beyond the break won't be able to print. Files can be shared in this configuration, but basically each message has to go up and down the line until a person sees the message directed to him or her.

Another classic topology is the **star**. Each computer is linked to a central computer, and all data must go through that hub. The disadvantage of this system is that one computer can bypass the central one, and if there is a lot of traffic, data travel may slow down. In complex networks, however, a modified star approach may be used as individual labs are connected to the central file server in star formation. (See figure B.)

The main feature of a **bus topology** layout is a backbone cable that connects all the computers. (See figure C.)

Each connection to the main cable is called a **tap**, and each end has a resistor to complete the circuit. While this may look suspiciously like a daisy-chain, the difference is that each computer can talk directly to every other computer—one break within the network does not affect the workings of the other computers. In fact, taps can be unused, like phone jacks, so it's a good system if you know you're going to add more computers and don't want to add wiring. Usually the backbone is hidden in the wall so people can't easily disconnect the main system. The backbone can be fiber optic for fastest throughput

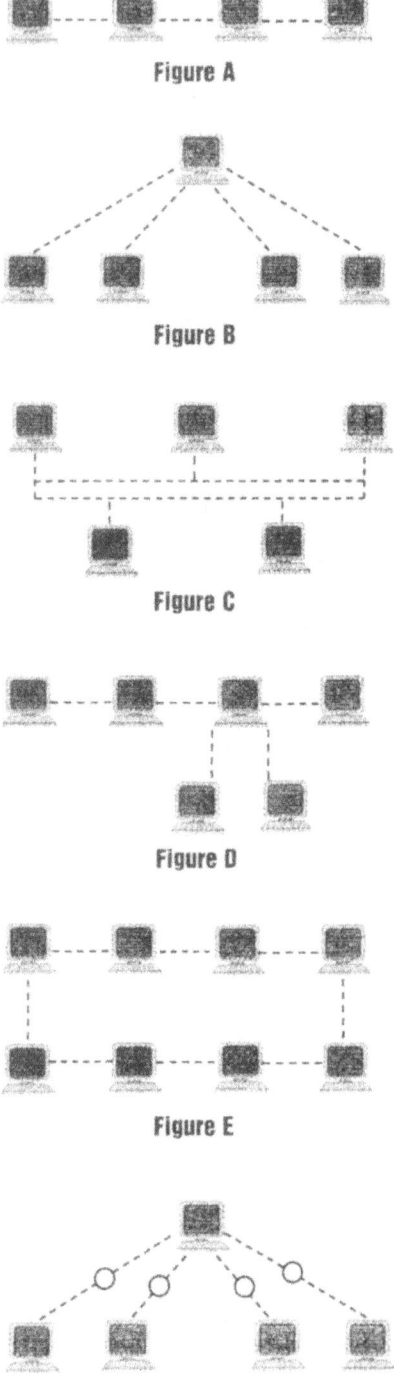

Figure A

Figure B

Figure C

Figure D

Figure E

Figure F

and have cheaper cabling at each station.

Logically, the layout of the **tree topology** is very much like the bus. It looks like a star-studded daisy. (See figure D.)

This layout is very flexible, and is quite robust. However, if a crash or malfunction occurs, it is hard to pinpoint the system that is causing problems.

Each computer in a **ring topology** is connected to two others, so high performance is possible. However, the same connectiveness can cause a system breakdown if one machine goes out. FDDI (Fiber Distributed Data Interface) is a newer form of ring topology which is actually a dual-ring system so recovery is easier. (See figure E.)

Token ring topology looks like a star. The wiring is a string of stars, but the communications path is actually a ring. (See figure F.)

Several factors need to be considered when deciding how to connect computers together into a network.

Which Topology Should I Choose?

Several factors need to be considered when deciding how to connect computers together into a network.

• **What are the needs of the users?** If e-mail and shared printing are the extent of use, then LocalTalk suffices. If lots of data will be transferred, then Ethernet is probably called for, especially if going across computer platforms.

• **What printing demands exist?** Expensive printers, such as high-quality color models, should probably be networked (maybe with some restrictions). Check how printers need to be spooled (queued).

• **What modem sharing is involved?** If many users need telecommunications, network-based modems may be cheaper.

• **How are files shared?** A centralized database, especially of library reference sources, makes sense. Group scheduling is another good candidate for a file-server system.

• **How are users grouped?** If computer labs are the main structure, then a bus topology should be used. Long distances may require repeaters and routers (to be discussed later).

• **What is the physical plant?** Can a hidden backbone be installed? Does present wiring pose a hindrance or an advantage? Does a secure room exist for the file server? What kind of noise interference can be expected from other equipment?

The Lowdown on Connect Time

So how are the computers actually connected? Regardless of the topology, certain equipment is needed at each machine and between each station.

First, each computer needs **network software**. If computers are linked as peers, without a central file server, several easy solutions exist. Macintosh's System 7 supports such networking. Other common software packages include *LANtastic*, Novell's *NetWare*, and *Windows for Workshops*. Networks that have cross-platform capabilities include more sophisticated software.

Second, each computer needs a **transceiver**, which sends and receives the network's signals. Macintoshes have built-in transceivers; an external connection box links to the transceiver's port. Other systems use a network interface card (NIC) or network interface unit (NIU), which connects by cable to a small box (as in thick-wire Ethernet). Thin-wire Ethernet and 10BASE-T (twisted-pair) Ethernet incorporate the transceiver into the NIC.

Third, cable connects the computers. For an AppleTalk network, regular telephone cables or LocalTalk cables with locking connectors can be used. Each has its own type of connector box. For Ethernet-type systems, three kinds of cables are available. **10BASE5 coaxial cable** (thick-wire) is not used much; it looks like the cable used to connect VCRs and televisions, but bulkier. **10BASE2 coaxial cable** (thin-wire) is constructed like 10BASE5 but is easier to handle and needs to have T-connectors. **10BASE-T** is actually a pair of cables twisted together to decrease outside "noise." It's either shielded (with a woven wire layer) or unshielded. It is probably the most used type of cable now. (Note: "10" means 10 megabits per second, "base" means baseband signals, "2/5" means how many hundreds of meters the cable can run.)

Fourth, a **network transport system** allows the data to be transferred across the cables. Ethernet is the most widely used system; basically signals are transmitted when there is no other traffic. Apple's counterpart is LocalTalk. Token ring cabling uses twisted-pair cable that runs between two computers per path.

Making Signals Go the Distance

Several pieces of hardware are needed if signals go a long way or cross platforms. Next month we'll be looking at routers, bridges, and gateways as the network picture develops. **TC**

Lesley S.J. Farmer is the Library Director of Redwood High School in Larkspur, California.

Growing Your LAN Piece by Piece

How to Connect a Library LAN to Other Rooms in the Building

Editor's Note: The basic topography of networks was discussed in the Networking *column which appeared in the November, 1995 issue of* Technology Connection.

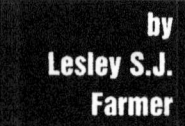

by Lesley S.J. Farmer

If your local area network (LAN) is contained within the library, chances are you are accomplishing all you need to do with a server, terminals with network cards, and cable. However, once you decide to connect with classrooms or other buildings, the picture becomes more complex. Even if you limit the LAN to the library media center, you may encounter a problem like mine: three rooms with large passageways and the need to string cables around room edges or across carpet. (In another library, we laid conduit *under* the floor with easy access so the wires could be pulled up where they were needed. Remember this if you ever have a chance to start from scratch.) If you have two computer platforms available for students, as I do (DOS/Windows and Macintosh), and want the two to connect, additional challenges are in store. Here are some details to consider.

The Task of Repeaters

Cable line performance suffers over long distances; a thin coaxial cable can run up to 185 meters, and a thickwire segment is good for 500 meters. Also, once a cable segment exceeds its allocated number of nodes, or connections to terminals and printers, signals deteriorate. That's when repeaters step in. A repeater is a device that takes the cable signal and cleans it up—through reapplication and retiming—so it can be transmitted to another cable, such as an extended segment of Ethernet cable. Even though a repeater is counted as a node itself, it enables several point-to-point segments to be joined in a star network so it expands network possibilities.

Repeaters can also make sure that breaks occurring over a segment do not compromise the entire system. The repeater disconnects the problem segment and lets the other segments operate. (In a bus topology, all nodes attached to that segment will be disabled, too.)

> Basically, a repeater takes the cable signal and cleans it up—through reapplication and retiming—so it can be transmitted to another cable...

Before you get too expansive about repeaters, however, you should know their limitations. Usually, the number of segments allowed with Ethernet is five; no more than three of the segments can have other network stations attached. Moreover, a chain of repeaters can cause system delays and signal problems. Bandwidth can also become an obstacle—that's when you need to partition the larger network into more efficient smaller sub-networks with bridges, switches, and routers.

Bridges Over Cabled Systems

Say you have two Ethernet systems. Perhaps one of them is connected with thin coaxial cable, and the other uses thickwire. How can the two segments of cable communicate? A bridge spans them so the entire network will seem transparent. Each bridge maps the nodes' addresses for each network segment, and then makes sure that only the necessary traffic needs to go over the bridge to the rest of the system. In that way, communication within a segment can stay local, thus speeding up signals and keeping overall traffic down. Basically, a "packet" of information is received by the bridge. It identifies the source and destination; if both source and destination reside on the same cable segment, the packet is dropped or "filtered." If the addresses indicate a transfer to a different segment, then the packet is forwarded. Bridges also filter "bad packets"—packets which are missing some bit of critical information. This process is called "store-and-forward" because the bridge looks at the entire packet before deciding what to do with it.

It's important to know that the bridge doesn't look at the message itself or examine the *meaning* of the address. It doesn't change the contents, so it works very fast. However, if many addresses are involved, the bridge may spend lots of time searching through them while it stores the packets.

Routers Provide Sophisticated Solutions

What if two or more segments have different protocols? Or what if you

The Technology Connection: Building a Successful Library Media Program | Chapter 2 Gathering the Tools: Library Media Specialist as General Contractor

have two networks that need to operate independently? A router is a more sophisticated solution. While they act like bridges to link segments, they can also process protocols and thereby forward packets more quickly by reading the language of the packets. Routers can determine the fastest or most reliable route to send packets because of this ability to read protocol information. However, the time needed to *read* the "extra" data results in slower network speed. A brouter is sometimes used instead. It has both bridging and routing capabilities—thus the name—and if it can't route the packet, it bridges it.

When You Need a Gateway

What happens if networks have different architectures, say IBMs and Macintoshes? Your school may have seemingly independent services, such as a mainframe and a mail service with different languages. Then it's time for the heavy software guns—gateways. These sophisticated systems convert and translate transactions as well as control the services and handle the physical connections between parts. Gateways can also contain bridge and router functions. Novell 4.1, for instance, can enable Macintoshes to use DOS/Windows files. Windows NT is a newer, cheaper competitor for that gateway function; with Windows 95 on the client machines, that approach is very attractive.

Together, They Spell Flexibility

And you thought networking was a simple process! Now you can have a secure network with one fast server, with CD-ROMs dumped into gigabyte storage, with that node server connecting to a central school server, that, in turn, can link remote Macintosh, IBM, and cross-platform labs to the Internet (through T1 lines) and selected library functions—with the potential for fairly easy videoconferencing. That's what's happening at my school site, thanks to the solutions described above. Black boxes can certainly contain a myriad of surprises inside—and between them! **TC**

Lesley S.J. Farmer is the Library Director of Redwood High School in Larkspur, California. She is the author of Creative Partnerships: Librarians and Teachers Working Together, *published by Linworth Publishing, Inc.*

NOTES

MANAGING  of/with TECHNOLOGY

Now That You Have the Technology, How Do You Keep It Up and Running?

By Becky R. Mather

After years of planning and scheming, the information network of your dreams is up and running. Teachers and students are comfortable using the media center's new state-of-the-art technology, and they expect it to be functioning every single minute. Alas! The inevitable crash occurs and the network goes down. Everyone is complaining. Students cannot complete their assignments. Teachers must devise alternate lesson plans. The media staff cannot check out materials on the computer and must record transactions with paper and pencil. The card catalog is inaccessible. How will you, the school media specialist, technology expert, handle this problem?

If the building or district employs a technician, who can have the network up and running quickly enough to end the grumbling and inconvenience, you are a rare and lucky media specialist. It's more likely that the district has an underpaid, overworked computer person with a list of more pressing problems. Help may be a day or two in arriving. And then there is the possibility that the technician will not be able to solve the problem and may have to call a tech support person. More down time. More frustration. Problems this serious are rare, but they are annoying and leave everyone feeling helpless and frazzled.

Most media specialists are not network-certified and able to work on serious problems. Network administration is time-consuming, and requires a specific and expensive education. Networks are not something for the novice to experiment on. Leave them to the professionals. Encourage your district to hire a network-certified person, or send an existing technician to be trained.

Another option is to contract with a network specialist for maintenance. Contracting usually means faster service by people who are specifically skilled in this area. Service contracts can be renewed or discontinued, and there are no costly benefits to pay since the person is not a school employee. Check with computer

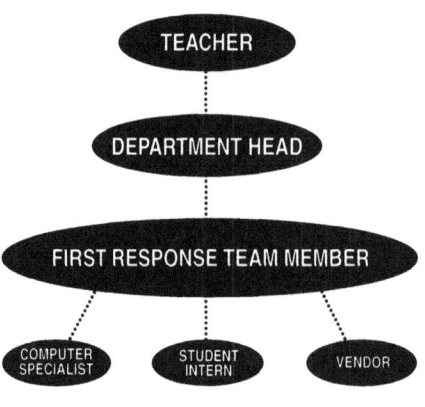

Figure 1

service providers in your area. Often they can provide network support and service contracts designed to cover specific situations for an agreed upon fee and time period.

If the people who did the original installation of the network are able to provide service, they may be the best choice. Always ask installers to provide documentation of their work. When changes or additions to the network become necessary, it will be important to know what was done in the original installation. A written schematic saves time and money. Maintenance tasks can sometimes be handled from a remote site via a modem. A technician can dial in and work on the system without leaving the office. This saves time and money.

If your school district can supply only limited technical assistance, consider forming a "first response" team. This team consists of acknowledged computer leaders in the district, those who are not afraid to tinker with the technology. Build on the skills they have acquired. Provide them with training on less-complicated tasks such as setting up new computers, adding memory, making cables, basic file server maintenance, checking orders for new equipment to verify compatibility with existing hardware, troubleshooting problems within the building, and routing those that cannot be resolved to the appropriate place.

Team members usually volunteer for these duties, and they may receive a supplemental salary similar to coaches, or accrue released time as compensation. The idea is to provide more computer help at minimal cost and designate the more difficult jobs to a computer specialist. The specialist provides some volunteer training, and outside experts are hired to offer additional education. Periodically, some team members are sent away for training. Certified or noncertified staff can become team members. Their training can be scheduled during inservice time or in the summer.

Team members are given a locally-created manual containing basic troubleshooting procedures and appropriate responses. The manual also contains a list of vendors' addresses and phone numbers and their areas of expertise. With this information, team members can determine a course of action and whom to call for various types of problems. (See Figure 1.) Educator price lists for computers and peripherals are included in the manual and updated regularly. Any job or request for information that can be handled at this level gives the computer specialist more time to deal with major problems.

Larger schools will want to have several team members with specific responsibilities. The media specialist should be in charge of the media center network and any other sites connected to its file server. If there is an administrative or other network, choose people who use that system and software extensively. Hardware repair also can be handled by a staff member. Additional formal training, as appropriate, is beneficial.

Setting sensible priorities is essential for the computer specialist and all team members. These priorities should be written and distributed to staff members. In general, a network that is down is first priority. Networks within a district or building are also ranked; for example, an administrative network has priority. Standalone machines are farther down the list. (See Figure 2.)

An often overlooked source of assistance is high school students. Many students know much more about technology than their teachers. Some turn to hacking because they are bored and need a challenge. With careful planning, these skills can be utilized constructively. Student hackers can become student interns who are indispensable to the media specialist. Even more important than computer knowledge is the student's integrity. Those chosen to be interns must be completely trustworthy. They will have access to every system password and an intimate knowledge of how things work, information that must be kept confidential for obvious reasons. Students may prefer to remain anonymous because they are harassed and teased occasionally by fellow students. An intern serves before and after school and during free hours. Compensation is independent study credit and the opportunity to acquire valuable skills.

We have two student interns, a freshman and a junior. Their obsession with computers was noticed early in their high school careers. The intern idea was created to give them constructive outlets for their abilities. We explained the concept to the parents, who were very supportive. Each intern is covered by a liability release stating they are not financially liable for any damage they may inadvertently cause. (A precaution that has not been needed thus far.) Both receive on-the-job training from the computer specialist and handle network, software and hardware problems. The downside of this is that they do have to attend class, and some days we could use their help all day long!

The older intern also makes house calls. Teachers have dial-up access to our Internet server from home, and many have needed help installing and configuring their communications software. They are happy to pay the intern a small fee for solving their problems. This exceptional young man has built his own computer and created a Linux server. He is able to dial in from home and work on fine-tuning the network. This is why we stress integrity so much. If we didn't trust him absolutely, he would not be allowed so much freedom. I have also hired him as a teaching assistant and troubleshooter in the graduate Internet classes I teach. He is also paid to work with the computer specialist during the summer months.

Student interns seem to have an intuitive sense about fellow students bent on causing problems with their hacking. Our interns frequently advise us to keep an eye on certain students whose behavior they have noticed. They are good at predicting misbehavior and setting up security measures to prevent attempts to break into the system.

Students with less training enjoy providing assistance to inexperienced network users. They also enjoy creating a page on the World Wide Web for the school. The page can feature athletic teams, organizations, and school departments. Establishing a computer club is one way to organize student talent. Do not overlook this readily available and largely under-utilized resource.

Most important, become as much of an expert as you can. Read magazine and journal articles on technology. Attend conferences. Ask questions. Watch and learn from the experts who work on the system. Keep a log of problems and their solutions for future reference. In a secure place, maintain a list of all system passwords. If you have Internet access, join a listserv such as LM_NET. There you can communicate with other media specialists and share concerns and suggestions. The key to managing technology successfully is to be creative with the resources available. TC

Becky R. Mather is Director of Media Services for Muscatine (Iowa) Community Schools and Media Specialist at Muscatine (Iowa) High School.

School District Computer Work Priority Chart

1. **Networks: Administrative**
   (Whole network nonfunctional)*
   Individual buildings, board office

2. **Networks: Class Dependent**
   (Whole network nonfunctional)*
   Media center and other labs

3. **Projects (Time sensitive)***
   Projects underway, Vendor/ Department coordination required

4. **Standalone Computers: Administration***

5. **Standalone Computers: Class Dependent***

6. **Class Supportive** (*Affects large numbers of students; labs*)

7. **Standalone Computers: Class supportive**
   (*Single classroom computer*)

8. **New Equipment** (*Nonreplacement; None in place*)

9. **New Equipment** (*Replacement/ Additional; Old still functioning*)

10. **Peripheral Equipment**
    (*LCD panels and so forth*)

11. **Nagging Problems**
    (*Functional but not quite right or requires tweaking*)

*Computer specialist should be paged

Networkese
Jargon You Need to Know

By Joe Huber

Dealing with computer network people sometimes can leave you feeling like a stranger in a foreign land. By following these few simple rules and learning a bit of "conversational networkese," you may save yourself some headaches.

Rule 1. Design your network for the future. Most people make the mistake of considering only what is in a room today instead of considering how that room may be used in the future. Since the main cost of your network will be the labor to run the wires through the walls, ceilings and under the floors, plan ahead so you only have to "pull wire" once.

Rule 2. Select a network designer who is familiar with the needs of schools. While networks in businesses may require only one or two data jacks per room, a school computer lab could need as many as 40 to provide one jack for each computer and printer.

Rule 3. Know the qualifications and the reputation of the person doing the actual wiring of your network. Since most designers contract with someone else to do the wiring, it is important to get references for the wiring contractor as well as for the network designer.

Rule 4. Consider walls and other obstacles when planning your network. If a classroom is located too far from the file server, you may not be able to send data to that classroom over plain copper wire. (For example, the greatest distance any ethernet signal can travel is 300 feet.) When calculating distance, remember to include the distance the wire has to travel up, down, and around walls, and from the wall to the computer.

Rule 5. Learn the language. While you may not become a fluent speaker of "network-ese," learning a few of these more common terms can help you more easily navigate through the project and converse with the "natives."

AAUI (alternate attachment unit interface) - the connection between the computer and the data network, found on most new Macintoshes, and many laptop computers

AppleTalk - the network protocol used by Apple Macintosh computers

ATM (asynchronous transfer mode) - a very fast cell-switched data network that when perfected should allow the user to send full-motion video over twisted pair wires

AUI (attachment unit interface) - the connection between the computer and the data network, found on some printers and some PCs and Macintoshes that are over 2 or 3 years old

Backbone - the wire or fiber optic cable that carries the data signal down the hall, much like a spinal cord with nerves running off it

BPS - bits per second

Bridge - a device used to create a physical connection between two networks using the same protocol

Bus - a type of network topology where each node branches off a main run. Used most often with LocalTalk.

Conductor - a single piece of copper wire

Ethernet - a type of network topology that can be used with AppleTalk, TCP/IP, or Novell. Data exchange rates from 10 MBS to 100 MBS.

Fiber (fiber optic cable) - very small diameter glass wires capable of carrying data when connected to appropriate transmission equipment

Hub - a device used to collect data from multiple nodes onto a common network

LAN (local area network) - the network in the same building or in a section of a building

> *Design your network for the future. Most people make the mistake of considering only what is in a room today instead of considering how that room may be used in the future.*

LocalTalk - a type of network topology used only in an AppleTalk network. The maximum data exchange speed is 230.4 BPS.

MBS - megabits per second

Node - a device (computer, printer, etc.) connected to a data network

Protocol - a set of procedural rules for information exchange over copper wire or fiber optic cable

Router - a device used to create a physical connection between two networks of the same or different protocols

TCP/IP (Transmission Control Protocol/Internet Protocol) - a network protocol developed by the U.S. government. TCP/IP is the network control protocol of the Internet.

Token Ring - a type of network topology that can be used with AppleTalk, TCP/IP or Novell. Data exchange rates from 4 MBS to 16 MBS.

Topology - the way a network is designed; the wires, connectors and electronics

Transceiver - the card or external device that attaches to a node that allows it to transmit and receive data

WAN (wide area network) - several LANs connected together **TC**

Joe Huber is Assistant Director of Technology for the Greenwood (Indiana) Community School Corporation.

NOTES

HANDS ON HANDOUT

Hardware TROUBLESHOOTING

By **Carol Simpson**

When you experience computer function problems, determining what the problem is *before* you call for technical support can save everyone a lot of time and frustration. Here are some tips to help the technicians help you:

Check the power first. Is the machine plugged in? Is the switch turned on? Do you get any indication the unit is getting power?

Check the network. Are you having problems accessing a network resource? Typical network problems may generate error messages such as "Error finding server" or "General failure on device network." If you get error messages, try taking these steps:

▶ **Turn the power off, then reboot.** Sometimes a computer's "brain" just gets tired. A power off/reboot can reset all the hardware and may solve many problems.

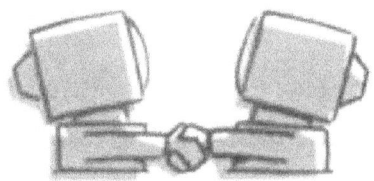

▶ **Reset the network wire.** Unplug *both* ends of the network cable. Replug firmly.

Where is the problem. If all of the computers have the same error, the problem is likely to be within the server or the building network.

If any of the computers can access the server, the problem is not with the server. In that case, check the hardware between the computer and the server: the jacks, wires, and hubs. Move the wire to a jack that you know is working. Does the machine work there? If so, the problem is with the jack. If none of the computers can access the server, and the server seems to operate properly (you can change screens, identify logged in users, etc.), the problem is most likely with the hub or network wire or with the jack to the server. If all of the computers log into the server, but can't access WAN resources (networked CDs, for example), try checking the network utilities. If you can see only your server, your building is off the network. Contact network support or follow instructions they have provided.

Check the hardware. Try exchanging hardware to determine where the problem lies by process of elimination.

For example, if you get a "keyboard error" message, or your keyboard doesn't work, the problem may be in the keyboard itself, in the keyboard connector, or on the computer motherboard (main board). The best way to eliminate all the possibilities is to try the suspected hardware on another machine. *(Always turn off power before changing hardware!)* If the keyboard doesn't work on another machine, the problem is the keyboard. If it does work on another machine, the problem may be the motherboard the connector. Sometimes just unplugging and replugging hardware connections will solve many problems.

 **Finally, before you call for technical support**

▶ Know the number of the machine.
▶ If there has been an error message, *write it down or print it out.*
▶ Be able to identify any steps you have taken to pinpoint the problem.

SEARCHING

How to Minimize the Dangers of Macro Viruses

Present macro viruses attack only the "Save as" command, but more advanced viruses could attack other features.

There are several differences between traditional viruses and a new type of virus called a macro virus. Traditional viruses are written in higher level programming languages such as BASIC, COBOL, or FORTRAN and target specific operating systems or CPUs. More importantly, traditional viruses are transmitted via executable files—those that run programs—and infect executable-only files. In DOS, they are indicated by .EXE, .COM, .SYS, and sometimes .BAT file extensions. In Windows, some files with the .INI file extension are also executable. Traditional viruses cannot infect non-executable files such as document and data files.

Macro viruses, on the other hand, are designed to hide within document and data files and attack the application that opens them. Present macro viruses attack only the "Save as" command, but more advanced viruses could attack other features. Macro viruses are platform-independent and attack their target application regardless of the hardware or operating system on which it is running. They can't be detected by traditional anti-virus software because these programs search only executable files and ignore document and data files. Because state-of-the-art applications programs can be used to write macros, any applications program—whether database, word processing, or spreadsheet—could be used to write a macro virus.

Macro Viruses on the Web

Last fall, several viruses—including two dubbed WinWord.concept and Word-Macro.nuclear—were discovered on the Internet and the World Wide Web. They apparently were written with *Microsoft Word for Windows* and they primarily attack this application, although they might attack other word processing or desktop publishing applications used to open the file. The specific damage they do is to alter *Word for Windows'* "Save as" command so that it saves files as infected templates, thereby propagating the viruses. Since this is a command common to all word processing and desktop publishing programs, it could infect other such programs if their import filers convert *Word for Windows* macros into their own native macros. The difference between the two viruses is that WinWord.concept is written in plain language, while the Word-Macro.nuclear virus is encrypted to avoid detection. Ironically, the Word-Macro.nuclear virus was listed on the Web as a warning about the WinWord.concept virus!

by
Paul A. Ekhaml and
Leticia Ekhaml

Monitoring files for unexplained changes in size or other activity is an effective way to see if virus-induced activity is present. Another simple trick is to maintain application files separate from document files on a separate, write-protected hard drive.

Dangers of Macros

The emergence of this new class of virus raises some ominous warnings. Macros can be used in text, data, and—of particular concern to school library media specialists—image files. More importantly, macro viruses could be written to attack system files as well as application features. They could also be used for "data diddling"—the surreptitious alteration of files. For example, someone with an anarchistic bent could write a macro virus that would search all files and replace the terms "President" and "Vice-President" with "Bozo" and "Vice-Bozo." Many traditional viruses are also capable of altering data in this manner.

Unfortunately, traditional anti-virus measures presently provide very limited protection. Firewalls—computers that monitor and restrict access to internal networks—have become the mainstay of state-of-the-art Internet security, but they are not practical in schools because they range in price from $7,000 to $25,000. Furthermore, macro viruses can be hidden in a document a user downloads from the Internet; a conventional firewall would let the document pass as an authorized item.

How to Protect Your Files

Backing up files is always good insurance for preserving critical ones. It also protects files that are costly to replace, such as application files. But backing up every file every day is quite time-consuming and you have to be careful to avoid backing up an infected file.

Monitoring files for unexplained changes in size or other activity is an effective way to see if virus-induced activity is present. Another simple trick is to maintain application files separate from document files on a separate, write-protected hard drive. This will prevent the propagation of macro viruses which rely on altering the "Save" and "Save as" features of applications. Also, if your operating system allows it, write protect as many of the remaining document files as possible.

It is hoped that the anti-virus software vendors will soon release programs we can put on our network gateways to scan for and block these viruses. Until then, rely on backing up, write-protecting, and other basic safety procedures. And because it's better to be safe than sorry, you would be wise to follow these procedures even *after* installing that yet-to-be-released anti-macro virus software. **TC**

Paul A. Ekhaml is a computer consultant and Leticia Ekhaml is Professor of Media Education at West Georgia College, Carrollton, Georgia.

Sources for Help in Preventing Infection by Macros

McAfee Associates Inc.:
http://www.mcafee.com/new/new/html

Symantec:
http://www.symantec.com/

Computer Security Institute
600 Harrison Street
San Francisco, CA 94107
Phone: (415) 905-2626
Fax: (415) 905-2218

NOTES

CHAPTER 3

Sound Footings: The Library Media Specialist Builds the Foundation

If you don't pay careful attention to the pouring of the footings and the construction of the foundation of a new home, you invite structural problems later on. Successful technology integration by teachers in your school requires a solid foundation in both technology content and pedagogy skills. Only by playing a pro-active role in the areas of mentoring, professional development, and technology support can the library media specialist bring this about.

Mentoring by library media specialists often allows teachers to observe in action what can be accomplished by the use of technology to support a lesson. Approach a teacher with an idea you have for using technology to enhance a lesson or unit, and take over the teaching for that day. Demonstrate how, although you are not the content specialist, you are able to target the information literacy skills needed to ensure students are thinking about *why* they are doing *what* they are doing. As a teacher observes engaged, on-task, active learners, perhaps he or she will come up with additional ideas for using technology effectively in the classroom. As Pope states in one article, "...news of a successful experience travels quickly, and other teachers will want to replicate their colleague's success...One of your tasks...is to continually show teachers the practical benefits of technology."

Providing formal and informal professional development is another way to ensure teachers have the foundation in the technological and information literacy skills. Classroom teachers were not trained in collection development, evaluation of materials, online searching, information sources, or reference interviews as library media specialists were. However, with the explosion of information available to teachers now via online databases and the Web, it is imperative they have these skills both to help them professionally and to allow them to mentor for their students. Many of the articles in this chapter provide models of professional development that have been successfully instituted by library media specialists. The models include one-on-one training, Saturday sessions, peer training, super substitutes, and district level initiatives. "Boolean Burritos: How the Faculty Ate Up Keyword Searching" describes an early morning search strategy session, followed by breakfast, that was both fun and informative.

Teachers need myriad technology skills to become successful technology users. ISTE has created national standards for teachers. This chapter includes checklists, rubrics, and collaboration forms to help library media specialists plan and carry out professional development activities that meet the needs of the classroom teacher. One thought-provoking article covers the pedagogical side of targeting both technology teaching and learning to the multiple intelligences.

By training teachers to comfortably use the hardware and software, to understand why technology and information literacy skills enhance a lesson, and to then move to the next level by internalizing these skills and processes, the library media specialist will have successfully laid the foundation they need to use technology to support and enhance classroom instruction.

NOTES

STAFF DEVELOPMENT

Fantasy and Fact in Computer Training

Lesley S.J. Farmer

We all know that students won't make the best use of computers unless they're required to use computer skills in the curriculum. And we know that teachers must be comfortable with computers in order to make assignments that take advantage of the technology. Furthermore, we know that sometimes neither scenario occurs. What's a computer literate librarian to do?

There are two options: a long-range, well-planned and implemented staff development model; or a "quick and dirty," train-on-demand model.

As a librarian, after years of working with teachers, I submit that the latter, though much less efficient and much more piecemeal, is the way to go. Sorry, folks. Even if the principal backs a thorough development plan, and there's a person to coordinate staff development, the most meaningful work is done one-on-one. Furthermore, it's driven by need and expertise.

What should the librarian do? Here are some ways to train teachers and students on-demand:

- Teach through students; identify student aides who can teach both peers and teachers.

- Teach for results; make sure that the resources presented fit the teacher's objectives for the upcoming lesson and facilitate the student's success (like poems on rats to complement Camus' *The Plague*).

- Advertise library services that teachers and students can plug into, like video productions of class readings.

- Create lots of "point-of-sale/use" flyers on how to use equipment. These may be augmented by library workbooks, audiocassette "tours" and brochures.

While the one-on-one approach may seem tedious, it can pay off because teachers hold a high stake in the process and outcome. Results are particularly exciting when teachers and students work as a team to understand and exploit the advantages of computer-based resources.

By training the adults in your setting, you can increase effective student use of the varied computer-based resources available. And the skills learned by teachers and students help them in their lifelong pursuits of knowledge.

What if *you* need the training? You can call on outside consultants or software packages, but the attitude you use to learn can help you whatever the format:

- taking notes on the concepts presented

- trying out the procedures enumerated in the software

- calling local or company experts for specific problems (and documenting the results)

- reading the documentation **TC**

Lesley S.J. Farmer is the Library Director of Redwood High School in Larkspur, California. She is the author of Creative Partnerships: Librarians and Teachers Working Together, *published by Linworth Publishing, Inc.*

Teacher Training is Key

By Paula Yohe

All the articles and books you make available on technology and all the vendor demonstrations you arrange will come to naught unless you can set aside at least one full day to train teachers.

At my school, we tried nearly every type of teacher training—demonstrations from vendors, planning period inservice by a variety of trainers, after school inservice, and summer training. Some teachers jumped on the bandwagon, but most did not. As one teacher put it, "Unless I'm told I have to use it (technology), I'm not going to. I just don't have the time."

Because their planning time is limited, they want software and equipment that requires minimal training. They want to drop in, create what they need, and run with it. That's why it's difficult to get some teachers to use a Macintosh or Windows/DOS machine instead of an Apple. Teachers can immediately get down to business on an Apple and quickly create a crossword puzzle, for example, whereas Mac and DOS/Windows will first lead them through questions about font size, style, and so on.

In response to these needs, we tried a new approach to training. We divided our faculty into six technology teams with six people on each team. A theme and logo were developed—"Tech Quest for Teachers" and "Tech Quest for Students"—and

Ten Tips for Attracting Teachers to Technology Workshops

By Robert Kirsch & David Miller
Lake Forest High School Library/Telecommunications Departments

To help teachers use technology more effectively, training is essential. Getting faculty to attend a workshop is often difficult. We find these strategies to be the most successful.

1 Target the faculty who most likely will use the media. Keep alert for potential users. When introducing television production services, we initially worked with the English department chairman who had some production experience and helped him develop his first few projects. Other teachers noticed his successes and began to use the technology for their courses. Teachers with such success experiences may demonstrate them in technology workshops.

2 Start with the simple and keep it that way. The card catalog, like Follett's Unison, is a familiar and straightforward place to start. Most electronic catalogs offer keyword searches in addition to a variety of other searchable fields. We have observed veteran teachers quake at their initial exposure to such easy programs, so offering the most "friendly" programs first alleviates some of this fear.

3 Build on your first presentation and connect it to subsequent technology programs. Beginning with your easiest database, lay out your complete program so that it progresses logically through various search tools like the local card catalog, a regional card catalog, newspapers, magazines, and special search subjects such as biographies.

4 Keep the groups small by using a departmental approach to technology. Specific search strategies may be applied to various databases depending on the subject and discipline being studied. In our case, retrieving movie reviews from magazine and newspaper CD-ROM products is a strategy which is applicable to the English and social studies curriculum.

5 Get an "expert" to give a presentation. Many software database companies like Follett, Wilson, and Newsbank will schedule one of their representatives to give a demonstration. Utilize this service! An outside speaker is new to staff and may offer some useful perceptive. The unknown authority always attracts the curious.

6 Identify the payoffs for teachers and their students. The rewards are many in using technology. Saving time may be one outcome. In teaching the software programs on word processing and proper word use like Grammatik, we stressed that teacher correction of word spelling, word tense, and run-on sentences would be reduced. Proper research techniques by students also saves time. In another case, one Spanish teacher was frustrated when her students didn't appreciate a novel they read. She responded to our suggestion that a video production might increase student interest. Her students did much better after dramatizing and producing a scene from the book.

7 Schedule the workshop at a convenient time. If a workshop is worth presenting, its timing should be ideal for the audience. Many schools use a late student arrival schedule so that workshops are scheduled in the morning. In our experience a deliberate, well-planned workshop is appreciated and is a success for participants. Attempting too much leads many times to frustration.

8 Take the terror out of technology. In technology many problems are easily corrected. The broken printer or the computer that doesn't work is often easy to "repair." Fear of technology often prevents quick action, which can resolve a small problem. The printer may need paper or may be unplugged from the computer. The computer may not be plugged in or may have a simple glitch, which a reboot can correct. A simple troubleshooting session is helpful to alert teachers to simple malfunctions that can be corrected on the spot.

9 Create and utilize incentives for your workshops. Many schools are moving toward a structured approach to technology workshops. These new "academy" programs provide either pay or hours of college credit on the teacher's pay grid. Such offerings are enthusiastically received by faculty and lead to a robust technology workshop program.

10 Food attracts and desserts attract teachers the best! We have found that offering gourmet desserts during lunch hours really promotes attendance. In introducing our faculty to the "Information Network" we went all out with chocolate pie, banana cream pie, brownies, and so forth. The result, about 97% attendance! *Reprinted by permission of Follett Software Company, McHenry, Illinois.*

we used these on all handouts. We placed logo/theme posters in a teacher work area and hallway to help foster interest. Then we hired substitutes for team leaders and provided a full day of inservice training on a variety of technologies and programs. They included the Winnebago Online Catalog, SIRS, Supertom, Jr, South Carolina Occupational Information System (SCOIS), Microsoft Works, Electronic Bookshelf, Print Shop, Print Shop Deluxe, Print Artist, Calendar Creator, Award Maker, and others. We also provided telecommunications training and showed teachers how to use the various interactive multimedia programs, as well as the Apple IIe component of the Macintosh LC. Each team leader received a training notebook with detailed instructions about each program and topic covered.

At the end of the day, team leaders were given time to practice and prepare themselves to, in turn, train their small groups. Since we cannot afford to hire subs for the other teachers, we are finding other ways to free up teachers for training. Two substitutes, two aides, and other teachers will cover classes of teachers being trained. No teacher will need to give up more than two planning periods and all teachers will receive a full day of training at minimal cost to our school. After completing their training, all teachers will be required to use one type of technology to replace textbook instruction in teaching a lesson.

By training teachers to use technology and then requiring them to do so, we are equipping them with the tools they need to help students enter the twenty-first century. **TC**

Paula Yohe is a Library Media Specialist at J.V. Martin Junior High School in Dillon, South Carolina.

TECHNOTRAINING

Stage a Well-Designed Saturday Session and They Will Come!

By Miguel Guhlin

Teachers may grumble about Saturday morning or after-school sessions, but they are so hungry for technology training they will come.

"What? Come on a Saturday? Are you out of your mind?" said one elementary teacher when I suggested that instructional technology-training sessions be held on Saturday mornings.

Several years ago that response would have discouraged me. But experience has taught me that although most teachers will claim that they will not attend technology training, the fact is, they will come on Saturdays and to after-school training sessions as well.

According to the United States Office of Technology Assessment, the role of the classroom teacher is critical to the full development and use of technology in schools. If teachers are not the focus of the technology training, then technology will fail. Happily, more teachers are recognizing the necessity of integrating technology into the curriculum.

Effective technology training begins with careful design of a staff development program. The following points must be considered in design and implementation.

1. Technology's potential is under-utilized. Over the years, various technologies have found their way into education. Most failed because administrators purchased them without involving teachers in the decision-making process or providing training in their use.

Although media specialists may write the proposal and technology plan, classroom teachers must be involved from the beginning because they will be the ones responsible for the actual integration. It is important to reassure them that extensive staff development will be provided.

2. Most teachers want to learn technology but lack time, access, and on-site support. In addressing this, it is wise to develop a campus technology plan that allows time for teachers to explore and learn to use a computer. Emphasize that while they may not become expert users, they will be able to use the computer and additional technology instructionally. Consider this staff development pattern:

a) Introduce ways to use technology for specific instructional tasks. Provide lots of hands-on time.

b) Provide individual follow-up modelling in the classroom.

c) Allow time for whole-class follow-up and sharing.

Training necessarily must take place before or after school, during the school day, and during the summer or on weekends. However, if a computer or the technology is not available in the classroom, teachers are seriously hobbled.

Research suggests that a classroom with one to four computers is a comfortable setting for teachers to begin using technology. Both students and teachers are more likely to use it when they need to, not when the computer lab is ready for them. Therefore, effective technology plans must allow teachers to earn hours towards obtaining computers for the classroom, and for weekend and summer use. This is a powerful incentive. Other incentives include providing copies of the software and manual that teachers are trained on, instituting educator computer purchase programs and providing summer and weekend loan programs.

On-site support is critical. Unfortunately, many technology coordinators are overburdened with classrooms and instructional technology duties. Site administrators must decide how to balance their load. Often, providing an extra planning period specifically for technology training works well. Coordinators can log their activities during that time and share them with the site administrator.

3. Lesson plans, related materials and curriculum guides must have clear and relevant objectives.

While hands-on training addresses a fundamental need to integrate technology, it has to be woven into the curriculum. In the beginning, teachers often take existing lesson plans and add technology. This approach works with some success, and it is a necessary developmental step for teachers. However, integrating technology will not be effective until it is used to do things that previously could not be accomplished without it.

Integrating technology involves **redesigning** lesson plans, a problem for the few teachers who use lesson plans from year to year without adjusting them to particular class needs. For the most part, however, teachers do change how they teach because they are genuinely concerned about their students' learning. The questions these teachers ask are: "How do we work technology into our already packed curriculum?" and "What do we do with the students once we start?"

The answer to the first question is not an easy one. Curriculum change is driven by what students need to know. In the past, math curriculums were driven by arithmetic and computation. Now, they are beginning to incorporate arithmetic and computation within the grander scope of creative problem-solving, decision-making strategies and cooperative learning. Technology is best suited to curriculum that involves discovery learning, developing higher-order thinking skills, and the comprehension and communication of ideas and information. If curriculum focuses only on lower-order thinking skills (basic skills) as a prerequisite to higher-order thinking skills (metacognition, problem solving and decision making), the computer will remain a drill-and-practice tutor.

The answer to the second question is much easier. After higher-order thinking skills are addressed, technology can become a tool for comprehending and communicating, serving both students and teachers. Nevertheless, writing lesson plans can be a difficult process. Developing databases that address these needs and assist in the development of lesson plans that incorporate technology is useful, but the job of integrating will fall on the classroom teacher and the curriculum writers.

As stated early in this article, the keys to integrating technology are the classroom teachers. Supporting them must be the first step in any technology training program. To quote the voice in the movie *Field of Dreams*, "Build it and they will come." Build a technology teacher training program addressing teachers' issues and they will come—after school, on weekends, during the summer, and in their free time. **TC**

REFERENCES

Finkel, L. (1990). Moving your district toward technology. The School Administrator Special Issue: Computer Technology Report, pp.35-38.

Office of Technology Assessment Report. Power On! New tools for teaching and learning. U.S. Government Printing Office, Washington, D.C. Stock #052-003-01125-5.

Snyder, T. (January, 1995). Technology is cool, teachers are cooler. Teaching with Technology NewsFlash; #33.

Solomon, G. (October, 1990). Share the Spirit: 15 Ways to generate excitement and support for classroom technology. Instructor.

Miguel Guhlin is District Instructional Technology Specialist for the Mt. Pleasant (Texas) Independent School District.

NOTES

TECHNOTRAINING

Singing the Praises of On-site Training

By Sandy Pope

Tailor-made training beats "one size fits all" every time.

During the past month, have you: Rescheduled a training session for the third time? Tried unsuccessfully to contact the vendor who installed your latest hardware or software? Searched for the elusive power switch on the network file server's UPS? Been asked by an administrator for a technology plan update?

If so, you must be the building or district media specialist/technology trainer/unofficial troubleshooter/tech coordinator! And chances are if you had to rank your most important task, training staff would be at the top of your list. In most schools, staff are at three different skill levels based on their personal computing experience, access to equipment, and acceptance of technology. Some are in the basic informational stage, others are ready to integrate technology and need practical help to do so, and still others are confident enough to try totally new methods.

Find Out What Teachers Want

Experience has taught me that the first step in designing or updating a relevant training program is to survey teachers about their current interests and needs. Also ask them to honestly evaluate the content and relevance of previous inservice offerings and the ongoing technical support they receive. We conduct an annual survey to find out what needs to be improved, what needs to be added, and what needs to be deleted from the training and support we offer teachers.

We've found that on-site training and support offer great advantages over "one-size-fits-all" seminars. It lends itself to the hands-on approach with demonstrations followed by guided practice. Another plus to keeping our teacher training in-house is that we *can* be flexible about rescheduling a session for the second, third, or even fourth time. We can also respond quickly to teachers' interest in learning to use new hardware and software. For example, if a PC-to-TV converter is purchased at the request of teachers having only one computer in their classrooms, they already understand the potential of that equipment. However, the actual connections and operation will remain a mystery until training (and color-coded dots) are provided. Plan the sessions to include examples of equipment and application use. Encourage practice during the sessions.

Provide Training That Meets a Variety of Needs

Teachers should be trained to use new equipment and software for their own personal or professional use as well as for instructional use in the classroom. Research shows that teachers want training in such applications as word processing, creating spreadsheets, and using grade book managers as well as in using computers to enrich, extend, or provide remedial help in their subject areas.

To make sure they've grasped the material, make sure your training sessions provide plenty of practice time. Those learning these applications skills in training workshops should complete a document using those skills. It's essential that teachers leave the final training session with a usable project. Similarly, they must find practical ways to integrate technology into their students' learning.

Offer Ongoing Support

You can support and extend what teachers learn in training by offering refresher courses or open lab time after school for them to work on their own individual applica-

> Teachers should be trained to use new equipment and software for their own personal or professional use as well as for instructional use in the classroom.

tions or on classroom projects. You may also want to offer follow-up by department or by grade level.

> It's essential that teachers leave the final training session with a usable project.

Often, a teacher will request technology training or support for a specific classroom topic or thematic unit. News of a successful experience travels quickly, and other teachers will want to replicate their colleague's success. For this reason, one-on-one tutoring and lesson development is a good investment of your time. You would also be wise to schedule one-on-one sessions with building administrators who are often too busy to attend any or all sessions of training workshops.

Whether you are the official technology trainer or the unofficial "techie" at your school, you are undoubtedly aware of the advances other districts are making. If progress is slow at your site, it's easy to become impatient. Remember, unless there's a good reason to embrace it, most people avoid change. That's why one of your tasks—perhaps the most important one—is to continually show teachers the practical benefits of technology. **TC**

Sandy Pope is the Coordinator of computer-assisted reading instruction at South Elementary School, Eldon, Missouri.

IS A WORKSHOP NECESSARY?

Have teachers asked for one?

Have you acquired new hardware or software?

Has your administrator requested one?

Have new teachers joined the staff?

Essential Training Workshop Components

A brief nuts-and-bolts explanation of the topic.

Hands-on practice during every session.

Written or verbal feedback.

A talk-and-walk-through demonstration.

Adequate time for hands-on practice, note-taking and questions.

Creation of at least one document, chart, lesson, or teaching tool.

NOTES

TECHNOLOGY PLANS THAT WORK

feature

A Model for Teacher-Directed Technology Training

By Barbara Siegel

In September of 1992, the Hardy School (K-6) in Arlington, Massachusetts, armed with a three-year grant from the U.S. Department of Education, implemented a successful plan for integrating technology into the curriculum. This model, which can be readily adapted by other schools writing technology plans for staff development, includes three key components. Each year during a three-year period, one-third of the staff is trained on integrating technology into the curriculum. A new lead teacher is chosen annually to oversee this training, and each subsequent year, the trained teachers act as mentors for other teachers.

Teacher Selection
The teachers chosen for the first-year training should be those most interested in using technology who will commit to working with future trainees to share what they have learned. They should understand the hardware, software and training support they will receive as part of this pilot program.

Before instituting any plan, decide what resources will entice teachers to commit to the program. Schedule meetings on a regular basis for the entire staff where teachers in this pilot group will have an open forum to discuss what's happening in their classrooms. When other teachers see the resources these teachers are acquiring, they will be stimulated to join the training program.

In the Hardy School model so many staff members became excited about the program that there were not enough openings to accept everyone who applied for formal training in the second year. This "bandwagon" effect allows the school to base selection of remaining teachers for the second and third years on desired grade distribution.

Before instituting any plan, decide what resources will entice teachers to commit to the program.

Lead Teacher Selection
A new lead teacher is chosen each year to oversee the training on using technology in the classroom. Since this individual is a member of the staff and does not evaluate the trainees, teachers feel comfortable working with one of their own colleagues and are more willing to accept help. Responsibilities of the lead teacher include selecting software and programs, modeling and co-teaching lessons, providing training and support, coordinating schedules for teacher planning, motivating the staff to use technology, and involving parents.

By having three different staff members assume a leadership role in this technology training and support, the school increases its own resources. After the "formal" period officially ends, the school has three strong leaders to spearhead future staff development.

Selecting Software and Programs
To have teachers integrate technology into their teaching, they must have access to and knowledge of appropriate programs. It is extremely important that the lead teacher work with the classroom teacher to assess curriculum needs in order to choose applicable programs. In this model, the lead teacher, after consultation with the classroom teacher, suggests programs at the suitable

level that are user friendly and meet the classroom teacher's curriculum goals. The lead teacher will assist the classroom teacher in integrating this software directly in the classroom. For example, one fifth-grade teacher at Hardy was instructing her class on the order of operations during a math lesson. The lead teacher suggested that she choose the software program *How the West Was One*, by Wings for Learning, as a resource for teaching this concept.

Modeling and Co-teaching Lessons

In this fifth-grade classroom, the lead teacher modeled *How the West Was One* with the entire class in a one-computer lesson. After connecting the computer to a large screen monitor, the lead teacher divided the students into small cooperative groups and assigned each individual in a group a role. Then she used the program with the whole class so the classroom teacher could see how effectively this program reinforced the concepts she was teaching. Later both teachers met and discussed the versatility of this software and how it could be set up in a classroom center.

In this process of training teachers to integrate technology into their teaching, the lead teacher generally begins by modeling lessons using the software. At the next stage, both the lead and classroom teachers plan units and co-teach them. Later the classroom teacher designs her own lessons with some consultation from the lead and other teachers. Eventually many classroom teachers are able to integrate much of the technology on their own and create their own lessons with minimal guidance from the lead teacher. Often trained teachers use this process as a mini-model for mentoring other staff.

Providing Training and Support

Teacher training can take place both on and off site. Throughout the school year, the lead teacher offers informal training sessions as well as scheduled workshops. Topics can range from learning how to use new programs in selected curriculum areas to explaining how word processing applications can be used for making revisions in process writing in a one-computer class lesson.

Teachers can go to workshops out of school and can observe teachers in other school systems using technology. The lead teacher takes responsibility for all arrangements and for providing substitute classroom coverage.

At the Hardy School, lead teachers were able to bring in outside trainers so the entire staff benefitted. Some of the subjects discussed were how to set up cooperative learning groups, how to use the one computer for the whole class, and how to effectively integrate simulation programs.

Coordinate Schedules for Teacher Planning

The Hardy School model realizes how important it is for teachers to spend time together to plan and communicate ideas. The lead teacher or her assistant teacher can cover classes for teachers so they can meet and discuss lessons encompassing technology. When much time is needed, substitutes can be hired to provide coverage. However, if budgets are limited, creative methods and flexible scheduling must be developed to allow teachers this planning time without hiring substitutes.

Motivating the Entire Staff

While officially only one-third of the staff is involved in technology training, the remaining staff cannot be isolated. The entire school community needs to take pride in what's happening in their school and to feel a part of it. At formal staff meetings all staff can brainstorm suggestions and work together. To make certain no one feels excluded, the lead teacher also goes into all classrooms and teaches mini-lessons using technology.

SOME ADVICE TO THE LEAD TEACHER

- Find out each teacher's comfort level with technology.
- Don't overwhelm anyone and respect entry levels. Praise goes a long way and gives people confidence to try new things.
- Be flexible and willing to make changes.
- Don't hesitate to change anything to improve upon it.
- Encourage staff to collaborate.
- Be a listener and a facilitator—let others share ideas.
- Stay true to your role as a staff trainer in integrating technology.
- Do not act as a fixer of equipment or a technician.
- Use students as resources.
- Communicate with the school community.
- Make all aware of what's going on and be open about any problems.

Involving Parents

Parents generally welcome the opportunity to help out in the classroom and are very supportive. Parents might work with small groups or individual students on programs. Some might type stories of pupils into a word processing program on the computer so that students will be able to revise them later. Others might free up a teacher so that she can work with other groups on technology. Of course, these parents must be trained by the lead teacher and a committee of other parent volunteers.

At Hardy, the school community was kept informed about the technology program. The principal sent home a bi-monthly news-letter which sometimes included articles from the lead teacher about how students were using technology in their classrooms. A local cable TV station filmed students describing and using technology.

Resources

Although the responsibilities of the lead teacher seem overwhelming, she has some powerful resources to help her meet her obligations. Her budget allows her to hire substitutes so that teachers can go to workshops, visit classrooms in other schools, and meet and plan with their fellow colleagues. The model also provides for an assistant teacher who can be used in numerous ways by the lead teacher.

Additionally, she also has some funds to purchase programs for individual teachers that fit into a special area of the curriculum. She should have discretionary use of these monies and carry the support of the administrator who appointed her.

At Hardy, the lead teachers were quite fortunate to have other powerful resources: the staff, the principal, and a technology consultant. Teachers were

To have teachers integrate technology into their teaching, they must have access to and knowledge of appropriate programs. It is extremely important that the lead teacher work with the classroom teacher to assess curriculum needs in order to choose applicable programs.

used to working with each other in a non-competitive environment and had developed a strong bond. The principal was also an ardent proponent of the staff development model and supported it in every way. The technology consultant (author of the grant) offered valuable guidance to everyone and brought vision to the project. Even if a school does not have all these resources, this model is an extremely effective one for staff training.

Mentoring Activities

Teachers who become first-year trainees make a commitment to work with other teachers. As their own self confidence grows, they begin to share more of their ideas with their fellow trainees as well as other staff. This first group begins to take on more leadership roles as the year progresses. Even before the end of the first year, many of these trained teachers are inviting others in to observe lessons they are doing. They begin to plan lessons with their grade-level colleagues. Eventually they work together on setting up units. For example, at the Hardy School, one teacher experienced in using technology planned a unit with her grade-level colleague on simple machines. In it they incorporated a CD-ROM program that explained how these machines worked.

The model also encourages teachers to use their students as resources in a variety of ways. They can work with one another within the class on technology. Students can participate in computer centers/stations and learn new programs to bring back to their own classrooms. Older students can mentor younger ones on computer activities which benefit both ages.

Finally, mentoring occurs among the three lead teachers who prepare each other for their new responsibilities. As the staff development evolves, so does the role of the lead teacher. She becomes more of a liaison for mentoring activities, and a coordinator of schedules so that teachers can communicate. By the end of the third year, training has become a collaborative responsibility shared by all.

Success Beyond

The Hardy School model has advantages beyond its official three-year training program. It establishes roots for an infrastructure of ongoing staff training through its mentoring activities. Since it is staff directed, it is more likely that the teachers will continue to take responsibility for their own professional development. **TC**

Barbara Siegel is a teacher at Hardy School, Arlington, Massachusetts. This grant was received under Barbara Fischer Long, principal of the Hardy School. It was written by Harvey Pressman, a technology consultant.

TECHNOLOGY PLANS THAT WORK

feature

Integrating Technology from the Classroom Up

Ownership results in teachers using technology to change the way they teach and, ultimately, the way students learn.

By Miguel Guhlin

For technology to impact student achievement, teachers must be empowered. To empower teachers, administrators must provide extensive staff development and training. Teachers must be allowed to write their own building and district technology plans, all linked to instructional goals. Teachers who have learned how to link technology with curriculum objectives must train less-experienced teachers. When these things happen, teachers will have assumed ownership.

This ownership results in teachers using technology to change the way they teach and, ultimately, the way students learn. This type of change requires a lot of work on the part of instructional technology specialists. Although most of us are rightly skeptical of formulaic approaches to technology integration, there are some approaches that have worked for me in three districts. Among them at the building and districts levels are:

Building-Level Technology Initiatives
Building-wide initiatives eventually lead to systemic change. Changes occur in the classroom—the site at which technology integration must occur. Initiatives at this level include:

- Peer Training. While district technology trainers can provide training for building trainers, their training is not as effective as a teacher's. Classroom teachers know what their peers need. More important, their peers are comfortable asking for their help.

- Super Substitutes. Using the super-substitute model, teachers who integrate technology go into another teacher's classroom and do activities related to instructional goals, facilitated by the use of technology.

- Building-level Technology Plan. Building plans emphasize the use of technology as a tool to gather information and to facilitate comprehension and communication.
- Parents' Technology Institute. Classes for parents can teach computer literacy and involve parents in the activities their children are doing in the classroom.
- Kids' Technology Institute. Theme-centered, content-driven use of technology allows students to use multimedia authoring software and other information management tools (word processor, spreadsheet, database). We began introductory training during the summer and continued the institutes throughout the year on Saturdays. Student participants also serve as "classroom technology facilitators."
- Computer Club. Students form a peer-training group that focuses on using technology to train other students. The key here is sharing how to use technology to accomplish personal goals, such as downloading a graphic or game off the Internet.

These activities at the building level, thrown into the mix all at once, will cause immediate changes. Teachers will feel the pressure as their peers, students, and parents begin to use technology. In a short period, perhaps half a year, teachers will begin to ask for more opportunities for technology training.

At this critical moment, administrators must intensify their efforts to provide teachers with the needed information and training. Administrators also must allow teachers to take school computers home over long breaks.

District-Level Technology Initiatives

Here are some suggestions for district-wide approaches to technology integration.

- Establish a district technology committee, composed of two classroom teachers from each building, and meet monthly to discuss current research. Some great resources include TECHNOLOGY CONNECTION and publications of the International Society of Technology in Education (ISTE). Discussion topics might include training on modeling the use of instructional technology in the classroom and using the computer as a cooperative learning group manager.
- Invite administrators to participate in instructional technology classes at colleges and universities. Provide "scholarships" for teachers from each building.
- Allow students to publish their work on the Internet. For schools without a direct connection to the Internet, some Internet service providers will give space to develop a Web page and publish student work. It is not difficult to set up a World Wide Web page using shareware products available on the Internet.
- Establish guidelines that allow teachers to take school computers home over the summer. Offer a three-hour class that covers the essentials of caring for a computer. Send modems home and prepare handouts on how to access the Internet. When the teachers return to school in the fall, ask them to share their experiences via e-mail with a district-wide list.
- Emphasize how technology can be integrated across content areas.
- Give technology committee members subscriptions to technology journals.
- Find a way to communicate electronically with teachers in the district. You can do this through your state's Internet service provider, a school-run computer bulletin board, or a local computer bulletin board that is willing to set up a special interest area for teachers.

Technology coordinators can help their districts reach "critical mass." Technology integration is similar to a tidal wave, growing silently in strength, then falling with an unstoppable roar upon those who paid no attention or showed little interest. TC

Miguel Guhlin is Education Specialist and TENET Master Trainer at the Education Service Center, Region 20, in San Antonio, Texas.

NOTES

Boolean Burritos
How the faculty ate up keyword searching

Only have a few minutes for staff development?
This early-morning faculty meeting provided enough time for a memorable lesson.

By Sherry York

The online catalog had been up and running in the library for more than two years. The old, maple card catalog was gone. Most of the high school teachers had received orientation on using the new electronic catalog, and some teachers had even used it. However, very few teachers and students were using the online catalog to its full potential.

My goal was to introduce keyword searching to the teachers. My window of opportunity was the weekly, 30-minute, early-morning faculty meeting. I wanted to teach a lesson in a fun way, with audience participation rather than simply lecture while the teachers sat passively, looking attentive but mentally going over their plans for the day. As anyone who has ever presented to an audience of teachers knows, they are a tough crowd!

My limitations included lack of sufficient time to do an in-depth, hands-on program and the early morning time frame in which teachers groggily clutched gallon-sized cups of coffee as they trudged up the stairs to the library. On the plus side, I had a supportive principal who not only allowed but encouraged me to do short, library-related staff development programs. The group was fairly small but receptive and eager to learn.

Because I am a strong believer in the Big6™ process of problem solving, I applied it to this situation. I had already defined my task (Big6™, step 1). I spent some time leafing through my files of "really good stuff" culled from journals, printouts of ideas from the Internet, listservs and the like. At this point I had sought, located and accessed information (Big6™, steps 2 and 3).

I remembered, fortuitously, that some clever person either on the Big6™ listserv or in a Big6™ newsletter related an activity using ham and eggs to illustrate keyword searching. Food is something that gets my attention, but here in the Southwest burritos are more common than ham and eggs.

Boolean burritos, I thought. Yes! (For readers unlucky enough not to know the pleasure of authentic breakfast burritos, you have my sympathy.) Now I was ready to use my information to get this program together (Big6™, step 4).

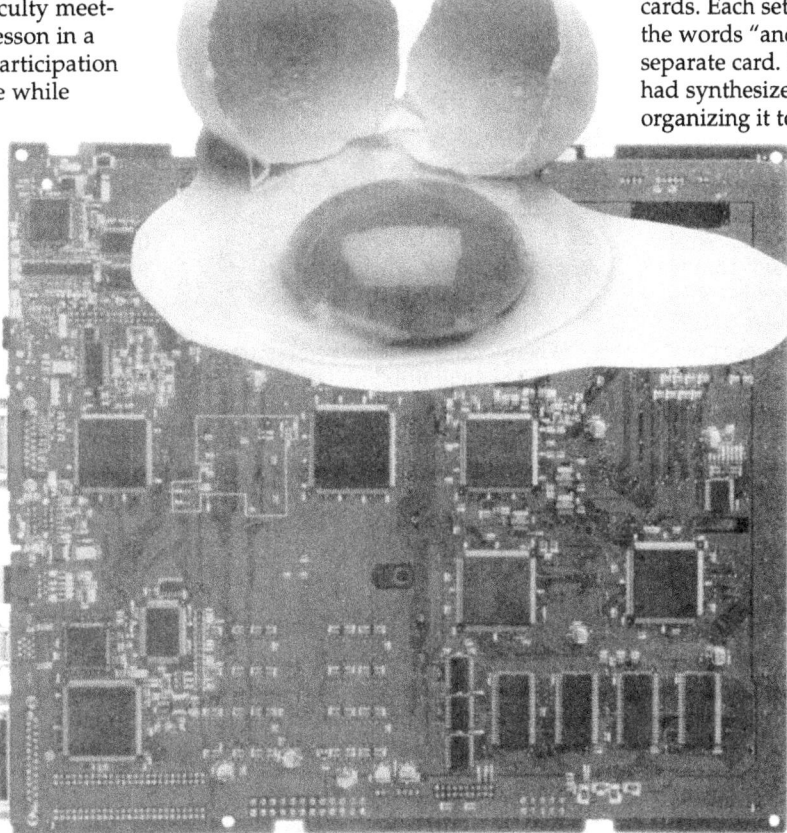

Yes, Boolean burritos it would be. I began by making some props. I made letter-sized cards using very bright, vibrant colors for both the background paper and the letters. My individual ingredient cards (letter-sized paper) included one each for egg, ham, bacon, potato, beans, and salsa. Then I made two identical sets of operator cards. Each set of operator cards had the words "and, or, not" on a separate card. Now I was ready. I had synthesized information by organizing it to create a performance (Big6Big6™, step 5).

At the meeting, I spoke briefly about the online catalog and its potential to help students (and teachers) locate precisely those books, videos, posters, picture files, and vertical files that they needed for reports and projects. I talked about George Boole, the English mathematician who helped develop modern symbolic logic. I pointed out that Boole's logic was used in algebra, reasoning and computers.

Then I quickly distributed the six ingredient cards to teachers by handing one to each table of teachers and asking them select a "holder." I assured them that holders didn't have to speak or act. All they had to do was stand up, come forward and hold up the card at the proper time.

Next, I gave out the operator cards. Operators, I explained, had to be able to do more than simply hold a card. They had to be critical thinkers who could choose the appropriate Boolean operator when it was called for. After two "best" teachers were selected to handle the operator cards, we were ready to start ordering. We were ready to make Boolean burritos.

I called on teachers at random to make an order. When the ingredients were called for, the two ingredient card holders were to step forward. Then the operator would move between the two and display the appropriate operator. We had an order for one ham and egg burrito. That was easy. Then someone wanted bacon and egg. Easy. Ham sat down and bacon stood up. The same operator was still being used.

Then someone wanted bacon and egg with salsa. Now salsa stood up and joined bacon and egg. A second operator was required for this combination. Now we had five people standing.

Then the vegetarian librarian asked for a burrito with beans only. How many operators were needed for that? None. Beans stood alone.

Then we got into more complicated orders. How about one for an easy-to-please customer, egg and bacon or ham? Egg, bacon, ham, and two operators stood up. Did it make a difference where the operators were placed? Could a bacon and ham burrito be the result if the operator was misplaced?

What about a burrito for the greedy person who wants a deluxe: egg, bacon, potato, and salsa. How many ingredients? Four. How many operators? Three. While three operators and four ingredients might be fine for a burrito, our online catalog has spaces only for two operators and three ingredients (terms).

> **Any time you can make teachers laugh before eight in the morning, you've been successful.**

When would we use the operator "not"? The operator "not" didn't have much value in our orders, we decided. If we said, "Everyone will have bacon and egg and salsa unless they order otherwise," then individuals might order bacon and egg not salsa or egg and salsa not bacon.

How many different combinations could we make? Would they all be feasible? edible? useful? palatable? But our time was running out. We really had fun with the "ingredients" and "operators" moving back and forth. Everyone laughed a lot, and most important, they thought about keyword searching and Boolean logic. I would like to say that we stayed afterward and actually made burritos; instead, I thanked everyone for their participation, the bell rang and we headed toward our respective first period classes.

(During the next exam-schedule day, I did provide breakfast burritos (preassembled), orange juice and reinforcement in the teachers' lounge. The food was accompanied by a sign that read something like, "These Boolean Burritos are provided by the library with the compliments of the high school students who provided financial support by paying overdue fines during this term.")

Finally, what about evaluation, the last Big6™, step? The program turned out pretty darn well, if I do say so myself. Any time you can make teachers laugh before eight in the morning, you've been successful. If they learned keyword searching and Boolean logic at the same time, it must have been worthwhile. BR

Sherry York is Librarian at Ozona (Texas) High School.

WEB PAGE EVALUATION: Views from the Field

By Nancy Everhart

Librarians-in-training spend countless hours poring over thick reference tomes to assess their quality in relationship to criteria prescribed by experts. We teach this skill so that the librarian-on-the-job will be able to evaluate new books and make good selection decisions. As the Internet invades media centers, librarians must acquire a new set of skills to evaluate sources on the World Wide Web.

Often access to the Internet for the entire school is provided in the media center. Librarians need to teach students and teachers how to discriminate among the plethora of sources available and, perhaps more importantly, when not to use the Internet. In many cases, the school library media specialist maintains a library or school Web site and must know how to choose appropriate links. Often, the librarian needs to convince administrators that print materials are still necessary even though the Internet is available. Having a tool to evaluate what is on the Internet will aid in each of these endeavors.

I could not find an evaluation tool for the school librarian's use. Commercial services give awards to Web pages, but the awards are based mostly on design considerations. Some existing evaluation instruments on the Internet are geared to students or Webmasters. So, I set about to create an instrument by drawing on other evaluation tools and with feedback from a panel of 40 Internet-savvy school library media specialists from throughout the United States. An explanation of the criteria found on the form [insert page numbers] follows.

1. Currency

The greatest strength of the Internet, as ascertained by school library media specialists, is that information can be updated so easily and frequently. News wire and stock exchange sites update their information every few seconds. Students looking for college facts may get more accurate information by visiting a school's Web site than by paging through printed college guides. As one school library media specialist stated, "Speed, accuracy, and timeliness are reasons that the Web is useful." Important considerations when checking for currency are the date of the last revision and dates for planned updates.

2. Content/Information

The next most important area of consideration is the information available at the site. Of particular concern is the second statement, "The information is not available in any other format elsewhere in my library." The school library media specialists noted that by the time one could locate, connect to, load and find the information on a Web page, in many cases it could have been found much more easily in the library's collection. But there is a lot of information available on the WWW not available elsewhere. This information must also support the curriculum or student interest, be thorough, accurate, clearly labeled and organized, be in good taste, and use correct spelling and grammar.

3. Authority

Determining who is responsible for a Web site and what their qualifications are can be extremely difficult. If the authors are not identified, you may be able to tell who the host of the site is by examining the URL. You can also look for e-mail addresses of the authors. Don't be fooled into thinking all sites with "edu" in their addresses are good, and those with "com" are bad. There are some terrific commercial sites that are comparable to reference CD-ROMs. There are also some awful sites originating on college campuses.

4. Ease of Navigation

Ease of navigation involves moving around within the site and out from the site using links. A sensible, clear, and clutter-free layout is key to finding relevant information. The user should be able to tell at first glance how the site is organized and the options available. If there is more than one page to a site, each supporting page should have a similar layout. Links back to the main page from supporting pages are helpful.

Links should be easy to identify without moving the pointer. The links should be grouped in some logical order, perhaps by subject. If a site links to another site, the linked-to site should be relevant to the subject.

Web Page Evaluation Worksheet

©1996 Dr. Nancy Everhart

Title of Web Site: _____ URL: _____

Directions: Use your judgment in allotting points for the various categories. Total the points for score.

Currency (0 to 15 Points) _____
    The site has the date of last revision posted.
    The site has been updated recently.
    Frequency of planned updates and revisions is stated.

Content/Information (0 to 15 Points) _____
    The information will be useful to our curriculum and/or student interest.
    This information is not available in any other format elsewhere in my library.
    There is sufficient information to make the site worth visiting.
    The information is clearly labeled and organized.
    The content effectively achieves its intended purpose.
    The information on the topic is thorough.
    The information is accurate.
    The purpose of the page is obvious.
    The information is in good taste.
    The page uses correct spelling and grammar.

Authority (0 to 10 Points) _____
    The authors are clearly identified.
    The authors and/or maintainers of the site are authorities in their field.
    There is a way to contact the author(s) via e-mail or traditional mail.
    You can easily tell from the domain name where the page originates.

Ease of Navigation (0 to 10 Points) _____
    You can tell from the first page how the site is organized and what options are available.
    The type styles and background make the page clear and readable.
    The links are easy to identify.
    The links are logically grouped.
    The layout is consistent from page to page.
    There is a link back to the home page on each supporting page.
    The links are relevant to the subject.
    The icons clearly represent what is intended.

Experience (0 to 10 Points) _____
    The page fulfills its intended purpose.
    The page is worth the time.
    The page is attractive.
    The page makes you want to continue exploring the site.

Use of Graphics, Sound, Video (0 to 10 Points) _____
    The graphics/sounds/video make a significant contribution to the site.
    The graphics/sounds/video are clearly labeled and identified.
    Each graphic/sound/video serves a clear purpose.

Treatment (0 to 10 Points) _____
    Any biases toward the subject matter can be easily identified.
    The page is free from stereotyping.
    The page is age appropriate for content and vocabulary for its intended audience.

Access (0 to 5 points) _____
    You can connect quickly to the page.
    The page is available through search engines.
    The page loads quickly.
    You can choose whether to download smaller images, text-only, or non-frame versions.

Miscellaneous (0 to 15 Points) _____
    The page has received an award(s).
    There are no per-use costs involved.
    Interactions asking for private information are secured.
    Information can be printed without the need to change your system configuration.
    Information is presented in short enough segments so it can be printed out without backing up the system for other users.
    The page has its own search engine for searching within the page.

TOTAL: _____

Scoring:
90-100	Excellent
80-89	Good
70-79	Average
60-69	Borderline Acceptable
Below 60	Unacceptable

Comments:

One library media specialist noted, "My favorite pages for library reference have tables of contents that help you locate information in a reasonable amount of time and are logical. I don't like using icons that stand for something known only to the creator of the page. I don't want to have to learn how to use a page."

5. Experience

Experience deals with the ability of the site to "draw you in." The site should be attractive but also worth the time it takes to explore it.

6. Use of Graphics, Sound, Video

Graphics, sound, and video were not particularly important to the library media specialists unless these features served a clear purpose and made a significant contribution to the site.

7. Treatment

Treatment deals with issues such as stereotyping, reading levels, point of view, and bias. Two criteria from the originally proposed list, "The page is impartial" and "The page is free from bias and stereotyping" were either dropped or changed because a majority of the library media specialists opposed them. Their reasons were interesting. Among the reasons stated were:

"You may want to check a page for a point of view that is not impartial. What is critical is that information is documented with a source address so the researcher can verify what a particular group or person represents."

"Why take the trouble to have a page if you don't feel strongly about an issue? It's more realistic to stress authority so biases can be recognized."

Obviously, media specialists have been using "biased" Web sites to obtain information from special interest groups, to obtain viewpoints that may be unavailable in print sources, and as a teaching tool. These statements affirm that approach to biased sites:

"I'm not concerned with biased information as long as it is clear that there is no attempt to portray the information as impartial. You just know certain pages are biased but that's o.k. if you're looking for information on that point of view."

"Although it is important to know whether or not the page is biased, once students have established a bias, they can work on this. Print sources are often biased—when students figure this out, they have used critical thinking skills."

Although it was important to the group to modify the statement on bias, they felt that the statements on stereotyping and appropriateness for the age of the audience should remain unchanged.

8. Access

Access to a Web site and the speed at which the site loads are often a function of the computer used or the time of day. The criteria in this category deal only with variables that the Web site can control. "You can connect quickly to the page" means you do not get frequent busy signals. Loading speed is often determined by the page's design, especially if it includes large graphics. This can be controlled somewhat by downloading small images, text-only, or non-frame versions of information. School library media specialists appreciate this feature when searching for facts. Another access feature, unrelated to speed, is availability through search engines. Trying to locate a page not available through search engines is like trying to find a book that is not listed in the card catalog.

9. Miscellaneous

This category encompasses a range of issues. Most school library media specialists appreciated Web sites where no per-use costs were involved. Some didn't mind costs if the costs were reasonable and known ahead of time. "Sites asking for private information" is a concern when dealing with young people. A time-saving feature of some sites is a search engine for searching within the page.

Two of the criteria are related to printing. School library media specialists value sites where information can be printed without changing the system configuration. They also appreciate short segments that can be printed without backing up the system.

The criteria listed here were developed in a systematic way by school library media specialists who have vast experience in using the World Wide Web. But as the Internet evolves, Web pages will evolve and so will methods of evaluating them. One media specialist took a futuristic view, "Perhaps we will see bibliographic Web sites on the Internet that will link us to credible sites for research." There has also been talk at library conferences about associations developing their own "seals of approval." But just as relying on book reviews doesn't substitute for examining the book yourself, these evaluation systems may not ultimately satisfy. It is important for you to acquire a new set of skills to make your own decisions. I hope this tool will help. **TC**

Nancy Everhart (nancye@ptd.net) is an assistant professor in the Division of Library and Information Science at St. John's University in Jamaica, New York. She is responsible for teaching and research in the areas of school library media centers and audiovisual production.

What Does It Look Like?

Part 1: The CODE 77 Rubrics

By Doug Johnson

Parents and administrators want computer-literate teachers. Students seek out teachers who meaningfully use technology, and teachers themselves acknowledge that computer skills are increasingly necessary and important in fulfilling their professional duties. The specific computer skills that comprise computer literacy, however, are rarely articulated. As it applies to teachers, computer literacy can easily remain ill-defined—a politically correct buzz word without meaning or purpose.

When Mankato Area Public Schools began its formal staff development program five years ago to train teachers to use technology, I wrote a series of rubrics, or graduated performance indicators, to describe what the district expected a computer-using teacher to be able to do after 30 hours of formal computer instruction and six to nine months of practice. The name of our program, CODE 77, stands for Computers On Desks Everywhere in District 77.

These rubrics primarily address professional productivity and are the foundation on which more complex technology and technology-related professional skills are built. Teachers who have mastered these skills are able to use the computer to improve their traditional instructional tasks, such as writing, record keeping, designing student materials, and presenting lessons. These

> *By examining the specific skills described, teachers know in what areas they need to take classes or to continue practice.*

skills also build the confidence teachers need to use technology to restructure the educational process. (For rubrics describing the Advanced Teacher Computer Use skills, see this month's *Head for the Edge* column.)

Each of the ten rubrics has four levels:

Level 1 Pre-awareness
Level 2 Awareness
Level 3 Mastery
Level 4 Advanced

We initially designed our training efforts with the assumption that most teachers would be at Level 1 or 2. By the end of the training, we anticipated that teachers would be at Level 3 or 4 in most skill areas and would have advanced at least one level in all areas.

These rubrics have served two purposes in our district. We have been able to judge the effectiveness of our staff development efforts by asking teachers to complete an anonymous self-assessment before and after training using the rubrics. Then simple graphs showing the percentage of training participants at each level before and after training are constructed to share the results with the staff development committees and the administration.

The rubrics also provide a "road map" for teachers to improve their computer skills. By examining the specific skills described, teachers know in what areas they need to take classes or to continue practice.

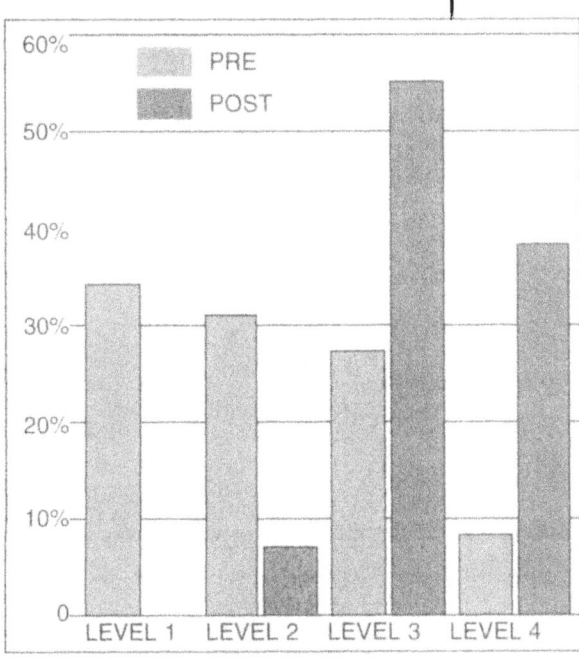

Below are both the instructions to teachers for completing a self-assessment and the rubrics themselves. Feel free to use and modify the rubrics for your district's needs and as technology changes. These rubrics can also be modified to benchmark student performance. (See Jamieson McKenzie's adaptation of these rubrics for that purpose at http://www.bham.wednet.edu/assess2.htm.)

Doug Johnson is the District Media Supervisor for the Mankato (Minnesota) Public Schools, and can be reached by e-mail at djohns1@west.isd77.k12.mn.us (or) palsdaj@vax1.mankato.msus.edu.

CODE 77 Self-Evaluation Rubrics for Basic Teacher Computer Use

Please judge your level of achievement in each of the following competencies. Circle the number that best reflects your current level of skill attainment. At the end of the training program, you will complete the same set of rubrics to reflect your level of skill attainment at that time. (Level 3 is considered mastery.) This tool is to help measure the effectiveness of our training program, and to help you do a self-analysis to determine the areas in which you should continue to learn and practice. Keep a copy of these rubrics to refer to during the training.

I. Basic computer operation
Level 1—I do not use a computer.
Level 2—I can use the computer to run a few specific, preloaded programs. It has little effect on either my work or home life. I am somewhat anxious I might damage the machine or its programs.
Level 3—I can set up my computer and peripheral devices, load software, print, and use most of the operating system tools like the scrapbook, clock, note pad, find command, and trash can (recycling bin). I can format a data disk.
Level 4—I can run two programs simultaneously and can have several windows open at the same time. I can customize the look and sounds of my computer. I use techniques like shift-clicking to work with multiple files. I look for programs and techniques to maximize my operating system. I feel confident enough to teach others some basic operations.

II. File management
Level 1—I do not save any documents I create using the computer.
Level 2—I save documents I've created, but I cannot choose where they are saved. I do not back up my files.
Level 3—I have a filing system for organizing my files and can locate files quickly and reliably. I backup my files to floppy disk or other storage device on a regular basis.
Level 4—I regularly run a disk optimizer on my hard drive and use a backup program to make copies of my files on a weekly basis. I have a system for archiving files that I do not need on a regular basis to conserve my computer's hard drive space.

III. Word processing
Level 1—I do not use a word processor, and I cannot identify any uses or features it might have that would benefit the way I work.
Level 2—I occasionally use the word processor for simple documents that I know I will modify and use again. I generally find it easier to handwrite or type most of my written work.
Level 3—I use the word processor for nearly all my written professional work: memos, tests, worksheets, and home communications. I can edit, spell check, and change the format of a document. I can paginate, preview, and print my work. I feel my work looks professional.
Level 4—I use the word processor not only for my work but also with students to help them improve their own communication skills.

IV. Spreadsheet use
Level 1—I do not use a spreadsheet, and I cannot identify any uses or features it might have that would benefit the way I work.
Level 2—I understand the use of a

spreadsheet and can navigate within one. I can create a simple spreadsheet to add a column of numbers.
Level 3—I use a spreadsheet for several applications. These spreadsheets use labels, formulas, and cell references. I can change the format of the spreadsheets by changing column widths and text style. I can use the spreadsheet to make a simple graph or chart.
Level 4—I use the spreadsheet not only for my work but also with students to help them improve their own data keeping and analysis skills.

V. Database use
Level 1—I do not use a database, and I cannot identify any uses or features it might have that would benefit the way I work.
Level 2—I understand the use of a database and can locate information within one that has been pre-made. I can add or delete data in a database.
Level 3—I use databases for personal applications. I can create an original database by defining fields and creating layouts. I can find, sort, and print information in layouts that are clear and useful to me.
Level 4—I can use formulas with my database to create summaries of numerical data. I can use database information to mail merge in a word processing document. I use the database not only for my work but also with students to help them improve their own data keeping and analysis skills.

VI. Graphics use
Level 1—I do not use graphics in my word processing or presentations, and I cannot identify any uses or features they might have that would benefit the way I work.
Level 2—I can open and create simple pictures with the painting and drawing programs. I can use programs like *PrintShop* or *SuperPrint*.
Level 3—I use both pre-made clip art and simple original graphics in my word processed documents and presentation. I can edit clip art, change its size, and place it on a page. I can purposefully use most of the drawing tools, and can group and un-group objects. I can use the clipboard to take graphics from one application to another. The use of graphics in my work helps clarify or amplify my message.
Level 4—I use graphics not only for my work but also with students to help them improve their own communications. I can use graphics and the word processor to create a professional-looking newsletter.

VII. Hypermedia use
Level 1—I do not use hypermedia (*HyperStudio*), and I cannot identify any uses or features it might have that would benefit the way I work.
Level 2—I can navigate through a pre-made hypermedia program.
Level 3—I can create my own hypermedia stacks for information presentation. These stacks use navigation buttons, sounds, dissolves, graphics, and text fields. I can use an LCD projection device to display the presentation to a class.
Level 4—I use hypermedia with students who are making their own stacks for information keeping and presentation.

VIII. Network use
Level 1—I do not use the online resources available in my building, and I cannot identify any uses or features they might have that would benefit the way I work.
Level 2—I understand that there is a large amount of information available to me as a teacher that can be accessed through networks, including the Internet. With the help of the media specialist, I can use the resources on the network in our building.
Level 3—I use the networks to access professional and personal information from a variety of sources, including networked CD-ROM reference materials, online library catalogs, the ERIC database, and the World Wide Web. I have an e-mail account that I use on a regular basis.
Level 4—Using telecommunications, I am an active participant in online discussions, and I can download files and programs from remote computers. I use telecommunications with my students.

IX. Student assessment
Level 1—I do not use the computer for student assessment.
Level 2—I understand that there are ways I can keep track of student progress using the computer. I keep some student-produced materials on the computer, and I write evaluations of student work and notes to parents with the word processor.
Level 3—I effectively use an electronic grade book to keep track of student data, and I keep portfolios of student-produced materials on the computer. I use the electronic data during parent/teacher conferences.
Level 4—I rely on the computer to keep track of outcomes and objectives students have mastered. I use that information in determining assignments, teaching strategies, and groupings.

X. Ethical use understanding
Level 1—I am not aware of any ethical issues surrounding computer use.
Level 2—I know that some copyright restrictions apply to computer software.
Level 3—I clearly understand the difference between freeware, shareware, and commercial software and the fees involved in the use of each. I know the programs for which the district or my building holds a site license. I understand the school board policy on the use of copyrighted materials. I demonstrate ethical usage of all software and let my students know my personal stand on legal and moral issues involving technology. I know and enforce the school's technology policies and guidelines, including its Internet acceptable use policy. I have a personal philosophy I can articulate regarding the use of technology in education.
Level 4—I am aware of other controversial aspects of technology use, including data privacy, equitable access, and free speech issues. I can speak about a variety of technology issues at my professional association meetings, to parent groups, and to the general community.

Rubrics for Restructuring (Continuation of The CODE 77 Rubrics) Part II

By Doug Johnson

Is technology being used in your school to accomplish anything that otherwise would be impossible? Other professions have used technology to make possible:

- banking services from home
- medical CAT scans custom-fitted
- blue jeans at a mass-production cost
- full-text searching for information in national databases
- the globalization of industries
- astronomical amounts of data from unimaginable distances
- customized news and information services
- distance training and customer support services.

Yet education is primarily using technology only to reinforce traditional educational practices.

Most teacher training classes are designed to give teachers a familiarity with the computer skills that help them improve their professional productivity: basic computer operation, word processing, telecommunication, and record keeping. (See *The CODE 77 Rubrics* in last month's issue.) But if technology is to realize its powerful potential for improving education, it must be used for more than just automating the traditional methods and practices of teaching.

The rubrics below are designed to help teachers move to the next level of professional computer use. Rather than the computer simply being a tool that allows a common task to be done more efficiently, these skills fundamentally change how instruction is delivered, how student performance is measured, and how teachers view themselves as professionals. The technology is used to restructure the educational process to allow it to do things it has never been able to do before. These include using technology to ensure that:

- all students master the basic skills of reading, writing, and computation
- all students practice authentic information literacy and research skills and the higher-order thinking skills inherent in them
- all students have access to top-quality resources, including human resources, regardless of location
- all teachers provide students and parents with
  - *individual education plans*

- continuous feedback on how well students are meeting their learning goals
- opportunities for virtual student performance assessments
- all teachers have the tools and ability to:
  - locate the research findings that will guide their use of technology
  - collect the data that measures the effectiveness of their practices.

These advanced rubrics are designed for the same purposes as the beginning CODE 77 rubrics—to help schools measure the effectiveness of their teacher training efforts and to guide teachers on their own learning path.

CODE 77 Self-Evaluation Rubrics for Advanced Teacher Computer Use

I. Instructional software use

Level 1
I do not use instructional software as a part of my instructional program, nor am I aware of any titles that might help my students meet their learning goals.

Level 2
I use a few computer programs as an instructional supplement, as a reward, or with special needs students.

Level 3
I use several programs (drill and practice, simulations, and tutorials) chosen by my department or grade level to help all my students meet specific learning objectives. The software allows me to teach or reinforce concepts more effectively than traditional methods. When it is available, I use the software's management system to help assess individual student performance. I use technological resources to meet the needs of students who do not respond to traditional methods of instruction.

Level 4
I seek new programs for evaluation and adoption. I know sources of software reviews and stay current on new developments in computer technologies through professional reading and conference attendance. I share my findings with other professionals.

II. Information literacy skills

Level 1
I am not familiar with the term information literacy, nor do I know why such skills are important.

Level 2
As a part of my curriculum, I have library research projects, and I support the library skills taught by the media specialist. I am aware that there are electronic resources available to my students.

> *If technology is to realize its powerful potential for improving education, it must be used for more than just automating the traditional methods and practices of teaching.*

Level 3
My curriculum includes multiple projects that have an information literacy component. These are team-taught with the media specialist. I understand the Big Six or a similar information literacy process and design student projects so they require higher-level thinking skills, use electronic information sources, require the use of computer productivity software, and are authentically assessed. I guide my students in accessing, evaluating, and using information and experts from worldwide sources through the Internet and videoconferencing.

Level 4
I am actively involved in curriculum-planning teams and advocate for multidisciplinary units and activities that require information-literacy skills. I share successful units with others through print and electronic publishing and through conference presentations and workshops.

III. Modification of instructional delivery

Level 1
I have one or two effective methods of delivering content or teaching skills to my students. I do not use technology that requires me to change my instructional methodology.

Level 2
I have tried units or projects that are student-directed, use small groups, or are highly individualized, but I primarily use teacher-directed, whole-group instruction.

Level 3
I use a variety of instructional delivery methods and student grouping strategies routinely throughout the year. I can design activities and approaches that best fit the learning objectives and the technology available to me. I can use small groups working cooperatively or in rotation to take advantage of student-to-equipment ratios of greater than one-to-one. I modify instructional methods to take advantage of the learning styles of individual students.

Level 4
I continually try new approaches suggested by research or observation to discover the most effective means of using technology to engage my students and meet curricular goals. I work with a team of teachers to create, modify, and improve my practices in this area.

IV. Assessment of student performance

Level 1
I evaluate my students using objective tests only.

Level 2
I evaluate some student performances or projects using subjective criteria. I save some student work for cumulative folders and

parent conferences and print some electronically-produced student work.

Level 3
I use a wide range of assessments to evaluate student projects and performances. I can create assessment tools like checklists, rubrics, and benchmarks, which help students assess their own performance and allow me to objectively determine the quality of student work. I ask students to keep a physical and an electronic portfolio of their work. Students and their parents have the means to continually access the recorded progress students are making toward their learning goals through networked grade books and portfolios. Students are given the opportunity to demonstrate skills through performance to a wide audience via data and video networks. I have a means of aggregating performance data for my class, which I use to modify my teaching activities and strategies.

Level 4
I continually try new approaches suggested by research or observation to discover the most effective means of using technology to assess student learning. I work with a team of teachers to create, modify, and improve my work in this area.

V. Individualization of the educational program

Level 1
I modify my curriculum or instructional methods only for students with identified special needs.

Level 2
I occasionally give students the choice of assignments in my class, but all class members (unless they are in special education) must meet the same learning objectives within the same time frame. Skill remediation is done during summer school or informally during or after school.

Level 3
With the assistance of the student, parents, and appropriate specialists, I create an individualized learning plan for each of my students. I track the accomplishment of learning goals in the plan using a computerized tool. I use this tool during parent conferences and for school or state reporting. Students and their parents have networked access to this tool for continual monitoring of progress and plan modification.

Level 4
I provide suggestions about the content and design of the individualized computerized planning and report tools.

VI. Professional growth and communication

Level 1
I do not use electronic resources for professional growth or communication.

Level 2
I can find lesson plans and some research in online databases. I use e-mail to correspond with parents and other teachers.

Level 3
I use the Internet and other online resources to obtain research findings, teaching materials, and information related to the content of my classes. I read electronic newsletters and journals to stay current on educational practices. I participate in electronic discussion groups and chat rooms that are related to my area of education, and I contribute to and use the best practices discussed there. I use a computerized presentation program when giving workshops or speaking at conferences. I use technology to take part in distance learning opportunities for my own professional development.

Level 4
I organize professional growth opportunities for other teachers and feel comfortable teaching other staff members about the use of technology.

VII. Research and evaluation of technology use

Level 1
I have not attempted to determine whether the use of instructional technology has made a difference in my students' learning or classroom climate.

Level 2
I gather, use, and share anecdotal information and observations about student use of technology in my classroom.

Level 3
I use action research and aggregated data to accurately determine whether the technology and methodology I am using has an impact on how well my students learn and on school climate.

Level 4
I participate in formal studies conducted by professional groups and academics on the impact of technology on student learning. I have designed such studies as part of my own professional education. I report to other professionals electronically and in print the findings of my research.

To help teachers master these complex skills will be a greater, more time-consuming task than the simple hands-on classes in which word processing, e-mail, and file management were taught. And it can't be done by the technology department alone. Staff development in technology will require a collaborative effort with experts in the content areas, child development, curriculum, assessment, research, and evaluation.

These challenging skills will take time, effort, and courage to master, but schools with teachers who do so will be in a superior position to meet future educational demands.

Doug Johnson is the District Media Supervisor for the Mankato (Minnesota) Public Schools

WORKSHOPS for Teacher Partners in Technology Integration

By Lesley S.J. Farmer

One of the most important partners in integrating technology is the teaching staff. Many librarians look for ways to encourage teachers to make full use of the computers and software available. This writer describes the characteristics of a comprehensive staff development program. You'll find good ideas for formal and informal training sessions for adults.

WHAT ARE THE BENEFITS of integrating technology in the classroom? Increased student performance, motivation of at-risk students, school-to-work skills, and new learning opportunities. For teachers, technology can facilitate individualized instruction, ease planning and administrative tasks, and increase collegiality and interest in teaching.

> Training should not exist in an intellectual vacuum; it should reflect current attitudes toward educational delivery systems.

If the benefits are so great, why aren't more teachers using technology? The main reason is lack of effective training. A comprehensive program of inservice training in technology is built on these steps:

- Develop short-term and long-term goals and objectives.
- Generate cooperation and interest among staff.
- Establish a coordinating structure and policies.
- Establish procedures for assessing, designing, and maintaining the program.
- Design and implement a planned sequence of "courses" in a variety of delivery modes.
- Establish training supports—a clearinghouse for information, a professional collection (preferably housed in the library), and time for practice/learning.

A comprehensive, effective inservice program requires much planning and support, much more than it requires in financial boosts. While administrative direction is obviously needed, the approach to staff development cannot be construed as a strictly top-down activity; the staff must "buy into" the program. A needs assessment completed by staff offers a beginning point for developing meaningful training. This input, together with insights gathered from classroom observations, provides the wants and needs that inservice training can address.

Sometimes the first task is to raise teachers' awareness of their need to improve their technology competencies. Next, the school must make sure that integration of technology is a high priority item in the curriculum; otherwise, no one will see the need for related staff development.

Inservice programs should be an integrated part of a total effort toward improved education. Training should not exist in an intellectual vacuum; it should reflect current attitudes toward educational delivery systems. Training and time for teachers to practice their new skills should be considered regular activities of the school routine. Training results should impact the entire school program.

ADULTS AS LEARNERS

Training adults requires recognition of the special characteristics and needs of mature learners. By addressing these characteristics, trainers can achieve their major task—to facilitate change. Some characteristics of adult learners are—

- Adults are experienced learners.
- Adults have limited time.
- Adults learn in response to their own interests and needs.
- Adults have strong habits.
- Adults need to see results.

DELIVERY SYSTEMS

A successful training program offers learning opportunities in several modes:

- manuals and how-to books
- videotapes (commercial and in-house productions)
- computer tutorials
- coaches
- workshops and classes

The critical factor in all delivery systems is thoughtful selection and evaluation of resources. Usually, the library media specialist works with the computer specialist and staff development coordinator to offer the best material. Planning and implementing workshops, though, requires more sophisticated and broad-based direction.

CONDUCTING WORKSHOPS

Probably the most important aspect of a workshop is its tone and climate. The presenters should be organized and enthusiastic. The room should be well equipped and provide a pleasant, comfortable setting. Programs should begin on time with a warm welcome and clear directions. Including time for questions and opportunities to share information ensures engagement and satisfaction. Ending on time and inspiring participants to action make for a satisfying end.

The workshop should take adult education principles into account as well as the course content. Experiential learning is the most effective means of learning for adults. This experiential model assumes that a person engages in

> One particularly good question to ask workshop attendees is: What do you want to learn now as a result of today's training? Their response providers direction for future programs.

an activity, reflects on and generalizes from it, and then applies it to daily life. The five points in experiential learning should be used in designing the sequence of activities for a workshop—

- experiencing an activity
- sharing reactions and observations
- processing by discussing patterns and dynamics
- generalizing by inferring principles about the real world
- applying skills and planning more effective behavior

Typically, learners work sequentially through the five points, or steps. Teamwork is important, particularly when hands-on activity or group input are part of the workshop. Working in small groups combines cognitive and affective learning and stimulates thinking and insights. Also, peer acceptance of new ideas is more meaningful to the adult learner than a superior's directive. Follow-up can be more effective, too, as small group interaction establishes information networks.

Some specific activities are well suited to small group work, such as discussion, problem-solving, case study, and brainstorming. In each case, different options are raised and considered so that sources for decision-making can be increased.

Managing small groups requires clear directions and time frames. In addition, each group needs to have some assigned roles, at least a facilitator and a recordkeeper. At the end of any small group activity, there should be an opportunity for each group to report its findings and incorporate insights into the total group process.

Workshops generally take on a rhythm or flow and often follow this sequence:

Early-bird Activity. Early participants need to feel involved from the start. Have handouts for them to read, food as a socializing focus, or last-minute preparation tasks that they can help with.

Introduction. The facilitator should introduce major presenters and agenda and take care of "housekeeping" details.

Warm-up. Workshop participants need to get acquainted with each other and the speaker. Sharing backgrounds and expectations helps focus participants.

Definition. The facilitator needs to explain the main concepts of the inservice program and their significance.

Main Program. The facilitator should often check for group understanding of the major ideas.

Practice and Application. The participants should practice and reflect on the concepts or skills presented. They should also have time to plan ways to transfer their learning to their classrooms.

Resources. Bibliographies and names of resource people give workshop participants ways to pursue the topic on their own.

Closing. The participants need a sense of closure. The main findings should be summarized, and follow-up strategies should be outlined. Participants should evaluate the workshop before leaving, although later follow-up contact can measure longer-term transfer of learning.

EVALUATING WORKSHOPS

Assessment of learning occurs on several levels. Both trainers and trainees can assess the quality and usefulness of a workshop. Evaluation time should be built into the workshop schedule. However, the real evaluation is the effect that the workshop has on student learning. This measurement is harder to obtain because a control group rarely exists.

Factors to consider in evaluation include attitudinal differences, test results, and levels of intellectual and affective engagement. Measurement tools can include observations, objective and standardized tests, teacher and student products, portfolio assessments, clinical supervision, peer and self-assessments, and focus group discussion.

Evaluation of the workshop itself is the key to knowing what worked and what didn't, and why. This will help you modify the content or the approach to better meet everyone's needs. Some factors to assess include

- content (level of difficulty, balance of theory and practice, level of usefulness),
- delivery (format, pacing, sequence, clarity),
- time (date, time of day, length of workshop, breaks),
- space (size, arrangement, seating, physical conditions), and
- resources (handouts, teaching aids, equipment).

One particularly good question to ask workshop attendees is: What do you want to learn now as a result of today's training? Their response provides direction for future programs. The subsequent workshop can then relate to the first one, either building on it or complementing it. For example, an Internet workshop could lead to student activities such as finding pen pals or it could lead to the use of Web sites across the curriculum.

The first workshop on integrating technology will have teachers begging for more! Ideally, a staff development committee would plan a logical series of related inservice workshops so teachers can progress systematically throughout the year. Often, inservice workshops are developed one by one in response to immediate needs. The first workshop is pivotal in either case, for its outcome will help determine whether there will be the support necessary to offer similar sessions in the future.

Lesley S.J. Farmer is the Library Director at Redwood High School in Larkspur, California. She is the author of Training Student Library Staff *(Linworth, 1996) and an Editorial Consultant and Columnist (Hardware) for the magazine* TECHNOLOGY CONNECTION.

A Planning Worksheet for Inservice Workshops

1. Define the objectives
   a. Content objectives
   b. Informational skills objectives

2. Define the learners
   a. Prerequisite learning
   b. Present level

3. Design the activity
   a. Where will it occur?
   b. What concepts or information will be presented?
   c. What resources will be used?
   d. How will the material be presented?
   e. How will it be sequenced?
   f. What is the time frame?
   g. What learning reinforcement will be provided?
   h. How will learners be grouped?
   i. How will instruction be individualized?
   j. How will learning be applied?

4. Design your assessment
   a. How will you evaluate the learning?
   b. How will you evaluate the instruction?

Partnering With Teachers For Internet Incorporation

By Lesley S. J. Farmer

Librarians need to carve out time to explore the Net and create Internet-rich products, such as interactive presentations on information literacy skills.

THE INTERNET IS NEW enough that some teachers still have misconceptions about its usefulness in education. While some view it as a panacea that contains all the information students need, others worry that students will merely download required assignments and will not develop critical thinking skills. And some teachers are even more skeptical about the Internet, believing either that it contains mostly rubbish or that it is more difficult to search than library shelves.

While these perspectives have validity, they are overreaching in their generality. Librarians who have worked with the Internet, and especially those who have helped students navigate the ether waves, have both blessed and cursed the Net and know that its viability depends on several factors:

- the information desired
- the ability of the user
- the access in terms of time and speed
- the teacher—through the content objectives, direct instruction (method and time), incorporation of the Internet into class activities, and the teacher's own ability to use the Internet.

At this point, all teachers should be comfortable with the Internet, but they may not have a full grasp of all the fine points. Teachers act similarly with the library's print collection. They tend to specialize in their own field of knowledge and typically do not know the entire DDC system or see the variety of incoming periodical articles. Savvy teachers plan with the librarian because they realize the librarian can make important connections with sources to broaden opportunities for student learning. Compare the limited number of access tools and strategies available to a print collection with the vast array of search engines and other access methods for Internet sources. Theoretically, teachers should be even more apt to work with Internet-experienced librarians in order to maximize student learning. Sadly, this is not always the case.

Since nothing succeeds like success, librarians who want to insure the incorporation of technology need to offer concrete ways for teachers to use media effectively. By building bridges for technology-based partnerships, librarians can provide better service and attain a higher professional reputation. Students will learn more.

Access to the Internet

Beginning Internet users can waste lots of time trying to find good information. Given enough time, most students can develop a sense of what is valuable on the Net, but in a one-hour class, especially where students have to share computer access, such time-intensive browsing doesn't result in immediate returns, and a student's grades may suffer in the short term. Particularly for students without home access to the Internet, every minute counts when the teacher schedules library Internet time. What's a student or teacher to do?

If the content objective is to glean information about a certain topic, then bookmarking good Web sites is a logical step. Of course, that means the teacher must let the librarian know ahead of time about the assignment, so the librarian has time to uncover good sites to be bookmarked. Obviously, the more detail the teacher can give the librarian, the closer the fit of the Web sites. Are pictures needed? Are primary sources preferred? Would sound bites be useful? Is a narrative or short-fact approach preferable? The more closely aligned sites are with the assignment, the easier it is for students to extract the information and see what constitutes as a good site.

Ideally, bookmarks can be stored on a disk and imported to all of the Internet-accessible computer systems. However, if labs are located away from the library, the librarian either has to give the disk to the teacher or aide or find a way to put the information on the local area network. As a quick fix, the librarian can print a Web site poster to be posted in each appropriate room. She also can develop and distribute a Webliography, listing both print and non-print sources along with Web sites. In these cases, the students must type in the addresses. While they may make mistakes, the kinesthetic process can help reinforce these valuable Internet addresses.

If the library has its own Web page, then lists of bookmarks and Webliographies can be easily imported onto the Net. With today's word processing programs, such as Word 97, simple documents can be saved as HTML files for easy Web inclusion. As an added benefit, such HTML documents can be read on either Macintosh or PC platforms. I also have put handouts and Webliographies in "common" folders for network access; however, the typical user didn't know how to convert the information into readable form.

Too busy to hunt for Web sites? CD-ROMs are now linking their content to the Net. Britannica's Encyclopedia, Grolier's Americana, and Microsoft Encarta are examples of offline encyclopedias that link to online information. Britannica also provides thousands of pre-selected Web sites through its Web site.

Pro-active Internet Use

If the librarian waits for the teacher to take the first step, then the library will be seen as a reactive place, rather than a vanguard of technology integration. Just as librarians should always be on the lookout for a good book, they should also keep a constant eye out for appropriate Web sites. An easy method is to keep Rolodex cards handy at all times; copy the URL onto the card and test it when the Net is accessible. Good sites then can be indexed by subject and inserted alphabetically into the Rolodex file. You also can create a binder by printing the first page of valuable Web sites.

If the library has a Web page, the entire list of Web sites can be posted. A good practice is to focus on noting and annotating sites that are well-reviewed lists of indexed or searchable Web sites. It is better to provide 100 excellent sites than 1,000 mixed-value URLs. Furthermore, you can easily update the list as new sites are found.

Finding good sites is another way to partner with teachers and students. Sending teachers a note or quick e-mail about good sites makes the library more technologically reputable. Librarians also should encourage teachers and students to share their Net treasures. Keep a stack of blank cards beside the Web rolodex for users to add to the virtual collection. However, it is a good idea to review these sites until you are certain the contributor is a critical reviewer. Greater participation in this effort results in greater ownership of the process and greater student learning.

What's Good about the Internet?

The most frequent curricular use of the Internet is as a source of information. Students could well be creating traditional five-page written reports with information found on the Internet. On the other hand, non-curricular student uses range from chat rooms to gambling, from Sailor Moon fan clubs to car buying, from last night's pro game results to video game cheats. In any case, the information needs to be examined for accuracy and authenticity.

The traditional library took care of that issue because each book and periodical was reviewed, evaluated, and selected by the librarian. On the Net, anything goes, and monitoring is not consistent. If librarians and teachers were to

> While the librarian often spends much time coaching individual students through research issues, student questions could be raised to a higher critical level if classes were given basic instruction on searching techniques.

select all the sites and deny student access to other addresses, they would not have time to do other tasks. More important, students would not learn how to examine and evaluate Internet sources critically.

Unfortunately, some teachers say there is not enough time to teach students how to evaluate sites, and students have to "pick it up" on their own. It may take several assignments where students wander aimlessly around the Net or pick false sites for teachers to realize the need for instruction in Internet evaluation. Again, the librarian can facilitate this process by diplomatically sharing observations with the teacher. The librarian is likely to note if students are off-task by recognizing frozen screens or interactive game sounds. And the librarian is likely to hear student dialogue, such as "I don't get how to do this," "Where do I begin?" or "How do I know if this is any good?"

While the librarian often spends much time coaching individual students through research issues, student questions could be raised to a higher critical level if classes were given basic instruction on searching techniques. Several methods may be used:

- Show factual and opinionated Web sites on the same topic side by side, and have students determine the critical differences.
- Demonstrate successful searches by using Net harvester programs to download procedures and results.
- Use PowerPoint presentations to show how to navigate the Net and find good resources.
- Have students search the same topic using different search engines and compare the results.
- Develop guide sheets on Internet navigation and interpretation.

Another option is to have students complete online tutorials on Internet searching. However, such self-paced instruction may go awry for students who are easily distracted or do not sense any kind of accountability. It is usually a better idea to walk through these tutorials with the class before letting students explore for themselves.

Making Active Use of the Internet

Another strength of the Internet is its interactivity. The most obvious example is real time "conversation" over the Net. Students can access user groups and chat rooms via the Internet. They can hold video conferencing sessions with experts worldwide. Global Schoolhouse is especially known for this practice. They can respond to mass media programs or events by accessing the accompanying Web site. In effect, students are witnessing information being created and are helping to create it.

This sense of original work empowers students in a meaningful way. Simple presentation programs, such as the newest versions of ClarisWorks and PowerPoint, enable students to incorporate Web sites into their work. For example, a student could present a background about Bosnia's troubles and then link to a present-day dialogue with a Bosnian student or a recent video clip of terrorist action in the country. Just the simple importing of images from the Net can enliven a paper or presentation.

Hypermedia programs, such as HyperStudio, HyperCard, and Digital Chisel, allow students to create sophisticated branching programs that meld text, imagery, and sound. And with the live links, the storage space needed to run these interactive files is relatively manageable. Each of these experiences enriches student learning, but each also involves additional skill in the accompanying software. Again, the librarian and teacher should work together to insure maximum learning with the least frustration. A number of issues must be addressed:

- Who will teach the authoring tools—the librarian, classroom teacher, or computer specialist?
- How will those skills be taught—as part of the content class, as a unit in a computer literacy course, or to a subset of the class as extra credit?
- How structured should the product be? Developing a template for students speeds their time, but requires more front-end work for the educator.
- How will classes be scheduled in terms of facilities—for computer labs, library research, Internet access (including video contact time), and formal instruction?
- How much does the teacher have to know about these technologies? Who else can help students in the process?

Who's Doing the Learning?

The incorporation of technology first requires educators to be comfortable with technology. Librarians need to carve out time to explore the Net and create Internet-rich products, such as interactive presentations on information literacy skills. But librarians also need to encourage teacher training through inservice workshops, online tutorials, local continuing education offerings, in-house mentoring, videotape courses, and user-friendly manuals. A binder of good Internet lessons can stimulate teacher ideas. Photocopying a particularly successful project description in the teacher's field of expertise can offer a model to replicate. Being a tech buddy is another effective way for two educators to help each other gain technological expertise. Once a successful application of the Net is made, the gateway is established to further Internet exploration and incorporation into the curriculum.

Lesley S. J. Farmer is the Library Media Specialist at Redwood High School Library in Larkspur, California

THE UPGRADE: EASING INTO TECHNOLOGY INTEGRATION

By Doug Johnson

Constructivists say you cannot learn something for which you have no frame of reference. One way to help your educators ease their way into integrating technology into their curricula is to help them take something they already do and add a technology "upgrade."

Below are ten common activities that teachers may already be doing and some ways technology can be used to "upgrade" the learning process.

Doug Johnson is the Director of Media and Technology at I.S.D. 77 Mankato (Minnesota) Public Schools.

Current Activity	Technology Upgrade	Benefits
1. Teacher Lecture	Computer presentation program (PowerPoint, HyperStudio).	Graphics, sounds, movies, and photographs to clearly illustrate concepts and heighten student interest. Easy to keep notes.
2. Student Writing	Word-processed, desktop published	Easily edited, spell-checked, handwriting-proof. Added illustrations or graphics. On-line peer review and commentary.
3. Student Research	Use electronic or on-line resources such as electronic encyclopedia, magazine index, or Internet resources.	Quickly accessed. Notes can be copied and pasted into rough draft. Sounds and pictures can be used in multimedia reports. Large number of resources means narrower focus on a topic and adds interest.
4. Book Reports	Use database with fields for title, author, publisher, date, genre, summary, and recommendation.	All students contribute to database. Concise reports can be used as a readers' advisory by future classes. Easily printed and distributed to class.
5. Math Problems	Use a spreadsheet to set up some basic math story problems.	Formulas and operations clearly visible. Charting and graphing capabilities. Convert data from original surveys into understandable information.
6. Plays, Skits, or Debates	Videotape the presentations.	Record for later analysis, sharing with parents. Editing possible. Save as example for future classes.
7. Create a Timeline	Use Timeliner or a drawing program.	Fast, simple, and easy to read. Possible to add graphics and modify time segments.
8. Student Speeches, Demonstrations or Lessons.	Videotape. Students use multimedia to accompany presentations.	Record for later analysis, sharing with parents. Editing possible. Save as example for future classes. Graphics, sounds, movies, and photographs can be used to clearly illustrate concepts, increase audience attention. Use slides in place of notes.
9. Drawings to Illustrate Concepts or Accompany Writing	Use a drawing or paint program.	Use features of drawing program to create meaningful original illustrations or modify clipart. Edit and use digital camera images or scanned images with writing for improved meaning.
10. Class Syllabus and Recommended Readings	Use a Web page creator and upload to school webserver.	Easily and quickly modified. Direct links to Internet readings. Can be accessed from home by parents.

PROFESSIONAL DEVELOPMENT THEY WILL CHEER FOR!

School Library Management in Today's World

By Linda Skeele

Teachers often get a pained expression on their faces at the mention of In-Service or Professional Development. In theory nothing could be better than spending a few days each year brushing up on the latest developments in technology and education, but far too often Professional Development (P.D.) is a dreaded term that brings to mind boring and irrelevant programs.

The media specialist, as the school's technology expert, must conduct many Professional Development classes. Technology, although inherently new and exciting, can be deadly dull if not presented properly. After years of attending and presenting such courses, here are some ideas and suggestions for technology Professional Development That They Will Cheer For.

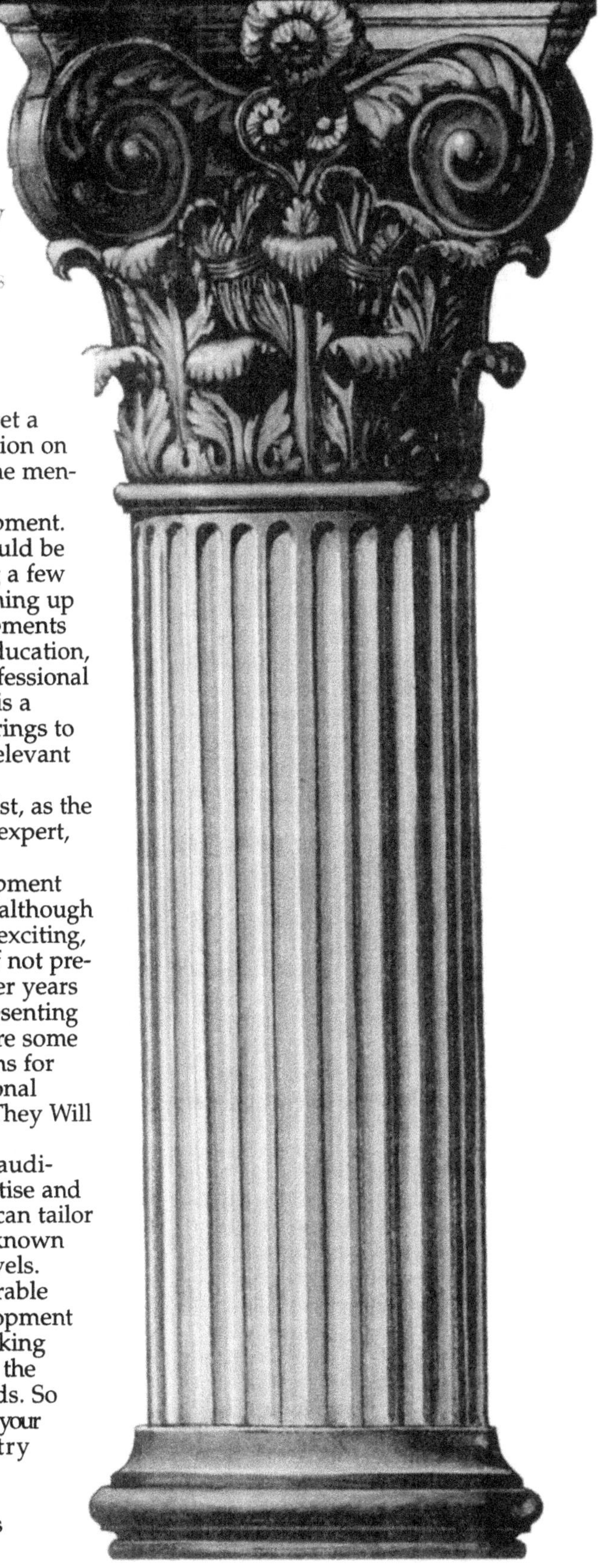

First, know your audience's level of expertise and interest so that you can tailor the presentation to known needs and ability levels. One key to a memorable Professional Development presentation is making the topic address the participants' needs. So while drafting your presentation, try to determine exactly how your teachers will use the information. How does this technology address their daily classroom needs? Why should they change their current methods to include this particular technology?

MAKE IT PRACTICAL

One of the best ways to address these goals is to make your examples something that teachers can use as soon as they leave. For example, I once taught a class on the spreadsheet function of ClarisWorks. How might a primary teacher use a spreadsheet for teaching? We came up with the Morning Weather Chart. All of our primary teachers spend a few minutes each morning putting weather statistics on a monthly chart, and most include a symbol to indicate the weather for that day.

To illustrate the spreadsheet functions, we made a large monthly chart to hang on the wall and symbols of each weather type. Instead of theory or general information about spreadsheets, we tied our entire lesson to the weather chart. The handout took our number of rainy days, snowy days, overcast and sunny days as examples for the teachers to follow as we led them through the process of creating a simple spreadsheet and printing a variety of graphs to illustrate the ratio of nice to poor weather days. Teachers left the session confident that they could recreate this simple spreadsheet with their classes.

Having selected as an example something that teachers can use in their classrooms, follow the introductory lesson with a work session in which teachers put their new knowledge to use. An hour-long work session for a six hour workshop is a good proportion. Post a few suggested ways to use the new software or equipment, and add to the list as teachers make suggestions during the presentation. These give participants a place to begin instead of wasting time trying to come up with an original idea for their project. Allocate time for each teacher/group to share their work.

LARGE vs. SMALL

Large class instruction is usually the least effective method for technology. Even with computers for all participants, trying to move around a room of 30 computers is less than ideal. However, small group sessions can be time consuming if the material has to be presented to an entire faculty. In this instance, a train-the-trainer model may work best.

Often technology sessions will cover several products. In this case try to find a different presenter for each item and rotate groups on a schedule. For example, you have four software programs and forty attendees. Teachers can divide into four groups and rotate through 30 minute sessions. We have successfully used this setup with as many as six different programs and types of equipment. With this arrangement, the technology expert is free to float and troubleshoot.

Someone who has just learned the material often makes an excellent teacher as this person knows the problems encountered, and what is really important for utilizing the program. One of our best Professional Development courses used this technique. We had received a number of pieces of new software at the end of school year. Each teacher in the school was given one to three of the new programs to take home for the summer with the understanding that the teacher would be responsible for presenting the programs to the rest of the school.

Don't always allocate the final hour as a Preview Time for teachers to go to the computers and work with the software themselves. If this is the last item on the agenda, there is a tendency for tired teachers to not stay on task. Try scheduling the Preview Times at earlier times. Consider having worksheets with specific questions teachers have to answer using the programs. Give a prize to the person who comes up with the best classroom use for the program. In small group work, think of ways to come up with different groupings. The classic strategy for this has always been counting off. Another tactic is to construct the groups ahead of time to come up with a good mix of teachers and abilities.

VALUE ADDED FEATURES

Print an agenda. Not only does it inform teachers where they are in the session, but it helps to keep the presenter on schedule. Use handouts to include the previously mentioned instruction guides, up-to-date price and product information, samples of what the product can do (such as generate crossword puzzles) and a tips sheet. A tips sheet can include shortcuts not covered in the session, information of interest to only some participants, and suggestions for using the program, such as tie-ins to other subjects.

> Introductory sessions should be bare bones basic. Save the shortcuts, enhancements, and seldom used features for another time. Go through the manufacturer's manual and cut, cut, cut. Bring the 60 page spreadsheet chapter down to a written Instruction Guide no more than one or two pages long. The goal is a written set of directions so clear that an elementary student could follow it. You want your teachers to be able to use their Instruction Guide months later without wondering what those hastily scribbled notes really mean.
> Our school purchased a loose leaf notebook for every staff member when we began our transformation into a high technology school. All Professional Development handouts are kept in this notebook near our computers. With the simple Instruction Guides in this notebook, it is seldom necessary to refer to the massive manuals that come with technology products.

Participants start with a positive impression of your session when they receive a handout with an attractive cover sheet that includes a few graphics, your name, address, and phone number. Instruction guides ensure that participants can concentrate on your presentation and not on to taking notes. Complete price and product guides eliminate the need to repeat and spell out the information several times. Software information should include the exact machine configuration needed for the program.

GUIDE ON THE SIDE

Any presentation to more than five participants can use an assistant. If the assistant knows the material, the two of you can carry on a dialogue and remind each other of any missed points and steps. Lacking a great partner, look to a teenage student, a fellow teacher or friend. The role of the assistant is to hand out and collect papers, bring late arrivals up to date, move equipment, and answer some questions.

TICK TOCK

Begin at exactly the minute the program was advertised. This way you start strong and positive, not, "we'll wait a few minutes while some more get here." The same thing applies after restroom and lunch breaks. Announce the time to reconvene and adhere to it. This tells the audience that both their time and yours is too important to waste.

Begin the session with a brief introduction of yourself (if necessary) and state exactly what the teacher should know by the end of the session. If it is a day long session, plan several activities to break up the tedium of sitting for hours. If you have only one or two computers and a large group, try selecting different people from the audience to role play as students. If necessary thirty people can sit on the floor around the computer to see.

Professional speakers suggest beginning your talk with a joke to relax the audience. Plan several humor breaks. If you can't remember jokes, have a repertory of "dumb things I've done" stories that you can tell when the presentation begins to languish.

In addition to breaking up the presentation with humor, contemplate giving out unexpected prizes. Most media specialists cruise the exhibitor's hall at conventions in search of freebies, and this is a perfect place to hand out pencils, note pads, balloons, mouse pads, posters and other technology freebies. After the first, "Great question Mary. You deserve a key chain for that," you will find the attention and participation level instantly higher.

At home, conduct a final check the day before the presentation to make sure everything is working. Repeat the check at least an hour before the session. When you go to another site, if possible, bring all your own equipment, no matter how much of it there is. There seems to be an axiom that if a program or piece of equipment is ever to give trouble, it will be during a presentation; therefore, always have a backup plan. Think worst case scenario (your only computer dies), and see if you can still conduct the session. If you have planned your handouts and displays well, the Professional Development can continue.

Be prepared to change your plans quickly. When presenting to an unknown audience, I conduct a quick survey asking for a show of hands with a couple questions to learn the background of the group. This information immediately tells me whether to cover the basics, or skip to the advanced details of a program. To do this, have several versions of your presentation ready. When the group turns out to have a better understanding than you were to led to believe, or when the group learns the material more quickly than anticipated, you have your tip sheet and displays with extra information ready to use.

EXTRAS

For different pieces of software, make banners with the name of the software and post all the sheets relating to that piece. Examples of student-generated work are a plus. I prefer displays to passing work around because when you pass out examples, those in the back of the class often never see the work.

Almost any technology In-Service is enhanced by a table display of related technology materials. This is the place for a collection of your books and audiovisuals on the subject, magazines on technology, and other software related to the session topic. This is both public relations for the media center, and fallback material for the times the session is completed early. These items can be included as a bibliography page in the handout.

If I had to give only two pieces of advice on a great Professional Development it would be K.I.S.S. and Donald O'Conner. K.I.S.S. is "Keep It Simple, Stupid," or stick to the basics. Donald O'Conner gave the classic audience-holding advice in the movie, *Singing In The Rain* when he sang "Make 'em laugh, make 'em laugh, make 'em laugh." If teachers leave your In-Service laughing, chances are they feel confident in their mastery of the material. This will make yours the Professional Development That They Cheer For!

Linda Skeele is a Library Media Specialist at Western Elementary School in Georgetown, Kentucky,

> *While drafting your presentation, try to determine exactly how your teachers will use the information. How does this technology address their daily classroom needs? Why should they change their current methods to include this particular technology?*

> *Almost any technology In-Service is enhanced by a table display of related technology materials.*

TOOLS OF THE TRADE

PHILADELPHIA LIBRARY POWER: Collaboration Form

By DEBRA GNIEWEK

Collaboration is a key theme in *Information Power: Building Partnerships for Learning* (American Library Association, 1998). According to *Information Power*, the information literacy standards for student learning provide "a concrete starting place for designing integrated instruction and for collaborative planning, teaching, and evaluation" (p. 63). In 1994 the School District of Philadelphia received a $1.2 million, three-year Library Power Grant for 30 elementary and middle school libraries. Each Library Power School has a librarian whose schedule is flexible. This provides teachers, students, and others ongoing access to the library, and it allows librarians to work with staff and children on research projects, to update collections and technology, and to plan projects that make the library media center invaluable to schools. When the library is used flexibly, collaborative planning between the librarian and teachers becomes essential. As Library Power evolved in the School District of Philadelphia, the Library Power librarians and Sandra Hughes, the Director of the Philadelphia Library Power initiative, worked to develop a collaboration planning form. The form is used by the librarians during monthly meetings with individual teachers and grade groups in order to create and teach units that integrate content and information literacy standards. The librarians found the form to be constructive for collaborative planning, and many of the teachers considered collaborative planning with this form to be a meaningful professional development activity.

Debra Gniewek is a librarian on special assignment to the School District of Philadelphia (Pennsylvania)

TOOLS OF THE TRADE
TEACHER / LIBRARIAN COLLABORATIVE UNIT PLANNING

Teacher/Team/Grade _____

▶ UNIT OF STUDY	▶ CONTENT AREA
Standards Addresses	Essential Questions, Goals, and Objectives *(What do you want your students to learn?)*
Resources (include URLs)	Proposed Learning Activities
Description of Culminating Task	Assessment
Responsibilities: Teacher(s)	Responsibilities: Librarian
Instructional Strategies	Resource Distribution

PLANNING TIMES: **LIBRARY TIME NEEDED:**

Editor's Note: In response to reader requests, we have initiated a new department called Tools of the Trade. Each month we will feature a one page reproducible item that is designed for you to share with your school community. It might be a lesson plan, a worksheet or game, or an executive summary of an important library-related issue for your administrators or colleagues. Each carries permission for you to reproduce the material within the building in which you work.

THE TECHNOLOGY CONNECTION:
BUILDING A SUCCESSFUL LIBRARY MEDIA PROGRAM

CHAPTER 3
SOUND FOOTINGS: THE LIBRARY MEDIA SPECIALIST BUILDS THE FOUNDATION

TEN TERRIFIC TIPS FOR ELEMENTARY TEACHERS

By M. Gale Lyons

How to Improve Students' Skills and Maximize Their Love of Learning

Are you just beginning to teach technology in your elementary school? If so, perhaps you can benefit from what I learned through trial and error during my first two years as a teacher in a high-tech elementary school. Our classrooms are equipped with EduQuest computers and we also have several in our media center and in each department. If your district has not already provided you with a large screen monitor and a converter that connects to a "teaching station" computer, you need to campaign to acquire such a setup.

It's essential to have a CD-ROM drive installed in this computer so you can use some of the many outstanding CD-ROM programs with your students. Among our favorites are *Storybook Weaver* by MECC, *3-D Dinosaur Adventure* by Knowledge Adventure, *Microsoft Encarta* and *Microsoft Works*, and *Around the World in 80 Days* by Electronic Arts.

Here are 10 tried-and-true tips for using technology with your elementary school students:

1. **Use size 36 point type to share favorite poems on your large screen monitor.** As students read poems aloud together, use your mouse to point to each word. Thus you have an electronic big book for teaching reading and phonics as you share the delights of poetry with the entire group.

2. **Type students' learning log information for them as they dictate their thoughts and print the on-screen information into their logs.** This really helps those reading and spelling skills!

3. **Select outstanding CD-ROMs and use them as teaching tools.** You can streamline time-on-task and actually teach three times as much information to students who are enthusiastic about learning.

4. **Use the large screen monitor to introduce a topic or skill, then give students time to practice it on their own computers.** During this phase of learning, the "Teacher Station" becomes a "Student Station" and is used along with the other computers in the room. Students will actually gather around the monitor and "reteach" themselves.

5. **Use a locking program to keep students from wiping out icons or deleting important files.** Our technology specialist wrote a program at home and gave it to us. The same program sells nationwide to high schools, middle schools and elementary schools and has been very favorably received. For more information, write to SuperLock Pro, JL Programming, 10551 Regent Circle, Naples, Florida 33942.

6. **Link up with keypals in another part of the country.** During our second year, we studied insects with our keypals, a second-grade class in New York State. They told us what they were learning in their insect research. We shared our adventures with Florida's abundant insect population and sent them a spiral-bound book with computer graphics about our experiences with aggressive red ants.

7. **Use technology to share your students' projects with others.** We used *LinkWay Live!* (IBM Corporation) to share students' reports on dinosaurs with the whole school.

8. **Improve your students' spelling with a talking speller program.** I used a pilot program, *Talking Speller* by JL Programming, to enter each week's spelling words on our large screen monitor. The program then took over quizzing students and giving such verbal feedback as "Excellent!" or "That's OK. Nobody's perfect."

9. **Encourage peer teaching of technology.** As second graders became more comfortable with technology, they frequently sat in what I called the "pilot seat" and acted as student teachers for their classmates. I was always there as needed for backup.

10. **Share your students' success stories with the community.** This can really pay off! Our school board, with the support of several community groups, recently okayed funding for $30,000,000 worth of technology, training, and support services for our district over the next five years. **TC**

M. Gale Lyons is a Grade Two Teacher at Laurel Oak Elementary School in Naples, Florida.

What's In A Name?

By Joe Miller

While end users think of file names primarily as a way to identify the content of a file, computer programs often assign special meaning to the file extension (usually a three-character string following a period, although it can be longer on some systems). For instance, on DOS/Windows machines, *MS Word* documents typically end in .DOC, *Excel* files in .XLS, and *PowerPoint* files in .PPT. *Netscape* (and other Web clients) recognize HTML pages on the Web as HTML files by the extension .HTM or .HTML. Although HTML files are simple text, they usually include links to a host of binary file types including graphics, multimedia elements such as sound and video, and special document formats such as *Adobe's Portable Document Format* (PDF) or *PostScript* (PS) files. The *Netscape* General Preferences Helper area reveals a long list of file types with corresponding file extension and how the browser will handle them. While *Netscape* can deal with some non-HTML files automatically, the usual action the browser takes when an unusual file type is encountered is to ask the user to identify the appropriate helper or plug-in application. A helper application is a separate program launched by the browser when needed for a specific task. The TELNET software, often needed to connect to a library online catalog, is one such helper. A plug-in program, such as *MacroMedia's Shockwave*, also extends the functionality of the browser but, unlike a helper, it runs seamlessly with the browser, not as a separate application that must be launched and then exited in its own window. The user must identify and configure these additional applications. While many of these programs can be downloaded from the Web, the process can be complicated by the fact that many are in a compressed file format requiring additional steps before installation.

Different Kinds of Files on the Web
Document Files

Most Web documents are HTML files—marked up text files that can be displayed by any Web browser. Other document file types that may be encountered are plain text files (.TXT), rich text files (.RTF), and standard word processing files (.DOC). Controlling the final appearance and display of a document is important to many publishers and is sometimes an absolute requirement (such as a government document like an IRS 1040 form). But the nature of the Web and HTML is that much of how a document will look is dependent on the platform, the type of browser, and the user's preferences. *Adobe PostScript* (PS) and *Portable Document Format* (PDF) files offer a solution to this problem, assuring the Web publisher that the information will display consistently. Common file extensions for PostScript files are .PS, .EPS, .PFA, and .PFB. While *PostScript* is excellent for document description, it is not as well suited to document interchange. The *Adobe* PDF format was developed for better portability and is more common on the Internet; it is widely used for government documents.

To be viewed in *Netscape*, PDF files require the *Adobe Acrobat* plug-in, which can be downloaded from the Adobe software Web site (www.adobe.com). This program is a self-extracting file (.EXE). It should be downloaded to a temporary location on the hard drive and extracted by double clicking on the file name. The setup program then runs, installing the program.

Images and Graphic Formats

Much of the appeal of the Web has centered around the creative use of graphics to enhance information. Many graphic file formats are associated with specific graphics programs such as *Paintbrush* (PCS files), *Corel Photopaint* (CPT files) or *Adobe Photoshop* (PSD files). Images are usually one of three types: bilevel (black and white), line art (cartoon), or continuous tone (photographic). Because image files can be extremely large, many have compression schemes built in. Some of these schemes result in a loss of image data and quality. The GIF file (CompuServe's Graphics Interchange Format) has become a standard for the numerous graphics often embedded in Web pages (called inline images in HTML), since it is often the case that rapid transmission of the image is more important than final image quality. GIF images are small files and small images. In addition, the image data gradually builds as it downloads, allowing the user to stop the transfer if it is not of interest. Two image file types that are better for large photographic images are TIFF (Aldus Tagged Image Format) and JPEG (Joint Photographic Experts Group). The TIFF structure lets an artist go quickly to a specific part of the image; JPEG's compressed format is good for storing graduations of color but since it is "lossy" compression, some data is lost every time it is used. Consequently, successive "saves" of an image using this format can cause significant quality loss. While *Netscape* and other browsers can display both GIF and JPEG files without additional software support, other image types such as BitMapped images (BMP files) and TIFF files will need viewers such as the TMS ViewDirector Imaging plug-in (www.tmsinc.com/download/index.html). Web authors usually convert image files to either the GIF or JPEG format to eliminate the need for the end user to locate another viewer.

Sound Files, Video, and Multimedia

While the use of sound on Web pages is sometimes of marginal value, well-used multimedia elements can enhance learning opportunities on the Web, make sites more accessible to the visually impaired, and provide entertainment. Some common sound file types are .WAV, .AU, and .AIF files. These files will require specific hardware (sound cards and speakers) along with appropriate media player software, which is usually included with the hardware. Some recent audio developments on the Web require special plug-in software, such as the RealAudio player (www.realaudio.com) for .RA files.

Video capture cards that allow the conversion of video from a camcorder or VCR to computer files have become fairly inexpensive and easy to use, but the use of video on the Web is still constrained by the large amounts of data that must be stored, transmitted, and displayed. The computer must move this data in a short time to avoid "jerkiness" of the video. Even with some of the techniques that are available to compress these files, large file size continues to make the use of video on the Web problematic. Some common video formats that may be encountered are AVI (Audio/Video Interleave—Windows), MOV (AppleQuickTime), and the MPEG (Motion Picture Experts Group) standard.

Many companies involved with multimedia authoring software are interested in developing Web capability for their products. Macromedia, Inc. has developed a browser plug-in called *Shockwave* that allows the display of multimedia presentations created using its *Authorware* and *Director* software packages. (The latter have Macromedia's .DCR extension.) Their Web site (www.macromedia.com/shockwave/) has interesting educational examples, including interactive books and programs, such as the *My Computerized House* story, an interactive expedition into Mayan culture called *MayaQuest*, and the science adventure *Tidepool to Tundra*. The site also has the needed plug-in software available for downloading.

Common Internet File Formats

Category	File ext.	Name	Type	Viewer/Program
Text	txt	text or ASCII file	text	DOS, any text editor
	rtf	rich text format	text	text editor
	doc	document	binary	word processing
	html	hypertext markup language	text	Web browser/text editors
	ps	PostScript	text	PostScript Printer, Desktop Publishing
Graphics	pdf	Portable Document Format	text	Adobe Acroreader, Amber
	gif	Graphic Interchange Format	binary	Many graphics programs
	jpeg	Joint Photographic Experts Group	binary	Many graphics programs
	tiff	Tagged Image File Format	binary	Many graphics programs
	bmp	BitMap Image	binary	Many graphics programs
	cpt	Corel Photopaint	binary	Corel Photopaint
	pad	Photoshop file	binary	Adobe Photoshop
	pcs	Picture file	binary	MS Paintbrush
Sound	au	Unix sound file	binary	Netscape
	wav	Windows sound file	binary	Media Player, sound editing programs
	avi	Audio/Visual Interleave—Windows	binary	Media Player, other video players
Video	mov	Apple QuickTime	binary	Apple/Mac
	mpeg	Motion Picture Experts Group	binary	Video for Windows, mpeg player
Compression	arc	archiving utility	binary	pkarc
	zip	archiving utility	binary	pkzip and pkunzip
	exe	self extracting	binary	DOS
Encoding	UUEncode	binary to text encoding	binary/text	unix program
	MIME	Multipurpose Internet Mail Extensions	binary/text	Built into many mailers such as *Eudora*

Compression

Because larger files take more time to download, making files as small as possible is important in the Web environment. File compression programs control the process of "squeezing" bytes out of a file to reduce its size and putting them back later when needed. It's the electronic equivalent of freeze-dried food—it's not ready to eat, but it is easier to carry. While some programs create file formats that automatically have some level of compression, sometimes the user wishes to apply compression to a specific data or program file for portability reasons (to fit on a floppy disk, for instance). Most of the programs downloaded from the Web are in a compressed format and must be extracted before they can be used. Fortunately, many of these are now self-extracting executable files. For Windows-based systems, these files will have an .EXE extension and only have to be run to be extracted. Macintosh sees the .SEA (self extracting archive) naming convention handled in a similar fashion. Typically, the user downloads the file to a temporary directory and then launches the program by typing its name and the RUN line in Windows or by double clicking on the name from the File Manager, Explorer, or Finder view. The single file will then expand into numerous individual files, one of which usually is a setup or installation file, which is then run. (Sometimes this will start by itself immediately after extracting.) After setup is complete, the temporary directory and compressed file can be deleted to free up hard disk space. Another common compression format is the ZIP file. These files require the shareware program PKUNZIP (www.pkware.com) or WinZip (www.winzip.com) to be expanded. On the Macintosh, .SIT and .SEA files are common compressed formats and are handled by the Stuffit Expander program (www.aladdinsys.com/).

Encoding Formats

Computers handle text files differently than binary files. E-mail systems are designed to move around text messages, not binary files. This limitation can be overcome by encoding, which is a process that allows the transfer of binary data through a text-only connection. Binary data is encoded into text and decoded back to binary at the receiving end. The UUEncode and UUDecode programs (UUE files) are one approach; BinHex is similar, but is used with Macintosh mail programs. The MIME (Multipurpose Internet Mail Extensions) system also is used by e-mail systems to automate the encoding and decoding of binary data. This process allows e-mail messages to have word processing documents or other binary files attached to them. Any e-mail software that has an Attach File option usually supports all of these methods. Of course, both the sender and receiver must have e-mail systems that support this process; older mainframe-based mail systems are notorious for displaying these attachments as gibberish. When that happens, the sender may have to send the ASCII equivalent of the document within the body of the message instead of an attached file.

Conclusion

Understanding the basics of how to create, save, view, and share computer files has always been one of the first steps to computer literacy. While most users have learned these basics in the context of working on their standalone machine, our growing dependence on the Internet has created a need to expand our understanding. While programs like *Netscape* make it easy to browse the Web, additional knowledge and skills are needed to take advantage of its full potential. In this new environment of networked resources, we must be not only computer literate but also Web literate. **TC**

Joe Miller is Coordinator of Computing Services, School of Library and Information Science at the University of Kentucky in Lexington.

For further reading:

Kientzle, Tim. 1995. *Internet File Formats*. Scottsdale, AZ; Coriolis Group Books. (CD-ROM included.)

Tittel, Ed, Susan Price, and James Michael Stewart. 1997. *Web Graphics Sourcebook*, New York, NY; Wiley and Sons. (CD-ROM included.)

Zhang, Allison B. 1997. *File Formats on the Internet: A Guide for PC Users*, SLA Press.

Web Sites of Interest
Plug-ins and Browser Enhancements:

www.*Netscape*.com	*Netscape* home page
www.download.com	CNET Site for getting many helpers and plug-ins
www.browserwatch.com	Internet World's Web Site for Browser Development
access.adobe.com/	Adobe Software
www.macromedia.com/shockwave/	Macromedia Shockwave site
www.realaudio.com/	Real Audio Web Site
www.pkware.com	pkunzip program
www.winzip.com	winzip program
www.aladinsys.com	Stuffit Expander

File Format Help on the Web:

www.matisse.net/files/formats.htm
www.jwpepper.com/multimedia.html
VTGinc.com/ebennett/

ALTERNATIVE EDUCATION

MATCHING TEACHING AND LEARNING STYLES

By Gil Caudill

All of our students learn in different ways. They process information uniquely, and when it is time to share that information, they have preferred ways in which they can best share. Therefore, varying our teaching methods to include at least three basic learning modalities—auditory, visual, and tactile—in our teaching presentations will meet the needs of most of our students. The problem is that on the days we are focusing on one modality, students who learn best in one of the other two ways may lose interest or have difficulty staying focused. It is preferable to include multiple modalities within each lesson, and technology can help us do that.

The idea of multiple modalities is demonstrated by Harold Gardner's multiple intelligences (*Frames of Mind*, Basic Books, 1983). While I don't necessarily agree that his listings are intelligences, they certainly are learning preferences and abilities.

Linguistic intelligence applies to someone who thinks in words and prefers to learn by listening, reading, and verbalizing. This type of learner would benefit from word processors, prompted writing programs, crossword puzzle generating software, speech output programs, and word games to capitalize on their learning and expressing strengths. Written or verbalized activities are especially appropriate for them.

Someone who likes to categorize and classify is said to have *logical mathematical intelligence*. These learners think conceptually and logically, look for abstract patterns, and enjoy arithmetic problems. They would benefit from database and spreadsheet programs, problem-solving software and activities, and strategy games. Concrete, sequential activities, such as "Read this paragraph and improve the idea," will help keep them focused.

People with *spatial intelligence* think in images and pictures.

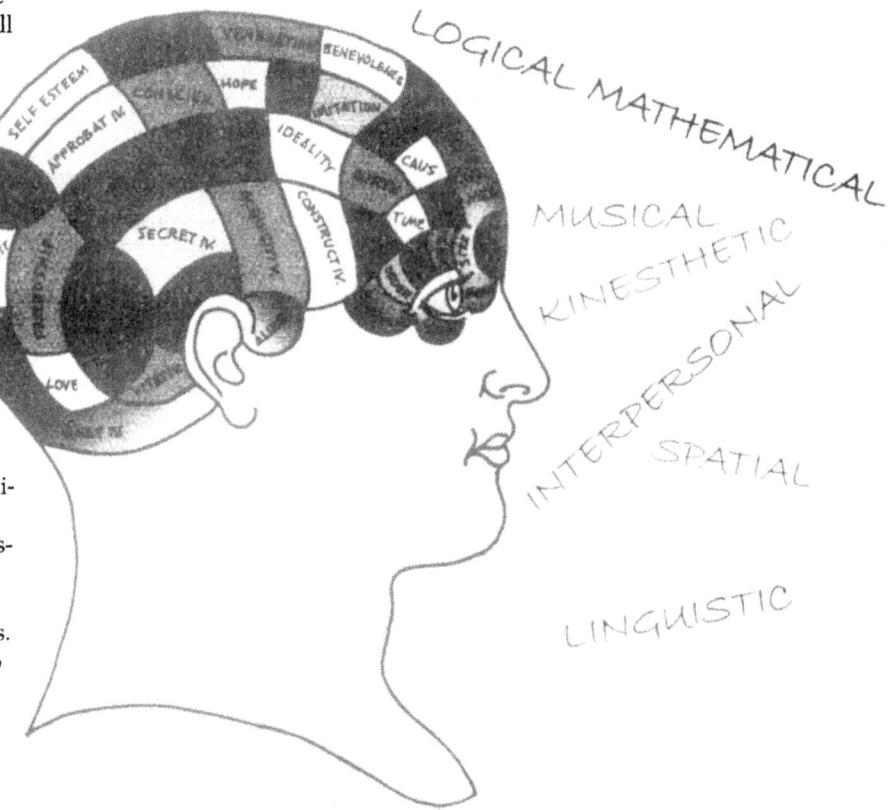

Learning for them would be easiest if it included draw and paint programs, maps, graphic production and hypermedia, and reading programs that use visual clues. Make appropriate software or materials with which to construct available to these learners.

Those who learn best with rhythm and melody possess *musical intelligence*. Reading programs with auditory or musical clues are good for them. Music as a reward, story-song combinations, letter/sound music association programs, and hypermedia would make learning easier for this type of learner. The ability to add music to their writing also will encourage these students to use their strengths.

Students with *kinesthetic intelligence* process knowledge through bodily sensations and learn best through movement, touch, and activity. Computer software that uses touch windows or a mouse or joystick will get them involved physically. Keyboarding, arcade-format instructional games, and animated graphics programs will hold their interest.

Interpersonal intelligence is demonstrated by interest in others. These are the students who always know what is going on socially. They learn best in cooperative learning environments, and they quickly become interested in programs that can be turned into social activities. Telecommunication, key pals, and social issues studies will hold their attention.

Intrapersonal intelligence is an independent-focused intelligence. These students prefer to work alone rather than in groups. They enjoy tutorials, self-paced programs, and computer programs that involve self-awareness or self-improvement. A possible formula for independent research is 1 person + 1 Internet + 1 multimedia + 1 letter + 2 books = project. This helps diversify their information-gathering, plus it requires us to teach them interviewing, business letter writing, multimedia, and Internet skills.

An important component for multiple modality teaching is to effectively assess our students. Educational assessment has historically focused on abilities versus disabilities. If certain scores were not achieved on tests, it was often assumed that learning had not taken place. Often, particularly in special populations, students are capable of performing the function but are unable to read the questions. However, portfolio assessment is primarily a demonstration of accomplishments of the students rather than identification of needs. If multiple media are used for portfolio assessment, it is easy to modify, update, and access.

Initial assessment of students could include performance tasks with optional media or materials available for students to choose. How students prefer to perform a task and how they choose to express it can tell educators a lot. When these preferences and abilities are incorporated into prescriptive plans, there is little need to further label students.

Future studies

Another teaching component of which we are increasingly aware is the need to include the study of the future. It should be our responsibility to include aspects of futures studies in each of our lessons. This is an integral part of preparing our students to be lifelong learners. In conjunction with futures studies, we need to give them skills in writing computing, and working with multimedia.

Activity examples
Visual activity:
1. Use barcode-making software to create a barcode that runs a videodisc segment without sound. (Pioneer makes freeware called *Enhanced Bar N Coder* for Macintosh, and other, more multifaceted barcoding software is available for $75 to $150.)
2. Ask the students to identify systems in the video. For example, there are several systems that are necessary for a city to operate: communication, transportation, governmental, health care, and economic.
3. Require students to draw their interpretation of how one of their identified systems will function 25 years in the future. (A longer class activity is to have students bring in building materials, such as cardboard and plastic containers, in order to construct a city of the future after they have studied the systems necessary for a city to operate.)

Auditory activity:
1. Play a segment from a movie, audiotape, or videodisc without the video.

> *It is preferable to include multiple modalities within each lesson, and technology can help us do that.*

2. Ask students to identify what is happening.
3. Ask students to record their interpretations on an audiotape of what it would sound like if it were from another planet, or to record their interpretations in a hypermedia software.

Tactile activity:
1. Create a box with a cover to keep students from seeing what is in the box.
2. Have students feel two or three different textures.
3. Ask students to imagine what these textures would feel like after 50 years in a stream or at the beach.
4. Ask students to write a scenario that explains the change, results, and possible uses for the object.

Scenarios could be the final part of most activities and could be drawn or written (visual or tactile), sung or recorded (auditory), or acted (tactile). They should be focused toward the future. The more students write about, consider, and study the future, the more they will realize they have the power to shape and affect it.

It is possible to use any academic discipline, such as social studies, science, or language arts, in these stations. And it is preferable to teach along a particular topic or with a particular theme in mind to give students a context in which to use the knowledge. It also is possible to focus on more specific learning styles than the three mentioned.

All of the activities may be mixed to give a significant number of possibilities. The idea is to tap the learning and expressing styles of all of the students. When coupled with future studies and the concept of scenario writing, we can give students skills and knowledge that will serve them well throughout their lives. **TC**

Gil Caudill is a Teacher at Ruediger Elementary School in Tallahassee, Florida. He presently serves as the chair of the Futures Studies Division of the National Association for Gifted Children.

HEAD FOR THE EDGE

By Doug Johnson

Teaching Ethical Technology Behaviors

Doug Johnson

Much to my children's embarrassment, I've never been shy about letting people know when I find their behavior impolite. My kids burrow a little deeper in their movie theater seats when I tell the talkers in front of us to pipe down. My son tries to look as unrelated to me as possible when I tell a group that their bad language is offensive. I've been known to explain to dog owners why they should pick up after their dogs, to students why they should say please and thank you to cafeteria helpers, and to smokers why they should believe signs that say, "No Smoking." My children don't understand why I am not popped in the nose on a regular basis. I don't really enjoy these little fits of Miss Mannerism, but I am firmly convinced that if everyone rationally admonished others of their bad behavior when they saw it, we would soon be living in a far more civilized world. As educators, this job of teaching polite, and more importantly, ethical behaviors, is not an option but our duty.

In direct and indirect ways, children begin to learn ethical values from birth. While the family and church are assigned the primary responsibility for a child's ethical education, schools have traditionally had the societal charge to teach and reinforce some moral values, especially those directly related to citizenship and school behaviors. And since most of the ethical issues that surround technology deal with societal and school behaviors, they are an appropriate and necessary part of the school curriculum.

Business Ethics magazine suggests that businesses take a proactive approach to ethical issues. That advice is also good for schools and classrooms: Media specialists and teachers must:

• Articulate ethical values related to technology.

• Clearly display lists and create handouts of conduct codes and acceptable technology use. The "Ten Commandments of Computer Ethics" by the Computer Ethics Institute at *http://www.cpsr.org/program/ethics/cei.html* is a good list to use as a model.

• Reinforce ethical behaviors and react to non-ethical behaviors. Technology use behaviors should be treated no differently than other behaviors – good or bad –and the consequences of student behaviors should be the same. It is important not to over react to incidences of technological misuse.

• Model ethical behaviors. Students learn more from what we do than from what we say. All rules of ethical conduct we expect from our students, we ourselves must model. Verbalization of how we personally make moral decisions is a very powerful teaching tool as well.

• Create technology environments that help students avoid temptations. Computer screens that are easily monitored (no pun intended), passwords not written down or left easily found, and the habit of logging out of secure network systems all help remove the opportunities for technology misuse in the media center or classroom.

• Encourage discussion of ethical issues. "Cases," whether from news sources or from actual school events, can provide superb discussion starters and should be used when students are actually learning computer skills. Students need practice in creating meaningful analogies between the virtual world and the physical world. How is reading another person's e-mail without their permission like and unlike reading their physical mail?

• Stress the consideration of principles rather than relying on a detailed set of rules. Although sometimes more difficult to enforce in a consistent manner, a set of a few guidelines rather than lengthy set of specific rules is more beneficial to students in the long run.

By applying guidelines rather than following rules, students engage in higher level thinking processes and learn behaviors that will continue into their next classroom, their homes, and their adult lives. Here are mine.

Additionally, students' understandings of ethic concepts need to be assessed. Technology use privileges should not be given to

> **Johnson's 3 P's of Technology Ethics:**
>
> 1. Privacy – I will protect my privacy and respect the privacy of others.
>
> 2. Property – I will protect my property and respect the property of others.
>
> 3. a(P)propriate Use – I will use technology in constructive ways and in ways that do not break the rules of my family, church, school, or government.

students until they have demonstrated that they know and can apply ethical standards and school policies. Testing of appropriate use needs to be done especially prior to student gaining online privileges such as e-mail accounts or Internet access. The school should keep evidence of testing on file in case there is a question of whether there has been adequate instruction about appropriate use.

Schools also have an obligation to educate parents about ethical technology use. Through school newsletters, talks at parent organization meetings, and through school orientation programs, the school staff needs to inform and enlist the aid of parents in teaching and enforcing good technology practices.

As information professionals, we are in a unique position to remind other educators that it is not enough to teacher our students how to use technology, but we must also teach them how to use it well. But don't do it around your children. It's embarrassing!

Doug Johnson is the District Media Supervisor for the Mankato (Minnesota) Public Schools and can be reached by e-mail at djohns1@west.isd77.k12.mn.us (or palsdaj@vax1.mankato.msus.edu.) Doug's new book, The Indispensible Teacher's Guide to Computer Skills, *will be published this month.*

Building the Structure: The Library Media Specialist as Carpenter

After the foundation is poured, a new house takes shape quickly. In a few days or weeks, the framing is constructed, walls are put up, windows and doors are put in, and the roof is shingled. The house looks almost ready to move into. However, the finish work inside the structure takes a long time. Electrical wiring, plumbing, insulation, drywall, taping, painting, molding, flooring, countertops, cabinets, and appliances require painstaking work, each by a different subcontractor.

The library media specialist's role is to teach the research framework and provide students with the technology and information literacy skills needed to complete the "finish" work of the structure. This chapter contains articles dealing with many aspects of creating this framework and teaching the information literacy skills necessary to sustain it.

The desired end result is problem-solving students who know how to formulate a task, search for information, evaluate whether the information is applicable, and then synthesize it into new meaning.

A number of models of effective student research practices are included in this chapter. By allowing students to "practice" within a formalized research framework, library media specialists are teaching them the skills they will need to be productive adults in an information-rich society. Other articles cover performance-based and standards-based assessments.

With technology available as an assessment tool, many classroom teachers encourage students to use multimedia presentations to present their findings. There is more to the use of these software packages than just regurgitating information. This chapter includes a model for effective student use of multimedia as an assessment tool, as well as articles dealing with technical aspects of multimedia use, rubrics that cover both technology and information literacy skills, and concepts to include in curriculum writing.

SEARCHING

How to Teach the 'Net

By Lesley S.J. Farmer

Internet has been described as a room full of books scattered all over the floor, with someone saying, "Go ahead and dig around—there are some great treasures." No wonder librarians are inclined to look with horror at the relative chaos of the Internet world!

How do we teach access to this ephemerous cloud of data? As with other reference tools, we must first learn to navigate it ourselves. Instruction methods include courses, conferences, collegial help, manuals, and—last but not least—cyberspace surfing.

Learn with a Collaborator

When teaching others, the key is hands-on, regardless of group size. For a large class, you can prepare simulated Internet sessions for the group to follow if phone access is a problem.

As you begin training, remember that those working closest with you can bounce back ideas most easily, and help you polish your delivery. In fact, for novice Internet-navigating librarians, collaborative exploratory sessions with a staff member or strong student aide techie are often the best method of instruction through learning.

There are two viewpoints about how to teach the Internet. One view holds that the Internet is a tool and access to it should be taught the same way that we might teach the characteristics of a dictionary. The other view is that application should drive the instruction, just as curiosity about a current event leads to instruction on how to use a magazine index.

Show the Entire Process

In the tool model, the learner tends to browse the Internet for interesting "stuff." In the latter, a subject approach is used in instruction. In either case, learners need to see the entire process: log-on, search strategy, database/file location, document retrieval and downloading, and log-off. They also need to see the breadth of sources: from weather forecasts to movie reviews, from Spanish-language news to Project Gutenberg, from educator chat sessions to federal health reform documents, from ephemeral memos to Steven King's latest book online.

To assure good results in front of your audience, it's a good idea is to store successful searches ahead of time, using bookmarks or personal folders. You can also save searches using file or screen dumps and later print out those search sessions to use as examples for your learners.

Learners also need to see the structure of the library's Internet gateway or "access road" and what applications are provided: e-mail, electronic bulletin boards, conferences, remote sites, online databases, and file transfer protocol (FTP). In fact, most telecommunications services include far more than Internet access. How are applications linked? Does front-end software enable the user to develop a search offline? These questions need to be answered when instructing users.

Include Theory and Practice

Instruction should strike a balance between theory and practice. Each concept should be introduced, explained, and tested out. A basic glossary is also a must. Other training aids include "cheat sheets" of commands, sample searches, lists of recommended Internet sources, and simulation tutorial disks. Overhead transparencies of Internet sessions are valuable backups when phone busy signals or equipment failures hinder instruction. Training sessions can also be videotaped and used again later.

The other major component of instruction should be to design lessons that complement the curriculum. The most satisfying approach is to work with an enthusiastic teacher to plan a model Internet session based on upcoming coursework, i.e., a unit on dinosaurs for which you can search the Internet for relevant sources. Current digs may be documenting their findings on the Internet (which is actually a common practice among those enthusiasts, perhaps because of "Jurassic Park.")

You can document and download those sessions to share with the teacher to illustrate Internet navigation methods. Even if the teacher is reluctant to personally use the Internet, you can suggest that he appoint a few students to act as Internet navigators for the class. If research is done in small cooperative groups, one student in each group can act as the Internet expert.

Build a Team of Student Navigators
Now let's look at making the best use of library instruction time. After a general discussion about searching for information, gather the student Internet navigators and show them how the system operates. Pull out saved searches with high-quality Internet "hits," and show them what information is available to them. Then let students loose, guiding them on their searches. As the searching progresses, have students describe what they are doing so everyone can see how search strategies evolve. Have them share what is happening as databases and files are located.

To save connect time charges, have students download what they've found to read later. After finishing the online session, students can copy the downloaded files onto personal diskettes to be further evaluated at personal computer workstations.

One benefit of this instructional approach is that a cadre of student Internet navigators is built naturally, and their expertise can be transferred to other coursework. They can also train their peers in Internet operations, thus freeing up valuable librarian instructional time. These same students are often the best instructors for their own classroom teachers. An Internet navigator card serves as a simple document to allow responsible students access to direct Internet connectability—and accountability.

Be Playful, Take Risks
Perhaps the most important factor in Internet instruction is risk-taking, by learners and librarians. We must take time to "play" in the Internet world, to make mistakes, and to cheerfully risk teaching others about this unruly and exciting tool. TC

Lesley S.J. Farmer is the Library Director of Redwood High School in Larkspur, California. She is the author of Creative Partnerships: Librarians and Teachers Working Together, *published by Linworth Publishing, Inc.*

CONNECTING WITH  THE CURRICULUM

Perfect Partners
Technology and Integrated Instruction

by Nadine K. Hinton
and Linda Orlich

Technology has forever altered the way we receive and process information. As a result, our schools have the formidable responsibility for training our young people to use this technology productively. Fortunately, authentic assessment opportunities abound. And by providing students with wider access to information, we can help them recognize that not all information is equally useful and that they must think critically and creatively as they examine the merits of different sources.

Curricula reform in our district emphasizes that technology is an integral component of instruction—not an add-on or replacement. Even with this philosophical commitment and modest financial support, we as teachers have often found ourselves overwhelmed by the sheer volume of ever-changing information related to teaching the new technology. From our experience with integrated instruction (and partly in self-defense!), we scoured the courses of study for all references to uses of technology in instruction. The results were still overwhelming. We then decided to distill the lists to identify elements that emphasized the importance of technology across curricular areas. We hope that other teachers, media specialists, technology coordinators, curriculum coordinators, and administrators can use this information as they plan for effective use of technology in instruction and to strengthen their proposals for increased budgets for technology.

Technology should be viewed as a tool to help students construct knowledge and to help teachers provide opportunities for more

HOW YOU CAN USE TECHNOLOGY ACROSS THE CURRICULA

effective, meaningful, integrated instruction. The time required to achieve these lofty goals and the dollars necessary to begin and maintain the system are substantial. However, we have found that incorporating technology into science, math, language arts, and social studies curricula is an outstanding use of both time and money.

Benefits of Integrating Technology:

EASIER SEARCHING

- Search nonprint sources to locate relevant information, including laser discs, CD-ROMs, and telecommunications.

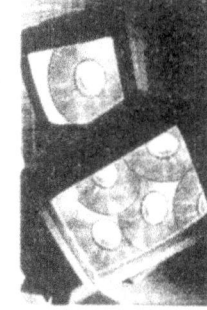

Many schools cannot afford to provide current print resources to all students. Laser discs and CD-ROMs offer an economical alternative for some references. Telecommunications, once modem connections and Internet links have been established, widen access to information, including access to towers of CD-ROMs available in many public libraries.

INCREASED PROPRIETY

- Write, edit, revise, and publish written work in an electronic portfolio.
- Display and publish enhanced written work.
- Integrate sound and speaking skills into students' presentations.
- Produce correct spelling.
- Choose fonts that enhance meaning and voice.
- Search for information and maintain records of their work for enjoyment, evaluation, and sharing.

Students should have access to their own filing systems, either electronically or on paper. Electronic portfolios (with "At Ease," disk and tape backups) provide a useful network system for storing files while addressing security needs within the school.

BROADER APPEAL

- Extend senses.

Vicarious field trips enable students to experience sounds via electronic technology. They add depth to learning and portray a more realistic experience for the learner.

WORLDWIDE COLLABORATION

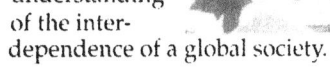

- Examine issues from diverse perspectives.
- Participate in individual and group projects, and simulations.
- Develop an understanding of the interdependence of a global society.
- Interact via telecommunications with others outside the classroom.

The global community is within reach. Technology can open doors that lead students to ever-changing sources of information.

CUSTOMIZED INFORMATION

- Collect, record, analyze, and synthesize information and numerical data.
- Quantify observations; create, organize, and interpret charts, tables, pictographs, and graphs.
- Use geometric shapes in drawing programs.

Production and manipulation of data internalizes learning. Using technology, students can process and reprocess information with ease, allowing opportunities to analyze which format best represents the intended message.

HORIZONTAL FOCUS

- Develop critical thinking skills and evaluate information.
- Develop graphic organizers such as webs, outlines, charts, lists, and maps.

Word processing gives students the means to create a finished product and, for proficient typists, transforms the nature of the writing task that is so laborious for some students. Word processing also provides support in spelling and grammar. Students can produce clearly illustrated materials that can be easily manipulated to fit the space and purpose of the project, thus allowing more student time to be spent on content rather than on production skills.

MULTI-DISCIPLINARY APPLICATIONS

- Integrate information across disciplines.

By integrating language arts, science, social studies, and math through the use of technologies, students can process and manipulate data and then prepare presentation materials quickly, professionally, and efficiently. Technology is integral to our instruction; it is not an addition to or replacement for current instruction.

INCREASED RETENTION

- Interact with text and graphics.

Computer programs such as *The Writing Center*, *HyperStudio*, *ClarisWorks*, and *Microsoft Works* enable students to combine their written text with clip art, reference graphics, student-generated art, or materials from level III laser discs, thus enhancing the appearance of the final product and more fully demonstrating mastery of the material.

WELL-ROUNDED RESPONSES

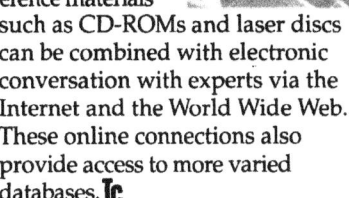

- Make inferences based on information from various sources.
- Use logic to solve problems.

Information collection from reference materials such as CD-ROMs and laser discs can be combined with electronic conversation with experts via the Internet and the World Wide Web. These online connections also provide access to more varied databases. **TC**

Nadine K. Hinton is a teacher at Emerson Elementary School and Linda Orlich is a teacher at Central College Elementary Magnet School, both in the Westerville (Ohio) City School District.

Harnessing Internet Resources for the Student Researcher

by Carol Simpson

hat the Internet entails and that it is an instructional resource, not a subject in itself, are two main concepts to understand before attempting to integrate the Net into a school's curriculum. New users sometimes have difficulty fathoming the expanse of the Internet's holdings. The school library may have one or two resources on a given topic. By contrast, the Internet may produce such a flood of information that the researcher is overwhelmed. And, if the researcher chooses to venture into the morass of data, the problem then becomes one of evaluating its quality and authenticity.

Compare the Internet to a large library. One wouldn't expect to be able to locate and retrieve all types of information at once. Learning to use the Internet is similar to learning to use a library; and, Internet skills, like library skills, are best taught in conjunction with real assignments. For example, for a lesson in maps one might look for atlases. For a lesson on weather, one might look for accurate and current Internet sites that provide constantly changing weather maps, radar data or temperatures. The actual resource, and even the type of resource, can be selected based on the lesson objectives, ages and maturity levels of the students, and the type of Internet connection available.

Selecting Services

Many users assume that using the Internet means using graphical browsers such as *Mosaic* or *Netscape*. These programs and their kin are powerful tools, but there are also other facets of the Internet that are appropriate for classroom use. Teachers should consider classroom organization before selecting tools. Will this be a cooperative and collaborative activity? Could there be work involving groups in different locations? E-mail, telephone, video or chat software might be appropriate for students in remote locations across town, across the country, or around the world who are working on joint projects.

Other projects might require more individual research. Especially in the middle grades, students are often permitted to select their own topics. Frequently students select topics for which the library has few, if any, resources. With the wealth of information on the Internet, especially on current topics, using one of the powerful Internet "search engines," software programs such as *AltaVista*, *Web Crawler*, *Lycos* or *Yahoo* will produce usable resources. All these "engines" are also available through nongraphical browsers such as *Lynx*, if your network connection does not support the heavy demands of graphics.

The age of the student is important when teaching Internet resources. Electronic mail lends itself well to interdisciplinary projects because writing, grammar and spelling skills come into play along with math, science or social studies content. Almost as soon as students begin to write, they can compose simple e-mail messages. Typing the message provides keyboarding practice, and sending it involves little risk of exposing students to inappropriate materials on the Internet, especially if the teacher establishes the correspondence between classes or locates and assigns keypals.

Other Internet tools such as gophers and Veronica permit students to locate information while training them in logical thinking and organization as they follow the sequence of menus. Intermediate students can navigate "nested" menus if they know there is a gem buried within. (Nested menus lead to other menus.)

Here are a few questions to ask before choosing the type of Internet service to introduce:

- What is the age of the student? Older students may be able to choose and use Internet services more accurately than younger ones.

- What is the goal of the lesson? Does this type of information support this goal?
- Can the Internet work effectively with the classroom organization pattern? Do students work alone? In groups?
- How will the lesson be evaluated? Student paper handed in? Group presentation? Project format? Can he information retrieved be used successfully to support the final product?
- Will students require graphics for their final product?

Evaluating Sources

The Internet is not always the best source of information for every topic. Research can still be successfully conducted in a traditional print library. The idea is to offer the Internet as another source, just as one would search *Readers' Guide*, the card catalog or the vertical file. The student then must evaluate the information and select the most appropriate information to support the thesis of the paper or project.

Students can use one of several models to evaluate an Internet site to determine its accuracy and authority. Teachers must also evaluate sites for appropriateness, content and presentation. Here are some questions to ask when selecting an Internet resource for a specific assignment:

- Does this site have all the necessary information for this assignment? If not, what will the student use to fill in the gaps?
- Is the reading level of the site appropriate for the students? Many sites are put up by and for university students who may use sophisticated vocabulary.
- Does the site offer links to games, chat rooms, or popular culture not associated with the assignment? Will students be lured from their task?
- Is the site reliable? Can you count on it to be up and active during your class time?
- Is the site heavily graphic? Some schools may find that accessing the graphic-intensive sites can be slow. Consider turning off graphics, using a text-only browser, or sticking with text-based resources such as gopher.
- Does this site have a search engine? How can a student locate additional information buried under several layers of pages? An index or search capability makes it simpler for students (especially young students) to be successful searchers.
- If you have a student who is not permitted to use the Internet, what resources will be available for him to use to complete the assignment?

Integrating the Internet into the curriculum is much like teaching library skills. The key is knowing what to teach, how to teach it, who is going to learn it, and why it is important. Thanks to new, comprehensive search engines, locating the resources will be simple. The hard part comes when students attempt to select the best information from the wealth that is available.

Carol Simpson is the Editor of TECHNOLOGY CONNECTION.

Turn On To Reading Through Technology

Reading Motivation: Using *All* Resources Available

By Lesley S.J. Farmer

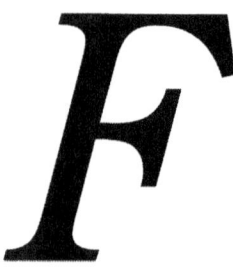

Fortunately, most young children want to read. Particularly if their families and teachers read to them, youngsters want to solve the mystery of those black lines on paper. However, some children take longer to unlock the key to reading, or they encounter a reading obstacle. If they don't soon experience concrete success, they are likely to turn off to reading. Incorporating technology can turn children on to reading and help them succeed in this lifelong skill.

Motivating Factors

What motivates kids? Something that gets their attention, like the bells and whistles of technology, certainly motivates them. In fact, in our technological world, electronic stimuli are competing constantly for their attention. Sound, text, and visuals offer multiple ways for students to pay attention. For that reason, any technology chosen for students needs to be of professional quality and visually arresting.

Of course, students need to act upon that attention. For that to happen, they need to be personally touched by either an emotional or intellectual connection. One key to technology's effectiveness is its interactive quality, so students can get involved with the content as they manipulate the media. Consider CD-ROM animated books, such as *My Grandma and Me*. Children take the two-dimensional story into another dimension, choosing which visuals and sounds to activate.

Choice of Technology

What kind of technology motivates students to read? Here are some points to consider when incorporating technology.

- Take advantage of the medium. Make sure that the media add value to the reading experience. Don't buy merely textual or drill-kill tutorial software.

One key to technology's effectiveness is its interactive quality, so students can get involved with the content as they manipulate the media.

- Encourage creativity. Enable students to move through and beyond the reading to share their responses. Sample utility programs are Kid Pix for presentations and MacPaint for illustrating reading.
- Link reading and writing. Let children use each skill to reinforce the other. Storybook Weaver is a good example.

Listening to Read

One of the main skills needed for good reading is good listening. Those story hour activities of rhythmic hand play and funny, repetitive songs sharpen those skills. Technology adds to this experience, both on the classroom and individual levels. Old technologies, such as records and audiocassettes, still help motivate children. Those little read-along picture books offer a link between sound and words. But they are no substitute for a real-life lap-read. CD-ROM interactive books constitute the next level of synchronized sight and sound. CD-I offered an interesting selection of titles, but that technological format hasn't really caught on.

Another spin on this approach is the audiotape-filmstrip combination. Weston Woods is probably the pioneer in this field. Most of its products are now available on videotape, which seems to be favored by students and teachers alike, even though the product may have changed little in the process. Many children's books adapt nicely into video form. In some cases, the books are fully animated while maintaining the spirit of the original book. Reading Rainbow offers several titles, and, in fact, many public libraries have good collections of such adaptations for families and schools to borrow.

Another existing technology is captioned TV. Many children's programs include this option, which gives children the opportunity to read the words while they watch the action. However, for some children, this kind of split attention is difficult to maintain. Try Reading Rainbow and similar shows. In some cases, schools have the right to record and archive the programs for an extended period of time.

Multimedia computers now also offer read-aloud options. Word processing files can be opened on the machine and read in a variety of voices. Some choices are distracting, such as a singsong bong sound. However, students enjoy picking out a favorite voice or comparing text in two different dictions. Depending on how sophisticated students are, they actually can scan a text using optical character recognition (OCR) software, such as Omnipage. The saved file is then read aloud by the system. Adaptive technology, although intended for students with special needs, can certainly help the struggling reader. Hardware may include imaging systems that amplify text size, read text aloud, and change fonts as needed.

Visualize to Read

Visuals are another natural "hook" to reading, both as a lead-in to the literature and as a way to share responses afterwards. Slides and transparencies can help students visualize the upcoming story. A rich selection of slides can be especially useful since they can be reorganized and cataloged along several dimensions. Furthermore, students enjoy working with the slides as they create links to reading.

Images also can be captured from the Internet. Some search engines, such as http://isurf.yahoo.com, focus on images. Suppose students are reading *Number the Stars*. They can find dramatic Holocaust images on the Internet. Some of the children's literature sites also include images for students to share. One option is for students to create a presentation about a story's background, such as a tall tale. They can get pictures from the Internet, or they can scan illustrations from library books to import into their project.

Pre-selected images, including video, are also available on CD-ROMs. The growing number of exciting curricular titles offers an array of visual information that can increase a student's interest in reading a story. The San Diego Zoo's *Mammals* is a natural lead-in for animal stories. Mindscape's *Oceans Below* serves as a stimulus for sea life tales. *Material World* gives students a concrete picture of life in other nations, which can help them understand multicultural literature.

Presenting to Read

Probably the most effective motivation, though, is sharing a good book. Technology facilitates this process in several ways.

- Students can type their book testimonials online to share in a common "good books" folder.
- Classes can be "key pals," sharing their favorite reading online.
- Students can videotape book talks or presentations, such as representing themselves as a book character or creating puppet plays about a story. These tapes can be archived in the library and shown in other classes.
- Students can create a Kid Pix show about a favorite book. Again, the file can be saved and accessed later by other students.

What motivates children to read? The answer is a good story and a friend to share it with. Technology can get and hold children's attention so they can use their imagination to connect with a great read.

Lesley S.J. Farmer is the Library Director of Redwood High School in Larkspur, California. She is the author of Training Student Library Staff, *published by Linworth Publishing, Inc.*

CONNECT YOUR STUDENTS ELECTRONICALLY TO LEARNING

feature

The Purpose of Information and Technology Assignments

Process or Product?

By Betty Dawn Hamilton

The U.S. Department of Labor Secretary's Commission on Achieving Necessary Skills (SCANS) report for America 2000, or "What Work Requires of Schools," clearly states five competencies that students will need in the work force. These five competencies include the ability to plan and allocate resources; work with others; acquire and use information; understand, improve, or design systems; and work with a variety of technologies. As teachers and school librarians team on assignments, each should reinforce what the other is doing.

Before the word processor, teachers ensured that students did their own work by identifying handwriting and certain sentence constructions that "sounded" like particular students. Now that students have access to word processors with spell check and even grammar check, student papers have become the product of applied electronic features as well as student thought.

The problem evolving from these electronic searches and electronically-processed papers is that students who are more skilled at using computers often are willing to do that part of the paper *for* students lacking those skills. This reinforces the skilled students while placing the unskilled students at further disadvantage.

In previous years, when papers were handwritten, students learned not only a process but also content as they read through books and made notes. In this age of technology, students may do a keyword or topic search, find a document with the words highlighted, scan the document to see that the content fits, print or download onto a diskette, and insert the text into their document.

In research, the purpose of the assignment must be clear. If teachers want only content and perfection, then the product is what they are seeking. However, if teachers want students to learn how to find, assimilate, and synthesize information into a document to meet certain technological as well as intellectual requirements, then those outcomes must be made clear to the students and everyone who works with the students on the assignments.

For example, once, when senior students rushed into the library computer lab in my high school, there was usually one person who keyed in information as the other students decided what to write. My concern was that students were not doing their own assignments. When asked about the assignment, the teacher said he did not care how the students produced the perfect résumé; he just wanted them to know what a perfectly designed and executed résumé looked like, and to have one they could present as they searched for jobs or entered universities. That teacher's goal was a product. In that particular assignment, we in the library computer lab did not need to concern ourselves with who was keying in data.

On the other hand, we have freshmen and sophomore students doing a research assignment where teachers are integrating technology into their assignment. Not only are the students learning how and where to find information, but they are learning how to use technology to produce a product. Yes, the teachers want the students to absorb information about the chosen topic as they research and make notes, but the process is the ultimate goal.

The question is: "How can educators arrive at a method for assuring that students learn what they are supposed to learn from the process?" When that question was posed to LM_NET, the discussion group for school librarians on the Internet, the general consensus was that a chart showing desired outcomes would be ideal. GenAnn Keller (gkeller@csn.net) of Elizabeth Middle School in Elizabeth, Colorado, suggests listing items or skills that must be mastered in producing the project. To the right of the list are columns titled "In Progress," "Basic," "Proficient," and "Advanced." Teachers could even attach letter grades to each, with "Basic" being a "C," "Proficient" a "B," and "Advanced" the coveted "A."

Another solution would be to have an end-of-year or end-of-semester test where students demonstrate they are able to perform those skills the teacher requires; however, designing such a test would not be easy.

One method that a teacher in our school uses is group instruction. Having 25 networked computers, she is able to have all students in a hands-on situation at the same time. Once the students have performed part of their research and have made notes, they begin to compose the document on the computer (one of the SCANS requirements). The teacher has each student create the title page according to her step-by-step instructions. The students then set up the document in the same way by completing the header and pagination and creating a "works cited" page. Each page is saved as a separate document on the students' diskettes. From that point, students begin writing on their own, but may ask for assistance if they encounter problems.

As more students have access to technology, the issue of product or process becomes more important, and the purpose of each assignment must be clearly stated. Only when students are able to perform skills required for the workplace will we be meeting the needs listed in the SCANS report. When students meet those requirements, they will be able to use the process to create a product acceptable in the information-intensive 21st century. **TC**

Betty Dawn Hamilton is a Learning Resources Specialist at Brownfield (Texas) High School.

HEAD FOR THE EDGE

Putting Computer Skills in Their Place

By Doug Johnson

What are the basic computer skills all high school students should master before graduation, and where, how, and by whom should those skills be taught? Can a student who operates a computer well enough to play *Doom* be considered computer literate? Will a student who has used computers in school only for running tutorials or an integrated learning system have the skills necessary to survive in college or in the work place?

One educational philosophy is that computer skills should not be taught in a separate "computer class," but should be integrated into the content areas. Yet to my knowledge, no comprehensive K-12 set of computer skills and model for integration exists. Too often computers are used only as electronic flash cards or worksheets while the productivity side of computer use is neglected or grossly underdeveloped. Productivity tools, such as word processors, databases, spreadsheets, graphics, and chart makers often are taught only in special classes like business or technology education—classes taken by a minority of students, despite the fact most of these applications could benefit all students.

However, many schools have successfully integrated information skills into the curriculum, with the best media programs being designed around cooperative projects jointly taught by the classroom teacher and the library media specialist. The inclusion of a comprehensive list of computer skills in an information literacy curriculum creates a model for a computer literacy curriculum, and eliminates the need for a separate computer curriculum.

Varieties of information literacy curricula can be found in several places, including the position paper on information literacy adopted by AASL, the Big Six information problem-solving models of Mike Eisenberg and Bob Berkowitz, and the Michigan State Board of Education information literacy model. In each of these models, the curriculum is a process divided into several steps, retaught at increasingly more sophisticated levels. One approach to integrating computer skills into the general curriculum is to revisit your school's current information processing model, and add specific computer literacy skills to supplement the more general information skills listed. Examples of such integration can be found in the ERIC document (EDO-IR-96-04), "Computer Skills for Information Problem-Solving: Learning and Teaching Technology in Context."

Computer skills within an information processing curriculum need to be stated separately and clearly for a number of reasons: Many districts already have some form of computer skills curriculum, and those skills that are valid should remain clearly stated. It is not realistic to expect most teachers and many media specialists to understand that information literacy automatically assumes computer literacy. Clearly stated computer skills help determine the resources needed to effectively teach a skill. If it is the expectation that information be communicated through a computer-generated graph, then the need for a certain number of computers, types of software, and level of teacher proficiency is more easily established. The business world, academic community and public are aware of the need for students to

> *Computer skills within an information processing curriculum need to be stated separately and clearly.*

have computer skills, but the need for information skills may be less apparent. The inclusion of readily understood computer skills may increase the acceptance of the information literacy curriculum.

Listing computer skills within a process framework is only a first step in assuring that all our children become proficient information and technology users. A teacher-supported scope and sequence of skills, well designed projects, and effective assessments are also critical.

Many library media specialists will need to hone their own technology skills in order to remain effective information skills teachers. But such a curriculum holds tremendous opportunities for library media specialists to become indispensable staff members, and for all students to master the skills they will need to thrive in an information rich future. **Tc**

Doug Johnson is the District Media Supervisor for the Mankato (Minnesota) Public Schools.

A Research Project Filled With Real World Technology

By Sharron L. McElmeel

When our elementary school was about to create a World Wide Web site, we considered whether to define our efforts as a technology initiative or as a research experience for our students. With the focus on technology, it is very tempting to define such projects as technology. However, in collaboration with the fourth- and fifth-grade students who worked on the project, it naturally evolved into a primary research project. The students compiled information from original sources and then shared it with the world via an Internet site. Classroom teachers, library media specialists, and resource specialists assisted students in researching information that met their objectives. In the process, they used a variety of technology and related skills.

Setting a Task and Staying with It

Defining a project goal gives the research a focus. With a goal, researchers can recognize when they have found enough information and whether it is appropriate. The students generated several lists of topics and categorized them into groups that provided an outline for the Web pages. They established a hierarchy of pages and formed research groups to work on specific topics. As some were working on the text, others were creating graphics and finding photographs that would complement the text.

Challenging Students to Think and Research

For many elementary students who have been involved in library skills lessons, the answer to every quest for information is in a book. The way to locate any book is to look in the library media center's catalog. Never mind that the topic might be so obscure that few if any authors will devote an entire book to the subject. For example, one student tried to locate the name of the newly elected mayor of Cedar Rapids, Iowa. The mayor had been elected in November and took office in early January; the date of the "research" was January 15. The library media center did not have back issues of local newspapers. Even if it had, few newspapers are indexed extensively enough for an effective search. The student tried to use the keywords "Mayor" and "Cedar Rapids" on the computer catalog, an inappropriate resource for the topic. In a research conference, the student was asked to think about other places to find the answer. He thought that the newspaper would have the mayor's name, or since the mayor had taken office, perhaps he could call the mayor's office and ask the secretary for the name and correct spelling. He did, and he got his answer. That is primary research. Technically, the strategy for locating that piece of information did not require library skills. Critical thinking and research skills were important.

Another group of fourth/fifth-grade students was beginning to gather information for the planned Web site on literacy. Their topic was "newly literate people," and they wanted to interview a few people who were newly literate and share some of their thoughts on the Web site. So the first question was "Where will we find people who have just learned to read and write?" They looked under "literate" on the computer catalog even though they didn't know what they were looking for. They had been given keyword instruction often enough that they used the topic, rather than the question, as their guide. It did not occur to the students that even if they found a book on literacy, it would not contain the information they needed: names, addresses, or telephone numbers of local people who were newly literate and willing to be interviewed.

The library media specialist helped the students back up and rethink the process. Where would an adult acquire the skills to read and write? With a little thinking time, the students decided to find local programs that might have taught some adults to read, and they called the public library. The response lead the researchers to a local community college where they made contact, by telephone, with a program director who put them in contact with two individuals who were pleased to tell their story. Once the researchers had arranged an interview time, they prepared questions for the interview. The material they needed came from the interviews, and the students added information about the program itself from a brochure. It was the primary research, the interview with the newly literate adults, that was one of the keys to a successful and meaningful research experience.

The Research

The students researched the information to be put on the Web site, they wrote the copy and designed the pages, and then worked with a web designer to compose and construct the pages. Their research took them to public libraries, to a bookstore established in 1893, through old newspapers on microfiche, into historical books and documents, and on interviews with real people. They read, conducted telephone interviews, wrote letters, and gathered information. Their findings were shared with the world on their Web sites. They learned about primary and secondary sources and about sifting information to find what is needed. These students used technology in the real world. They learned to scan pictures, create graphics, save the pictures and graphics in a specified format, write with word processors, spell check their narratives, and e-mail messages. The students and the educators found that technology means much more than using the Internet and that research skills transcend the basic library skills. The final products that were generated from the students' research and their use of technology can be seen on the World Wide Web at http://www.cedar-rapids.k12.ia.us/Harrison/harrison.html and at http://www.aea10.k12.ia.us/literacy.

The following is a summary of selected pages the students researched with a notation about the technology they used during their research.

For many elementary students who have been involved in library skills lessons, the answer to every quest for information is in a book. The way to locate any book is to look in the library media center's catalog. Never mind that the topic might be so obscure that few if any authors will devote an entire book to the subject.

Research Topic: History of Harrison School

Search tasks:
- Locate archival newspaper articles about the school and its origin.
- Interview former students of Harrison.
- Interview former staff members to obtain pictures of the school and other artifacts related to Harrison School.

Technology skills used:
- Reading microfiche of archival newspaper articles.
- Telephoning to contact potential interviewees and arrange for interviews.
- Audio recording to tape interviews for verifying written notes.
- Scanning to digitalize photographs.
- Word processing to compose permission form for quoting from interviews and using photographs on-line.

Research Topic: Iowa's Schools of the Past as Compared to Today's Schools

Search tasks:
- Locate and research information about an old or "oldest" school in Iowa.
- Locate and interview former students of one-room school houses.
- Learn about the educational testing services that are based in Iowa.

Technology skills used:
- Using electronic periodical index to locate articles about one-room schools and older schools in the area.
- Telephoning to arrange for interviews and to contact the caretaker of the oldest school in the county.
- Using camera to photograph the site of the school and the former students.
- Scanning photographs.
- E-mailing to communicate with the spokesperson for the American College of Testing organization.

**Research Topic:
Books (and connections to Iowa)**
Search tasks:
- Locate mayors in major cities and ascertain their favorite childhood books.
- Locate and investigate a relatively new public library in our state.
- Locate and investigate an early bookstore in Iowa.
- Locate books (particularly children's books) that are set in Iowa.
- Identify children's novels or nonfiction titles to be recommended as read-aloud titles.
- Identify children's picture books for sharing.

Technology skills used:
- General computer catalog skills to identify books that fit the structure of the book recommendation pages.
- Boolean searches in the computer catalog to locate and identify books with an Iowa setting.
- Modem connection to search the local public library's online catalog to identify specific titles.
- Word processing to write a letter to the mayor requesting the title of her favorite childhood book and to compose a survey.
- Reading microfiche indexes to locate articles about historical bookstores.
- Using local newspaper electronic indexes to locate articles about construction of new libraries.
- Telephone skills to contact a donor to a new public library and arrange for a presentation and interview and to contact the current owner of a book store.
- Speaker phone skills to conduct a group interview with a bookstore owner.
- Calculator skills to tabulate the results and figure percentages of the responses to the survey taken about school days in Iowa.

In addition to acquainting students with the resources in their local media center, library media specialists should discuss other resources such as telephone access, area libraries, people, and the Internet.

Research Topic: Authors/Books/ Children and Links in Iowa
Search tasks:
- Identifying and learning about nationally known authors with an Iowa link.
- Identifying and annotating books that describe pieces of Iowa's literary past.
- Profiling themselves as Web makers.
- Identifying and selecting Internet sites that provide information about Iowa.

Technology skills used:
- General computer catalog skills to identify books that fit the structure of the book recommendation pages.
- Internet search techniques to identify Web sites about Iowa.
- Using electronic post office or telephone book sites to locate authors identified through books and newspaper articles.
- Word processing to request permission to interview authors and to follow-up the interview with a letter and to compile their own collective profile and to compose a list of Internet sites.
- Audio cassette recording to tape interviews to verify notes. **TC**

Sharron L. McElmeel often writes about literature- and technology-related issues. Her recently released Research Strategies for Moving Beyond Reporting *(Linworth, 1996) shares strategies for developing research activities that provide real world applications. McElmeel is a library media specialist in the Cedar Rapids (Iowa) Community Schools.*

HEAD FOR THE EDGE

The Changing Face of Student Research

Consider these research assignments:
- High school students trace the history of buildings on their town's main street.
- A middle school class researches and recommends a location for the new city landfill.
- Elementary students use e-mail and the Internet to collect holiday customs celebrated by students from around the world.

These projects are not unusual. The first comes from Minnesota's new performance assessment package for inquiry; the second is from California Media and Library Educators Association's book *From Library Skills to Information Literacy: A Handbook for the 21st Century* (Hi Willow, 1994); and the last is a typical project coordinated through the Internet's Global School House http://www.gsn.org/. Do you notice any similarities? I can think of three attributes that make the projects both powerful and potentially frustrating. They are qualities that invite media specialists (again!) to rethink their roles as information specialists.

By Doug Johnson

1. Increasingly, research focuses on topics of local significance. Whether researching a building, person, ethnic group or custom, the emphasis is on things in the students' immediate geographic area, if not in their own households. Even when the topic is of national or international scope, such as pollution, the global economy, the Gulf War, technology, or health issues, teachers are asking students to assess the impact of policies and events on their own families and communities.

2. As a result, researchers are being asked to use primary rather than secondary resources. Local history is scanty in most school media centers. When it does exist, as in back issues of the local newspaper, often it's not indexed. Primary information sources such as the county courthouse, a local university, original surveys, government statistics (published on the Internet), and the memories of local "experts" are being used more and more.

3. Each of the examples above is purposely designed to be meaningful to the student researcher. The issues of recycling and pollution become relevant (and exciting) when the new landfill might be located next door to one's own house or favorite recreation area. The genuine voices of another culture's students speak louder than any text or reference book.

So, is there still a place for the school media specialist as research becomes primary-source based? When the school's collection is not adequate or relevant to the task at hand, what does the "information specialist" contribute?

Quite a bit, actually. The tasks involved in the inquiry process, regardless of the source of the information, remain pretty much the same. Students still need to formulate good questions and identify what information is needed. They will continue to gather, record, organize, and analyze the data, whether with paper and pencil, video camera, database or e-mail. More than with secondary information sources, the primary data should be critically evaluated. For example, a student felt she had hit the jackpot when she found a woman on the Internet who was willing to share her adventures as a fighter pilot in Vietnam. Later, the student discovered through other research that there were no female fighter pilots involved in that conflict.

As performance-based assessment becomes a standard means of evaluating student work, communicating the research results becomes increasingly important. Students need guidance to decide the best medium to display their findings, whether they compose thoughtfully crafted charts and graphs, a multi-media presentation, computerized slide shows, or even web pages.

Many teachers were probably not asked to do primary source research until they were in graduate school, if then. The use of original research and the use of primary sources may be as new to them as it is to their students. Our job as information specialists may well involve as much teaching of good information literacy skills to the teachers as to the students.

So, will the reference books sit dusty on the shelves? Will the library catalog monitor burn out and not be reported for months? Will our carefully made lessons on using the CD-ROM periodical guide mold in a drawer? No more state reports or posters of African animal facts or "social problem" term papers? I hope not. As excited as I am about constructivist, hands-on, experiential teaching and learning, I also firmly believe real education demands that students learn both process *and* content. And information technology (and technologists) will help with both. TC

Doug Johnson is the District Media Supervisor for the Mankato (Minnesota) Public Schools.

Empowering Young Women Through Technology

By Lesley S.J. Farmer

In your school, who dominates the Internet, writes the Web pages, troubleshoots the computers, and does the videotaping? In other words, who is the technology expert in your school? In most cases, it is a male. If the "expert" is drawn from the student body, chances are it is also a male since students mimic what they see in the adult world.

Now, what gender are most librarians? At least in the United States, the answer is female. Do these female librarians control the technology scene, or do they rely on males, both adults and students?

Since librarians are in the business of learning, they have a responsibility to learn about gender issues. But the central issue really is pluralism—how different perspectives can be respected, accepted, and embraced. The first stage is consciousness about inclusion and exclusion. Does the technology collection acknowledge the contributions of women and other under-represented groups? Does the content note the conditions and circumstances of women across classes and cultures? Is learning approached in a cross-disciplinary way so more transference of learning can occur?

Gender issues also influence teaching and learning methodologies. Do librarians facilitate learning by providing a supportive climate rather than dictating the *right* way to learn? Do students have the opportunity to work collaboratively and independently? Is process as important as product? Does learning transfer to real world and relational skills? Instruction also translates to student staff training. Do students work as pairs, and do they help one another and their peers? Do all students have a chance to develop their mechanical and troubleshooting skills?

Gender-equitable practices broaden the scope of technology and equip young people with the skills they need to succeed in a widely diverse and changing environment. And libraries are a logical and inclusive place to model gender-equitable technology. The Center for Children and Technology did a series of studies on gender attitudes about technology, and the results reinforce societal expectations.

- Males see technology as a source of power. Females see technology as a medium to connect.
- Technology is appealing to males because it fosters command and control. Females are attracted to technology's expressive qualities.
- Males see the computer as a one-way trip to the world. Females see computers as a means to converse.
- Males see technology as a positive force conquering nature. Females worry about technology's effect on nature.
- Males are more likely than females to take risks and fix computers.
- Males focus on the machine; females focus on the social function of technology.
- In general, females are more ambivalent about technology and so are less likely to choose it as a possible career.
- Males see technology as an end; females see it as a means.

How does that translate into the real world? If your library is like mine, more boys than girls monopolize computers. Let's look at some library issues relative to technology and gender. Technological curriculum is a major factor in insuring gender equity. Content must have personal meaning for females as well as for males. Female role models and women's approaches to life must be represented in content for it to have educational meaning for young women. Again, the more closely females can identify with the content, the more easily they will learn, and the more profoundly they will connect with the material. Gender issues should be addressed consciously. It is not enough to subtly incorporate it into the collection. Otherwise, students will not develop the consciousness needed to overcome present social inequities.

Since most teaching is concept-based, the stimuli for learning should be rich in variety and approach to reflect the spectrum of human experience. Since technology is one launching pad for learning, librarians and students should examine technology for gender sensitivity. Gender-biased materials distort reality while gender-equitable technology expands gender role attitudes and behavior as well as increases student motivation and comprehension. The following aspects can guide students as they conduct content analyses of technology sources.

- Language (use of pronouns and titles)
- Content (percentage of text devoted to males vs. females; status of genders portrayed)
- Perspective (variety of approaches; contextual information)
- Illustrations (variety of males and females in terms of appearance, roles, settings, and status)
- Authoring (expertise by gender)

If a technology-based resource lacks gender awareness, students can note the need for other resources to provide a more well-rounded perspective on content. The library should be seen as an opportunity for gender-equitable content as it provides different ways to examine and connect with content. Of course, the librarian has a special responsibility to provide those varied approaches to topics of learning by acquiring a rich collection of technology materials for students to use. Technology resources should reflect different ways of learning as well as different perspectives to information. Selection policies should be established to ensure a balanced collection.

One of the bright lights of collection development is resource sharing through the Internet. The Net allows people to contact one another and share ideas—an activity highly valued by girls. Interestingly, if the Internet is viewed as a search strategies game, then it's more likely used by boys, but if it's used as a means of communication, then girls will warm up to it.

Often, access to technology is gender-biased. When my library opens, it's the boys who run into the computer area and occupy all the machines. Most girls are too intimidated to tell a boy to give up a workstation. One solution is scheduling. Librarians can establish a system where each gender gets the computer for a half hour. If the stereotype of girls being more organized than boys holds, then girls will be more likely to plan ahead and schedule time accordingly. In some schools, there is a girls-only period or a corner designated *girls only* and decorated by the girls in a territorial gesture. While some people may deem such actions as sexist, I prefer to label them affirmative action measures.

Another subtle issue is technology self-competence. Notice how boys are more likely to say, "The computer is broken," while girls will say, "I think I broke the machine." Conversely, if everything works well, boys will assert, "See how great I am!" while girls will say, "Computers are great—I'm lucky." It's a difference in the focus of control and responsibility. The safest approach is an objective one when dealing with student behavior around technology. The following statements offer a perspective that can challenge emotionally charged students:

- What do you want to accomplish? What did you want the machine to do?
- What happened? At what point did something not work the way you expected?
- Show me.

Resist the temptation to say, "I was never any good at this either."

Of course, the best way to raise self-confidence is to teach students how to use technology. Technology skills are seen as tools, and information literacy is context-embedded, just as a needle isn't useful to study unless used to sew, remove splinters, or otherwise manipulate. A basic tenet in feminist scholarship is that students learn by gathering data in a variety of ways from a variety of perspectives. They consciously examine the values and beliefs in which information is embedded, and they incorporate those perspectives into the total multi-faceted and ever-changing picture. With technology providing information in so many forms, its presence can be liberating for girls.

Moreover, technology skills can be seen as relational. Students find relationships between pieces of information, they relate information to themselves, and they relate information to the world around them. This connectivity provides a deeper meaning to the information found and engages the whole person. Presentation software exemplifies technology's ability to provide a way to show relationships between ideas and images.

> *Technological competencies are required of today's librarians, and those high-level responsibilities need to be credited by supervisors.*

Let's consider some of the steps in information literacy, such as locating information. First, students must decide how to find the facts. In the research process, students may consult some kind of index or catalog as a first step to find the source itself. The research step of key words is essential here since many indexes use a controlled vocabulary to organize the indexed sources. It should be noted that computerized indexes and catalogs rely less on this abstraction step. In either case, female verbal ability can be promoted, and girls can take the lead in this step.

Traditional research has concentrated on sequential, factual print material. Such narrowly defined resources do not address the learning styles and interests of many students. Therefore, teachers need to value and encourage the use of nonprint resources, such as videos and CD-ROMs.

Physically accessing the information within the source is a separate procedure. For books, students need to look at tables of contents if the topic is broad and indexes if a specific fact is being researched. As students try to find specifics, they should also look at the source's arrangement of information—whether it is arranged alphabetically, chronologically, or thematically. Technology-related materials pose different access situations. CD-ROMs often include random-access searching software. Videos, on the other hand, usually require sequential scanning. Interestingly, girls may find themselves the experts in these non-traditional access methods since they are often expected to ascertain non-verbal or literal cues.

Presenting information requires translating the synthesis into terms that others can understand. On a practical level, this transformation of information ensures that students understand what they read and make it their own. Plagiarism is rarely an issue if meaningful presentation incorporates the transformation of gathered data into an original form. Students should be encouraged to explore alternative means of sharing their information, such as skits, debates, simulations, multimedia presentations, videos, white papers, and games. Often these presentations are team efforts, which reinforce feminine awareness of relational learning and group responsibility. Such collaborative results can be used to assess social as well as academic tasks. Technology lends itself to such collaborative efforts. Multimedia products, in particular, merge text, graphics, and sound in creative sequences, which reinforce female relational approaches to learning.

As classroom and library teachers design and facilitate the learning environment, they model the kinds of technological use they want from their students. The main consideration is clarity; all parties must know what is going on. Let's look at a generic situation.

One teacher looks at a classroom of students and discovers how gender is affecting perception or behavior. Maybe girls aren't doing enough risk-taking, and perhaps boys are condescending toward girls. Probably more male than female role models are being presented in software. The library teacher notices that boys use the media center's computers more frequently, and the two genders approach research and handle frustration differently, to the detriment of the girls. The two teachers want to change the students' behaviors by addressing gender issues. On a more general basis, lessons or activities should be built on the teachers' assessment of student needs and, as much as possible, the students' self-assessment of needs and desired outcomes.

The content arena is usually the responsibility of the classroom teacher, particularly in high schools that are department- or content-driven. The teacher looks at what the students should be able to do and at what they know and don't know at this point in order to achieve the specific action. Prerequisite knowledge should be ascertained so all students can start on a somewhat equitable playing field. Teachers should be cognizant of possible gender-sensitive technology. Can both girls and boys relate to the topic? What prior experiences do they bring to the subject matter of the technology? Are gender stereotypes reinforced, such as "motherly instincts" or "manly arts"? Are gender differences acknowledged, such as cooperation expectations or attitudes toward violence?

Next, library teachers, as experts in resources and information literacy, typically identify student competencies and prerequisite skills related to technology. Usually the library teacher reacts to the assignment rather than initiates the planning dialogue. Librarians need to talk with teachers to determine at what level students are performing relative to technology skills. For instance, if the information skill entails locating and comparing two magazine articles, do students know how to use computer magazine indexes? If not, the assignment may need to be changed or modified.

Librarians also need to be sensitive to possible gender inequities relative to technology skills. For instance, boys may be more comfortable using computers for Internet searching because they may have had more experience taking risks with remote online databases. In this example, a separate training session might be given to girls in order to provide a level playing field for all students using computers.

In planning, teachers transcend the students' daily behavior and look at the underlying long-term ramifications of the content and information-processing skills to be learned. What will capture their interest? Why should students learn

> *Student staff use of technology should underscore the library's mission: technology is a means to information and ideas, not an end in itself.*

this, and how will this activity empower them? How can gender equity be fostered through this activity? Separate Internet training can be beneficial for girls because librarians and teachers can show sites and functions that girls will enjoy without reinforcing female stereotypes, such as fashion models or the Barbie site. For example, www.girltech.com brings girls into the world of technology that is fun and adventurous. Librarians can highlight more interactive sites, especially those that allow e-mail or two-way dialogue. A girls-only videoconferencing can be another powerful learning experience for young women.

Lesson structure

Grade Level: The two teachers need to make sure skills are appropriate to the students' age or readiness. Do the students have the prerequisite skills or experiences to master the activity?

Time Frame: Both the content skills and the information skills require time to assimilate, so the total time allotment must be negotiated. In some cases, students will work in the library media center, assess their progress in the classroom, and return to the library media center to process information at a more sophisticated level. Time to learn a new technology must be counted into the total instruction time frame.

Resources: The librarian typically guides the process. In fact, the classroom teacher benefits by examining available technology and shaping the lesson to accommodate local resources within the school and the community rather than designing an activity that frustrates students' research efforts.

Grouping: Because classroom teachers see students daily, they usually determine the group or team arrangement. However, different technology skills may call for different ways to divide the assignment, which the library teacher can help determine.

Activities: The use of small heterogeneous groups facilitates student learning because students can build on their individual strengths and help their peers with more challenging skills. Learning styles also may be considered. Teachers should incorporate a variety of approaches to learning to accommodate individual needs. Providing opportunities to learn through different senses and personal interactions expands the students' learning and coping skills and reinforces recognition of individual strengths relative to technology.

Another major area for technology gender equity is the librarian's use of student library staff. All students, even those who initially fear mechanics, should have basic technology training because technology-related jobs can vary greatly. For example, desktop publishing requires different skills than cleaning a printer; connecting video editing equipment uses different skills than training a student to edit a videotape. Both genders need exposure to these technologies; their interests may be piqued, and the librarian can match the student's potential to the medium.

Fortunately, technology has always played a part in the library, from the lowly stamper to the barcode scanner, from the pencil sharpener to the photocopier, and from the slide projector to the multimedia computer station. Today, library technology continues to augment library productivity and student learning. Today's students have lived with technology from infancy. Student staff use of technology should underscore the library's mission: technology is a means to information and ideas, not an end in itself. That message is actually comforting for girls. Other messages also ring true for female student staff: that equipment needs to be handled carefully, that documentation of steps and changes is necessary, that details must be considered, and that staff is there to help other students and adults.

Finally, technology equity has to do with librarians themselves. The librarian's role has traditionally been associated with female clerical skills and mothering abilities, such as storytelling. Too often, the rest of the community does not realize the changes introduced into the library science profession. Technological competencies are required of today's librarians, and those high-level responsibilities need to be credited by supervisors. We librarians also need to be more assertive and pro-active in order to insure that our technology skills are well used within the work scene. Female librarians, in particular, need to model the power of information professionals. Strong librarianship is a testament to the career opportunities for diverse, capable people.

In fact, the library can serve as a neutral, safe ground for technology learning, use, and career potential for girls. Girls can become technology experts without losing their femininity and can share their knowledge with others in a helping environment. When you think about it, several traditional female stereotypes do get played out in the library under the umbrella of technology: service, detail work, written and verbal skills. That melding of "high-tech" and "high touch" provides a powerful base for gender equity and self-confidence. **TC**

Lesley S.J. Farmer is the Library Director of Redwood High School in Larkspur, California. She is the author of Training Student Library Staff, *published by Linworth Publishing, Inc.*

> *In some schools, there is a girls-only period or a corner designated girls only and decorated by the girls in a territorial gesture. While some people may deem such actions as sexist, I prefer to label them affirmative action measures.*

Why Students Should Use MULTIMEDIA

Not every report or research paper is best prepared with the glitz of multimedia. Like other information mediums, it has its appropriate and inappropriate uses.

What are the benefits for teachers and librarians?

Multimedia presentation software can be used to produce attention-getting, dramatic, audio and visual lessons and reports. Using solid instructional design principles (objective, content outline, materials list, storyboard, and so forth), a teacher or SLMS can produce a variety of multimedia instructional materials that should keep the interest of most students. Librarians can produce library orientation, reference guides, and skills instruction programs that students and teachers can use at any time.

Why should students use this software?

Let's go back in time several centuries to the year 1560. Gutenberg's invention of moveable type has been in existence for over 100 years. Yet, in a small room in a monastery, an apprentice scribe bends low and laboriously copies a book by hand.

Hearing the master scribe enter the room, the weary apprentice asks why the monastery does not use the technique discovered by Gutenberg. Then, many more books could be produced and learning would spread. The master replies that Gutenberg's idea is just a passing fancy and will never really catch on. Its product just cannot compare to a handwritten text, and, besides, copying by hand is a good exercise for the mind.

By Katherine Bucher

Now move back to the end of the twentieth century. Think about some of the reasons you may have heard against allowing students to produce multimedia presentations instead of written reports. Do you see any of the master scribe's logic in them? After all, how many "term papers" does the average person write once he or she completes school? Compare that to the number of presentations to clubs, church groups, civic organizations, and government agencies (city council, school board) that the person will probably give. Don't the presentations outweigh the research reports?

Contrary to some opinions, allowing students on all levels to create multimedia presentations to replace or supplement written reports does not mean the death of books and learning. In researching the information needed to prepare a multimedia presentation, students use the same print and electronic sources that they use to create a written report. In addition, students are able to combine traditional library/information skills (i.e., selecting and narrowing a topic, preparing an outline) with the higher level thinking skills (i.e., critical thinking, problem solving, and decision making) when they are actively engaged in authoring their own multimedia presentations. If they work in groups, they are developing cooperative learning skills.

Giving students this opportunity also takes advantage of the students' various learning styles. Often, we forget that many high school students are tactile-kinesthetic and learn best by actually doing things.

To see how school librarians have worked with their teachers to help students make multimedia presentations as part of their assignments, watch school librarians Connie Scott and Star Wolven at Hampton High School in Hampton, Virginia, as they work with an English class that is studying American poets. These dynamic librarians are fortunate that a Macintosh computer lab is located off the library and that Connie has become quite proficient in using *HyperCard*.

- In the classroom, the teacher has assigned groups of students to report on specific poets.
- Using the library's reference collection (print and CD-ROM), Star guides the students as they gather information.
- Since most of the members of this class had used *HyperCard* in their social studies class in the fall, Connie meets the groups in the Mac lab, reviews the basics of presentation planning, and helps the groups organize the information that they found through their research into a computer multimedia presentation.
- Students work on their presentations in the lab with their teacher (and sometimes Connie or Star) during their class periods and during other times when the lab is available.
- The scanner is used as one group decides to use a portrait of the poet in its presentation while another wants to incorporate some artwork that the students think illustrates the mood their poet tried to convey in some major works.
- Another group wants to incorporate a brief audio selection into its presentation.
- Finally the presentations are ready and are used as the groups present their reports to the class.

While both librarians agree that a project like this takes time, they also say that it is worth it. It's exciting to watch students become involved in their work and teach each other how to use the computers, software, and references. Everyone seems to be learning. Students who often are the first out the library door, now return after school to polish their presentation or to try to find one more piece of information that they need. In fact, students who have been allowed to use the computers to create a multimedia presentation in one class help convince other teachers to try it.

What can students do?

With a little help from teachers and the SLMS, students in elementary, middle, and high school can use multimedia presentation programs. Although some teachers may be reluctant to allow students to create multimedia presentations because they are not familiar with the software or are not sure how to evaluate the product, with a few suggestions, most are willing to give multimedia a try.

While presentations can be created on almost any subject, here are some suggestions for various curricular areas.

Social studies:
- Research local history. Supplement the text with illustrations that are scanned in from postcards.
- Present a person in history, including a picture, the reading of a famous quotation, a brief part of an important speech or, for recent figures, a film clip.
- Select a time period and present an overview of it. Include music (audio) and art (visual) as well as information about important historical events.
- Prepare a brief economic report on a major U.S. corporation that is listed on the New York Stock Exchange. Include graphs and charts as well as illustrations of its products.

English:
- Select a favorite poet. Provide biographical information and a visual interpretation of one of his poems.
- Select one novel and have different characters tell their side of the story.
- Develop a multimedia book report that will encourage others to read the book.
- Write a short story that includes options for the reader. (Think of this as a computerized "choose your own adventure.")

Science and math:
- Prepare a short tutorial that other students can use. Include an information section, an activity, and a short quiz.
- Create a tutorial to help others learn basic science terminology.
- Illustrate a mathematical concept or formula.
- Using Mammals as a guide, prepare a report on an insect, bird, or fish. Use the results as the beginning of a class science encyclopedia.

Foreign language:
- Instead of a written report on a foreign city, create a visual one. Any narration should be in the foreign language.
- Prepare a tutorial stack that shows items or actions and then describes them in the foreign language. Then try the reverse by making a statement in the foreign language and letting the user click on a button to see what it represents and hear the English translation.

Art:
- Prepare a biography of an artist and include samples of his or her major works.
- Select one of the basic artistic elements (form, line, shape) define it, and show how several artists used it. **TC**

Katherine T. Bucher is an Associate Professor at Old Dominion University, Norfolk, Virginia.

Reprinted from Computers & Technology in School Library Media Centers, published by Linworth Publishing, Inc.

Guidelines for Effective Multimedia Design

By Elizabeth Downs and Kenneth Clark

The affordability of multimedia presentation programs has led schools to purchase programs such as *PowerPoint* (Microsoft), *Astound* (Gold Disk), and *HyperStudio* (Wagner). The media specialist often is called upon to help faculty and students in the design and production of programs. The following guidelines are designed to be used by media specialists in helping others use these programs effectively. The central themes of the guidelines are simplicity and appropriateness. Novice users tend to go overboard when they discover the many color, text, graphics, and special effects options available. You must help them understand these effects are not an end in and of themselves but tools to help them to get their message across.

Color

Use color with care. Color should be used to create a realistic effect or to focus attention. Most computers are capable of generating millions of colors. As a result, the designer can quickly overpower the viewer with confusing hues and values.

Text

Again, the user is confronted with many options, including font, size, color, placement, justification, case, spacing and style. Designers should consider the content being delivered when deciding on the screen text format.

Graphics

Graphics should be used only when they support the topic being covered. Keep in mind that developmental level influences the viewer's ability to understand the graphics. Consider the type of graphic with respect to its message. Do you need a pie chart or a photograph? A major consideration is the degree of realism of the graphic representation. For example, graphic representations can be simple black-line drawings or complex full-color images of a real person, object or event. If one of the latter is your subject, then use the most realistic representation available.

Special Effects

Special effects such as transitions and "builds" should be minimized. Transitions are the time variables and screen designs selected to move from one screen to the next. The screen designs include wipes, dissolves, split screens and checkerboard effects. These can prove to be distracting. Consider the audience's attention span when choosing transition speed. If the designer chooses slow transitions, the audience may lose interest. Builds are special effects used to bring text onto the screen. Builds for text can include "flying" text, dissolves and checkerboard text. These can help direct the learner's attention to the relevant material if the builds are not distracting. When using transitions and builds, be consistent throughout the program, and only to enhance the content.

DESIGN PRINCIPLES

Simplicity is the best model to apply when adding elements to a single screen. At the same time, creativity is important, and the designer should be encouraged to try a variety of techniques. By incorporating some basic design principles, you can provide suggestions for faculty and students to consider as they create a multimedia program. Try offering these guidelines:

COLOR

- Limit the selection to two colors per screen for everything other than graphics.
- Use a text color that will contrast with background color.
- Use solid color background for screens; avoid textured or designed backgrounds.
- Be consistent throughout the program in use of colors for text and background.
- Use color to direct the user's attention.

TEXT

- Use simple block fonts that do not contain endstrokes.
- Select a text size that is 18 points or larger.
- Limit text to six or seven lines per screen.
- Present a single concept or topic per screen.
- Choose a text color that will contrast with the background.
- Left-justify text.
- Use headings and subheadings to provide hierarchy of the content.
- Use a combination of upper and lower case letters; avoid using all upper case.
- Use a minimum of 1½ spaces between lines.

GRAPHICS

- Choose a graphic that is directly related to the content of the text on the screen.
- Consider the developmental level of the viewer when selecting the complexity of the graphic.
- Use realistic graphics when content is dependent on visual detail.
- Limit the number of graphics per screen to one for most topics, two if showing a contrast or comparison.

SPECIAL EFFECTS

- Use special effects sparingly.
- Be consistent in use of builds and transitions throughout a program.
- Avoid builds that use overpowering effects such as flying or walking text.
- Avoid effects that are slow transitions from one screen to another.
- Avoid transitions that change the viewer's focus of attention such as checkerboard dissolves or diagonal wipes. **Tc**

Elizabeth Downs is Assistant Professor and Kenneth Clark is Associate Professor in the Department of Educational Leadership, Technology, and Research at Georgia Southern University in Statesboro, Georgia.

Authentic Assessment of Information Literacy Through Electronic Products

Electronic resources make it easier for students and teachers to demonstrate to a skeptical public the depth and diversity of schooling.

By Lesley S. J. Farmer

THE DEMAND FOR tougher standards for high school graduation, by both local and national constituents, signals the need for school accountability. Parents and the community demand that a diploma mean more than a certificate of completion of a certain number of hours.

How can learning become authentic? One possible solution is outcomes-based education that uses authentic assessment. This article explores this concept and its implications for information literacy.

What is Outcomes-Based Education

Essentially, outcomes-based education embraces the concept of measurable goals-setting. When developed and stated clearly, outcomes specify what schools want students to accomplish. Outcomes describe standards that graduates will meet or exceed. Outcomes are set within a framework of performance, which is measured against an objective standard rather than in relationship to the abilities of other students.

Additionally, outcomes use an assessment tool to determine whether or not a student achieves the standard. Outcomes tend to be stated in global terms. Typically one to ten outcomes would describe a course. On the other hand, the performance indicators more resemble instructional objectives; they are detailed and specific.

The Education Task Force (ETF), a consortium of K-14 public schools in Marin County, California, has been developing a series of outcomes to drive education and provide seamless articulation between school levels. One of the outcomes generated by ETF is:

> **Authentic assessment is not a one-time event. Just as in the work world, assessment in schools is an ongoing activity.**

Using technology as a tool to access information, analyze and solve problems, and communicate ideas.

To put the outcome in concrete terms, each element is given a descriptor:

The student demonstrates competence in the use of authoring tools, graphic applications, and telecommunications. Uses technology in many disciplines to solve problems. Selects and employs a variety of electronic technology resources for research and communication. Creates products using technologies. Uses technology responsibly, legally, and ethically.

Another step specifies the performance indicators demonstrating that the student has achieved that outcome. For high school graduates, technology indicators include:

Within a curricular context the student will produce a solo project which exhibits mastery of the following technologies, authoring tools, graphics, telecommunications plus items from at least two different technology categories. Students may propose projects that encompass such processes as design, construction, and modeling. Or, the student will develop a portfolio that incorporates the use of three or more technologies with sample works from at least four subject areas.

Two other indicators fill out the list. Additionally, benchmark indicators are identified for second, fifth and eighth graders. For instance, the fifth-grade benchmark includes "cross-curricular project presented by a small group, utilizing at least two authoring tools plus two other technologies."

Standards

While it is not the intent of this article to focus on standards, certainly standards play a role in authentic assessment. Schools and educational groups are already busy creating standards, from the classroom to the national level. Such standards describe the level of acceptable or desired competence but vary widely in their perspective. Standards can be analogous to "setting the bar": an athlete is expected to high jump (outcome) a five-foot bar (standard).

The Mid-continent Regional Educational Laboratory (McREL) distinguishes between content and performance standards. The critical difference is that a performance standard describes a task that a student is supposed to accomplish in order to demonstrate his or her knowledge or skill. In terms of fractions, a content standard might be "the ability to use fractions to solve problems"; a performance standard might be "a student should be able to accurately calculate how to share two pies among seven people equally." Content standards most closely resemble outcomes. Performance standards correlate to outcome indicators. Subcomponent standards refer to benchmarks, just as with outcomes-based educational terms.

Authentic Assessment

Assessment, in general, refers to gathering and analyzing information about students in order to determine their abilities. Assessment is a basic part of education because it enables one to determine whether students "get it," whether they meet the standard. Not surprisingly, outcomes are directly associated with authentic assessment. The underlying theory is that outcomes need to be authentic: that is, true to life and reflecting lifelong learning skills. Outcomes should also answer essential questions and use high-order thinking skills. Thus to measure outcomes, authentic assessment is usually called for, referring to a complex set of performances. It's the difference between describing how to ride a bike and actually putting the foot to the pedal and pumping down the street. Thus a scantron "bubble" test would be an unlikely authentic assessment tool; a student-directed play would more closely correlate to real life, and a Junior Achievement business venture would constitute a still more authentic assessment, especially as students count their profits.

Authentic assessments can assume many forms. In his book *Assessing Learning in the Classroom*, McTighe categorizes assessment items as

Product: lab report, story, poem, art exhibit, model, videotape, spreadsheet.

Performance: dance, demonstration, athletic competition, debate, recital.

Process: conference, interview, journal.

The assessment task itself should have these characteristics:

- multidimensional and complex in nature
- incorporated modalities of learning
- demonstrated progress over time
- learned with practice rather than based on native talent
- built on practice and feedback
- aligned with school outcomes and goals.

This approach to accountability not only helps students see the relevance of their learning but also reflects society's demands for education that prepares students for the world of work. Authentic assessment helps bridge the two worlds. By designing substantial projects, students demonstrate their ability to work with peers and accomplish specific tasks. They show that they can apply theoretical concepts to solving lifelike problems. As a result, education doesn't seem to operate in a vacuum; it truly prepares students for the rest of their lives. Real learning for real results.

Authentic assessment is not a one-time event. Just as in the work world, assessment in schools is an ongoing activity. As a person creates a draft or

---

With the surge in educational technology, information literacy skills can be assessed in new and creative ways.

---

a model, that effort is analyzed and feedback is given so the product will be the best possible. So, too, in education; as students make a first attempt in a project, teachers should provide meaningful feedback. Students should assess their own work and their peers' to insure the best final results.

Rubrics

The next question that arises is, how does one assess projects objectively? Outcomes-based education typically includes rubrics that describe the performance at different levels of competencies. These rubrics are developed at the same time as the outcomes so that everyone involved in the outcome has a clear understanding of what is being measured and the degree of competency required at each level. A sample rubric for the ETF outcome quoted above appears in the box (page 13).

As the sample shows, the difference between levels of competence often lies in degree or thoroughness, such as "wide variety" versus "diverse" or "some" versus "many." These key words act as critical features to distinguish one level of competency from another. As teachers and students develop rubrics, they identify what is "good" by identifying these critical differences. Concurrently, rubrics are "anchored" in actual products or performances, so everyone knows what a "4" looks like in comparison to a "3" or "2" or "1." How different is this approach from the practice where a teacher gives an abstract goal or assignment and doesn't show any examples of the desired product at the beginning!

Electronic Projects

Key to achievement in outcomes-based education are the benchmarks that demonstrate authentic learning. The design and development of a product or presentation becomes the contextual vehicle for learning concepts and skills. Typically, a project spans several lesson units and crosses subject disciplines. Because of the amount of research and synthesis involved, products may demand an extended period of time. Products are often developed by a group of students, and the teacher acts as a facilitator. Thus, the product to be assessed also needs to be open-ended enough to allow each student to bring to it his individual gifts and to maximize individual learning.

Implications for Information Literacy

With the surge in educational technology, information literacy skills can be assessed in new and creative ways. The following examples highlight the potential for authentic assessment of information literacy skills using electronic products.

Newspaper or magazine simulation. Students recreate another time period or historical events by producing a newspaper or other publication of the day. For instance, a simulated paper on the day that Julius Caesar died might include scanned pictures of ancient Rome. Students would need to research Marc Antony, the Roman Senate, Roman mythology, and maybe Roman cuisine. They might find out about Roman entertainments, such as the Coliseum attractions, and incorporate advertisements for them. They would need to organize their findings in the form of newspaper layout and report writing. Students would probably use a Roman typeface, including the use of "V" for every "U"

Technology and Product Rubric

OUTSTANDING 4	HIGHLY COMPETENT 3	COMPETENT 2	NOT YET PROFICIENT 1
complexity in defining problems and stating thesis	clearly defines problem/states thesis	defines problems/states thesis	does not define problem/state thesis
accesses relevant information from a wide variety of sources	accesses relevant information from diverse sources	accesses relevant information	does not access relevant information
shows thorough understanding of the problem, concepts and processes	shows good understanding of the problem, concepts and processes	shows general understanding of the problem, concepts and processes	shows little or no understanding of the problem, concepts and processes
provides an exceptionally clear, coherent, complete, and organized explanation	provides a clear, coherent, complete, and organized explanation	provides a reasonably clear, coherent, complete, and organized explanation	provides an unclear or incomplete explanation
rarely contains technical errors	contains few technical errors	contains some technical errors	contains many technical errors
contains relevant information	contains relevant information	contains relevant information	contains very little information
uses correct language mechanics and usage	uses correct language mechanics and usage	uses correct language mechanics and usage	contains many errors in language mechanics and usage
production and composition are excellent	production and composition are good	production and composition are fair	production and composition are poor
integrates diverse technology effectively	integrates technology effectively	integrates technology	does not integrate technology

(since "u"s hadn't been invented yet).

Videotape production. Students can tape interviews with local experts about regional environment issues, and compare/contrast the talks with videos of affected nature. The video essay can demonstrate student ability to locate primary sources, identify main ideas, distinguish between fact and opinion, synthesize and sequence their research, and visually communicate what they learned.

Computer-Aided Design (CAD). Students can develop a model neighborhood, which could demonstrate their knowledge of community services and interrelationships. The project can be strengthened by introducing a crisis, such as a fire or major layoff. Students could also complement their CAD project through the use of spreadsheets to quantify the neighborhood economic "ecology." This added project shows how students have located and applied statistical information.

Multimedia presentation. Students can design a political advertising campaign on *HyperStudio* (Wagner) or other software program. Cards showing the candidate's background and political stance would concretely demonstrate student research results. Pictures portraying issues would show the student's ability to locate and select visual sources. Multimedia presentations can result in particularly useful assessments, for students would be learning globally or rationally rather than sequentially.

Web page publication. Students can create "WebQuests" about a topic, providing an electronic equivalent to a bibliographic essay. Selecting and describing significant Web links demonstrate the student's ability to locate and evaluate Internet sources. Web pages can also show how students organize their information for easy access.

Ways to Get Started

Here are some ways you can begin to introduce authentic assessment in your school.

■ Collect examples of authentic assessments of electronic products.

■ Build on existing strategies that incorporate electronic products. An easy method is to videotape a simulation; for example, students re-enacting a U.S. Senate proceeding instead of writing a paper about a Senate bill.

■ Collaborate with another teacher to design an interdisciplinary unit that weaves in authentic assessment and electronic products.

■ Brainstorm with students to identify electronic products that would demonstrate deep learning and also apply to daily life.

■ Use phrases such as "What does it look like?" "What do you feel when. . ." "How do you know?" as you think about and discuss assessment.

■ Start with a clear-cut presentation, such as a lab procedure or a step-by-step demonstration, and develop two rubrics, one that describes competence of the content and another that describes the presentation itself.

■ Have students develop electronic portfolios of their work in which they have to choose items that show progress over time and represent their best efforts. Then have students write reflective letters explaining their choices and assessing their own progress.

Lesley S.J. Farmer is the Library Media Teacher at Redwood High School in Larkspur, California. She is also the consulting editor for the Professional Growth Series published by Linworth and an editorial consultant to the magazine TECHNOLOGY CONNECTION. She is the author of a number of books, including Workshops for Teachers: Becoming Partners for Information Literacy *(Linworth).*

MULTIMEDIA

Yes, They Put on Quite a Show,
BUT WHAT DID THEY LEARN?

by Joanne Troutner

Have you heard of the Kansas City Monarchs, the Pittsburgh Crawfords, the Indianapolis Clowns, or the Homestead Grays? These teams were part of the Negro baseball league formed in the 1860s. The link with racism is obvious to most students. However, the link with Adolph Hitler requires a slightly more astute youngster.

Students in history at Battle Ground Middle School are finding a number of links between their favorite topics that are not usually covered during the short school year. Josh is class expert on the Negro baseball league. Susan did her research on Ellis Island. Shannon has acquired in-depth knowledge about Adolph Hitler. Janet's project provides a look at the life of George Washington Carver.

These hypermedia projects span the school year and are presented to the entire class during the month of May. Motivation runs high because the students can choose the topic that interests them most, and they use IBM's *Linkway*, digitized images, and sound to develop their history projects. When all the projects are completed, they are put on the instructional network in the school and serve as reference tools. In this way, all the students can see the work of their fellow students.

Technology, in the guise of *Linkway*, has invaded the history class. Students, the teacher, and the library media specialist all function as a team during development of these technology projects. The research portion is facilitated by the library media specialist. The classroom teacher and the library media specialist provide some initial instruction in the use of *Linkway*. The students are given one day a week throughout most of the school year to work on the projects.

> *Students, the teacher, and the library media specialist all function as a team during development of these technology projects.*

While this sounds like a good use of technology, and it is, you may well ask, "How are these projects assessed? How do you know that students learned anything from them?" These questions were asked by the educators at Battle Ground Middle School and the other three schools using hypermedia for student projects.

For several years a team of educators in the Tippecanoe School Corporation has been working on incorporating the use of hypermedia at the secondary level. In the first two years the educators learned to use hypermedia themselves and discovered methods of successfully integrating hypermedia projects into social studies, history, geography, and science curricula. The third and subsequent years of the project found the group discussing, investigating, and developing assessment methods to use with hypermedia projects developed by students.

The discussion of assessment began with these questions: How do we know what the students are learning? How do we justify the amount of time spent on these hypermedia projects? The yearlong process of developing assessment tools began over lunch. The following questions were discussed:

- What are the existing paradigms for assessing hypermedia projects?
- What strongly held beliefs color our assessment?
- What strongly held rules color our hypermedia use and assessment?
- What assumptions do we have about assessment?

This discussion led to more questions. In order to continue the development of an assessment process, we held a daylong retreat facilitated by an outside expert on assessment. We also used some of the Grant Wiggins videotape series on assessment, "Standards Not Standardization." During the day, we developed two lists. The first list described the actions we wanted to assess as students developed hypermedia projects; the second list explained what these actions looked like and how we would recognize them. The list of desired goals included research, links in knowledge, decision making, self-reflection and assessment, creativity, design techniques, and technical computer skills. We ended the day with a tentative list of areas we wanted to assess, characteristics associated with these areas, and brief descriptions of how we would know it when we saw it.

> "How were these projects assessed?" and "how do you know the students learned anything from the time spent on them?"

From here began the detailed work of developing our scoring rubrics (see page 17). During a series of four after-school sessions, we developed scoring rubrics for presentation, cooperative learning skills, computer skills, and content knowledge. Discussion was lively, sometimes heated, as work continued. Changing from a traditional scoring method or from a method that relied heavily on evaluating computer skills alone was not easy. The topic of how to explain the assessment process to parents was discussed frequently. Finally, we had scoring rubrics we were ready to pilot test.

Pilot testing was done in several areas. First, one group had the students use the computer skills rubric as a peer assessment tool midway through the hypermedia project development. This session proved invaluable to the educators and the students. We found the scoring rubric worked well. However, we quickly discovered the need to hone students' skills in the area of peer assessment. Second, some of the group took the concept of our scoring rubrics and developed assessment tools for other classroom assignments. Student feedback was extremely positive as were the feelings of the educators involved. These kinds of comments from students were common: "Boy, Ms. K., now I really know what you want from our debate!" "Mrs. Trujillo, how can I not get an A on this project? You're telling me exactly what you are looking for."

One of the most rewarding and effective public relations tools was the pilot test involving parents. We had a parent assessment night during which the parents actually used the computer skills rubric to score a child's project. During the course of the evening, the scoring rubrics for knowledge, cooperative learning, and presentation were also discussed. The success of the event was gauged by the fact that parents were very reluctant to leave. They wanted to continue exploring the social studies references created by the students. In addition, the discussion among the parents about how concrete the evaluation was and how students could not claim they did not understand what was expected of them proved that our scoring rubrics and the assessment process accomplished what we educators had envisioned. Assessment of these projects had moved from a simple summative assessment of computer skills to a formative assessment of the complete project. The scoring rubrics also helped build, from the start of the project, student understanding of the expectations.

Final assessment of the projects was done by including the parent assessment, a peer assessment, the

> *How do we know what the students are learning and how do we justify the amount of time spent on these hypermedia projects?*

content area teacher assessment, the library media specialist assessment, and the assessment of another teacher, the principal, or a central office administrator. Student reaction to this comprehensive assessment was astounding. Often, the students would comment on the feeling of importance it gave them to have so many people examining their work. The students were very particular about the final product knowing that their audience would include more than the classroom teacher.

As we educators completed the first year of using these assessment tools, we proclaimed the experience of developing them as one of the most powerful forms of staff development we had ever experienced. We felt our growth as educators was phenomenal. Finally, as we planned, the group has continued to share, with at least one educator, the new assessment strategies. The work of integrating technology into the curriculum, as well as changing assessment, has begun in the Tippecanoe School Corporation. Technology, assessment, and a team approach that included the library media specialist were the catalysts for the change. **TC**

© *Joanne Troutner, 1996.*

References:

Wiggins, Grant. et al. (1991) *Standards, Not Standardization Volume I: Rethinking Assessment.* Genesco, New York: Class.

Joanne Troutner is the Director of Technology and Media at Tippecanoe School Corporation, Lafayette, Indiana.

RUBRIC FOR PRESENTATIONS INCORPORATING TECHNOLOGY

Criteria: Students' use of technology
1) Accurately reflects the ideas presented.
2) Communicates clearly.
3) Contributes meaningful content to topic presented.
4) Is technically/mechanically competent.
5) Reflects higher-order thinking skills.
6) Is appropriate to the audience.
7) Is well-developed and organized.

Scale
A: Fully accomplishes the purpose of the task; is well done; exceeds requirements
B: Substantially accomplishes the purpose of the task; is adequate; meets requirements
C: Partially accomplishes the purpose of the task; needs revisions; meets limited requirements
D: Makes little or no progress in accomplishing the purpose of the task; should restart; meets little or none of the requirements

Assessment of Presentation

Section	Description	Rating Key
Oral	• Good eye contact • People at back of room can hear • Demonstrated ease with topic • Smiles, shows enthusiasm in voice	1 Unsure/poor eye contact 2 Limited eye contact/some questions 3 Poised/answered questions
Mechanics	• Punctuation • Spelling • Grammar—Basic verb tenses • No slang • Graphic further explains or clarifies text • Supported facts	1 Poor grammar/spelling 2 Some problems 3 Complex sentences/correct grammar
Matching Information to Presentation	• Graphics help explain text • Graphs/charts best form to convey information • Graphics serve a purpose	1 Graphics distracting 2 Graphics superfluous 3 Graphics reinforce information

Assessment of Cooperative Learning Skills

Section	Description	Rating Key
Shared Labor	• Contributes orally in class • Contributes with written material to the group project • Contributes ideas to group • Willingness to contribute	1 Little contribution 2 Adequate contribution 3 Equitable contribution
Dependability	• Attends class • Meets deadlines • Brings supplies	1 Sometimes 2 Usually 3 Always
Integration of Work/Collaboration of Effort	• No bickering or whining • Ability to compromise • Willingness to adapt work as needed • Revise work as needed to fit group project • Accepts constructive comments • Ability to tactfully provide constructive comments • Gives positive feedback to group	1 Sometimes 2 Usually 3 Always

Assessment of Computer Skills

Section	Description	Rating Key
Screen Design	• Button placement consistent • Type contrast pleasing • Type style appropriate • Icons appropriate • Arrows point correctly/sized • Picture size appropriate • Graphics understandable/appropriate	1 Can't read it/inconsistent 2 Okay/usable but confusing/can navigate folder 3 Clear/appealing/navigate easily
Program Operation	• Contains Menu or Quit button on every page • Buttons work as stated • Pop ups, if used, are clearly marked • Sound, if used, is clear	1 Doesn't work/has lots of bugs 2 Works but has some bugs 3 Pretty bug free
Program Design	• Has title page with credits • Appropriate use of branching • Pop ups appropriate • Branching opportunities • Returns to a recognizable point, i.e. menu • Uses intuitive icons as much as possible	1 Many deadends/doesn't flow 2 Works but could be better 3 Pretty well designed/logical flow
Use of Linkway Resources	• Uses pictures/graphics appropriately & often • Uses sound appropriately • Uses paint feature appropriately • Uses types of buttons appropriately	1 No graphics/sound/links 2 Acceptable use/missed opportunity/few links 3 Optimal use

Assessment of Knowledge

Section	Description	Rating Key
Research	• Uses varied sources—books, magazines, vertical file, databases • Has notes with source documented • Has bibliography • Cites sources • Avoids plagiarism	1 Has less than required number of resources 2 Has required number of resources 3 Has more than required number of resources
Subject Knowledge	• Mentions factors leading up to or resulting from topic • Relates topic to time period • Historically accurate	1 Little or no understanding of where topic fits in history 2 Some understanding 3 Clear understanding
Organization of Information	• Logical progression of information • Thesis is clear • Introduction clearly states purpose • Conclusion clear • Graphic further explains or clarifies text • Supported facts	1 Strange connections between information 2 Limited connections between information 3 Logical connections between information
Content and Accuracy	• Facts are up-to-date • Pictures accurately tie to text • Sound ties to text • Demonstrates depth of knowledge	1 Inaccurate/lack of ties 2 Accurate but partial requirements 3 Accurate and fits requirements

Head for the Edge

By Doug Johnson

Getting What You Ask For

I've discovered a great technique for getting what I want for Christmas. I describe the hoped-for gift—precisely. I've learned that if I simply ask for a tie, heaven only knows what I'll receive. If I ask for a red-and-gray tie, my chances improve. But if I lead my daughter by the hand to the Jerry Garcias at the local department store and ooh and ah over one or two, I am pretty sure to get something to my taste.

As educators begin to work with students on performance skills that cannot be evaluated by standard paper and pencil tests, their ability to write an assessment instrument that clearly articulates a desired quality level becomes critical. Whether in the form of a rubric, a checklist, or a benchmark, creating tools that describe what is expected of learners can help educators dramatically improve instruction.

Library media specialists have a leadership role in implementing these new forms of assessment. Having experienced project-based learning, we can use our experiences to teach teachers effective means of evaluating performances and projects, both through inservice workshops and by modeling the assessments of joint library/classroom projects. Our media specialists and teachers are becoming increasingly proficient at writing good assessment instruments. Here are some of their secrets:

1. Describe what you want in observable terms. Remember the tie analogy? The more specific you can be with the indicators of quality, the easier it will be for students to determine quality for themselves. A hypermedia stack about a historical period might include checklist items such as:
- location and years
- proper clothing
- correct transportation
- tools and weapons
- people doing their daily work
- key events—what happened that was so important we're still studying it?
- main geographical features
- symbols (religious, job-related, or holiday) that were important to people in your region
- important or famous people, sayings, or documents.

2. Use two strands of assessment: content and container. Remember getting back English papers that had one grade for content and one for mechanics? Projects that use technology to help communicate the content really need two separate sets of assessment criteria—one for the content and one for the electronic container of that content. Whether it is videotape, hypermedia stack, electronic slideshow, word processed document, desktop published brochure, spreadsheet, or database, you need to develop an assessment tool that describes the effective use of the container. Quality container criteria for the hypermedia stack above might include:
- a minimum of eight cards, each with a uniform background and layout style
- easily seen and understood navigation buttons
- a logical organization and structure
- readable text
- graphics, sounds, and movies to add to the understanding of the topic

3. Use examples of past high-quality work. Students need to see or read actual examples of high-quality work. The "critical elements," as Mankato media specialist Kathy Wortel describes them, need to be listed. One of the dangers of using examples is that students may be tempted to copy them too closely. To prevent their doing so, change the assignment enough to make that impossible. If a research assignment looks at the attributes of effective leaders, one year ask students to choose scientists as subjects, the next year social activists. If geographic regions are the topic, questions one year can be about environmental issues, the next year about the effect of geography has on living conditions.

4. Give criteria to the learner at the time you make the assignment. Assessment tools need to be shared with students at the time the assignment is given, not after it is complete. That way students have a roadmap to follow as they work on the project. The goal should be *no surprises*. Here is the task. Here are the quality indicators. Go to it.

5. Use the assessment tool to help guide revisions. Jean Donham at the University of Iowa reminds us that the term assessment has its roots in a Latin word that means "to sit down beside." One of the great philosophical differences between doing an assessment and an evaluation is, an assessment is a tool that encourages continued growth rather than simply judging a completed task. The assessment tool should help students see where they are strong and where they can improve. And by using these tools while the project is in the works, rather than simply when it is completed, you can actively encourage such growth and improvement.

6. Use multiple assessors. The best checklists I've seen have places for input from multiple sources. The teacher, of course, should comment on whether a quality indicator has been met, as should the student. The media specialist can add his or her unique perspective. Parents should be given the opportunity to review with their children the progress of the work. And in special cases, experts in either the subject of the research or the use of the media can provide insights unavailable elsewhere.

7. Revise your tools each time you use them. No assessment instrument is perfect the first time it is used. Criteria might be unclear. Too many indicators might restrict creativity or originality. We have found and eliminated nearly all uses of superlatives (good, better, best) in creating rubrics. The terms are empty without precise descriptors of what actually makes something "better" than something only "good." Keep your assessment tools in digital format, a word processing document, or database, for easy updating and reuse.

Writing good assessments takes time, practice, and thought. And that goes not just for instruments that measure student performance, but also for tools that measure the quality of programs and professional performance. The more experience we as educators have in articulating what we hope to get, the better chance we have of getting it. Remember Johnson's Law of Assessment: You'll only get what you want if you can describe what you want. And that applies to both Christmas ties and student performance.

Doug Johnson is the District Media Supervisor for the Mankato (Minnesota) Public Schools. Doug's new book, The Indispensible Teacher's Guide to Computer Skills, has just been released by Linworth Publishing.

TECHNOLOGY: IT'S ELEMENTARY FOR YOUNG LEARNERS AND THEIR TEACHERS TOO

feature

Tailoring the Internet to Primary Classrooms

By Kathy Tobiason

Walk into any primary classroom and you'll notice little chairs, tiny tables, and waist-high drinking fountains. Accommodations like these allow young learners to go about their work comfortably and productively. Rather than keep children home from school until they grow into their desks, we've recognized the need to scale down the environment to fit the learner. At our school, we're trying to do the same thing with the Internet.

The American School in Japan (ASIJ) is a K-12 international school in the suburbs of West Tokyo. Since our student body is drawn from a high-tech business community, we are blessed with abundant technology resources. As we've tackled the challenge of meaningfully integrating technology into an already bulging curriculum, a few basic principles have come to light. First, technology tools are treated as resources within the structure of our resource-based teaching. Second, the use of these tools is determined by the learning and problem-solving activities that take place within integrated, thematic units. Third, we try to adapt our technology tools to make them more accessible to young learners.

An example of this customization is the main menu in the elementary computer labs. To log on to the lab server, kindergartners type the letter "K." This gives them access to a submenu listing the programs that are used at their level. Third graders type "third" and get a more extensive list of choices. By fifth grade, students have access to the entire gamut of applications and programs.

The next challenge was to customize our access to the limitless resources of the World Wide Web. We wanted to scale down the tool to fit young learners. Sounds daunting, doesn't it? Over the course of a school year, with a little experimentation and a good deal of collaboration, we came up with a strategy that is helping us meet these goals.

Originally, with leadership from third-grade teacher Cathi Matthews, our efforts were focused on identifying and bookmarking appropriate Internet sites. Cathi and others were spending hours each day prospecting for high-quality Web sites to support our instructional units. Before long, the elementary lab computers had lengthy lists of bookmarked sites. Cathi took the next step and organized the bookmarks into folders by units and topics. The end result was an excellent collection of URLs, plus staff and student enthusiasm for using them.

At the same time, another group of teachers focused on developing material for our elementary school home page. Fourth-grade teachers Jeff Harrits and Patty Nakagawa ran a student publishing activity that reported the events of their Japanese Culture unit. Ultimately, the student-written articles plus Quicktake photographs became the "Focus on Japan" segment of the ASIJ Elementary School home page (http://www.asij.ac.jp). Fifth-grade reporters, led by teacher Bridgette Fincher, developed a student-oriented Web page describing the school from an 11-year-old's perspective.

With all of this activity taking place in the same room, naturally some cross-fertilization took place. The after-school atmosphere of the elementary computer lab was charged with a spirit of exploration, camaraderie and collaboration. As a result, the idea to integrate bookmarks into an HTML format ultimately emerged. At first, this took the form of linking Cathi's Bookmarks to the elementary home page. It wasn't long before another idea surfaced: use HTML to organize the bookmarks. That eventually led to the format we are using today.

With the start of this school year, ASIJ gained classroom Internet access through a campus-wide network. We naturally wanted to maximize appropriate classroom use of this resource. We also wanted to minimize the possibility that students would encounter inappropriate material. Unlike Internet access in the computer labs, where there was direct supervision, classroom access was likely to take place while the teacher was occupied with other students.

How could we customize access to keep students on task and out of unproductive or unsavory territory?

The answer actually came in response to another question: Why doesn't somebody make a Web site with links to all the great rain forest information in the world? Eventually we realized that we could do this for ourselves.

Having used numerous weather web site bookmarks the previous year, Jeff took the next step and created an HTML web page devoted to the fourth-grade weather unit. Basically the page consists of the unit title and links to the URLs used for unit activities. The unit Web page acts as an organizer of the URLs (similar to bookmark folders) and structures student use of the resources. The unit Web page is set up as the classroom computer's home page, and students boot right to the tools they need. As Jeff says, "It focuses student's attention and focuses their access."

This prototype Web page became the model for how we maximize student access and minimize the problems inherent in independent student Internet use. Based on his weather home page, Jeff created a template that enables teachers to paste in active URLs for sites supporting unit activities. Now that a separate home page is set up for each unit of instruction, the URLs are organized by topic in a way that's easy for students to use. By simply clicking on the appropriate link from a page full of links on their topic, students access an appropriate site. In the elementary library, we've been able to facilitate unit home page development in a variety of ways. When a materials request for an instructional unit is made, the procedure for gathering resources includes running keyword searches through Alta Vista, and

checking Yahoo by category. We also check the *Internet Kids' Yellow Pages* (Osborne) and the *Educator's Internet Companion* (Wentworth). As new issues of *Classroom Connect* and *Electronic Learning* reach the library, we comb through them for recommended sites.

When promising sites are located, they're bookmarked as the first step to capturing them for the unit home page. After each site is previewed by the classroom teacher, the URL is copied, pasted into Works, and labeled with the name of the site. We can then save these on disk for teachers, along with print and AV materials for the unit. Teachers can upload the Works file and paste the active URLs into the unit home page in their classroom. Over the course of the year, we hope to create a unit home page for each major instructional unit.

We've added the process of building unit home pages into our training sessions on Internet use for teachers. ASIJ's elementary library and technology staff recently sponsored a Saturday Seminar, targeting search strategies and the unit home page process. The number of teachers willing to give up their Saturday to pick up this skill was proof that we're on the right track.

For further information contact Kathy Tobiason, ASIJ Elementary Librarian at: library@asij.ac.jp. **TC**

Kathy Tobiason is a Librarian at The American School in Japan.

ANOTHER OPINION...

By Barbara D. Stahl

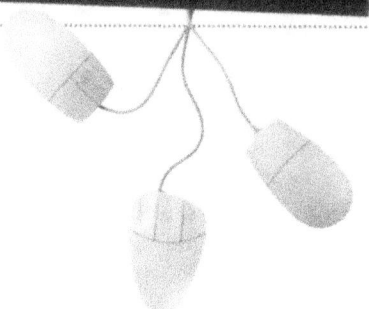

Quick! May I Go to the Internet?

Why use permission slips for Internet access? After much thought, research, and review of current literature, I believe it is wiser not to ask parents to sign acceptable use agreements for their children to use the Internet.

Students should use the Internet only for class assignments or approved independent study projects within the school curriculum and then only under supervision. Because exploring the Internet without direction is not an efficient use of instructional time, students should not be allowed to just "surf."

Staff and students must understand netiquette and online ethics, and must know how to determine appropriate sites. Proceeding without permission slips is not taking an easy way out, but it seems to be most realistic in the long run. Educating parents and community members becomes essential.

We don't ask a parent's permission for students to use encyclopedias or other reference books, so why single out the Internet? I'm not suggesting we should be naïve or stick our heads in the sand about the controversial and inappropriate sites on the Web. Responsibility and ethics are part of what we must teach our students. Although we may try to avoid them, explicit, violent, racist, outdated, and gender-insensitive print materials can be found on our shelves as well as in electronic resources.

The Internet is one more tool with which to gather information, but it shouldn't automatically be the first place we search for an answer. For all the Internet's popularity and attraction, most reference questions can be answered more efficiently by using encyclopedias, dictionaries, or other such common reference books.

Parental permission slips or filtering software for the Internet can create a false sense of security for instructors. With permission slips safely filed away, a more relaxed atmosphere may exist, allowing students to navigate the Net alone. And with filtering software, adults may think students will always be in an Internet "trouble-free environment." Neither of these scenarios is true.

Filtering software is not foolproof. It may block access to useful sites while at the same time allowing students into inappropriate sites. We have all heard of students being unable to access "breast cancer" or "sex roles in the workplace" because the words "breast" or "sex" were among the blocked words.

From a management standpoint, keeping track of who has submitted permission slips and determining if permission slips have been forged can become issues. Who keeps the master list? Who checks to be sure a student has permission to use the Internet? What if a student does not have permission, and the Internet is the only source needed to complete an assignment? What if a student who has a signed permission slip reaches an inappropriate site, and the parents still become furious.

Isn't it better to teach the value of the Internet while acknowledging that there are some unsuitable sites on the Web? Students need to learn how to make choices and how to sort the valid from the invalid and the credible from the incredible. We must give them the tools to evaluate sources. This alone can be a valuable lifelong skill.

There are two strategies that can be used to make the resources of the Internet safe. Teachers can bookmark sites they want students to use for a particular assignment. Those sites can be saved on a disk and opened online, and students would be instructed to go only to the designated sites.

The second strategy—and the safest way—is to use Net harvesting software, such as WebWhacker (ForeFront Group), which copies a desired portion from the Internet. Multiple menu levels can be saved. When the student uses the saved site on a computer, it acts exactly like being online. A great deal can be saved, but it can occupy a large amount of file space. This method confines and structures students' usage to only those Web sites previously collected by the teacher.

It is mandatory to get permission from the site owner to harvest Web pages, but the use of e-mail makes this process fairly painless. When you e-mail the Webmaster and describe how you plan to use the site with your students, most Web page creators are flattered and are willing to grant permission for educational applications.

Taking responsibility for one's actions is an admirable character trait. Perhaps educators can help foster that responsibility in our students by teaching ethical usage of the Internet. We cannot hold their hands throughout their lives, but we can try to give them systems for sifting and sorting through the massive amounts of available information. As library media specialists, our problem is no longer locating information. It is interpreting, evaluating, and discriminating to separate the valid from the invalid.

---

*Barbara D. Stahl is the Director of Library and Educational Information Resources at the Oneida City School District in Oneida, New York, and can be reached at **bstahl@oneida-admin. moric.org or barbsta@aol.com***

Editor's Note: Occasionally we invite authors to voice opinions on controversial or pressing issues that we feel are important for our readers. The opinions expressed in this column are those of the authors alone. We invite your participation or rebuttal. Send letters or questions to: 480 E. Wilson Bridge Road, Suite L, Worthington, OH 43085 with the subject: Another Opinion.

WHAT DO THEY REALLY NEED TO KNOW?

Adventures in Curriculum Writing

By Amy Pritzl

A year ago I took a high school library media position that required me to start from scratch in terms of philosophy, discipline, teacher cooperation, collection and, of course, curriculum. I spent the first year dispelling the ghosts of librarians past, ruthlessly weeding the collection, working with teachers, fighting for a larger book budget, cleaning up a disorganized and unkempt computer card catalog, and training two new part-time library aides. With those problems confronted, I decided it was time to begin writing a library media curriculum.

Building on Experience

Many school library media specialists have put off writing the curriculum, hoping that it would write itself. But with the push for meeting standards and benchmarks and maintaining up-to-date curriculums, the task can no longer be put off. Perhaps, in typical library media fashion, you began gathering and hoarding information on standards and curriculum. You may be surprised to learn that writing a library media curriculum really comes down to one's knowledge as a professional and what you think the students need to know.

Finding a book or an article listing the basic library information skills that ninth through twelfth graders need to learn is a difficult, if not impossible, task. It is easy to find a multitude of books on different methods for the research process, books on integrating information skills into the curriculum, and books on cooperating with teachers. Using the Internet, it is even easy to find stacks of ambiguous state and national standards that rarely seem to apply to our jobs. Very few, if any, of these resources get down to the nitty gritty job of identifying a minimal list of basic skills.

So what is a librarian to do? Lesson planning seems to be hit-and-miss when we don't have a core foundation upon which to build. As professionals, we are more than capable of developing lessons and projects to teach the skills, but first we need to identify the specific skills that need to be taught. What library information skills do ninth through twelfth grade students need to know?

In answering these questions, a library media specialist must trust his or her instincts, experience, and training. Deep down, we know we can identify students' weaknesses and the skills they need. Start

> Writing a library media curriculum really comes down to one's knowledge as a professional.

keeping a notebook of ideas or problems that you notice when working with students and classes. For example, when working with one class, I realized that the students did not use the index or table of contents in most of the books. They seemed to feel that everything should be alphabetically arranged as in the *World Book Encyclopedia.* Another problem I noted daily was the lack of effective electronic database and Internet search skills. Keeping these ideas and problems in a notebook makes it easier to compile a list of basic skills without trying to remember things off the top of your head or searching for misplaced scraps of paper.

Having access to copies of other school library curriculums is helpful, though they will have to be customized for your programs and resources. This will be another problem you encounter in your quest for information. Emphasis on computer, video, and multimedia production skills seems to be increasing. Quite often, these skills do not fall into the realm of the library media specialist's job. Many computer courses and skills are now taught through Business Education or Computer Technology departments, while Technical Education and English departments often teach the basics of video production. Because of your school's course offerings, your job as the library media specialist may focus on managing the library, purchasing and maintaining audiovisual equipment, and teaching information skills rather than technology skills.

Organizing Your Resources

After you sift through the course descriptions at your school and identify your niche in the curriculum, it is time to gather all your notes, books, articles, standards, and curricula and to write your curriculum. First, skim through all the information you have gathered, taking notes as you go along. Rather than writing notes on index cards, type them into the computer using a large font and the "columns" feature. When the notes are printed, simply cut them apart to be sorted and categorized, keeping an eye out for duplication and overlap. After sorting everything, choose a heading to best fit each category.

After all the searching and pondering and worrying, the basic information skills I settled upon are listed on the following pages.

As professionals, we are more than capable of developing lessons and projects to teach the skills, but first we need to identify the specific skills that need to be taught.

Library Use:

- ✓ Understands the role(s) and expertise of the library staff
- ✓ Demonstrates proper library conduct
- ✓ Demonstrates an understanding of the procedures for checking out and returning materials
- ✓ Understands the importance of returning materials on time
- ✓ Recognizes the arrangement and location of materials within the library
- ✓ Comprehends the purpose and arrangement of the Dewey Decimal Classification System and can locate materials using this system
- ✓ Utilizes the computer card catalog to locate materials
- ✓ Identifies information on the card catalog:
  - Call Number
  - Title
  - Author
  - Status
  - Subjects
- ✓ Demonstrates knowledge of available print and computer resources
- ✓ Demonstrates proper use of library materials, including books, periodicals, electronic resources, and equipment
- ✓ Utilizes the school library resources and available materials
- ✓ Utilizes the public library and other available community resources, such as interlibrary loan and distance education

Literature Appreciation:

- ✓ Understands literary terminology:
  - Genre
  - Fiction
  - Nonfiction
  - Biography
  - Autobiography
  - Annotation
- ✓ Recognizes award-winning, college-bound, core classics, and other distinguished books
- ✓ Reads for classroom assignments
- ✓ Reads for personal and recreational purposes

Resources & Researching:
Selection of appropriate resources

- ✓ Comprehends the need to read for different purposes
- ✓ Identifies a wide range of print and computer resources
- ✓ Understands the purpose and use of different types of materials
- ✓ Identifies the strengths and weaknesses of different types of materials
- ✓ Understands the advisability and feasibility of print versus computer resources and applies this knowledge
- ✓ Selects the most appropriate types of materials for completing research and classroom assignments
- ✓ Utilizes the most appropriate types of materials for completing research and classroom assignments

Research Strategies and Tools

- ✓ Recognizes different research process strategies
- ✓ Applies a research process strategy when conducting a research assignment
- ✓ Understands the difference between keyword and subject searching
- ✓ Selects appropriate keywords or subjects when searching
- ✓ Utilizes Boolean logic or other operators/limiters to narrow searches
- ✓ Understands cross-referencing
- ✓ Utilizes cross-referencing to locate information
- ✓ Utilizes complex or advanced features of print and electronic resources
- ✓ Identifies resources with varying viewpoints
- ✓ Understands the difference between primary and secondary resources

Utilization of Print Resources

- ✓ Understands basic terminology:
  - Periodical
  - Concise
  - Collective
  - Abridged
  - Bibliography
  - Glossary
  - Appendix
  - Table of Contents
- ✓ Understands the various formats of reference materials:
  - Alphabetical
  - Chronological
  - Topical
  - Single or Multi Volume Indexes
- ✓ Utilizes the various features of print materials to locate information, including the table of contents, index, appendix, glossary, and bibliography
- ✓ Utilizes basic reference tools:
  - Collective biographies
  - Almanacs
  - Atlases
  - General and specialized dictionaries
  - General and specialized encyclopedias

Chronologies

- ✓ Understands the purpose and arrangement of the vertical file
- ✓ Utilizes the vertical file to locate information
- ✓ Utilizes a variety of print materials to locate information
- ✓ Selects the most appropriate print materials for completing research and classroom assignments
- ✓ Utilizes the most appropriate print materials for completing research and classroom assignments

Utilization of Computer Resources

- ✓ Understands basic terminology:
  - Database
  - Boolean logic
  - Boolean operator(s)
  - Keyword(s)
  - Abstract
  - Full-text
  - Listserv
  - Standalone
  - URL
  - JPEG, GIF, and other file formats
  - Icon
  - Search engine
  - E-mail
  - Network
  - Reboot
  - Reset
  - Minimize
  - Maximize
- ✓ Identifies computer research resources available in the library
- ✓ Utilizes computer research resources to locate information
- ✓ Compares and selects appropriate search engines when using the Internet
- ✓ Utilizes strategies and search tools when searching computer resources:
  - Boolean operators
  - Keywords
  - Symbolic operators (for example, " ", +)
  - Help menus
  - Function keys

- ✔ Utilizes advanced search functions (if available)
- ✔ Understands the difference between subject and keyword searching
- ✔ Understands the purpose and format of various computer resources
- ✔ Identifies the strengths and weaknesses of various computer resources
- ✔ Selects the most appropriate computer resources for completing research and classroom assignments
- ✔ Utilizes the most appropriate computer resources for completing research and classroom assignments

Ethical and Legal Issues:
- ✔ Understands terminology:
  - Copyright
  - Bibliography
  - Censorship
  - Fair use
  - Plagiarism
  - Citation
  - Freeware
  - Shareware
  - Commercial software
- ✔ Credits sources for all quotations, visuals, major ideas, facts, and data
- ✔ Identifies and locates the necessary elements of a bibliographic citation
- ✔ Compiles bibliographic information using an approved format
- ✔ Understands the importance of crediting sources
- ✔ Identifies issues related to censorship
- ✔ Understands issues related to censorship
- ✔ Understands copyright and fair use regulations
- ✔ Applies copyright and fair use regulations
- ✔ Understands the legal restrictions on electronic media
- ✔ Understands when copyright permission needs to be obtained
- ✔ Understands how to obtain copyright permission
- ✔ Understands the concept of intellectual freedom

Evaluation of Resources:
- ✔ Evaluates resources and information for:
  - Reliability
  - Timeliness
  - Bias
  - Accuracy
  - Relevancy
  - Authority
  - Stereotyping
- ✔ Distinguishes between fact, opinion, point of view, and inference
- ✔ Utilizes specific techniques for evaluating Internet resources
- ✔ Understands why Internet resources need to be evaluated more closely than other resources
- ✔ Evaluates the appropriateness and effectiveness of resources used
- ✔ Evaluates the research process and determines how it could have been improved, expanded, or modified

Independent Learning:
- ✔ Conducts independent research on topics
- ✔ Independently locates materials in the library
- ✔ Independently selects materials for classroom and personal use

The curriculum writing process is reminiscent of writing a high school or college research paper—the information gathering, the note taking, the revising and revising and revising. But like any good research project, curriculum work will never really be "finished." More revising and adding will always need to be done. The skills still need to be broken down into grade levels, and lessons and projects still need to be developed in cooperation with the classroom teachers. Use a basic skills inventory to determine the ninth graders' entry-level skills so the curriculum can be adjusted accordingly. These tasks are easier once a list of basic skills has been developed. Once you become serious about the task of writing a curriculum, you can accomplish quite a bit in just a few weeks. You may even wonder why you ever dreaded this project at all!

Amy Pritzl is the Library Media Specialist at Southern Door County High School in Brussels, Wisconsin.

NOTES

Making the Most of E-Mail

HOW TO BE CONCISE, COURTEOUS, AND CORRECT ONLINE

by Leticia Ekhaml

Electronic mail has become a popular and indispensable method of communication. However, it has a few disadvantages. It can sometimes cause misunderstandings because, like letters, it offers no clue about the sender's facial expressions, body language, or tone of voice. A second problem is that you cannot send a message without knowing the receiver's e-mail address. Finally, you need to check your e-mail frequently, since the quantity can quickly overwhelm you.

Readers hesitate to read unusually long messages. Don't be a blatherer.

When you type a message on a text editor of the e-mail system and send the message, the program tells you, the sender, that the message has been sent. The message goes to the mailbox of the receiver on the same central computer. After the receiver reads the message, he or she can choose to reply to the sender, forward the message to someone else, delete the message, print it, file it, or simply quit.

Avoid These Mistakes

- Inaccurately typing the receiver's address. "Addressee unknown" or "undelivered mail" messages specify this problem.
  Remedy: Always check the person's address before mailing.

- Failing to give an appropriate subject line to the message. A subject line helps the receiver identify the summary or importance of the message. Examples of inappropriate subject lines are:
  Subject: Your June 6th response
  Subject: Your reply yesterday
  Subject: Urgent message
  Remedy: Summarize your message in a phrase on the subject line or use key words in your subject line. Some authors recommend that you tell the receiver what to do instead of what your message is about. For example: Subject: Send copy of the July 26th Minutes.

- Using conventional greetings such as Dear Sirs, Dear Madam, Dear Jane.
  Remedy: If you know the person well, address the person by the first name without the "Dear." If you know the group of persons you are writing to, write "Greetings." If you are writing to someone you don't know, use Mr. ___ or Ms. ___.

- Using long paragraphs or long messages that occupy more than one screenful. Readers hesitate to read unusually long messages. Don't be a blatherer.
  Remedies: Break a long paragraph into several short paragraphs to increase readability. Limit your message to one or two screens. Make use of journalists' *inverted pyramid* style—that is, put the who,

Misspelled words can be annoying or confusing and give the impression that you are sloppy, incompetent, or careless.

what, why, when, where, and how in the first paragraph. Use subject headings and double line spacing before and after a heading. Use double line spacing between paragraphs and do not indent paragraphs. Use bulleted or numbered lists. Include an *executive summary*, a short, beginning paragraph that summarizes the key points of the message. You can also break up your long message into several short messages.

- Using space bar spaces to align numbered lists or bulleted lists and to separate them from the text. This can cause problems in displaying the message on the receiver's screen.
  Remedy: Use tabs.

- Misspelling words. Misspelled words can be annoying or confusing and give the impression that you are sloppy, incompetent, or careless.
  Remedy: Check your spelling with the help of your spelling checker (if your e-mail system has this feature) or use your dictionary.

- Using all capital letters in the message. This can cause readability problems.
  Remedy: Use both capital and

lowercase letters when writing.
- Using font features such as boldface or italics. Some receivers' computers and e-mail systems cannot reproduce these effects.
Remedy: Use an asterisk on each side of a word or phrase, indicating that it is italicized or boldfaced. If you need to emphasize important ideas, use boxes consisting of hyphens or asterisks or pipe characters. (Example shown below.)

```
*************************************
*                                   *
*   Send Minutes as soon as         *
*       possible for approval!      *
*                                   *
*************************************
```

- Failing to delete unwanted messages immediately which can take up disk storage space.
Remedy: Delete all unwanted messages.
- Using conventional methods of closing. "Sincerely yours," "Yours," "Yours truly," "If you have further questions, contact me" are not used.
Remedy: Close with "Thanks" or "Regards," plus your signature or initial. It is recommended that you put one or more hyphens before your name to separate this line from the body of the message. For someone who does not know you well, include your title/position, the name of your organization, and your e-mail address. Some people even include the number of their voice mail. Avoid elaborate graphics in your signature.
- Not answering e-mail messages promptly.
Remedy: If you need more time, send a quick message to let the sender know that you have read the message and that you will soon reply.
- Sending a file when an e-mail message is sufficient. Some receivers' e-mail systems may not handle this. Sending a file also requires extra work on the part of the receiver since the receiver will need to decompress and download the file, then start an application and open the file.
Remedy: If you have to send a file, compress the file and let the receiver know that the file is compressed. Make sure the receiver has the same compression program to decompress the file.
- Using jargon or technical words to impress the reader.
Remedy: Write simply. If you need to use jargon, make sure the reader understands it. If you need to explain the jargon, explain it in simple, layman's language.

Be a professional and competent communicator! Avoid these mistakes. Get to know more about e-mail rules and conventions. Happy e-mailing! **TC**

Leticia Ekhaml is Professor of Media Education at West Georgia College in Carrollton, Georgia.

NOTES

SEARCHING

Adventures In E-Mail Land

When It Comes To Developing Interpersonal Skills, E-Mail Speaks Volumes

I've been surfing the Internet for about four months and have traveled to telnet sites all over the world. But there's no place like home—my favorite spot to visit is my own mailbox.

My Listserv

On LM_NET, I have found a community of friends who help me with all my professional problems. I am the only librarian in my building, and the only high school librarian in my district. But—thanks to my listserv—I am not at all isolated.

My online colleagues have offered advice on how to load software, provided grammar tips, and argued good-naturedly about whether it's better to start as a school or public librarian. I've gotten the low-down on what to read, what to buy, and how to get along with teachers. I've gotten the scoop on everything from locating great sources for government documents to finding German-speaking "keypals." There have also been some wonderful ideas on what to do with those old card catalogs. My mission for this year is to get many other teachers matched happily with the right listservs.

Keypals

I have gathered around me a group of diverse students—some considered popular, some whom others consider "nerds," and some with a variety of disabilities. All have discovered that e-mail is blind. This anonymity has been refreshing. Even students who "hate to write" love to write e-mail.

However, there is a trick to motivating high school keypals. It really helps to match older students with the opposite sex. A bit of flirting may help to break the ice online.

This is exemplified by an incident with our Tasmanian friends. A number of the boys asked for metric conversion tables. Thrilled with their new interest in exploring math, I dug up tables and formulas. Can you guess the reason for this interest in things metric? The Australian girls had been sending their measurements! We discouraged further activity of this nature.

Another of our students, upon realizing that he was brighter and more affluent than a counterpart in North Carolina, wrote a letter expressing a "superior air." His keypal's response expressed hurt feelings. Our student was shocked that his short note had such an impact on another person. No lesson from me was needed there.

To avert these types of situations, I now monitor all e-mail and my students know it! I'm proud that other, perhaps more relevant, cultural exchanges have taken place—we've learned a lot about the climate in Australia, cultural differences, Tasmanian devils, and slang expressions.

We're now embarking upon a new creative writing project with our keypals from North Carolina. After linking students by interests, communicated via a database, those involved have exchanged friendly letters to get to know each other. They are now collaborating on writing suspense stories online. To round out our keypal program, we are planning e-mail relationships with high school students from Japan. This will be particularly exciting because of a new Japanese language program in our district.

Other interesting e-mail happenings:

1. Debate students are sharing tips on the national topic of immigration with students from other states.
2. Exchange students are communicating with their families and friends abroad.
3. Students are practicing foreign language skills with native speakers or others studying the same language.
4. Students and teachers are communicating with children and friends away at college.
5. Students are tracking concert schedules of their favorite groups through e-mail addresses they've discovered inlibrary directories.
6. I make embarrassing apologies the cowardly way—through e-mail—and avoid face-to-face contact.
7. I can now easily contact my colleagues to change or verify dates for committee meetings.
8. We are now exploring mentorship arrangements with local businesses and established e-mail "experts."

E-mail has built our students' self-esteem and opened a world of new friends beyond our library. It's little wonder that they have learned to love e-mail as much as I do! **Tc**

by Joyce Kasman Valenza

Joyce Valenza is the media specialist at Wissahickon High School Library, Ambler, Pennsylvania.

Inspections: The Library Media Specialist as Building Inspector

As stated in the introduction, another of the library media specialist's roles is to teach students to look at all information with a critical eye, similar to the critical eye of the building inspector when he comes to inspect the newly built house. The building inspector has a checklist of items he is going to inspect, and checks off each part of the work that meets regulations.

Authority, authenticity, accuracy, and applicability to purpose are the checklist that students must learn to use to evaluate the vast amount of information published on the Internet-- by anyone and for anyone in the world to see.

This chapter includes articles dealing with effective search strategies and the acquisition of lasting search habits. These articles deal with both how to search (the technical aspects) and what to search (identifying the search terms before beginning to search).

The rest of the articles in this chapter offer checklists of criteria for students (and teachers) to think about when considering using a site and models for including these skills in the information literacy curriculum.

When evaluating sites for inclusion in my Guide for Educators (http://discoveryschool.com/schrockguide/), I have a set of criteria that I have identified as important to determining if a site is authoritative and accurate. I have also included a two-page checklist for you to use for evaluation of Web sites (pages 190-191).

When you examine sites with the building inspector's critical eye, use these models and checklists of information. If they pass the inspection, they're ready to be used!

▶ URL UPDATE

The Honeymoon Is Over: Leading the Way to Lasting Search Habits by Melissa Pierson

Infoseek: http://infoseek.go.com/

Magellen: http://magellan.excite.com/

It Must Be True. I Found It on the Internet! by Kathleen Schrock

FDR Cartoon Collection:
http://www.nisk.k12.ny.us/fdr/

Kathy Schrock's Evaluation Instruments
http://discoveryschool.com/schrockguide/eval.html

Brush Up on the Internet Lesson Plan
http://discoveryschool.com/schrockguide/brush/brush.html

UC Museum of Paleontology T-rex Exhibit
http://www.ucmp.berkeley.edu/trex/trexpo.html

WebWhacker
http://www.bluesquirrel.com/products/whacker/whacker.html

The ABC's of Web Site Evaluation
By Kathy Schrock (kathy@kathyschrock.net) ©2000

URL of page:	Y	N	N/A
Authority			
• Can you tell who is providing the information?			
• Can you find out information about the person providing the information?			
• Is the author a recognized expert in his or her field?			
Bias			
• Is the language free of emotion-rousing words?			
• Is any bias clearly identifiable?			
Citations			
• Is a bibliography of sources included?			
• Are full bibliographic citations given?			
Dates			
• Is the date of creation included?			
• Is the date of last update included?			
• Does the date make a difference to your purpose?			
Efficiency			
• Does the page download quickly?			
• Is the site reliable?			
• Is the site useful for whole-class instruction?			
Fallacy			
• Is only part of the information included?			
• Does some of the information seem to be presented out of context?			
Graphics			
• Do the included graphics serve a purpose?			
• Are graphics clearly labeled and identified?			
• Do the graphics aid in meeting lesson objectives?			
Handicapped access			
• Is the site usable with a screen reader?			
• Is the type large enough for a visually impaired user?			
Information availability			
• Does the type of information you need seem to be found on the Web?			
Jerrybuilt			
• Are the spelling and grammar correct on the page?			
Knowledge			
• Does the information on the Web agree with what you already know?			
• Does the information on the Web change what you know about the topic?			
• Does the information on the Web add to the existing body of knowledge?			
Links			
• Is rationale given for the inclusion of certain links?			
• Are the links appropriate for the scope of the page?			
• Are links to related sites included?			
• Do all the links work?			

	Y	N	N/A
Misinformation			
• Does the site utilize persuasive tactics (i.e. opinion verbs, oversimplification, etc.)?			
• Does the information seem to change rapidly on the page?			
Navigability			
• Is the page usable by the intended audience?			
• Are navigation icons present and understandable?			
• Is a search tool available for the site's content?			
Online research model			
• Do your key concepts or words appear on this page?			
• Is the information found relevant to your stated purpose?			
Quantity of information			
• Is the rationale given for inclusion or exclusion?			
• Does this site grow each day due to user input?			
Requirements			
• Does the site require a registration?			
• Does the site state that it collects data about the users?			
• Does the site require use of a certain browser due to proprietary extensions?			
Scholastic reviews			
• Is the site reviewed in a print journal?			
• Are the awards received by the page reputable?			
• Do others have links to this page? (link:URL in Altavista search box)			
Thoroughness			
• Does the resource cover the subject matter adequately?			
• Are there obvious gaps in the information?			
Uniqueness			
• Does the resource contain any original work?			
• Does the resource consist of more than a list of links to external sites?			
Verifiability			
• Is the information on the site verifiable in a reputable print source?			
• Are citations included to verify primary source materials used?			
5 W's (fast evaluation of a site)			
• Is it easy to tell who wrote the page and if the writer is an expert in the field?			
• Does the author include the purpose of the site?			
• Can you tell when the page was created, updated, or last worked on?			
• Can you tell where the information comes from?			
• Is the information useful for your purpose?			
Xtra information			
• Does this site need special criteria for evaluation because of its type?			
Yahoo			
• Did you find this page by using a general or subject-specific directory?			
• Did you find this page by keyword searching in a search engine?			
Zen			
• Would it have been easier to find this information in a print source?			
• Was it difficult to locate the information you were looking for?			

6 Steps to Simplifying Student Searches

By Joyce Valenza

Databases are multiplying by the minute and mastering research skills is becoming as fundamental to students' success as learning to read and write. Online searching can be intimidating, however, so we must break down these skills so they can be taught logically. I use the following six steps as a model for simplifying the thinking steps needed for seeking and retrieving online information.

I introduce this process one step at a time at ninth grade orientation, using five to ten minute minilessons and reinforcing these sessions as I walk around and peek over shoulders. I have developed a worksheet which includes "or" and "and" fill-ins and the steps described in this model. If you have any suggestions for improving it, please send e-mail to jvalenza@mciunix.

1 Identify the problem.

I'm surprised at how many students dive into their research before they even think about their problem. That's why we librarians are always asking the types of questions we hope students will eventually internalize and ask themselves. What type of information do you really need? How much information do you need? Do you need an overview or perhaps a point of view, for a debate or persuasive speech?

2 Select the appropriate database.

This decision could be a big one—especially online. DIALOG, for instance, offers hundreds of choices. Even offline, on CD-ROM, students need to choose thoughtfully. Subject is certainly the main consideration, but the student also needs to consider scope of coverage in terms of date and types of journals indexed. If the database is not full text, are journals available physically? Are available journals too difficult for students to comprehend? If they can't make sense of the title or abstract, odds are students won't be able to make any sense of the actual article. You must help students make a number of basic CD-ROM choices as well. Would the best choice be a newspaper, magazine, encyclopedia or other specialized database?

3 Brainstorm keywords.

Now is the time to map out synonyms and related terms ("ors") in columns and link them to additional words, phrases or concepts using "ands" in other columns. How shall we handle plurals, variant spellings or other word forms if we are searching by keyword? How will our strategy be affected by wildcards or truncation devices? How should proper names be handled? Will the strategy be different if the database is full text? Consider which databases you will be searching. If you are in a sports database, the word "sports" would be meaningless. It is best to have this all mapped out on paper to avoid the dreaded "freaking out online" syndrome.

4 Search by subject or keyword.

Almost every CD-ROM database a student approaches poses the initial question: Do you want to search by subject or keyword? The answer will take into account a number of factors, and in some cases the user may need to try both approaches. This one decision is crucial to conducting a successful search, so put special emphasis on it. Generally, when more than one concept is being searched and flexibility is needed, keyword searching should be the first choice. If you are browsing for an appropriate manageable topic for a paper, Subject/Topic searching is best. If you are unsure of spelling, topic searching functions as a type of thesaurus if you can get the first three letters right.

5 Refine your search (online).

Here, I emphasize to students that searching is an interactive process. If your plan is in front of you, you can easily refer to other words and concepts when the first approach falls flat. Clues are all over the database. Choose your very best hit as a "guinea pig." Examine the descriptor/subject field. Look for related proper nouns that keep surfacing. In a search about euthanasia, for exam-

The Technology Connection: Building a Successful Library Media Program

Chapter 5
Inspections: The Library Media Specialist as Building Inspector

ple, the name "Kervorkian" might provide many additional hits. If your subject begins to seem unworkable, note related topics for which more information is available. When you're exploring, there are no mistakes! Even the most experienced searchers must re-evaluate and refine their searches.

Some simple things to consider at this point: Were your initial keywords spelled correctly? Is there an online word list that might offer some spelling help? Very important: Consider the number of hits! Is there too much or too little material? Should you add additional keywords to narrow your search, or think of broader terms to enlarge it?

Evaluate your search. Plan another attack.

This is the "what if?" step when you analyze the printout to separate the important from the trivial and identify the strengths and weaknesses of a search strategy. Ask yourself whether your search met your needs. Online time is costly, and students need to learn to use it wisely. Even with CD-ROMs, they have limited access to workstations during class periods and consequently should be thinking about their problems and successes offline.

Some good evaluation questions for students to ask themselves: Which part of my strategy worked well? Were there keywords I should have thought about? Are there descriptors on my printout I might be able to use next time? Did I select the best database? How available are the resources on my printout? Were the resulting hits relevant? Timely? Credible? Biased? Readable? What's my next step? Our goal is to train students to search efficiently and learn from previous experiences. **TC**

Joyce Valenza is the media specialist at Wissahickon High School Library, Ambler, Pennsylvania.

Search Strategy Worksheet

1. What's my problem?
Express in one sentence.

2. List appropriate databases:

3. Brainstorm keywords/topics:

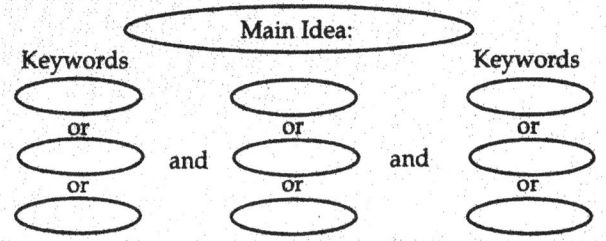

Consider synonyms, related terms, phrases, spellings, plurals or singulars, and truncation.

4. Topic vs. Keyword search:

5. Refining the search (online):
Other usable keywords:
Terms to narrow or broaden:
Proper nouns to search:

6. Evaluation (offline)—What worked, what didn't:
Ideas for the next search:

BONING UP ON BOOLEAN SEARCHING

By Linda Turrell

Too often, students who've been assigned research projects enter the library, switch on the computers, and ask "Now what?" Computer neophytes are usually clueless about how to construct search strategies and evaluate their search results. It's essential that all students learn to perform a few types of Boolean searches, along with simple keyword searches. It's equally important that they understand the logic behind these searches so they can choose the type of search that best suits their purposes.

They need to understand, for example, that a Boolean search using the keywords "ecology" AND "soil pollution" will retrieve information on soil pollution and how it impacts ecology. A Boolean search using "ecology" OR "soil pollution" will yield results about one or the other, or both. A Boolean search using the keywords "ecology" AND NOT "soil pollution" will yield information about ecology with no references to soil pollution. To successfully access information about ecology and soil pollution outside the United States, the Boolean connectors need to be changed.

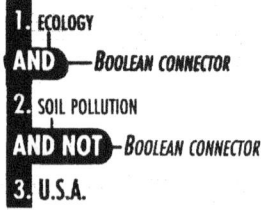

It's helpful to give students sample Boolean search circles. Creating sample worksheets that require students to think through their research questions also helps, as does requiring them to analyze research questions to see if they fit in a simple search or Boolean format.

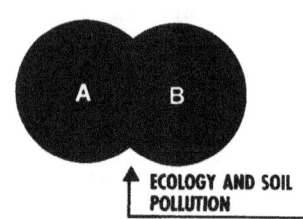

ECOLOGY AND SOIL POLLUTION

Such questions will guide students as they analyze the value of their own research questions. They need practice, practice, and more practice in the higher-level thinking skills required to create these questions and to select appropriate keywords. The simple commands required to conduct the searches are easily taught. **TC**

Linda Turrell is the national winner of the 1995 Texty Award for Academic and Instructional Materials, and an Educational Media Specialist at Raritan High School in Hazlet, New Jersey.

SAMPLE STUDENT WORKSHEET

Think about each of the following research questions and decide whether you would do a subject search or Boolean search. Explain your choice.

- What information is available about the giant turtle?

- Find general information about turtles and list the places where they are endangered.

- How much information can you find about Amelia Earhart?

- How does crime affect U.S. teenagers?

- How is use of chemicals in the rainforest related to soil and water pollution?

THE HONEYMOON IS OVER
LEADING THE WAY TO LASTING SEARCH HABITS

By Melissa Pierson

While your students may appear to be "Web-literate," are they truly making the most of the resource? If your school is fortunate enough to have had access to the Internet for a time, you may have noticed that teachers and students have reached a comfortable plateau. Computers are turned on, and teachers have found a few interesting sites that relate to curriculum. Students have meandered from one link to the next. There was a time when this was enough, but not any longer. While surfing is fun, and occasionally students stumble upon a valuable gem of a site, it is also aimless and extremely time consuming in an already-too-full school day. Invaluable searching skills need to be taught to help students and teachers become intelligent researchers of the wealth of information available online. If you are the technology leader in your school, whether officially or by default, it will most likely be your task to move your school's online practices to the next level.

Searching Tools

There are two approaches, beyond haphazard surfing, to find information on the Internet. The first is to use a hierarchical subject directory, like *Yahoo!*. A subject directory is handy if you want quick, general information. Users are first presented with a list of very general subjects. Choosing one of these subjects takes the user to another, more specific, list where another choice can be made to narrow the search until Web page links are given. The directory designers may have a different idea of the organization of information than you do, so be prepared to spend some time looking through the threads of topics to find what you want.

The other, more directed, approach to finding information on the Internet is to use a search engine, such as *Excite*, *Lycos*, *AltaVista*, or *HotBot*. Clicking on the search button in your Web browser should take you to a site with links to all of the largest engines. Search engines are actually enormous indexes of information locations that have been amassed by computer programs designed to automatically find these sources. Search engine sites allow you to input keywords, or search strings, to guide the search of the indexes. All of the available search engines vary according to size, speed, options and how documents are indexed. In addition, each site has its own unique look in terms of page layout and presentation of search results.

Countless articles have been written comparing and rating the efficiency of the currently available search engines. As a test, the reviewers generally enter the same keyword query into each engine and compare the results for accuracy and relevancy. Curiously, a review of several of these comparisons reveals that there is no clear winner among search engines. An engine that performed admirably in one test was able to find no matching results in another. Complicating matters even more, search engines, as with everything else on the Internet, are evolving and changing so rapidly that a site that offers the best results one month could very well be surpassed by another engine the next month. No one search engine will serve your needs in every circumstance. Ideally, a desired term should be entered into several different search engines to ensure a complete

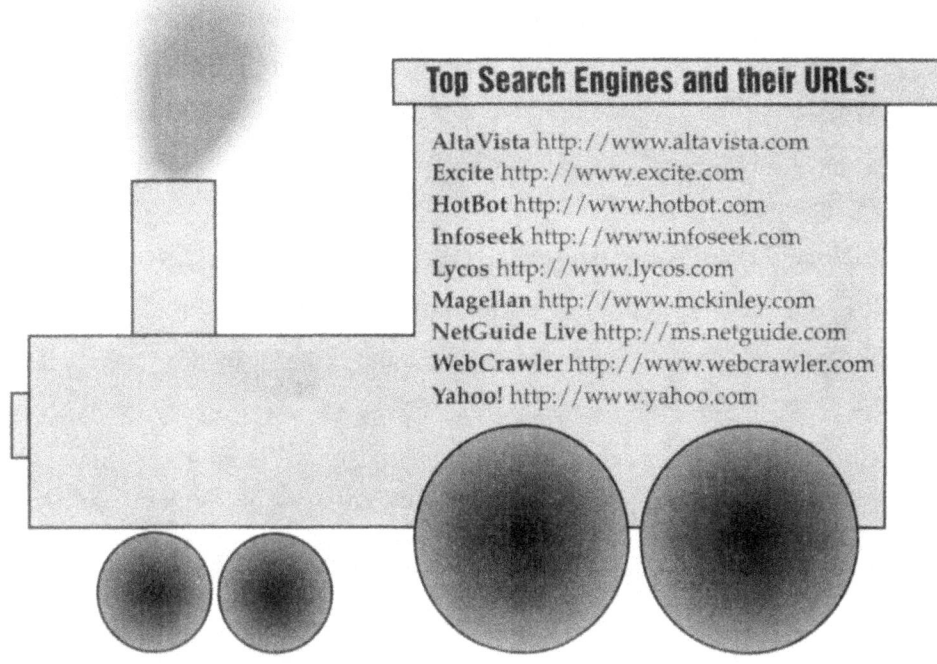

Top Search Engines and their URLs:

AltaVista http://www.altavista.com
Excite http://www.excite.com
HotBot http://www.hotbot.com
Infoseek http://www.infoseek.com
Lycos http://www.lycos.com
Magellan http://www.mckinley.com
NetGuide Live http://ms.netguide.com
WebCrawler http://www.webcrawler.com
Yahoo! http://www.yahoo.com

Instruction	Example
Search for the singular form of a term; you also will get the plural form. This search will give you both *castle* and *castles*.	castle
If you are not sure how to spell a word, or if the term for which you are searching has more than one known spelling, enter all of the spellings you think might apply, separating each by a space.	Hanukkah Hanukah Chanukah
To search for a phrase, enclose the entire phrase in double quotes; otherwise the engine will find every occurrence of each individual word.	"Albert Einstein"
Be as precise as possible. Entering a common word, such as "book," would give you far too many useless sites. Including the word in a specific phrase will help to narrow the search.	"book publisher"
Many engines allow you to narrow your search by requiring or prohibiting a term.	
• A required term means every document found must contain that term. To require a term, precede it directly with a plus sign (+).	+adoption
• A prohibited term means that no documents found will contain that term. To prohibit a term, precede it with a minus sign (-).	-betting
• One search string can require some terms and prohibit others. This example will give you documents about adopting greyhound dogs, but will not include anything about Greyhound buses or gambling on greyhound races.	greyhound +adoption -bus -betting
Some engines allow the use of wildcard characters at the end of a phrase to substitute for several missing letters. *AltaVista*, for example, uses the asterisk (*) as a wildcard character. This search will give you *earth*, *earthquake*, and *earthworm*.	earth*
Boolean searching uses the word operators *and*, *or*, *not* or *and not*, and *near* to narrow searches. These word operators can be entered in either upper or lower case letters, but it is a good habit to use uppercase letters, so the operators stand apart from the keywords.	
• Use *and* to find documents containing more than one term occurring together.	lions *and* tigers
• Use *or* to specify one term or the other found separately.	saguaro *or* "prickly pear"
• Use *not* or *and not* to exclude a term from the search.	"polar bears" *and not* zoo
• Use *near* to find documents which contain two terms in close proximity to each other, usually within ten words.	"George Washington" *near* "apple tree"
Combine Boolean operators and phrases into logical groupings with parentheses. This search will give results on the economy of Uruguay and results on the economy of Chile.	(Uruguay or Chile) *and* economy

search. Therefore, rather than expecting the faculty and students at your school to remember the unique characteristics of every available search engine, it is a good idea to become familiar with general properties and basic search strategies common to most search engines.

Searching Strategies

Once you have located a search engine site, check the help section for search tips specific to that engine. The following table provides a description of search tips along with an example of the search string you would enter into the search engine.
entered into several different search engines to ensure a complete search. Therefore, rather than expecting the faculty and students at your school to remember the unique characteristics of every available search engine, it is a good idea to become familiar with general properties and basic search strategies common to most search engines.

A Training Plan for Searching

Let's assume that you have already accomplished the task of getting teachers in your building to turn on their computers regularly, and many are exploring the Internet with their students. The following three-step plan will help you turn your passive surfing school into a community of researchers.

STEP 1

The teachers at your school need to understand what search engines do and where they can be found. Compare using a search engine to searching for a term in a print encyclopedia. We would never turn one page at a time hoping that the word we were looking for would be on the next page. Instead, we have learned reference skills to find the ideas for which we are looking.

Next, show the engines at work. Whether this means conducting an inservice with the entire faculty or simply gathering a few teachers around one machine, don't start by presenting a long list of do's and don'ts for each search engine. Begin by following the lead of those reviewers who have tested the search engines. Have the group develop several topics, ranging from simple to complex. Put the same keywords into at least three or four of the most common engines and compare the results. Do the same engines consistently produce the best results? Keep a tally of acceptable results for each engine to provide visual proof of the variability.

Now try to search for some of the same topics on a hierarchical subject directory. How long does it take to arrive at useful sites? Discuss what situations would call for which search tool. This activity also can be done with groups of students, or even with mixed groups of teachers and students. They should see how to access the search sites, how to enter the search strings, and how to interpret the results. Allowing for age appropriateness, have students discuss the sites that are found. Can students develop a rating system of their own to distinguish between the engines? To both teachers and students, the concept should be stressed that results between engines will vary, so if they want a thorough search, they should always put their terms into several engines. The most important thing for this step is that students and teachers are made aware of the search tools available to them.

STEP 2

Now that the idea of a search engine is familiar, demonstrate both basic and advanced search strategies. Show what different results can be obtained just by enclosing a phrase in parentheses or by narrowing the search with a *not* operator. Even young students can understand the idea of Boolean searching. Introduce it as a kind of code. Have them give examples and predict what the results will be. Give them a complex topic and challenge them to develop a search string that will lead to successful results. Understanding the logic of this smart searching will empower teachers and students to make the most effective use of their time and will result in the most useful information.

STEP 3

Create schoolwide enthusiasm for this newfound searching skill. epending on age appropriateness, make "cheat sheets" of examples of the search strategies to laminate and keep next to each computer. Post charts around the school where students can tally engines that gave them useful results. Conduct contests where the engines are put to the test. This air of excitement will transfer over to the writing and reporting that prompted the research. A community of learners discussing these strategies together will ensure students who are proficient in finding information for themselves. **TC**

Melissa Pierson, Arizona State University, Educational Media & Computers

THE INTERNET: CONNECTING WITH THE CURRICULUM

feature

It Must Be True.
I Found It on the Internet!

By Kathleen Schrock

"Look at the copyright date."

"Is the author an authority on the topic?"

"Is a bibliography included?"

These questions are familiar to library media specialists. We use a set of criteria to evaluate a print item for purchase and know how to instruct students in critiquing an item for use in research projects. However, another set of standards is needed for evaluating information taken from the World Wide Web. Users need to learn to evaluate the technical aspects and subject content of a World Wide Web page to determine whether it meets their needs.

Training students to evaluate this new medium means blending media literacy skills with library reference skills. The bottom line is that before accepting information they find on the Internet, students need to verify it with a second source. If the primary source material is found only on the Internet, like the FDR Cartoon Collection (http://www.wizvax.net/nisk_hs/departments/social/fdr_html/FDRmain.html), students must decide whether an item has been altered from its original state.

I have designed a set of evaluation instruments for use at the elementary, middle, and high school levels. These instruments may be found at http://www.capecod.net/Wixon/eval.htm, along with two essays dealing with the topic of assessing a Web page. The two essays will help readers determine which elements of a Web page should be evaluated.

Lesson Preparation

I recently conducted a four-lesson Internet unit with six fourth-grade classes and incorporated the critical evaluation of a Web page as the third lesson. The lesson plan and a copy of the evaluation tool for the elementary grade level are included here. In the future, I will post the entire four-lesson unit on my home page, Kathy Schrock's Guide for Educators, at http://www.capecod.net/Wixon/wixon.htm.

To replicate this lesson, you need some HTML-writing knowledge and a standalone HTML editor or word processing program, a graphical Internet account (PPP or SLIP), and a copy of *WebWhacker*, software that allows you to "grab" a Web page address (URL) while surfing online and then "whack" (download) the entire page, graphics included, to your own hard drive.

Later, you can simply open your graphical browser and view the whacked page as a static HTML document. In this way, you can simulate the Internet experience even if you don't have a connection in your classroom. All you need is a computer with a Web browser. You can download a 30-day trial copy of *WebWhacker* at http://www.ffg.com.

[Editor's Note: There is considerable controversy over the copyright implications of copying Web pages. At the time of this writing, the U.S. Congress is holding hearings on modifications to copyright law and practice to protect Internet documents.]

To design a lesson on the critical evaluation of a Web page, I used a topic that most fourth-grade students know a little about and are interested in—dinosaurs!

I first went to the UC-Berkeley Museum of Paleontology site (http://ucmp1.berkeley.edu/trex/special-trex2.html) and used *WebWhacker* to download the entire page about *Tyrannosaurus rex*. I then opened my HTML editor (*HTML Assistant Pro* by Brooklyn North Software) and proceeded to edit and create six different versions of the page: one version was the original page; one version had a lot of spelling errors; one version had completely erroneous information (*T. rex* was a plant eater that weighed 50 tons); the other three versions were unsigned, with no updates and no author information.

I printed out one color copy of each of the six different pages and laminated them. So that each student could have a copy, I photocopied four copies of each page. I also made a copy of the critical evaluation form for each student.

Remember to obtain permission from the Webmaster of the page you want to use and will be "whacking." A short note explaining what you are teaching and how you are going to edit the pages will usually result in permission to use the material. If not, try another page and another Webmaster!

Conclusion

With the advent of new technologies, there is always a new set of skills to be learned. Anyone can publish and distribute information on the Internet and the World Wide Web. It is imperative that library media specialists provide students with the skills needed to evaluate the accuracy, authenticity, and applicability of information found on the Net. **TC**

Kathleen Schrock is a Library Media Specialist at Nathaniel H. Wixon Middle School in South Dennis, Massachusetts.

> *Users need to learn to evaluate the technical aspects and subject content of a World Wide Web page to determine whether it meets their needs.*

The Lesson Plan

Brush Up on the Internet Week 3: Critical Evaluation of a Web Page

Purpose: To have students realize that Web pages need to be looked at critically and evaluated for content accuracy and authenticity.

Materials: Six laminated Web pages; a set of four photocopies of each laminated page; 24 copies of the critical evaluation checklist; one overhead transparency of each laminated page; Internet connection or *WebWhacked* Web page that meets all of the criteria for a good Web page; large screen projection device for class viewing

Procedure:

1. The library media specialist will poll the students to see if they know some of the methods for critically evaluating a print source (copyright date, bibliography included, information about the author included, and so on). The library media specialist will remind students that the Internet is a huge repository of information, but students need to be able to verify whether the information presented is accurate and useful for their purpose.

2. The library media specialist will project on the large screen an exemplary Web page that includes all criteria. These include, but are not limited to, a descriptive title, a photograph or drawing, a date of last update, a signed page, information about the author, sources used to prepare the page, and links to other related sites. Using the checklist, the library media specialist will model aloud how to critically evaluate the Web page.

3. The library media specialist will present students with the scenario that they are doing a report on dinosaurs and will need to evaluate information on that topic found on a Web page.

4. Working in six small groups, students will evaluate the copy of the page at their table by filling out the checklist. Encourage students to use traditional print sources to verify questionable information. Each group will then present its results to the class using the overhead copy of its particular page. (Some of the questions on the evaluation checklist, such as those on sound or loading, will not be applicable for this static Web page lesson.)

Summary: Using *The Important Book* by Margaret Wise Brown (Harper, 1949) as a model, ask students to fill out the following summary sheet. (This picture book identifies the key characteristics of common objects.) Students will give the main concept in the first and last statements and three supporting details in the middle. For example,

The important thing about Web pages is you need to check the information.

They **should be signed.**

They **should be current.**

They **should contain a good title.**

But the important thing about Web pages is **you need to check the information.**

Critical Evaluation of Web Site: Elementary School Level

Designed by Kathleen Schrock

1. How are you hooked to the Internet?
   ___ Computer and modem
   ___ Direct connection at school
2. If you are using a modem, is the speed 2400 9600 14.4 28.8?
3. What Web browser are you using?_____
4. What is the URL of the Web page you are looking at?
   http://_____

How Does It Look?

5. Does the page take a long time to load? YES / NO
6. Are there big pictures on the page? YES / NO
7. Is the spelling correct on the page? YES / NO
8. Is the author's name and e-mail address on the page? YES / NO
9. Is there a picture on the page that you can use to choose links? (Image map) YES / NO
10. Is there information in columns on the page? (Table) YES / NO
11. If you go to another page, is there a way to get back to the first page? YES / NO
12. Is there a date that tells you when the page was made? YES / NO
13. Do the photographs look real? YES / NO / NO PHOTOGRAPHS
14. Do the sounds seem real? YES / NO / NO SOUNDS

What Did You Learn?

15. Does the title of the page tell you what it is about? YES / NO
16. Is there an introduction on the page that tells you what is included? YES / NO
17. Are the facts on the page what you were looking for? YES / NO
18. Would you get more information from the encyclopedia? YES / NO
19. Would the information have been better in the encyclopedia? YES / NO
20. Does the author of the page say some things you disagree with? YES / NO
21. Does the author of the page include information that you know is wrong? YES / NO
22. Do the pictures and photographs on the page help you learn? YES / NO / NO PICTURES

Summary

Looking at all of the questions and answers above, write a paragraph telling why this Web site is helpful, or is not helpful, for your project.

_____
_____
_____
_____
_____
_____

NOTES

Easy To Find *But* Not Necessarily True

By Steve Baule

Finding information has long been one of the "cornerstone" skills of librarians. "Asking the librarian" was a common step in the student's research process ten years ago. However, many of us have found that technology has changed this. No longer do we regularly face a line of students needing assistance to find books on wolves, genetic engineering, drug abuse or whatever is the topic of the week. The teachers haven't stopped making these assignments; the kids are gone because they are surfing through cyberspace.

Besides the solid information on wolves they found at the Natural History Museum site, they have also found "true" stories of werewolves, a new punk band named Black Wolf, and statistics on Wolf, South Dakota. To the eighth grader, the werewolf information may be the most interesting. And since it is on the Internet, it must be true.

We now face a greater challenge in helping students evaluate the information they find. This becomes particularly difficult when students are sifting through hundreds or even thousands of items that might be found with a simple keyword search on the World Wide Web.

Our first task is to teach young people to look at four aspects of evaluating information found on the Web:
 1. The purpose of the article or other information
 2. The author's credibility
 3. Publication date and the date of the last updating
 4. Wording of site titles.

The Purpose of the Article

You should help students learn to determine the purpose of information they find on the Internet. Teach them to ask questions such as, Is the site trying to sell a product? Who sponsors the site? Is the sponsor a library, a museum, or other organization that provides solid information? What is the purpose of the site? Does it specialize in information on the research topic or is this information part of a program on other topics?

The Author's Credibility

When teaching about the credibility of a source, use the bizarre. Ask the students where they would go for information about UFO sightings in Arizona and give them a sample listing of articles to choose from. Use a range of sources, such as *Time* or *Newsweek* and tabloid newspapers. After a few minutes of discussion, you may be amazed how well students understand the reliability of popular news sources.

Some further questions for teaching young researchers to evaluate sources are: Was the information developed by a student or teacher of the topic? Did the author identify himself or herself? What does the author's willingness to identify his or her credentials say about credibility?

Publication Date and Date of Updates

When was the information published or posted on the Web? Is the information current? Was the information posted before or after the event you are researching occurred? If we could reach every student with these questioning techniques, the nation would probably have fewer conspiracy theories.

Wording of Site Titles

Students get better search results if they look for their research topic or keyword in the title of Web pages. This eliminates many irrelevant treatments of their topics. In addition, teaching students and teachers how to narrow searches and make the best use of search engines is a good use of time. Make sure they know where to find the "help" feature for each of the search engines.

Going Back to Print

Going to the Internet for every information need may be trendy, but it isn't always a good use of time. Searching for the name of the capitol of India on the Internet is not as efficient as using an almanac from the bookshelf. One assignment that recently came through our library required the student to find a picture of the first atom bomb. When the librarian started for the shelves, the student told her that the teacher said the picture had to come from the Internet.

Promoting good print materials and non-Internet electronic sources for each assignment to both students and teachers is essential. One method is to develop "pathfinders" or research-helper handouts that list the appropriate sources for assignments. Among the resources, list books, electronic resources, and World Wide Web sites. Work with teachers to ensure that students include at least one or two references from each type of source listed in the handout.

Asking teachers to avoid Internet-only assignments is another method to encourage students to use the best source. Make sure the teachers understand the need to allow students to use the best source for their assignments. Explaining to teachers that, in the past, they seldom required students to use only one resource in a research assignment may drive home the point that requiring an Internet search may not be the best directions.

When explaining the new dimensions of finding information, remember to end your instructions to students and teachers with "and if you need assistance, ask a librarian."

Steve Baule is Director of Information Technologies, New Trier High School in Winnetka, Illinois. He is an editorial consultant for Technology Connection. *His book* Technology Planning *is available from Linworth.*

Where on the World Wide Web is the Library?

Seduced and Abandoned on the Web

(or How Users Are Seduced by the Internet and Then Abandon Their Critical Faculties)
By Mark Williams

BUT MR. WILLIAMS...it has to be true. I got it from the Internet!" The sound you now hear is a frustrated librarian banging his head on a nearby wall. This student and I had been working for weeks on a major paper, and he had proudly asked me to give it one final look before he turned it in. In the first three paragraphs, there were three serious factual errors that rendered the paper worthless.

I have become increasingly concerned about the abuse of the Internet as an information source for classroom assignments. Why do students who would normally do at least some minimal checking of sources for accuracy and relevancy abandon such behavior when dealing with information from the Internet? This phenomenon is not limited to students; more than a few adults, including faculty, also are guilty.

Of course, we should apply the same standards to information regardless of its source, but why does information obtained from the Net seems to seduce students into blind acceptance? I think it is partly because of the seductive nature of computers. Kids love them and often prefer them to print materials. Partly it is the ease with which young people learn to work with electronic equipment, and partly it is because the media have portrayed computers as a kind of magic bullet that will cure all problems and answer all questions. And, of course, it involves the fact that when they

> **Why is it that information obtained from the Net seems to seduce the student into blind acceptance?**

are working at their best, computers are undeniably good at retrieving bits of information from a welter of material.

One of our most important jobs as librarians is to teach both students and staff to evaluate the sources of their information. Nowhere is this more important than when dealing with information from the Internet. Our students and adult patrons have come to expect that when they walk into a library they will find accurate, balanced information because someone professionally trained has selected the materials for accuracy, currency, and relevancy. We have no such assurance on the Internet.

Anyone with a few dollars, a computer and a bit of experience can launch a professional-looking web site and fill it with whatever (mis)information he wants. The advent of web page authoring software obviates the need for extensive knowledge of HTML encoding. You cannot judge by appearance alone. Both good, solid information and trash can, and often do, come across the computer screen looking equally professional. We are accustomed to instructing students in methods of evaluating print resources. I suggest that we must be equally vigilant in doing so with electronic resources, especially with web sites.

But the interactive nature of the medium adds another dimension. Although accuracy must be our top concern, the way information is presented in a web site can make that information either easy to find and use or difficult in the extreme. So other considerations enter into our evaluation. I have found it helpful to break evaluation rubrics into four broad areas: content, source, access, and structure.

> Teachers are encouraged to incorporate the serious evaluation of Web sites when they discuss the evaluation of other sources in preparing their students for research projects or assignments.

CONTENT

This important criterion strikes at the heart of any evaluation. What information is contained in the site and how comprehensive is it? Does the site present an overview of the topic or does it go into detail? Is the level of detail consistent, or are some areas covered well and others poorly? How current is the site? Is the most recent revision date clearly stated? How complete and accurate are links to other sites? (Of course, this will involve taking the time to pursue those links and applying the same criteria to them that were applied to the original site.) Are the URLs for the links still valid, or do you get the dreaded "404 Error" message when you attempt to go to the site? How does the site compare to print sources? Does the site present information that is not readily available in other formats? Are the multimedia elements relevant?

SOURCE

Equally important is the source of the information presented. Librarians naturally tend to look at this criterion before others.

Is the author of the site clearly stated? Do you have some indication of this person's or organization's credentials and level of expertise? Is the site sponsored or co-sponsored by a reputable organization? Are documents quoted directly or paraphrased? Are quotations fully credited? Are pictures, graphs, and charts clearly labeled as to source and date? Is there any evident bias, either in the information itself or in the sources selected for presentation? Are links clearly identified as to authorship? Again, all the criteria used for evaluating the original site's sources should be applied to any links.

ACCESS

This criterion is based on the assumption that the even best sites are worthless if they cannot be found easily or used by the typical user.

Is the site indexed on major search engines or only on the more esoteric ones that access only a limited number of sites or index a narrow range of topics? Is there a text-only option to speed loading of the site? This is especially useful where the Internet connection is slow, where there are a limited number of stations available for patron use, or when a site is heavily laden with multimedia goodies that do not relate directly to the information presented.

Has the author used standard HTML formatting and codes, or are proprietary extensions used? This can cause some parts of the site to display in ways greatly different than the author intended or not at all. Is downloading time reasonable? This is often a function of the service provider, but it also relates to the placement of multimedia elements in the site itself. A large graphic at the beginning of a site may slow the loading of any useful information below it.

Is the site stable? Is the URL consistent, or does it move from server to server? Note that service providers do go out of business, and site owners may be forced into changing the URL for their pages. But a site that seems to have a new address each time you access it may indicate questionable authorship.

STRUCTURE

As a visual person, I pay close attention to the way a source looks. Students tend to rank this area highest because it grabs their attention. In reality, the way the information is presented on a page does not affect the accuracy of the source or the value of the information. But if the page is unreadable because of a poor choice of background color or typeface, or if it is so poorly organized that it is frustrating to use, then the site is not helpful regardless of how it ranks on the other criteria. Pages that are "busy" with graphics or animations may impede effective use of the site.

Is the site clearly organized? Are descriptions of what the user can find located near the top of the site? Are directions for navigating the site clear and concise? Are there easy ways to move from one place to another, or must the user scroll endlessly to get from one part of the site to another? Can a novice navigate the site without the need for constant help? Can an expert user quickly retrieve information from various parts of the site and develop a trail of information from link to link? Are help dialogs or screens readily available for novice users?

Are the graphics and multimedia elements functional or merely decorative? While decorative isn't necessarily bad, it shouldn't be overdone because graphics take time to download. What elements of creativity are evident? Does the site do anything better than print sources. Of course, a primary reason for web sites is the ability to bring together sight, sound, and movement in a compelling presentation of factual information. Are background patterns and colors suitable? Do such background patterns or colors interfere with the reading of material? Can sounds be turned off? Is the typeface and size appropriate? Are key elements readily discernible? Are links clearly indicated with some form of contrasting typeface color or size or a graphic? Is the "look" of the page exciting and involving?

So what is the best way to get students and faculty to apply these critical criteria to web sites? One approach is for faculty and the librarian, either at the site or district level, to develop a rubric for the evaluation of Internet resources. This is an excellent chance for the school librarian to build influence on campus by demonstrating some of the principles that Gary Hartzell discusses in his book, *Building Influence for the School Librarian* (Linworth, 1994), particularly those of shaping perceptions at the site and district level. Although this does reinvent the wheel somewhat since there are numerous Internet sites that display ratings sheets and rubrics for evaluation, there is great value in local groups creating their own rubrics. Groups that develop their own rubrics are much more likely to apply them than if they simply are handed a canned set of criteria.

A useful tactic is to have the group meet and discuss some potential problems that would arise from the blind acceptance of material from the Internet. I like to illustrate this with a site that purported to show that the dictator Pol Pot had asked for and received political asylum in Sweden. Although professionally done, the entire site with photographs and video clips to accompany the "news release," is a fabrication. A more complete discussion of this site can be found by accessing Andy Carvin's posting of July 7, 1997 in the LM_NET listserv archives with the subject heading "Getting the truth online: Pol Pot in Sweden."

After reviewing the four broad criteria—content, source, access, and structure—the group is broken into four sub-groups, and over a 20-minute time block, the goal is to develop specific criteria within their category. The sub-groups present their lists to the whole group as individuals record them on a worksheet. Suggestions and comments are encouraged. At the end of this process, each group member has a completed worksheet that is, in essence, a rubric for evaluating web sites.

Ideally, the group will then immediately move to a lab setting and apply the newly-created rubric to several pre-selected sites. Discussion and further refining of the rubric may follow, and in the remaining time, they can surf the Net and apply the refined rubric to sites they find.

Another aspect of this process is the need to educate parents and the public about the need for critical viewing of Web-based resources. We all have heard the horror stories of students accessing inappropriate sites and the school being taken to task for allowing such incidents to happen. One way to fend off some of the criticism is to take a proactive stance and inform the public about the need for care when using web sites. This can

---

SITES THAT HAVE EVALUATION GUIDES:

Kathy Schrock's excellent Educator's Guide site...
www.discoveryschool.com/schrockguide/eval.html

Ohio State's guide for site evaluation...
www.mansfield.ohio-state.edu/writecu/webeval.htm

Duke University's guide...
www.duke.edu/~de1/evaluate.html

The UCLA evaluation guidelines, required of students in certain courses...
www.library.ucla.edu/libraries/college/instruct/critical.htm

SITES THAT ARE "FALSE" FOR USE IN DEMONSTRATIONS

www.tass.net (Note: this site has NOTHING to do with the ITAR-Tass news agency in Russia)

134.29.12.207/NewHartford/tour.html (Note: someone went to a LOT of trouble with this site..it is filled with all sorts of nice stuff......there IS no New Hartford, MN....a tip off is that none of the businesses profiled have phone numbers, and the map uses county highways that don't exist.)

SITES THAT SHOW EXAMPLES OF POORLY DESIGNED WEB SITES:

www.webpagesthatsuck.com/index3/html
www.worstoftheweb.com/

be done through parent workshops conducted in conjunction with PTA meetings, newsletters, and flyers. Letting the public know that we are teaching students to critically evaluate the information they retrieve from the Internet can help foster a view of schools and school libraries as responsible users of technology.

Local cable access programs sometimes can be used for such training. Service organizations often are looking for short programs for lunch or evening meetings.

Presenting a brief version of a workshop detailing the rubric your site or district has developed not only can provide them with useful information but also can garner some positive publicity for your school. Communities want to feel good about the schools their children attend, and such outreach can help develop those feelings. It also lets people know that school librarians do more than stamp dates in books.

Instructing students to use a rubric to evaluate sites is more difficult. Sometimes it is simply overkill to give students a complicated rubric to use with each site they access. I conduct a short lesson with classes using my current faked site to demonstrate the perils of swallowing unquestioned what they find on the Net. I give the students a handout that details selected questions listed under the content and sources sections of the larger rubric, and we discuss these as a group. Students then are better equipped to evaluate what they find.

Teachers are encouraged to incorporate the serious evaluation of web sites when they discuss the evaluation of other sources in preparing their students for research projects or assignments. If this is done through the library, I always stress that all information should be subjected to the same critical appraisal.

It took us years to get library users to routinely evaluate the sources of information they access. We need to continue that effort with the wealth of information available to them on the Internet.

Mark Williams is a Librarian at Colton (California) High School.

NOTES

Producing Information Consumers: Critical Evaluation and Critical Thinking

By Kathleen Schrock

IT IS WIDELY ACCEPTED that, at the end of the 20th century, we have become an information society. It is more important than ever, therefore, for educators to provide students with the awareness and skills required to critically evaluate the tide of information that floods our culture. This is especially true of the information that can be found on the Internet, because so much of it does not undergo any type of review process. Students must be able to evaluate the quality of such information, which means that they must be able to think critically.

In their online essay, *"Tactics that encourage active learning"* (*Center for Critical Thinking*, <www.sonoma.edu/CThink/K12/>, September 22, 1996) Paul Richard and Linda Elder suggest that "critical thinking involves learning to realize how one thinks and forming opinions and perceptions based on this process. Students need to be presented with lessons which actively engage them in thinking and evaluating the content of a particular topic. They should be able to relate this content to their own knowledge, make connections between related concepts, summarize what an author or teacher has said, and give examples to clarify what they, themselves, have stated."

Elizabeth Kirk in her online essay, *"Evaluation information found on the Internet"* (*Milton's Web*, <milton.mse.jhu.edu:8001/research/education/net.html>, September 22, 1996), states: "Establishing and learning criteria to filter information on the Internet is a good beginning for becoming a critical consumer of information in all forms."

If students look at the layout and content of an information source, and then ascertain whether the information is appropriate and useful through a guided evaluation process, they should acquire the skills to become these "information consumers" and have the knowledge to critically evaluate information of all types.

In the case of the Internet, the evaluation of content and appropriateness is a bit different than the same process with the printed word. Books and journals are usually evaluated first by editorial boards and then by review sources, before they are purchased by librarians for a reference or subject collection.

Commercial databases are often created and evaluated by subject matter specialists and indexers. Producers of these databases are careful to check the authority of the author and the authenticity of the content before an addition to the database is made.

Given the global, distributed nature of the Internet, material found on the Net is not likely to have gone through any such review process before being published. Anyone may publish on the Internet, so some additional criteria need to be considered by students when evaluating Internet pages. Because of the proliferation of World Wide Web pages, the focus will remain on evaluation of the type of information found on the Web.

Before starting any research project, students and teachers need to recognize the current limitations of information found on the Internet. Book and magazine publishers are not likely to have full-text copies of their information available freely on the Net. There may be portions or supplementary material available, but students must realize that printed materials will still be their primary source of information.

Most information on the Internet is recent. There have been some compilations of historical data put on the Net, but the majority of statistical and empirical data presented is still post-1993.

Due to the varying limitations of bandwidth on the Internet, most of the useful information is in text or photograph form. If a student wishes to view a video of the Hindenburg airship disaster, a CD-ROM, videotape, or videodisk would be the most appropriate place to begin.

Once students recognize the type of information that will be found on the Internet, they should formulate a search strategy by identifying the information that is necessary to complete the project at hand. Teachers can facilitate this process by providing a simplified reference interview to allow students to recognize what information is being sought.

Once a search has been conducted and a site has been identified, each level of student (elementary, middle, and secondary) should evaluate the site using the same set of criteria. The evaluation questions may be phrased differently for each level, but the concepts will still be the same—evaluation of author authority, content, and presentation.

Authority of Author

The author should be recognized as an expert in the field. Some items to consider include:

- Has this author been cited by others?
- Can the students find the author's name attached to print resources?
- Does the author list his or her qualifications?
- Is an e-mail address given so the author may be contacted for further information?

Content, Bias, and the Authenticity of Information

Because the content is the most important aspect of the site for students collecting information, these questions should be taken into consideration:

- Does the author state a purpose for the site?
- Does the author describe the audience that the site is intended for?
- If the content is controversial or biased, does the author give an explanation for this?
- Can the content be verified in a print source?
- If currency is important, is the information current?
- Is the page dated with the date of last update?
- Is a lot of information presented or just an overview?
- Is a bibliography included for verification of information or further research?

Presentation

Due to the varying speeds of Internet access, types of browsers, and ages of students, the presentation of a site on the Web is also important.

- Is the page easy to use?
- Is the information on the page well organized?
- Is the page pleasing to look at?
- Is the page free of spelling, grammatical, and HTML errors?
- Do included graphics enhance the presentation or supplement the content?

Evaluation tools for students at the elementary, middle, and secondary school levels may be found at <www.capecod.net/schrockguide/eval.htm>.

After students have evaluated the author, content, and presentation of a site using these evaluation instruments, they should be able to judge whether the information is applicable to their purpose. Using some higher-level thinking questions, students are asked to justify the use of the site for their project.

Have students compare the information they outlined as important in the beginning reference interview with the sites they have critically evaluated, and come up with a rationale for using or not using the site in their project.

By training, and modeling for, our students how to become critical evaluators of information that we find, we shall be producing the well-educated "information consumers" of tomorrow. Given the massive amount of information and information sources available, this is truly an important skill for the 21st century!

A great Internet site that has links to many pages of critical evaluation of Web page research is *Teaching Students to Think Critically About Internet Resources* <weber.u.washington.edu/~libr560/NETEVAL/index.html>.

Kathleen Schrock is a Technology Coordinator at Dennis-Yarmouth Regional School District in South Yarmouth, Massachusetts, and can be reached at kschrock@capecod.net

NOTES

THE BIG6 NEWSLETTER presents:

How to Use Soda Pop, *The Blair Witch Project*, and Other Methods to Help Students Learn to Evaluate Web Information Critically

By Kathleen L. Spitzer

"Hey, Ma! There's this really scary movie that I want to go see. It's called The Blair Witch Project."

"Oh, I haven't heard of it. What's it about?"

"You haven't heard of it? Everybody's talking about it. There're these three students who are making a film, and they get lost in the woods. Then they disappear. And what's really scary is that it really happened!"

"It really happened?"

"Yeah. They found the videotapes locked in a trunk, and it was buried under the foundation of a house that was built in the 1800s."

"Where was this?"

"I dunno. I think it was in Maryland."

"Hmm. I never read anything about three students being lost in the newspaper. It's hard to believe that wouldn't have made the papers."

"It's real! They have a Web site and everything!"

This conversation is the perfect example of a "teachable moment." It is an opportune time to teach an essential skill that permeates the Big6 process—critically evaluating information. Did *The Blair Witch Project* really happen? It's got a Web site, so it must be true, right? Wrong.

As an educator, you have likely seen evidence of students' indiscriminate use of information found in one form or another. This is even worse in regards to information on the World Wide Web. Many students believe that if something is on the Web, it must be true. It is therefore imperative that we provide our students with some guidelines to help them learn to evaluate information found on the World Wide Web.

Our challenge is to demonstrate the necessity of critical evaluation and help students learn to do so. What better place to start than with something familiar? Students make countless decisions on a daily basis—among them, what soft drink to choose. So, for our lesson on evaluating Web sites, we'll start with soft drinks and follow up with a lesson connected to a topic that the students will be studying.

Introduce the lesson by holding up two cans of different soda pop brands (e.g., Coke and Pepsi). Ask students to work in pairs or groups to develop a list of factors that influence them to purchase a particular brand of soft drink. Tell the students that each group will share the factors developed with the rest of the class, and ask each group to choose a spokesperson. Allow a few minutes for the groups to create their lists. Students enjoy this activity, and as you walk around the room you will probably hear some interesting conversations.

When the conversation seems to be dying down, stop the activity and ask the spokesperson from each group to contribute one item from its list. These factors can be written on a chalkboard, a whiteboard, a pad on an easel, or displayed electronically by typing them into a computer connected to a large screen TV or monitor. Continue rotating around to each group until all factors have been listed. Ask students to review the compiled list generated and select only those factors that deal with the quality of the product itself. As students make suggestions, place a check mark next to these factors. (See Figure 1 for a sample list.)

Comment on the fact that the students have come up with a lengthy list of factors that influence their purchase of a type of soda pop. Now that you have students' attention, note that it is no less important to use discretion when "buying into" information. Remind students that Step 4.1 of the Big6 is to read, hear, or view information in a source. At this point, students must make a judgment about the information.

To demonstrate the criteria that students can use in evaluating information found on the Web, use a slideshow such as *PowerPoint*. This is a particularly effective tool if you have Internet connectivity and can click on selected links to visit in the course of the demonstration. As previously mentioned, the lesson should be related to a topic that the class is studying or to an upcoming paper or project. With this in mind, use the slideshow to demonstrate each of the following criteria:

➤ Who is the author or sponsor of the Web site? (Hint: You may have to scroll down to the bottom of the page to see if you can find anything about the author or sponsor.)

- What authority does the author or sponsor have to write this type of material? (Hint: Is there a link that tells you about the author or sponsor of the Web site?)
- Does this information tell about the author's background, education, or credentials?
- Does the author or sponsor provide a source for the material that was included in the Web site? Is that source reputable? (Hint: You may have to scroll down to the bottom of the page to see if a source for the material is listed.
- Is there any bias evident in the information? Is the information one-sided?
- Is the information fact or opinion?
- When was the site last updated? (Hint: This is often located at the bottom of the page.)
- Is the material relevant to your need?

Figure 1: Factors that affect the purchase of a particular type of soda pop.	
Cost	Calories*
Taste/Aftertaste*	Advertisements
Company reputation	Ads—Placement in the store
Marketing	Fizziness*
Packaging	Caffeine*
Amount of carbonation	Coupons or on sale
Size of bottle	Can or bottle
Glass	Promotions
Color	Amount of sugar*
Availability	Smell*
Reputation of brand	Habit
Ingredients*	Age of the product
Recycle-ability of the can/bottle	

* factors that affect the quality of the soda itself

In putting together the *PowerPoint* show, search out Web links that demonstrate each of the criteria. For example, to demonstrate a site that provides the source of information, go to <http://www.biography.com> and search for a biography of a famous person. At the bottom of the page, note that credit for the source of information is provided.

Following the *PowerPoint* demonstration, provide students with a worksheet that requires them to visit sites that you have pre-selected. At the top of the worksheet, provide a list of the criteria that were demonstrated in *PowerPoint*. Students should then evaluate the information found on these sites using three criteria. If your students have access to computers with Internet connectivity, the worksheet can be in electronic format. For example, you can use *Microsoft Word* to create the worksheet and distribute it to students on disk. An electronic worksheet saves time by allowing students to simply click on a URL to visit a Web site. They can also type in their response directly on the electronic worksheet.

Be sure to select the sites for the worksheet according to a topic the students are studying or sites that are related to a paper or project they will be doing. In putting together the worksheet, select a number of sites that will challenge students to apply the criteria presented in the *PowerPoint* show. For example, for a biographical research project, you could select links about Dr. Seuss. There is a wide variety of information about Dr. Seuss on the Web—everything from fan tributes to critical examinations of his work. If you have electronic access to full-text magazines or to sources such as *Current Biography*, include links to these as well. They can provide an example of information that is reliable.

After students have a chance to complete the worksheet, discuss the sites together. If possible, display the sites that are being discussed via computer projection. Ask them what they have learned to be sure they are starting to evaluate information from the Web more critically.

Critical evaluation of information is a fundamental skill of the information age. Students need to be critical consumers of information, so they will be skeptical and able to see beyond the hype and glitz of Web presentations, such as the earlier mentioned site about *The Blair Witch Project*. Teaching from a Big6 perspective means developing critical thinking across settings and situations so that students constantly question the reliability of information sources and the accuracy of information within various sources.

Kathleen L. Spitzer is a Library Media Specialist at Cicero-North Syracuse (New York) High School.

Webliographies

Much More Than Just a Bibliography

Creating a webliography can give students the experience of evaluating sources of information as well as learning technology skills.

Nancy Robinson Marino

YOU ARE LOOKING for information on the Internet. Even if you go to a search engine, such as *Webcrawler, AltaVista* or *Lycos,* you find yourself with hundreds, thousands, or even a million sites. Finding a useful, reliable source on a particular topic can be frustrating even for the most experienced searcher. Any experienced searcher knows there's a lot of garbage out there. So, how can you help students find relevant and useful sources on the World Wide Web? One method is to create webliographies.

Webliographies are a collection of Internet sites on a particular subject. They can be printed on paper, placed on a home page, or entered into a computer-accessible file so that students can automatically link to relevant Web sites. The similarities to a bibliography cannot be overlooked and the learning advantages are similar. By examining and evaluating sources, students improve critical thinking skills.

One way to start a webliography project is to begin a lesson on how to evaluate information. Students naturally make decisions regarding the validity and relevancy of information in their daily lives. Make students aware of their evaluative abilities by playing the "Who Would You Believe Game." Students are given a question or problem to solve and a choice of two possible sources of reliable information. Have the students decide which source they would believe and why. Here is an example of questions and information choices:

WHO WOULD YOU BELIEVE?

Questions	Sources of Information
Why are dinosaurs extinct?	Your little sister or a scientist
What you are having for dinner?	Your parents or a scientist
What are the coolest fashions?	A 1985 book or this month's fashion magazine
Will the United States will ever pass a federal law regarding the Internet?	The President of the United States or the Mayor of your town
Will a traffic light be placed at an intersection near the school?	The President or the Mayor

> *The similarities to a bibliography cannot be overlooked and the learning advantages are similar.*

This exercise can be used to begin a discussion on why some information sources are more valid than others. It can also point out that no one is an authority on everything. While the scientist may be the expert on dinosaurs, mom (or dad) is probably the expert on what's for dinner. By explaining why they would believe their source, students begin to develop a criteria for evaluating information. This criteria should include organization of information, currency of information, and authority of the source.

When students decide on a criteria, review some Web sites together. Unlike books and magazines, which are generally the product of professional writers and editors and often the subject of review, the World Wide Web is a vehicle for anyone who has something to say. Web pages can be created by anyone who has a little knowledge of computers. Therefore, students must be careful when evaluating their use and relevancy. To illustrate this point the Reference Department at the B. Davis Schwartz Memorial Library, C.W. Post Campus, Long Island University, uses the example of two "whitehouse" Web pages. http://www. whitehouse.gov is the official White House page. http://www. whitehouse. org is a spoof of the official White House Web page.

These web pages look very similar and have very similar addresses, but are quite different in purpose and usefulness.

One way to help decide if a Web site will be useful is to look at the domain name. The domain name shows the purpose of the organization where the Web page originated. Using the White House examples above, the domain name "gov" shows that one page comes from a government agency. The name "org" shows that the page comes from an organization.

Other examples of domain names are .edu (educational organization) and .com (commercial organization).

Several new domain names may be introduced in the near future:

.firm (for companies or firms)

.store (for companies selling goods)

.web (for organizations involved in Web-related activities)

.arts (for organizations involved in arts and cultural activities)

.rec (for organizations involved in recreation and entertainment)

.info (for those providing information services)

.nom (for individuals)

Before beginning the actual webliography project, have students spend a class session comparing and contrasting two Web sites on a particular subject. Students can choose their own subject, perhaps one they have a special interest in, and evaluate each site. The students could create a table with the criteria for evaluating the pages listed on the side and the names of the Web sites as a heading.

Another way of organizing this information is by creating a Venn diagram. Each circle represents a Web site with their common elements in the overlapping area.

When you're ready to start the webliography project, students will begin to search the Web. In addition to search engines such as *Lycos* (www.lycos.com) or *AltaVista* (www.altavista.com), students can use *Yahooligans* (www.yahooligans.com), a search engine for children. Don't overlook print sources. Directories, such as *The Yellow Pages for Kids and Families* by Jean Polly (McGraw Hill, 1997) and *Internet for Kids* by Deneen Frazier (Sybex Inc., 1995), offer lists of kid-friendly Internet sites. Another excellent source is the *Internet Resource Directory for K-12 Teachers and Librarians* by Elizabeth Miller (Libraries Unlimited, 1997). Miller's book is designed for adults, but the easy-to-use format makes it an excellent source for children.

Using print sources in the webliography project helps to reinforce the fact that information comes in many forms. The children may discover that they need to integrate print and Internet information to find some of the best lists of Web sites. Also, by examining print sources, students learn about the elusiveness of Web sites. What was on the World Wide Web yesterday, may not be there today.

During the search part of the project, students can work in collaborative groups. Some students can search the Internet while others review print sources. Some can write summaries while one or two students can be the Web masters, who place the sites on a file that can be accessed through *Netscape* or *Microsoft Explorer.*

A Web page can be created using the program *Notepad*, which is on Windows and Windows 95. For an easy to create, basic Web page, follow the step-by-step guide above. This page can be embellished with graphics, colors and backgrounds.

Once you have created the page, make sure to save it in Notepad as an HTML file. Do this by pulling up the "save as" menu and typing the name of your file with an htm extension (filename.htm). If you do not have

How to Set Up A Webliography Web Page

After opening up the Notepad program, type the following:

```
<HTML>
<HEAD><TITLE>Title of Your Project</HEAD></TITLE>
<BODY BGCOLOR="#FFFFFF"
TEXT="#000000"
LINK="#8B0000"
ALINK="#6B8E23"
VLINK="#96FB98">
<BR>
<BR>
<BR><CENTER><FONT SIZE=5><B>Title of your class project</B></CENTER></FONT>
<BR>
<BR>
<FONT SIZE=4>
<UL>
<H3>Subheading for your webliography</H3>
<LI><a href="http://www.firstweb-site.xxx">Na me of first web site</a>
<BR>
```

Type a description of your first web site. This can be as long as you want. When you are done with the description, type

```
<LI><a href="http:secondwebsite.xxx">Na me of second Web site </a>
<BR>
```

Type description of your second Web site.

```
<BR>
<H3>Second subheading for your webliography</H3>
<LI><a href="http://www.firstweb-site.xxx">Na me of first Web site </a>
<BR>
```

Type description of your second web site.

```
<BR>
</UL>
<BR>
</BODY></HTML>
```

access to an Internet server and cannot load your page on the World Wide Web, you can still use it in your library. After the file is saved, you can open it in *Netscape* or *Explorer*. The file will look like a Web page. Of course, if you have access to a server, place the file on the World Wide Web.

The webliography can be an ongoing project since the Web is constantly changing. Students should frequently check that the sites are still located on the Internet and still contain relevant and useful information. Next year, other classes can use the old webliography projects as a starting point for their own.

Nancy Robinson Marino is Assistant Professor, Library Faculty, at the C.W. Post Campus of Long Island University in Brookville, New York.

HTML Used in the Web Page

For those not familiar with HTML, below is a description of the HTML commands:

HTML—Declares that this is HTML.

HEAD—This is the first part or heading.

BODY—This is the body of the page.

BGCOLOR—Background color (this is followed by the code for colors). In this instance the code is "#FFFFFF" or the code for white.

TEXT—Text color (the page above uses the color black.

LINK—Color of the links (the page above uses blue).

ALINK—Color after the link has been used (the page above uses green).

VLINK—Color while the link is being used.

BR—Break command (unlike word processors, HTML doesn't word wrap. You have to tell it where to break.)

B—Bold.

CENTER—Centers the text.

FONT SIZE—Determines how big the font size is going to be. Sizes range from 1-6. 6 is the largest.

UL—Unordered list.

LI—Listed item.

H3—Headline size 3. (Use this to create subheadings. They help students organize information.)

a href=URL.../a. Command for linking a URL to your page. Anything before the /a will be linkable. If you click on the words between the anchor and the /a you will go to another Web site. Anything after /a is not linkable.

Any command with a slash (/) in front of it stops the previous command. For example, <B> is the command for bold; </B> ends the bold command. <Font size=5> commands the font size; </font> ends the font size. All commands are placed in <>.

NOTES

CHAPTER 6

The Open House: Library Media Specialist as Host/Hostess

Once the new house has the building inspector's okay, it is time to invite the public in to see the results. As library media programs change and grow with the addition of technology and information skills curriculums, public relations is important in all areas. Publicizing successes with student research reports and school-wide initiatives is a good way to hook teachers on your library media program. Traditional newsletters, invitations to visit, or use of a Web page are good ways to keep parents and community up-to-date on your "new house," ensure continued fiscal support, and create a feeling of community.

The articles in this chapter deal with myriad public relations topics: selling your program to the teachers in your school; starting the year off with positive public relations events; using students and technology to publicize your library media center; creating home pages for student, staff, and community support; and much more.

Other articles deal with the quantitative data that need to be regularly collected for reports to school boards, committees, and administrative staff. By having empirical data at your fingertips whenever asked, you'll have the tools necessary for reporting, budgeting, and justification for purchases and continued fiscal support. Knowing the copyright date-ranges of the items in your collection can be invaluable when you're writing a grant proposal to obtain more up-to-date science and technical books for the collection. The number of students served and the numbers of items circulated will support your request for additional staffing.

The library media specialist's role is to support the information needs of students and staff. You need to publicize the fact that you are there for them any time, any place, and anywhere. Public relations is not just a weekly newsletter to staff about new acquisitions but a consistent, positive, helping attitude throughout the school day and throughout the school building. Any help you can give one-on-one, whether in the library media center, the hallway, or the teachers' room, makes you the "hostess with the mostest." Administrators, staff, and students will quickly realize how valuable a service you provide.

▶ URL UPDATE

Parent Internet Driving School:
Using Technology to Increase Parent
Involvement in Schools by Debbie Abilock

Sendit USA Schools
http://www.sendit.nodak.edu/usa.htm

ALA Intellectual Freedom Statements
http://www.ala.org/alaorg/oif/celebrating.html#ptftr

Mudfellows
http://nuevaschool.org/curric/

Southwest Tribe Study
http://nuevaschool.org/humanities/archaeology/

HP Telementor Project
http://www.telementor.org/hp/

NOTES

Getting the Year Off to a Good Start!

By Jacqueline Seewald

One day in the faculty cafeteria, a teacher said how much she had enjoyed a very expensive dinner at a local French restaurant. Another teacher insisted that this particular restaurant served very small portions and wasn't worth the money. The first teacher then replied, "It's all in the presentation." I believe she meant that how something is perceived is significant. In the context of the media center, it is possible to do the most incredible job, but if you don't sell your program properly, your efforts will be taken for granted. Then you will not get the financial support you need to run a first-rate program. The people who allocate the budget have to be sold on your program and its value. How you present your program from the beginning of school is important. And yes, little things really do mean a lot.

Advocacy of the media center, learning center, or educational information center begins before school ever opens officially. It begins even before the other teachers arrive. If you want to get things off to a good start and show what the media center is all about, you have to make a sacrifice. Happily, it is not necessary to offer up your first-born on an altar. It is merely necessary that you get to the media center a day earlier than the rest of the staff.

First, consider what your desk looks like, the catalogs that have been arriving, the junk mail accumulating, the general clutter. Try to separate the wheat from the chaff. Getting organized is crucial. When the teachers come in, the media center should have a "together" look about it. The teachers will ask for services immediately, and you need to be prepared. Have a set procedure for dispensing equipment. Place request forms in every mailbox, preferably before school starts.

Another reason to come in a day early is to meet new staff members. They are always required to come in ahead of the regular staff. They will also need to learn media center procedures. Chances are, they are going to ask you for equipment and materials right away.

It's also important for the administration to know that you've come in early. It's definitely good PR for the media center. By being there, you present an image of the media center as a place where staff can get strong support services. The key to good PR for the media center is the perception that the staff is organized and helping from before day one.

If at all possible, set up your display cases before the staff arrives and certainly before the students come in for their first day. Choose attractive new books for display. Several themes suggest themselves. "Something for Everyone" allows for a variety of fiction and nonfiction to be put on display. Another good choice is "Welcome Back." New bookmarks should be out on the circulation desk in plain view. Orientations for the newest students usually begin sometime during the first month of school. Set up a schedule with the English teachers, since everyone takes English. It's a good idea to close the media center to study hall, lunch students and other classes during orientations so that you assume the characteristics of a regular classroom as much as possible. Since you do work in something of a fish bowl, expect that other staff members and administrators will be walking through. Because you are always on display, it is important to present the image of an outstanding teacher.

There are always going to be staff members who think that the media specialist is "just" a librarian. It's important for them to realize that this is not the case, that we are actually master teachers, besides being librarians and AV and technology experts. If handled correctly, the orientation demonstrates and showcases our unique abilities. The first day of student orientation should be fairly regimented. Here are some suggestions that have worked well for me:

- Set up an overhead and a tripod screen so that you can use transparencies or a computer data projector.

- When students arrive, tell them where to sit, preferably facing the screen so they can hear and see you.

- Be attractively and professionally dressed. Clothes do make the media specialist to some extent. Remember, as the teacher said about the expensive French dinner, "It's in the presentation."

> **The key to good PR for the media center is the perception that the staff is organized and helping from before day one.**

- It's okay to smile right away. You're not their regular teacher. A pleasant but firm manner is needed. Appear confident. This is your media center.
- Give handouts of what you are about to discuss.
- Explain what hours you will be open, what behavior is expected, how I.D. or library cards are handled, loan policy, fines, location of circulation desk, and school rules as they relate to media center use.
- Give out maps of the media center.
- Point out such things as where the photocopier and vertical file are located.
- Display interesting, attractive examples as you discuss the following resources: Reference books, fiction, short story collection, nonfiction, biographies, paperback collection, and periodicals. Point out their locations and explain how they are cataloged.
- Introduce the media center staff so students will know who actually works in the media center.

As you do your presentation, involve students by asking questions and listening to their answers, occasionally restating answers when students speak too softly to be heard by the group. Questions such as "What is a collective biography?" or "What is a periodical?" can be asked to elicit participation.

Also, show rather than tell whenever possible. For example, when I explain to students how valuable a CD-ROM like the *Readers' Guide* can be, I pile up 10 bound volumes representing the last 10 years. Then I explain that all this information is available with just a touch of the enter key on the computer. Students are usually impressed.

I use audiovisual materials during the orientation. Originally, a sound slide show created by teachers and students at the high school was shown. However, I find that a video is much more appealing and easier to use. You can enlist other teachers and students to help create an appropriate video that introduces the media center. It need last only 10 to 15 minutes. A listening guide should accompany this video. Students will be required to answer the questions on the guide in written form on the worksheet as they watch and listen. The accompanying English teacher grades this as a classwork assignment. Here are some sample questions from our listening guide:

- List some of the resources (materials) in the media center.
- What books are labeled "B"?
- In what section are encyclopedias and dictionaries found?
- What is the vertical file?

A second day of orientation involves students with hands-on activities. Again, the students will be required to complete a worksheet. This time, they will be using media center resources. Here are some sample questions you may wish to include in your orientation task sheet:

- Find a title and a call number for a fiction book.
- Find a call number and title for a nonfiction book.
- Find a title and a call number for an individual biography.
- Find a call number and a title for a collective biography.
- Find a title and a call number for a reference book.
- List two magazines (periodicals) that we have in our media center.
- Go to the computer network. Use the *Readers' Guide to Periodical Literature* on CD-ROM to locate the number of articles about Mike Tyson.
- Use the card catalog on the computer network to search the computerized card catalog.
- Who wrote the book Black Dance in America?
- Search the SIRS CD-ROM using a keyword search. How many articles are there on the subject of drug abuse?
- Select the Internet connection. Type in the subject of "rose gardens." How many references do you find?

Explanations to students are necessary for the computerized part of the activity. All the effort involved in this will pay off because students will be much more confident and independent when they come in to use the media center either on their own or for class research. Our goal is always to enable our students. This says a great deal for our services and our significance in the school.

Before the students leave, hand out bookmarks—and include the teacher. We had bookmarks made up especially for us by the print shop. The Dewey Decimal system is on one side and the school logo on the other. Remember, everyone likes a gift, no matter how small. It promotes good feeling and positive PR. If you follow these suggestions, I believe you will have a memorable opening of the media center for the school year.

Jacqueline Seewald is an Educational Media Specialist at Red Bank Regional High School in Little Silver, New Jersey.

> In the media center, it's possible to do the most incredible job, but if you don't sell your program properly, your efforts will be taken for granted.

Don't Forget PR!

Katherine T. Bucher

"I don't know what all the fuss is about computers in the library. We're just throwing our money away on that stuff when all we really need are books."

You may have overheard a comment like this at a faculty meeting or at the grocery store. But it doesn't matter where it was said. What does matter is the misunderstanding and even resentment of the new technologies that are entering school libraries.

Technology changes things that we do in libraries. The focus of our work frequently shifts from the acquisition of materials (buying books) to accessing information in a variety of formats (online, CD-ROM, videodisc). However, many of our users are not aware of that switch.

Remember, a major reason that technology fails is that the potential users do not accept it. (A recent survey found that 55% of Americans suffer from technophobia or fear of technology.) Many adults do not know how to use it and do not want to appear stupid by asking for help. While students may flock to the computer, adults are often much more reluctant. That is why it is important to set up a good technology public relations program.

Before starting any PR program, review a few basics:

Create an image that you want people to have of the use of technology in your library. Then develop a program to "sell" that image. Perception is reality. What people perceive becomes their reality, even if it is not true.

Learn from the business world. Take some tips from the folks who can afford to hire a PR firm. Be *visual* with graphs, charts, and flyers. Be *vocal* with catchy, nontechnical sound bites. Keep the jargon to a minimum. Publicize the *image* with slogans and a logo. *Time* your promotions to get the best effect.

Think big, start small. Hook one teacher or student on the technology. While you want to sell everyone on the benefits of technology, you can start with one person.

Insure success. Do not set yourself up for failure by trying to sell the person who boasts that he can live without the computer. Start your training with a willing learner.

Try Some of These Ideas

Here are a few ideas that you can modify for your own PR.

Provide "answer people." Take a hint from the answer desks that do-it-yourselfers look for in hardware stores. Train a core group of teachers and students to use a certain technology and let them teach others. Advertise the services of the "answer people." Provide them with "Ask me about . . . " buttons or badges.

Offer before- or after-school specials. Try an ongoing series of workshops for teachers with a different focus each week. Provide time for hands-on practice. Several short sessions are better than one long one.

Give rewards. Provide incentives for teachers to attend workshops. You might offer recertification points, the first chance to use a new piece of equipment, a gift from a local business, or one hour of planning time with the librarian. In a series of workshops, let each person put her name in the hat at each meeting for a prize drawing during the last workshop.

Prepare a short videotape or audiotape on the operation of equipment. Encourage people to view or listen to the tape when they work with the hardware.

Publicize programs. Stay up-to-date about workshops offered by the state department of education and professional associations. Share this information and more in newsletters.

Cooperate with others. Build relationships with other school groups and other schools, both public and private. Work with them to offer special programs such as demonstrations of advanced searching techniques. Offer a program for parents and teachers on buying computers or multimedia for home use.

Provide temptation. Put the new technology (hardware and software) in the teachers' lounge for a few hours each day and see what happens. You might want to insure success by arranging for an experienced user to be in the lounge during that time.

Promote success. Host a technology fair. To show administrators and the community the benefits of technology, have teachers, students, and staff members demonstrate how successfully they can use it.

With a good PR program, the next comment that you overhear might be about the wonderful things that are happening in the school library because of technology. TC

Katherine T. Bucher is an Associate Professor at Old Dominion University, Norfolk, Virginia.

Technology - a - Goldmine For Positive PR

Showcasing Technology

By Rocco Staino

Each day when you read the paper or tune in to local news, you'll usually see at least one school-related story. Although education is clearly a hot topic, many of us are so busy trying to get technology up and running that we overlook the great potential it has for building positive public relations.

If you can find time to send professionally written news releases that combine the word "students" with "Internet," "CD-ROM," or "telecommunications," you're sure to capture the eye of a news-hungry assignment editor.

An appropriately prepared news release always lists in the upper right-hand corner a contact person and a phone number (which reporters tend to use rather than tracking down quotes in person) where that person can be reached. It should also include the time, date, and location for the activities described in the release.

Here are some ideas for preparing a news release on technology:

Students and Technology

Students are using the Internet in a variety of newsworthy ways. For example, students in my area found the music and lyrics to a song for a countywide competition on the Internet. High school seniors have been using it to find alumni from their school who are attending colleges that interest them. And middle school students have been corresponding with their siblings attending college. (This project encouraged family values and showed that more communications took place electronically than face-to-face.)

Community Benefits

Community members, especially those without school-age children, lack a clear understanding of what a school library media program is and how it positively affects students' learning. The best way to bring these people up to speed is to provide community access to your media center. In some communities, the school's media center provides Internet access for the entire community. In others, community members can dial into the school's online catalog, place a reserve on a title, or browse the electronic periodical index and access full-text articles from their homes. This may not seem like news to *you*, but to many in the community, this is a new frontier.

Technology Twist to a Familiar Theme

Technology can be used to add a new dimension to the way adults relate to their school experiences. You may remember "class pen pals"... Well, add the word "electronic" and you have a whole new story. Students are now communicating electronically with others across town, the state, the nation, and the world.

Library research is another such shared experience, although one which is not so fondly remembered. Today's shift from merely locating information to critical *use* of information definitely has news appeal. Showing how easy it is for students to locate articles through today's media center technology will enlighten adults and give them a new view to library research.

Put Technology in a Nontechnology Event

This year, in celebration of the Christmas holidays, our school decoration was a wreath made of hand cutouts. Each hand held a wish for the new year. Our news release regarding this event contained examples of a number of wishes. The wish for Internet access captured one reporter's eye and was included in an article.

Our annual bookfair also took on a new twist when we began selling software along with traditional items, prompting the local press to write about our event.

Develop a Relationship with the Media

To become media savvy, you must take some time to read, listen, and view your local media. Become familiar with the types of stories particular reporters tend to favor. Make note of those who seem interested in the stories you

The wish for Internet access captured one reporter's eye and was included in an article.

have to offer and program their numbers into your fax machine or phone file. Feed these individuals story ideas, especially on Mondays (traditionally, a slow news day). Finally, always have a story idea waiting because you never know when a reporter may show up on your doorstep! **TC**

Rocco Staino is the Director of the Keefe Library in the North Salem (New York) Schools.

NETWORKING

Library Home Pages: A New Knowledge Environment

Creating a Web home page boldly says that the library is the center of information access. It places the library in the forefront of educational technology. What kinds of information and services can such a home page provide? How can you make it work for you, especially in your role as instructional leader?

The opening home page serves as a four-second first impression of the library. The library's name should appear exciting and distinctive—and welcoming. To accomplish this, explore options in font style, size, and color. A sharp-looking graphic would complement the title. Note that variations in World Wide Web appearance can alter the graphic; so be sure that the visual isn't too big or wide. The next line should give a 25-word "sound bite" about the library's role. Make sure that the description sounds flashy and impressive because you have very little time to hook a potential library user.

By Lesley S.J. Farmer

The main body of the home page should show the variety of library services and resources. The easiest approach is to develop a short list of linked options. That way you can point to a number of important pieces of information without making your users plow through details that don't interest them. These links may refer to embedded "pages" or to external files. This menu approach also insures that the page will be interactive; the user is in control of the knowledge environment. Here are some topics to consider:

- Library resources, rules and regulations, statistics
- A floor map
- Staff and volunteers (get permission if you include photos)
- The newsletter
- New print and nonprint resources, services, or staff members
- Announcements of upcoming events
- Book reviews and booktalks
- Book or CD-ROM of the week
- URL (Uniform Resource Locator) of the week
- Trivia contest
- Reader's advisory booklists
- In-house databases (hotlines or community contacts)
- Pathways>>>>WebQuests (see below)
- Links to other school pages

Remember to give users a way to contact the library, by phone, U.S. mail, or an e-mail connection. One effective approach is to encourage students to ask the librarian questions via e-mail. It can be as easy as this: "Can't find what you need? Ask the librarian by clicking on this address: accountname@domain.address." The account is an active link so the student can type in a specific request. Of course, this feature requires the staff to answer in a timely manner. Otherwise, the benefit is lost. The student must also have an e-mail address to receive his answer. For students who do not have an address, you can provide a generic student account with one name/address, such as student@school.edu. This single account works like an electronic bulletin board; all messages are public to anyone who knows the account name. Students can check their messages at any time from any site. Before attempting this option, though, you will need to know your constituents and security systems well, in order to avoid communication abuse.

A Study in Detail

Pathway guides are used by many librarians and teachers to help students locate resources on a topic. (See sample below.) Now you can use the guides in a new way: transform them into Web pages and expand the library's role in information literacy instruction. Such online guides can direct students to print resources and other holdings as well as remote sites. With some creative thinking, you can make sure the Web pages do not just duplicate the paper version; color, clip art, and linked information make the new format more attractive and useful.

Selecting and evaluating the useful Web sites requires skill. If other library staff or aides work on this task, make sure you check their results. A simple method is to examine their search history, which will be indicated in most Web browsers. In some cases, you may want to show end users the line of strategy, such as going from a general directory to a more refined topical set of files. In designing the pathways page, begin with an overview of a broad subject, such as "Science" or "Renaissance," and list resources that give a general treatment. Then you can subdivide the topic yourself, or use an index such as Yahoo to list more specialized references.

What Does It Look Like?

The difference between a traditional paper document and a Web page is the interconnectivity. The electronic form provides a more complex set of links than a print document would typically offer, even with a good index. Because it is so easy to go from link to link, it is important that you keep those connections straight. One way to maintain an overall perspective is to draw a flowchart of the various pages, so you and your users won't get lost in the information web.

The appearance of the page is as important as the quality of the content. A dull-looking screen will be an instant turn-off. The goal is to make your Web page "zing" without looking chaotic. Basically, visual elements should help users find information, not distract them. Here are a few principles:

Keep the type face simple. Use only a couple of font or typeface styles, and make sure they are easily read. Stick to commonly used fonts so remote machines will be more likely to translate the text. Use only a couple of font sizes, and be consistent in their use. That way, they can act as a visual cue to the importance of the content. Thus, headlines would have a larger size than the main body of the text. Use boldface and underlines sparingly, since these features don't always transfer well to other systems. A good practice is to develop a style sheet. In that way, library aides can enter information in a consistent manner.

Use color and texture for emphasis. Keep color variations to a minimum; some colors may change when picked up by other systems. Textured backgrounds can lend atmosphere to a page. Make sure, though, that any background is light and subtle so the viewer can decipher the text through it. Be sure to check the resolution and color range of graphic images so they are easily read by other systems. One trick is to test the appearance of the Web page by calling it up on another, unlike system.

Watch edges and columns. Because monitor size varies, try to have all elements arranged so the user doesn't have to scroll across the screen. This is another case where it helps to test the Web page on different systems. Because columns can also be unpredictable, it is safer to list menu items in a single column or with center justification.

Go for the uncluttered look. The ideal is a home page with one page of introduction and one page of menu links. That way people don't get lost. (The backup button is much easier to use for navigating than long scrolling fields.) The number of menu choices should be limited to eight or fewer so users can remember their options.

Use graphical organizers. Most HTML languages permit horizontal bars to separate text blocks. Newer mark-up programs include frames to group related text together. Remember, though, that older systems might not be able to read these frames. Also, background color and texture may not carry over to all systems.

Explain yourself. Links should either be self-explanatory, such as "Library Map," or they should include a brief annotation to explain them. For instance, the option "What's New?" might be followed by "Get lists of latest books and CD-ROMs that have arrived in the library." Images should also be self-evident or captioned. Note: make sure you have permission to use a graphical element, and cite that permission if it is required.

Maintaining the Home Page

Maintenance tasks rise to a new level of timeliness on a Web page. Users' expectations for current information and novelty rise dramatically. As new materials come into the library, announce them immediately. Pathway files can also reflect new holdings as they go into circulation. Be sure to review links to resources at least monthly to make sure the resources haven't disappeared or moved. And, new URLs need to be added as well. If e-mail is offered on the library home page, examine messages daily.

As users become accustomed to pathways for research, the demand for more such guides will increase. If teachers notice that students use the guides and improve their research skills, they may ask for more.

Sample Pathway Guide

1) For general background information, use an *encyclopedia*: [title of encyclopedia]
2) Generate a set of *keywords or terms*: [suggest terms]
3) For specific facts, use *specialized reference books*, such as: _____. Some *CD-ROM reference titles* in this field include: _____.
4) For current information, consult *periodicals* by using a magazine index, such as _____.
5) Some specific periodicals in this field include: _____, _____.
6) For current information, check the *Internet*. Remember to evaluate what you find because quality varies greatly. Some good sites include: http://_____ gopher://_____.
7) For in-depth information, examine *books*. Use your keywords to locate books through the library's catalog. Some Dewey Decimal Classification call numbers in this field include: _____, _____.

Obviously, updating and expanding the library home page will have an impact on staff hours and efforts. Some maintenance tasks can be handled by student aides and volunteers. If given the information, they can enter it into the computer. Students may find helpful URLs and pass them along to the librarian for future inclusion on the home page. Such suggestions confirm user interest and involvement. Students may even try their hand at developing research guides. (If you include students' work, be sure to give credit to them.)

Professional time is needed to develop high quality Web pages. The impact of such effort is great because it is potentially accessible to a broad spectrum of users both on and off campus. If anything, producing Web pages demonstrates the critical and highly developed skills that librarianship offers. And it offers a unique service to the school community. **TC**

Lesley S.J. Farmer is the Library Director of Redwood High School in Larkspur, California. She is the author of the forthcoming book Training Library Student Staff *to be published by Linworth Publishing, Inc.*

NOTES

SCHOOL TECHNOLOGY AND THE COMMUNITY

feature

PARENT INTERNET DRIVING SCHOOL: USING TECHNOLOGY TO INCREASE PARENT INVOLVEMENT IN SCHOOLS

By Debbie Abilock

According to a recently released 10-year study of high school students, parents are one of the most critical influences on a teenager's performance in school (*Beyond the Classroom: Why School Reform Has Failed and What Parents Need to Do* by Lawrence Steinberg, Simon & Schuster, 1996). However, it also reports that many of the parents in the study did not know what their teenagers did after school hours or how they were progressing in school, and 40% of them had never attended a school program.

THE VIRTUAL PARENT

Some educators predict that telecommunications will invite parents into schools in new ways. "Parents who would never come to a PTA meeting or a school-based event" will participate in "virtual parent-teacher conferences and informal social interchanges," predicts Chris Dede in "Distance Learning—Distributed Learning: Making The Transformation" (*Learning and Leading With Technology*, April 1996). While currently only the most affluent and technology-savvy families might have the equipment to participate in "virtual" parent conferences, technology may still be a useful bridge between home and school.

For the past three years, The Nueva School in Hillsborough, California, has held two-hour workshops called "Parent Internet Driving School" during parent-conference days. Team-taught by the librarian, the assistant librarian, the computer specialist and the systems administrator, it exposes parents to the Internet and builds support for school programs. Scheduled to repeat four times during the day, a one-hour discussion is followed by a hands-on hour in the lab. During the second hour another discussion begins in the classroom so that classes are conducted simultaneously. Since we have 20 computers in the lab, we can run 80 parents a day through the program. However, a school with a larger lab or several labs could increase the number of parents during each session.

DRIVING SCHOOL

Parent Internet Driving School motivates parents to come to school to develop their skills, to learn what their children are doing on the Internet, and to increase their confidence in parenting in this technological age. We have tailored the content of the parent program to fit our curriculum and acceptable use policy. For example, because Nueva does not use any filtering devices at school, we feel it is important to explain our policies and practices, as well as the American Library Association's Intellectual Freedom statements (gopher://ala1.ala.org:70/11s/alagophx) and the Supreme Court's hearings on the Communication Decency Act (http://www.eff.org/pub/Censorship/HTML/hot.html#cda). Because learning takes place during unstructured time exploring the Net, Nueva has always supported dial-up accounts for both children and their parents. But offering access without discussing "techno-parenting" strategies, or providing information on the pros and cons of software filters or the trade-offs on various connection options, does not provide the support that parents need to do their job in a society permeated by technology.

Another of our goals is to acquaint parents with examples of

how the Internet is integrated into our curriculum. In science, for example, elementary students from several sites collaboratively studied the San Francisco Bay mud in a program called "Mudfellows" (http://www.nueva.pvt.k12.ca.us/~essci/). This year a middle school humanities research project is asking students to examine modern Native-American issues (http://www.nueva.pvt.k12.ca.us/~debbie/library/curriculum/wk97.html) and younger students are investigating various tribes from a historical perspective (http://www.nueva.pvt.k12.ca.us/~kathryn/TribesProject/). A successful new program matches our sixth graders with mentors at Hewlett Packard (http://mentor.external.hp.com/) as they carry out semester-long science projects. During the spring, some of these mentors will become the subject of their students' "Mathematician's Report," in which students will ascertain how these engineers and scientists use math in their careers. The mentors will help the children understand a mathematical topic which they, in turn, will teach to their peers during a class demonstration. By showcasing the unique suitability of the Internet for information collection, collaborative problem solving, information literacy and mentoring, we help parents understand the value of the Internet to our school, to their children, and to their own lives.

The second hour of our Driving School takes place in the computer lab. Parents get a taste of e-mail using their new accounts and explore a series of bookmarks on subjects we believe will be of interest. We point out each child's work on our Web pages, as well as The Nueva Library's help pages on Internet searching(http://www.nueva.pvt.k12.ca.us/~debbie/library/research/research.html). One hour in a lab will not turn novices into competent computer users; however, Parent Internet Driving School creates a bond and a common understanding among the members of our school community.

KEEPING INTEREST HIGH

As a follow-up to Driving School classes, we contribute information to our school newsletter about interesting sites, new networking developments and curriculum projects. Generally, we try to be available for help with searching and on configuring systems, although the latter is a daunting task that we hope will eventually be shouldered by the Nueva Parent Association. This year, for the first time, parents are requesting both beginning and advanced classes in such topics as search strategies, advanced e-mail and creating 0Web pages.

Here are some tips for planning parent education workshops:

1. Make sure you have the support of both the administration and the people with whom you will teach, including the systems administrator.
2. Brainstorm an outline of the workshop with team members to decide what each member wants to teach.
3. Share the content and structure of your part of the workshop with other team members, so anyone could teach any section of the workshop in the event of illness.
4. Brainstorm the checklist of responsibilities and let your team members choose their roles. The person who has to leave early may want to sign up parents in advance, photocopy handouts, put up notices, or come early to set up equipment.
5. Set aside time after the event for evaluation. Take notes on what worked, what needs follow-up, and what you forgot to include on the checklist.
6. Don't forget to report back to your principal. It's a chance to demonstrate productive teacher collaboration, garner support for your next project, and give your administrator a positive agenda item for the next school board meeting. **TC**

Debbie Abilock is a Librarian at The Nueva School in Hillsborough, California.

HEAD FOR THE EDGE
By Doug Johnson

Techno-Parenting

Just last week I got this in my e-mail inbox:

Hello Parents and Guardians,

We are coming to a close on our mental health unit. Throughout the unit, the students have been writing in a journal every day. Next Tuesday, Nov. 16, this journal is due. They must have 11 journal entries and the journal must have a cover that relates to their journal. Also, the students have been creating a PowerPoint *presentation. They are coming along wonderfully. Tell your child what a great job he/she has been doing in health!*

Jane Doe, Health Teacher

That message is just the latest in an almost weekly series of reminders I've been getting from the teachers in my son's school. I've been asked to help with homework and projects; forewarned of upcoming tests and their content; and advised of upcoming field trips. And do you know what? My son's schoolwork is better as a result.

This is just one example of how technology can help forge terrific alliances between teachers and parents. Neither alone can offer a child the best possible learning experiences. It takes, if not a whole village, at least a couple of huts to educate today's kids.

E-mail is just one way technology can help the communication process. True, not all parents have e-mail. But a surprising percentage do, and that percentage grows each year. Parents who can't afford home computers may still have access to them at work or at their public library.

E-mail has some advantages over other means of communication. It's the rare e-mail that gets lost on the way home. A single e-mail message can be sent at a keystroke to dozens of parents without the hassle or cost of photocopying. Parents can respond to e-mail as soon as it is read. E-mail messages can be indexed, stored, and rapidly retrieved. (A memo is sent not only to inform the reader, but also to protect the writer, remember?)

The telephone is still the premier means of communicating with individual parents. It's easy to use, found in almost every home, and personal enough to say you care. Teachers should have a classroom telephone along with a good voice mail system. If your district can't afford to put a phone in your classroom, ask to borrow a student's cellular phone.

Web-based information systems allow parents to check their children's password-protected grades in real time. It's not hard to imagine this scenario: "See Jimmy flop on the couch with remote in hand, claiming that he's doing swell in all his classes. See Mom log on to his teacher's grade book and discover he is an assignment or two shy and did a less-than-stellar job on the latest test. See Jimmy hit the books—under Mom's supervision."

School Web pages currently provide school contact information, course descriptions, lunch menus, policies, and schedules. Teacher-designed Web pages contain classroom newsletters, assignment logs, spelling lists, and course notes. Web sites produced by media specialists give parents and students links to study guides, homework help sites, and reference materials. These pages are colorful, current, and extremely useful.

What's the next step in Web-based communication? A year ago, I met a teacher in Iowa who is pioneering a way that parents can participate in the assessment of their children's performance in real time. He gives the parents the URL where they can watch their lil' darlings perform, then connects a Web camera to his computer while students give oral presentations. My guess is that the amount of preparation goes way up knowing that Mom, Dad, and possibly Grandma might be watching. Far-fetched? Web cameras are being used in child day-care centers and preschools today.

While our district, like many others, *is* making progress with school-home communications, both traditional and digital, we need to continue to grow. I received another e-mail recently—this one sent by a parent:

Dear Teachers,

I have recently received an update on Beth's progress in school. I am disappointed, but not surprised. Beth always believes that she is doing better than she really is. The only way that I can help her stay organized with homework is to have you send me a list of her assignments. This would include upcoming tests and quizzes. Please e-mail this information every week. Hopefully we can make a difference in her grades.

Thanks for your cooperation.
Jane Doe
e-mail jdoe@hotmail.com

Why should the teachers go to all this trouble to help folks like Beth and her mom? I'll give you a list of reasons:

- home schooling
- charter schools
- virtual schools
- vouchers
- open enrollment

Parents are already choosing their children's schools here in Minnesota. Most parents understand that more than any time in history, an excellent education will be crucial to the success and happiness of their children. Schools that become more effective by harnessing the communication power of technology will have parents who are active and satisfied consumers. How long before your parents will be selecting their children's school by the quality of its communication and its ability to make parents and teachers partners in the learning process? I have a dollar that says it won't be long.

Doug Johnson is the Director of Media and Technology at I.S.D. 77 Mankato (Minnesota) Public Schools

GUERRILLA LIBRARIANSHIP
Hold the Camouflage!

By Joyce Valenza

A long-time "pacifist" borrows some tactics from the more belligerent.

Wake up comrades! These are times of real conflict. We are being attacked from all fronts. We must wage our own battles, mount our own campaigns. Indeed we must begin to fight against:

- those who close our schools of library education;
- those who believe the Internet will replace the need for libraries;
- those who are afraid of the Internet;
- those who believe our budget and staff are expendable in tighter times;
- those who expect us to fund both technology and print resources from a budget that has not grown in 10 years;
- those who believe the super bookstore in the mall can replace the school or public library;
- those who create turf issues such as pitting school librarians against technology teachers in the fight for funding;
- those who divert our effectiveness by forcing us to operate on too many fronts—managing two or three facilities;
- those who attack our philosophy to the core with the banners of "family-friendly" on one front and "political correctness" on the other.

Forgive these fighting words from a long-time pacifist, but I have seen too many librarians take the threats to our profession with a polite smile. I think it's time we mount a little subversive warfare of our own.

Guerrilla wars are little wars where each soldier may fight on his own or in a small group. Indistinguishable from the rest of the community, guerrilla warriors don't wear uniforms. The technique has been traditionally used by the militarily weak as a method of defense against invaders or occupiers. Guerrillas use flexible tactics and rapid maneuvers. Attacks are not always military; they can be political, psychological, social or economic. I think we school librarians can borrow some of these tactics.

Guerrilla Marketing

Perhaps we need to take a lesson in marketing from the successful book store chains. The superstores are reeling in customers, sponsoring functions that have historically been ours. Our collections may not have the scope of the superstore, but we have many items they do not carry and services they could never replicate. We need not serve coffee, but we can look at our facilities and see how we might make them more inviting to young people and their parents. We might even consider hours that meet the needs of students who work after school. The big bookstores' signs are bigger than ours, and their newsletters are more impressive. There is nothing stopping us from creating bigger signs and better newsletters. Certainly, there should be no problem providing better service! We have to let our community in on the secret.

Training: Readiness for Combat

Are you well-trained for combat in this environment? If not, catch up fast. Take courses, read professional journals, and join a discussion group on the Internet, such as LM_NET for school librarians. Working on your own familiar terrain, prepare yourself for action. Make sure you have modern ammunition and tactics. Is your technology up-to-date? When was the last time you looked at your curriculum or checked to make sure that information skills are written into the content area curriculums?

Guerrilla Fund Raising

As talented and well-intentioned as you are, you cannot have a successful program without materials, and you cannot have materials without money. When normal funding channels don't work, find a way to fund yourself, if only in a small way at first. The National Investment in Education program, sponsored by many banks, has provided my library with

---

Joyce Valenza is the librarian at Wissahickon High School in Ambler, Pennsylvania. Her book of resources for school librarians, Power Tools, *will be published by ALA Editions this summer.*

computer equipment, with almost no effort on our part. Investigate those supermarket receipt collection programs that provide schools with money or equipment based on the total amount of the receipts collected. Contact businesses in the area. Many are looking for ways to recycle their computer hardware and peripherals. They may not provide you with a lab of multimedia dream machines, but you may gain some good basic word-processing and CD-ROM workstations to meet student needs.

Volunteer to field test new products. Volunteer to review software for journals like THE BOOK REPORT or TECHNOLOGY CONNECTION. Reviewers keep the software. You can use the opportunity to engage your students in developing critical evaluative skills.

Bagels and cream cheese bring in about $100 a day at my school. We sell them between 7 and 8 a.m. with parent volunteers doing the serving. The sales create a friendly morning atmosphere with parents, teachers and students noshing and chatting together.

Guerrilla Public Relations

Guerrillas cannot fight without popular support. Make sure that support is strong before the battle begins. Form alliances. Develop Friends of the Library groups, school library committees, and student advocacy networks.

Be shamelessly honest and unafraid to boast. Your administrators may have no idea what you do. Write goals and monthly reports even if no one has asked for them. Copy your principals, superintendent and school board members. Be visible. Get on those key committees. You must be on the strategic planning committees and committees to draft the Acceptable Use Policy. Not only will your viewpoint be represented, you will be able to mingle with community members who would not otherwise understand your importance. Get your newsletters out to teachers and make sure the information is useful. Highlight the best Web sites in curriculum areas, download and copy lesson ideas, create rubrics for evaluation, and forms for organizing student research or cooperative group activities.

Make sure you know the key parents in the school, and do nice things for them. At parent council meetings, remind them that the library can serve the entire school community.

Guerrilla Advocacy

The American Library Association has produced packets of material for getting your word out. There are great quotes, sample letters, speeches, clip art and press releases. Tips on how to conduct an advocacy session and answer those tougher questions are also useful. For more information about the association's PR materials, call 1-800-545-2433 or e-mail pio@ala.org.

Learn to translate jargon for parents, teachers, administrators and students so that they will understand information skills. Do not assume that every parent or administrator is "on the same page" as you when it comes to technology. The Pennsylvania School Librarians Association recently published the pamphlet "Internet: Myths and Facts" to counter attacks from both the Internet-terrified and the forward-thinking who believe the Internet is the only library our children will ever need.

Be the one in your district to handle that "Internet Parents' Night." Describe the incredible resources the Internet can provide and explain those it won't. The battle cry must be sounded against those who believe that children can find their way around the Internet without guidance and training. They need to learn skills in problem definition, access, analysis, evaluation and communication that are the center of the library program. Go above and beyond the call of duty and hold Saturday morning or evening community workshops on a regular (quarterly?) basis.

Make sure you are balanced in your approach to collection building and that you have a collection development policy in place. When the community decides to challenge an item, you should be able to whip out your selection policy and your complaint form. Make sure you know who to call if the fight becomes hot.

Communicate with Other Guerrillas

Know when the time is right to come out from behind the trees to join forces with others. We must build our communications networks. No one need fight alone. If a library is about to fall in the forest, make sure someone (everyone!) can hear it fall. When small groups link up, they provide a better defense against larger armies. Get yourself on LM_Net and let others know when you or your program is about to be threatened. Phone key people in the state and national organizations quickly, even if you are not a member.

Know your powerful allies in advance. Who would you phone if your library books were being challenged? Who would you phone when a layoff appears imminent?

Pep Talk

Never stop at "no." Work until you get to "yes." Guerrilla fighters attack like bees. Opponents can tolerate a sting or two. But when the bees return every day, persisting with missions "to die for," they are awfully tough to resist. Smart guerrillas realize: a defeat today does not mean a defeat tomorrow. The war can be won with persistence and tactful aggression.

MAKING Friends IN HIGH PLACES

By Cynthia K. Dobrez & Lynn M. Rutan

These librarians have devised a quick and easy method of giving administrators a readable and entertaining glimpse of the library- in-action.

"THE TROUBLE IS THAT THEY just don't understand all the things we do!" How many times have we heard that lament from our colleagues or thought it ourselves? When the "they" we are frustrated by are the people who decide our budgets, staffing, and assignments, it is a serious concern indeed. Even the most supportive principals, superintendents and school board members need to be reminded of the wonderful happenings in school libraries. Many of us have believed for far too long that our importance to children's lives and education is self-explanatory. The real truth is that these busy people are often unaware of the many facets of our jobs or how critical good libraries are to student learning.

We work in a middle school (grades 6-8) in a fast-growing district and are fortunate to have a supportive administration. Last fall, with one of our positions a new one, it was important to find a way to demonstrate what the additional staffing enabled us to do for students and teachers. With several new administrators, we also wanted to ensure that they understood the role libraries play in the educational success of our students.

As we were discussing methods of achieving both goals in a reasonably efficient way, we remembered that the high school librarians write an impressive annual report. We decided to try writing short reports that would present the highlights of each month's library activities. (Reactions to this statement are easy to imagine. "A monthly report that no one made you do? You must have a lot more time than I do!")

Time, or the lack of it, is one of the key issues in any librarian's life. With nearly 1,600 students and over 100 staff members, time is definitely a factor for us too. We knew that any report format we established must have easily obtained data and be quick to plan, write, and distribute. We also knew that our administrators had piles of reports, documents, proposals, legislation and professional journals of their own to wade through each month. Our new report would have a lot of competition. It would need to be concise, relevant, and even entertaining; it should be as easy to read as it was to write.

Determining the Scope

We asked ourselves what were the most important of our library activities and how could we group them for easy organization. We established five categories: curriculum connection, committee and school involvement, reading incentives and public relations projects, special projects and vital statistics. Bulletin-like highlights of each month's activities could then be listed under each category. We have not changed these initial categories as they worked well for us.

Curriculum Connection is the category under which we list the kinds of research and curriculum projects that have taken place during the month. This list is not exhaustive, rather we highlight just some of the activity. This gives us an opportunity to show the types of research and projects being done in the library. A sample entry reads:

Mrs. B's 6th graders tested our botany and biology knowledge as they researched the plants and animals for their habitat displays. For a week the library was crawling with beetles, bugs and leaves we hoped were not poisonous.

This section also gives us an opportunity to highlight some of the creative work being done by our teachers in designing units and to bring these teachers to the attention of administrators. We can also stress how well the new materials are being used. For example:

Mrs. A's 7th graders researched chemical elements with a new reference set that was delivered just in time. The books were ripped out of the box and put in the student's hands, and now that the project is over, we will catalog them.

The Committee and School Involvement feature is a list of the committees and activities that we are involved with on a building and district level. But this is also an important section as it illustrates the many hours that are spent on activities outside the daily operation of the library. It may also be a little startling to you to find out how long that list can be!

Reading Incentives and Public Relations Projects is where we highlight our contests, bibliography creation, bookmarks, bulletin boards, book fairs, and other reading-related events. Here is how we reported a contest that was a great favorite with our students:

Sob-O-Meter contest and display. Our students gleefully ranked their favorite tear-inducing books in order of sadness: sniff, weep or sob.

This is also the section where we report public relations projects. For example:

"Get Wrapped Up in Books," a holiday book and computer selection evening parent program featuring booktalks, computer program demonstrations, and displays by three local vendors just in time for Christmas.

Special Projects is our miscellaneous category. Here we slot items that don't fit neatly into the other categories but are important to report. Here we put library management tasks that are vitally important, most often done after school ends and seldom thought about by nonlibrarians! We have used this section to explain the importance of weeding and inventory, to discuss the book selection process, and to report how we deal with overdues.

With a list of overdue materials split between us, we spent many evenings calling parents to request their assistance in getting materials returned to the library. This is a true lesson in life and something they never tell you about in library school!

We also use this category to report on staff training, the creation of manuals, grant applications and the arrival of new equipment.

The last section, Vital Statistics, has the important numbers dear to everyone's heart. We include five sets of statistics: classes taught by us, classes using the library for research, booktalk sessions, books circulated, and books cataloged and processed. Our library management program allows us to run the last two statistics at any time. We have found this section useful when we want to compare statistics over the months and when we plan for our class scheduling needs.

The question of how to acquire the information for the report proved to be simply solved. Our teachers sign up for time on the library schedule on a calendar in our office. Because of the high volume of library use, we have always included a descriptive notation about research projects to help us prepare for the classes. These entries remind us of the kinds of research and class projects that took place during the month. We just tear off the calendar page when the month ends and use it to compile the report.

Our personal planners provide reminders about meetings we attended and special projects we planned and implemented. Another simple but useful technique evolved in the first few months. Since we wanted to inform our administrators of our public relations and reading incentive programs, we decided to make additional copies of any event, contest, training or special project information that we were distributing to staff and students. These copies are then put into our "monthly report" file and

> Our new report would have a lot of competition. It would need to be concise, relevant, and even entertaining; it would need to be as easy to read as it was to write.

can be pulled out at the end of the month and attached to the report without creating a lot of extra work for ourselves.

We also began to keep a list in the file of things we wanted to be sure to include in that month's report. We have gotten in the habit of jotting down reminders throughout the month and putting them in the file. This greatly reduces the chore of remembering everything we did at month's end.

Because the district has been trying to pass a bond issue, public relations has been one of our library goals over the past two years. We worked hard at generating news articles about the library and school activities. We include copies of any newspaper articles or other publicity achieved in the monthly report.

Getting It Down On Paper

After the initial work of setting up the format, we have found that it takes us about an hour each month to write the report. We take turns writing it, depending on which of us has the least amount of home-life chaos that month. Through the school mail, the report goes to the building principal and assistant principals, the superintendent, the assistant superintendents of finance and curriculum, and the director of technology and staff development. These are the people who approve our budgets, evaluate our performances and support our programs.

After a year and a half of monthly reports, we believe that this hour-a-month chore is one of the most important things we do to promote the library. The administrators have responded positively and often comment on how much they appreciate the report. Don Clavette, assistant principal, says, "A year ago I was shuffling through my mail and I came across something new, Library Monthly Report. I was truly awed at what I was reading. The short bursts of information are very helpful to an administrator in learning how the librarians work with teachers and curriculum and how they use library materials, technology and research skills each month."

Our superintendent enjoys the report as well and includes information from it in his weekly school board packet. After several months of reports, we asked our readers, by note and by voice mail, to let us know if they didn't want to receive the report. Not one of our administrators asked to be removed from the list and we continue to receive their enthusiastic comments. Rosemary Elvine, assistant superintendent for instructional services, wrote, "I greatly value the librarians' monthly report. It not only provides a snapshot of statistical information regarding book circulation, but it further delineates the commitment to a seamless link between the library and the classroom...Our librarians are high-energy individuals who have truly created an environment that is viewed as the educational hub."

This is flattering, of course, but we think it is the kind of response that you too can have when you let people know what is happening each month in your library.

Cindy Dobrez and Lynn M. Rutan are Librarians at West Ottawa Middle School in Holland, Michigan.

Successful Public Relations Efforts
Using the Departmental Meeting as a Resource

By Jacqueline Seewald

AS AN EDUCATIONAL MEDIA SPECIALIST, I look for ways in which the media center can develop and promote better public relations within the school community because we need support if we are to get necessary funding to implement our programs. There often are misconceptions about the services the media center can and will provide. Some people still refer to me as the librarian, which, of course, I am; however, it is important for our faculty to know that I can provide many more services for the school.

One way to develop good public relations with members of the school community is to establish a rapport by visiting departmental meetings. Full faculty meetings are too large and impersonal and many things must be discussed by supervisors and administrators. Departmental meetings are smaller and much less formal, and more attention is paid to individual speakers.

Since most meetings are held at the end of the school day when teachers are tired and eager to go home, I like to begin by assuring each department that I don't plan to talk long. Also, supervisors are not always pleased to have outsiders take over their meeting for any extended period of time. Although Ben Franklin said fish and visitors begin to stink after three days, speakers at departmental meetings become odious after about three minutes.

We have recently added new computers and upgraded our hardware, putting in a more powerful file server, an extra CD-ROM tower, and new software programs. At the departmental meetings, I explain how this

Although Ben Franklin said fish and visitors begin to stink after three days, speakers at departmental meetings become odious after about three minutes.

will benefit teacher preparation and student research. I've discussed our newer, faster Internet access and have handed out a dictionary of terms, a bibliography of books related to Internet, and a list of useful educational Internet addresses. I also have handed out an updated list of CD-ROMs in our network and have offered to work with anyone interested in using the network. In addition, I have distributed copies of our CD-ROM manual, which explains how to use the various programs.

Because many teachers are still unfamiliar with various CD-ROMs, software, and computers, they cannot fully use what the media center has to offer in support of the curriculum. It is important that staff members feel welcome and comfortable using media center equipment, whether they're using word processing to prepare lesson plans, maintaining an electronic grade book, or bringing their classes in for research. By receiving an informal invitation at the departmental meeting, teachers are encouraged to use our facilities.

Many staff members approach me after departmental meetings or later and ask about particular CD-ROMs they feel would benefit their teaching. For example, our art teachers were unaware of two new art CD-ROMs that were requested by teachers in the humanities. A guidance counselor who had never used our services before asked to look at our career CD-ROMs. A few weeks later, she arranged to bring in special needs students to research career opportunities.

While that's all well and good for those of us who are fortunate enough to have new equipment and materials to promote to the faculty, what about those who are not as fortunate? There generally are valuable materials in the media center that go unused for one reason or another. Promoting valuable but neglected resources is still another purpose for speaking at departmental meetings.

For example, several years ago, I ordered workbooks on coordinating writing skills with the research process. When these books came in, I mentioned them to teachers I thought might be interested, but for one reason or another, no particular use was found for them. I brought these books to the English departmental meeting. Since it was term paper time and all 11th-grade students had to write an American literature paper, interest was shown in these books. Several teachers borrowed the books, thinking they would benefit their lower-ability students.

If you feel you have something that would benefit the curriculum, you should advertise it, and one good way is by showcasing it at the departmental meeting. It may not be new, but as the song lyric goes, "everything old is new again," made new by our efforts.

I also like to suggest at the departmental meetings that teachers think of planning lessons with me when they involve media center research. I let staff members know that I consider it a privilege, not a chore, to work with them and that I am never too busy. Taking on the extra work is not the result of a masochistic nature but rather a desire to make certain that the research proposed is within the realm of possibility. Sometimes demands are simply unrealistic. Other times, by knowing in advance what is needed, I can put together new research materials where adequate sources might have been too thin for class use.

For example, the social studies teacher involved in a lesson on immigration let me know well in advance that she would be doing research on the immigrant experience in America. We discussed exactly what she would need. Our books in reference and non-fiction were adequate, but I discovered that our vertical file on immigration had disappeared. Therefore, I began creating a new one. I had the opportunity to collect newspaper and magazine articles and put valuable photocopies in the new file. I also sent copies of the particularly useful new articles to the teacher in charge of the research.

Another reason to speak at the departmental meetings is to remind staff of the availability of the interlibrary loan network, a truly valuable resource to the educational community. Every year, I emphasize that if we don't have materials, we can order books and journal articles through interlibrary loans for students, teachers, and administrators. If we haven't got it, we can usually borrow it.

I also state that I am interested in discovering what books, periodicals, or audiovisual materials we don't have that are needed to support the curriculum. Often teachers do not respond to the form I send each spring. A better method of solicitation is going to departmental meetings and asking teachers to let me know what we don't have but should be able to offer. By convincing teachers that their input is important, I get a much stronger response. And teacher input is extremely important. Since I don't teach their subjects, I can't always know the best things to select to support the curriculum. The benefits of meeting in this manner are mutual.

My purpose is to establish a high trust level, so teachers will discuss assignments and be willing to let me share in the conception, planning, researching, and teaching. To be fully integrated into the curriculum, the media center must understand educational needs. The best way to promote good public relations with members of the school community is to demonstrate how useful and important our services are to every department and faculty member.

Attending departmental meetings is one effective way to have our message heard, so we are no longer considered merely support staff by administrators and teachers but are essential to the educational process.

Here is a brief checklist of ideas for educational media specialists to present at departmental meetings.

✔ Indicate that you will speak briefly and stick to that plan.

✔ Explain any changes that are being made in the media center (new equipment, hardware, or software).

✔ Provide handouts that offer more detailed information or that simplify the use of new materials.

✔ Briefly explain what each handout represents without getting too technical. (Give staff credit for being able to read on their own.)

If you feel you have something that would benefit the curriculum, you should advertise it, and one good way is by showcasing it at the departmental meeting.

✔ Emphasize any software or CD-ROM that has special value for the department you are visiting.

✔ Promote or advertise older materials that have been ignored or neglected but that you feel would be useful to this department.

✔ Remind teachers that you are more than willing to work with them on lesson planning, developing worksheets, and research strategy in relation to assignments for their students in the media center. Encourage teachers to think of such teaching as a team effort.

✔ Remind staff members of the value of the interlibrary loan network for themselves and their students in regard to obtaining research materials that are not physically present in the media center.

✔ Finally, ask if there are any questions. If there are, answer them briefly. If someone requests a more detailed answer, suggest that person see you individually unless everyone else is eager for more specifics.

Jacqueline Seewald, Educational Media Specialist, Red Bank Regional High School, Little Silver, New Jersey.

Build Library Support With T.L.C.

Pat Miller

Are you invaluable or invisible to your staff? Do you integrate technology into lessons you plan with teachers? Do you provide resources, suggest Web sites, and co-teach lessons? All these are powerful ways to become useful to your overworked colleagues. However, nothing seems to build good will and support more than old-fashioned tender loving care. Try a few of these ideas to spoil your faculty, and notice how teacher involvement with library programs increases.

Many of your teachers, particularly the new ones, may not know what an asset you are. At the beginning of the school year, make business cards for each teacher, using a word processing program and sheets of perforated cards that can be purchased at an office supply or computer store. Attach a note to the sheet of cards saying, "Let us personalize your library service!" Then list many of the things you can do for teachers to help them with lesson planning and instruction. After we printed this list on colorful computer paper and distributed it, we had many teachers visit the library to say thanks and to take advantage of the services we had promoted.

You can increase interest in the library collection by publishing teacher favorites. For Children's Book Week or National Library Week, ask teachers to provide a list of their 20 favorite children's books. These should be titles available in your library. Type each list in a bookmark form. Under a treasure chest filled with books or a similar picture, add the title "Mrs. Smith's Favorite Books." Make copies for each class, and give them to the teacher to distribute during the national reading week. As an incentive, we gave a coupon for a free book at our upcoming book fair to all teachers who turned in their list by the deadline. We had high teacher participation, numerous student requests for the books, and many positive parent comments.

Special attention is most appreciated during times of stress. To boost teacher morale and attract attention to the library during the week before the Christmas holiday, invite your staff to the library for spiced cider and cookies. I bought a large tin of fancy European cookies, made the cider in a crock pot, and set out plates, cups, and napkins on a festive cloth. Feature holiday books as a backdrop for the refreshments. This inexpensive treat provides a needed break as well as some handy quick reads for those busy days. Something similar could be done for Valentine's Day or before spring break.

A handmade coupon book given to me by one of my preschoolers inspired me to design one for each teacher for the new year. Coupons include things such as "I will teach a jointly-planned lesson in your classroom," "Good for one guest read aloud by me," or "Good for $1.00 off at the book fair." The cover of the coupon book is a bookmark, and all coupons expire by the middle of May. This approach initiates communication, gets you into the classrooms, and brings teachers to you to claim services you are willing to provide.

When you receive a delivery of new books, celebrate with your teachers. Send them an invitation to see your new arrivals. Make the invitation like one for a baby shower. Set the new books on counter tops as well as in bassinets, bathtubs, and strollers borrowed from some of your mothers. Add refreshments and perhaps a door prize and bask proudly as teachers admire your newest additions.

You can show teachers some personal attention by remembering their birthdays. For a special day, place a bookplate in the book of their choice from your collection. Then visit the class during the birthday to read it aloud. This is a hit with students as well as teachers. Make an announcement the morning of the birthday so everyone can wish the teacher well throughout the day. For summer or holiday birthdays, pick an unbirthday. Teachers will enjoy your thoughtfulness and the quiet read-aloud time, and the only cost is the bookplates.

Tension is highest for most teachers during the week of state achievement tests, but you can provide a stress remedy. About two weeks prior to the tests, put a plastic medicine bottle filled with candy in each teacher's mailbox. Buy the bottles from a nearby pharmacy and add a label. Under the name of your library, spelled vertically in capital letters, type *RELIEF*. For each letter, name resources or services in the library suitable for the test week. Library relief can also be used to introduce the library at the beginning of the year or to relieve the doldrums of late winter. On each label, add an Rx for two refills. If teachers bring their bottles back to the library, refill them with candies. As you do, mention any resources or services you think may be appreciated by your "patients." Each refill gives you an opportunity to become invaluable to your colleagues.

Though we are all harried and overwhelmed by our own tasks, the time and effort invested in these perks are definitely worth the return in good will and appreciation. They might be just the thing to take you from invisible to invaluable.

Pat Miller is the Library Media Specialist at Walker Station School Library in Sugar Land, Texas.

Building Influence in the School Library

A newsletter filled with timely and relevant information from a creative and enthusiastic LMC staff can further create a positive image of LMCs.

EXTRA! EXTRA!
Library Newsletters Make Good News!

By Pat McAbee

A successful library media center (LMC) does not operate in a vacuum. As library media specialists, we try to reach as many teachers as possible with up-to-date information on activities and services, new technologies, and recent collection additions. Inundated with paperwork, planning, and committees, in addition to daily teaching duties, a busy faculty is not always able to take advantage of all the resources offered. One method of promoting activities and creating a positive image for our profession is through a library media center newsletter.

According to *Information Power*, "Ensuring consistent positive visibility for school … library media programs is of critical importance." A newsletter filled with timely and relevant information from a creative and enthusiastic LMC staff can further this goal. In a newsletter you can:

1 Request faculty input on collection development. Let the staff know you welcome their expertise and suggestions when ordering new books, periodicals, computer and AV software, videos, and professional library materials. When new materials arrive and are ready for circulation, list titles in the newsletter.

2 Feature a computer software program. As CDs are added to the media collection, publicize one in each newsletter. Include possible curriculum uses and a brief description, such as, "Discovering Careers and Jobs is a computer program that assists students in job searches and career planning, providing access to over 1,200 job titles in over 250 careers. Students will find job descriptions, salary information, training and educational requirements, and lists of publications, organizations, and services related to their chosen career."

3 Include a book talk. To promote literacy and a love of reading, have a student or LMC staff member spotlight a current bestseller, timeless classic, fast-paced thriller, or intriguing mystery with a brief introduction in the newsletter. Match books with seasonal themes, such as a popular new love story in February's issue, or include the latest Newbery, Edgar Allen Poe, or National Book Award winners. Invite teachers to write their own book talks or recommend titles for inclusion.

4 Keep faculty apprised of current laws and policies pertaining to the use of instructional material. In each issue of the newsletter, include information in question-and-answer format on possible copyright infringements: "May I photo-

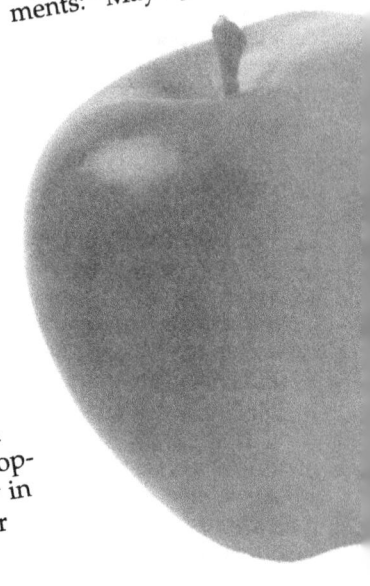

copy materials for an absent student?" "Are e-mail messages copyrighted?" "As a music teacher, may I copy the first movement of a modern symphony for an exam question?" Invite questions from the staff to be answered in upcoming issues.

5 Say thanks. Acknowledgment in the newsletter will be appreciated by students, LMC helpers, adult volunteers, clubs and departments that decorate LMC bulletin boards and showcases, custodial staff, and teachers who frequent the LMC with their classes.

6 Promote special events. During Banned Books Week, educate staff about censorship. Celebrate National Library Week. Publicize local book fairs, technology conferences, and book signings by authors.

7 Provide current Web sites. With access to professional library journals and new periodicals geared to electronic sources, the LMC can be a clearinghouse for the latest Web sites to support the school curricula. Cite Web addresses geared to specific academic areas, such as the Virtual Frog Dissection Kit (science), <george.lbl.gov/ITG.hm.pg.docs/dissect/info.html>; PAWWS Financial Network (business),<pawws.secapl.com>; and Internet Center for Mathematics Problems (math), <www.matpro.com/>.

8 Spotlight a faculty member. Publish brief biographies of new teachers. They'll enjoy the attention, and other faculty members will get to know them better. I learned that among *our* faculty there is a judo expert, frog collector, gourmet cook, gospel singer, and devoted Trekker.

9 Spread the word about successful LMC research projects. Publicity of a unique or especially rewarding class project is a good public relations tool. Let teachers know the LMC staff is eager to collaborate with them when planning lessons that involve LMC research. For example, by spotlighting a U.S. history project on the Roaring '20s (from Buster Keaton, flappers, and ragtime to Al Capone, yo-yos, and Charles Lindberg) that proved to be an exciting and successful collaboration between the teacher and library, the media specialist might increase usage of the LMC and promote other instructional partnerships between the library and teaching staff.

10 Use a book quote, cartoon, or humorous anecdote as filler between longer articles or to add to an attractive layout design. Insert amusing stories, quotes, or cartoons that involve books, reading, and libraries. Faculty will look forward to "Media Mirth" items. Be sure to follow copyright laws on reprinted material. ■ ■

PRESENTATION TIPS

Use brightly colored paper, fonts of different styles and size, and appealing visuals and graphics.

Create a catchy title and logo.

Edit carefully for grammar, spelling, and punctuation errors.

Before distributing newsletters to the staff, be sure to get the principal's approval.

For a professional look, use a good computer desktop publishing program.

Pat McAbee is a Library Media Specialist at Princess Anne High School in Virginia Beach, Virginia.

Partners in Learning

TWO FOR THE ROAD

By Ann Dempsey

Taking a car trip can be seen as a metaphor for the process of teaching. A vehicle (classrooms, learning resources) is used to get teachers and students from where they are (the beginning of each school year) to where they want to be (the end of the school year, having obtained a set amount of information along the way). In this scenario, teachers are the drivers.

ON THE ROAD AGAIN

Let's think for a moment about the process of getting from here to there. Usually, some sort of navigation is required, but have you ever tried to navigate yourself while driving? It requires either attempting to read a map while in transit or pulling to the roadside frequently to check the map. A more efficient way is for the driver to rely on a passenger to help navigate. With one person reading the directions and two people interpreting them, the driver has a better chance of getting where he wants to go.

Now think about getting to your destination. If the driver doesn't have a firm destination in mind, he may wander through many cities and states before finding a site that meets his expectations. If the driver knows exactly how to get to a destination, many wonderful sites along the way may be overlooked out of sheer habit.

Let's say the driver has a passenger help with navigation. Has the driver ever traveled with this person? If not, he may not know if this person can be trusted even to distinguish north from south, let alone calculate mileage in six-point map font. In this situation, the driver might want to go on day trips with the navigator before relying on him to get them cross-country. Eventually, the driver will learn that the navigator is able to be of real help.

On the road of learning, schools should provide a smooth journey for students. To accomplish this, teachers — the drivers — select destinations based on curriculum, keep abreast of current teaching techniques, and make use of the resources that fit best with their

• • • • • • • • • • • • • • • • • • • •

Trade in your jalopy for a new model and reeducate your faculty and administrators about your contributions to the instruction at your school.

• • • • • • • • • • • • • • • • • • • •

objectives. Given such huge navigational tasks, however, teachers should collaborate with other teachers, instructional specialists, and media specialists — the navigators — to ensure that the students' journey is as productive as possible.

Teachers often try to navigate and drive simultaneously, however, instead of relying on the experience of media specialists, who make great "copilots" on this trip. With knowledge of resources outside the four walls of the classroom, familiarity with teaching information skills, and an understanding of objectives, media specialists can complement teachers to build an effective navigational team. It will take work, time, and patience to convince teachers that you make a great copilot, but the rewards — for you, the teachers, and the students — are worth the effort.

POTHOLES ALONG THE WAY

Why don't teachers collaborate with media specialists more often? There are four common reasons. First is a lack of preplanning on the part of teachers. Last-minute lesson plans and requests for media may produce lessons by Monday morning, but they don't allow time to find appropriate media to meet the teaching objectives nor to collaborate with the media specialist.

The second reason is a lack of time. Teachers are already overwhelmed with paperwork and meetings. The last thing that they want to do is initiate another meeting or project. If anything, teachers will informally collaborate with the media specialist in hallways or at lunch. This may not lead to teaching lessons collaboratively but it is a start.

The third struggle teachers face is to change the way they teach from one year to the next. Teachers need to evaluate the abilities of each new group of students, then adjust their instruction, techniques, and media to meet those abilities. The media specialist is a great resource for matching media to student abilities. Yet, if the media specialist is new to the school or to the profession, it may be hard for teachers to trust his judgment or even to ask for his opinion. This is the fourth pitfall in collaborative planning.

ROAD REPAIR

Media specialists, whether seasoned or new, can patch all of these holes with a little public relations work. Three actions that will help are building an area of expertise, informing teachers of how you can assist them, and letting administrators know about your important role in the instructional process.

The key to successful collaboration is building a working trust with teachers, and defining your area of expertise will help you develop a good relationship. If you are a trustworthy source of knowledge and resources in one area, teachers will begin to rely on you for information about that field and others, as well. (A suggestion: You may not want to put all of your expertise into troubleshooting technological problems. This easily could turn into a full-time job. Prioritize by helping only with a technical problem that is interrupting instruction at the moment.)

The other two public relations tasks are linked. Neither teachers nor administrators get any formal training on the role of the media specialist in a school. Teachers are usually inherently interested in media center procedures because these procedures affect their students. A great time to generate teacher interest in the media center is at the year's first faculty meeting. Take that opportunity to let teachers know you are interested in working on lessons with them and to encourage informal and formal planning. If you let teachers know what you have to offer and how you can help them, they just might take you up on it.

On the road of learning, schools should provide a smooth journey for students.

• • • • • • • • • • • • • • • • • • • •

Administrators don't have quite the same stake in the media center as teachers do, but they can become interested allies. Find your administrator's favorite way of communicating (e-mail, memo, in person) and keep him or her updated on media center events. Try passing along interesting articles about topics concerning your media center.

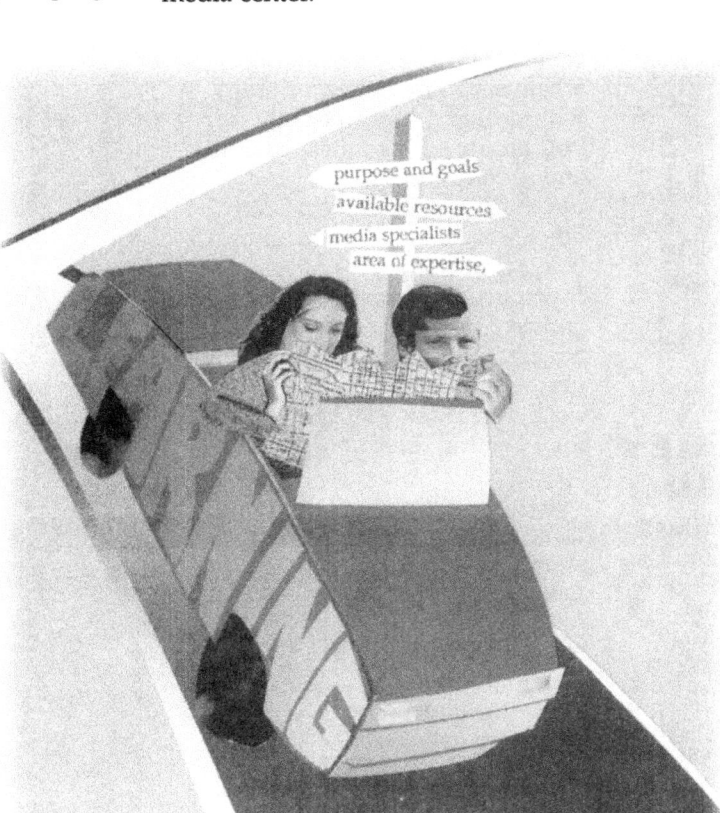

FINDING ROAD SIGNS

Many teachers are unaware of the resources available at their school and beyond. Provide information about the resources you have to offer, such as books, models, or Web sites, by including a "resource of the day" component in your school's daily news announcement. If your school utilizes a closed-circuit broadcast system, post an announcement on the television screen and leave it there all day. Create links from the library Web page to outstanding instructional sites. Or create links to classroom Web pages, which are increasing in popularity. Assist teachers in creating a Web page for publishing student work.

Once teachers are familiar with the wealth of available resources, they may be more comfortable consulting with you on ways to use those resources during instruction. Ultimately, some teachers may come to trust and rely on you so much that they will choose to collaborate with you not only on planning lessons but also on teaching lessons.

A good place to begin planning a co-teaching lesson is with a form that provides the necessary information and allows you and the teacher to formulate the lesson's purpose and goals. The last thing a teacher wants to do is fill out another form, however, so create one as simple as possible. The form that has been helpful for me has a top portion for information about grade level, unit of study, length of study, objectives to be met, and skill development, and a bottom portion divided into teacher responsibilities and media specialist responsibilities. The teacher has to complete only the top portion.

In addition, the left side lists steps for teaching information literacy. These steps could be adapted to the Big Six™, "I Search," or any other information skills model you use. If the teacher has already planned some parts of the unit, those ideas can be listed next to the appropriate step in the process. If not, the media specialist can start the ball rolling by jotting down a few suggestions in either the media specialist or teacher responsibilities section. As you and the teacher add to the unit, the form can be jointly updated.

A suggestion: When co-teaching lessons, make sure the logistics are clarified beforehand. Never assume that your collaboration form has made everything clear. Some teachers assume, for instance, that if the media specialist is teaching, they aren't needed and are free to leave. Teachers need to understand that the part of the unit you will teach is not a stand-alone lesson. Teachers need to be present so that they will be able to build on the information you're teaching when they take over again during later lessons.

SOME FINAL THOUGHTS BEFORE YOU HIT THE ROAD

Even if you've done everything you can think of to communicate with teachers (such as attending team and curriculum meetings, and corresponding via e-mail), there will still be teachers who are reluctant to collaborate, either closely or at all, with media specialists. Such teachers may fear that you will ask them to teach with a resource — especially a technological resource — that they are not comfortable using. If this is the case, offer to train these teachers to use technology and other resources so they will feel less intimidated by them. Such training will also save you from some emergency calls asking for your help with technological problems.

As you work toward changing teachers' awareness of your usefulness, keep in mind that their

Will the teachers at your school be able to depend on a collaborative partnership with you, their media specialist, to help them reach their destination or will they drive in circles, not trusting you to copilot?

initial perceptions of you will affect how willing they are to attempt collaboration. As they observe you each day in the media center, they'll be determining whether you manage your job with skill and control or whether you simply have too much to do and spend most of your time responding to emergencies. In other words, they'll see you as being either proactive or reactive. If you usually serve as a resource gatherer for a project that is already underway, a technical troubleshooter/repairperson, or a storyteller during planning time, you probably are perceived as being in a "reactive rut." Although all of these tasks are part of our job, they should not consume it. All faculty members profit from a proactive media specialist. Being proactive also makes your job less stressful.

Will the teachers at your school be able to depend on a collaborative partnership with you, their media specialist, to help them reach their destination or will they drive in circles, not trusting you to copilot? If you've been in a "reactive rut" as a media specialist, trade in your jalopy for a new model and reeducate your faculty and administrators about your contributions to the instruction at your school.

Ann Dempsey is a Media Specialist at Golden Isles Elementary in Brunswick, Georgia.

NOTES

Public Relations: Celebrating Your Library

By D. Jackson Maxwell

In this time of educational reform, library media specialists can play a proactive role. An idea central to nearly all reform models is the need for community-school interaction. As media specialists, we can serve as catalysts for creating this interaction. The word "media" starts with "me." By assuming the role of liaison between our schools and the media, we can project to the community positive images of the library and school. By publicizing accomplishments, librarians can help build strong community support, increase student self-esteem, and provide records of success for our schools.

Introduction

Hamilton Elementary is an urban, community-based public school in Memphis, Tennessee. It serves 750 students. Hamilton Elementary entered the reform process four years ago. Surveys told those in charge of school redesign that the stakeholders did not feel they were adequately informed of school activities. They were unaware of many programs designed to enhance learning, both within the school and the community.

At this point, I took up the challenge of establishing better community-school contacts. To this end, I have actively sought media partners to broadcast Hamilton Elementary's messages of success. These examples demonstrate how media partnerships promote the school.

Newspapers

The local newspaper is a good initial partner. The rewards of getting to know education reporters are great. Too often, all we see are negative articles about schools and students. One reason is that no one is informing the newspaper of the good news. Reporters are seeking positive stories, so send a fax or e-mail to let them know about worthwhile events happening at your library. You will be surprised how many of these suggestions make it into the newspaper.

Hamilton Elementary averages 10 newspaper articles per year. Reporters now contact me when they are looking for stories. The articles promote creative student programs and reward volunteers through press coverage of their charitable work.

Television and Radio

Like newspapers, television and radio are looking for good stories. Children who succeed make good press. Establish contacts through phone calls and press releases. Press releases are short news accounts telling the name, date, time, and purpose of an event with a description of why it is newsworthy. Television and radio stations need a week lead time, so make sure the assignment desks are informed early.

Use radio stations to announce awards. Talk/News stations have been very receptive to school news. Following these broadcasts, your school will probably receive some congratulatory messages.

Seek television coverage for more visually stimulating events. At some stations, a reporter may be assigned to report only good news. Get to know this reporter and make sure he is aware of programs like a puppeteer troupe, the school carnival, and library media center special events. My experience has been that television coverage materializes every other time you request it, so persistence pays.

Electronic Media

As technology proliferates, the educational community finds itself telecommunicating more and relying less on traditional interaction. Electronic publications are another excellent way to connect with stakeholders. Extend the library's message by establishing a home page, publishing in e-zines and electronic journals, and providing an e-mail address.

Web sites provide an additional link between community and school. Use the site to inform parents of teacher assignments, upcoming events, school calendar, and extracurricular activities. Create pages dedicated to the library media center that describe special programs, feature pictures of student accomplishments, and list library achievements. Today, user-friendly software such as *PageMill* makes home page construction relatively simple, so you might consider serving as Web master.

Electronic or online publishing has also become easy. Students or teachers can submit work to an ever-increasing number of online publications (examples include *Kid Pub*, <www.kidpub.org/kidpub>, or *Cyberkids*, <www.cyberkids.com>. This is a quick way to put out quality work for public viewing. Use *ERIC Documents* to publish research findings, technical reports, and instructional materials resulting from projects at your school. Instructions for ERIC authors are available at <ericir.syr.edu/ithome/bnauthor.htm>. Online publishing keeps the community aware of exciting learning occurring in your school. Always include your e-mail address on library correspondence so readers can contact you.

Newsletters

Newsletters can be utilized for brief mentions of your latest success. School newsletters, school board and state publications, and college and professional newsletters can all be used to spread information. Many of these mailings come with a form requesting news of school activities. These publications offer the opportunity for librarians to announce their accomplishments far and wide. School board and state education newsletters allow "bragging," including pictures and descriptions of student projects.

These publications are also a good place to announce grants. Once you announce in a newsletter that your school or library has received a grant, teachers and others will approach you to learn how to write similar grants. Academic and professional newsletters allow librarians to notify others of recent publications and awards. Newsletters can keep your name in the news. They can also introduce you to colleagues.

Journals and Magazines

Journals and magazines provide an opportunity for professionals to share their accumulated knowledge. Through either formal research or informal practitioner reports, we can make others aware of programs we have developed.

Assume the role of liaison between your school and the media to project positive images of the library and school to the community.

• •

Numerous library, education, child psychology, teaching, and technology publications seek practitioner articles from experienced educators on a variety of topics. These venues provide a global audience with whom to share your school's successes.

Conferences, Meetings, and Workshops

Conferences can serve to showcase library accomplishments. These events bring together many of the top people in the education field. By presenting research you have conducted, you can inform others of your undertakings. Conference and roundtable formats permit discussion of issues with peers and introduce programs and projects to wider educational circles.

Meetings and workshops provide a chance to meet and interact with parents and community members. Parent Teacher Association (PTA) gatherings are great places to announce library projects. PTA meetings can be used to notify stakeholders of area resources, public library services, and adult education courses. Presenting technology workshops for teachers, students, and community members helps build positive lines of communication and good will toward the library and its services.

Honors and Awards

Nominating students, fellow teachers, administrators, community members, and other librarians for honors and awards lets others know they are appreciated. This is an inexpensive way to recognize achievements. Even if they do not receive the honor, most nominees are notified of their consideration as a candidate, which in itself is an honor. Additional awards may come from collaborative efforts between media specialists and teachers in the form of recognition or monetary gains.

Conclusion

"Media" starts with "me," and it is up to each of us to make positive changes in the learning environment. Library media specialists are in a unique position to serve as information brokers and providers for their school. We have the resources and the skills to locate and generate positive news coverage for our libraries and schools. By promoting the accomplishments of students and teachers, you create a positive image of your school in the community, district, city, and state. Working with the various media outlets develops powerful allies, should your school ever need them.

Library media specialists can step forward and take a proactive role in the reform process, helping to make our schools more effective environments for learning. By broadcasting to the community what is right and good about our libraries and schools, we take a huge step toward creating positive self-images and pride in our educational institutions. By taking the lead in promoting and celebrating our schools' successes, library media specialists can help increase our stature as invaluable professionals in the eyes of our communities and in the field of education. LT

D. Jackson Maxwell is a Library Media Specialist at Hamilton Elementary School and an Adjunct Professor at the University of Memphis (Tennessee) and can be reached at <maxwellj01@ten-nash.ten.k12.tn.us>.

NOTES

Public Relations: Celebrating Your Library

Parent-Friendly Web Pages

By Lesley S. J. Farmer

Who wants the best education for children? Who wants children to have state-of-the-art technology? Who is scared about what children are learning? Parents. As the Internet becomes more ubiquitous in schools, parents wonder: "What is my child accessing? Is my child safe? How can I help my child?" To a large extent, what parents are feeling is a lack of control.

Not surprisingly, some school librarians share that same fear. No longer can the librarian review all materials before students can get their hands on any of them. While some librarians cope with this Internet issue by using software filters or secure gateways, most have concluded that education, in evaluating and selection resources, is a more positive and proactive solution. This approach mirrors the "I can't control the universe around me, but I can control my response to that universe" way of thinking.

Thus, librarians can help parents in their educational role as "first teachers" by showing them how to become more knowledgeable ab out the Internet themselves. From librarians, parents can learn how to guide children in their Internet use and teach their children to become technologically independent. All parties gain more control of interactive processes—and I promote self-control.

But how can librarians and parents work together? PTA meetings typically have set agendas, but some parents don't attend those events—let alone "extra" parent education workshops. School bulletins may—or may not—be read. Moreover, a parent might not have any interest in the Internet when the librarian brings up the topic, but that same parent might frantically seek help when their child reports that "some man talked dirty to me on the computer."

These issues and constraints point to the potential of instructional 24/7 Web pages, that is, interactive professional information available anytime, 24 hours a day, seven days a week. Even if parents don't have access to the Internet at home, they usually can get their hands on a machine at work, in a public library, or at the school itself. Frankly, parents are more likely to access the Internet than take time to talk with the librarian. Once they know that the library has such a service, parents are more apt to use that information—and will return to the site if it helps them. Particularly because parents are busy people who want information on-the-spot (rather like students with papers due the next day), those Web pages must answer parents' questions—and be "parent-friendly." Children benefit indirectly when their parents have sufficient access and understanding of the Internet. Here are some tips to make access better for kids—through their parents.

First Impressions

The first impression upon opening a Web page is an important one. People make assumptions about each other upon first glance, for example: "He looks tired" or "She's really in a hurry." So, too, do they make assumptions when they open a Web page for the first time. Is the page easy to read? Does it look cluttered? Are there typographical errors? Does it have inviting graphics? Is this page for me?

Library Web pages for elementary grades can fall into the trap of looking so cutesy that a parent thinks that it's ONLY for children. If all that shows on the opening "splash" screen is a reading teddy bear, parents may wonder if they happened upon a literate "beanie baby" site. The library's intent must be immediately apparent. A simple introduction is needed such as "Welcome to 'Ourtown' School's Library Web Page. We're here to tell you about the library, and how you can get information from around the world to help you and your family." Fortunately, most youngsters don't mind sharing "their" library Web page with their par-

> *Librarians can help parents in their educational role as "first teachers" by showing them how to become more knowledgeable about the Internet themselves.*

THE TECHNOLOGY CONNECTION:
BUILDING A SUCCESSFUL LIBRARY MEDIA PROGRAM

CHAPTER 6
THE OPEN HOUSE: LIBRARY MEDIA SPECIALIST AS HOST/HOSTESS

ents, so an opening heading or button marked "Special for Parents" is usually acceptable for students. Teenagers may warrant a "Teens Only" site, with parents accessing the main school page for library information pertinent to their needs. In fact, every library should be sure that its page is linked on the school's first Web page screen. Fortunately, with more schools using "frame" scripting, headings for different aspects of the school are easier to incorporate in the "front page." In any case, the library must clearly appear available and accessible to parents.

Professional-looking graphics enhance the page, and should help tell the library's story by showing students and adults working together and illustrating different types of resources and services. What images characterize that library? Graphics should not overpower the page, and they need to be downloaded quickly, especially by families with slow modems. Smaller images, use of simple background color, or colored text can add dash without adding hours of load time. (Note: JPG files are better for photos and gradated graphics; GIF files are better for line art and icons.) Images can also be misleading, particularly if parents are not familiar with icons. Novice Web users may not even realize that they should click on the image in order to get information. Thus, descriptive terms should accompany any image, for example: "information" beside a question mark, "librarian" beside the national library symbol, or "sports books" beside a basketball. Additionally, if parents primarily use a language other than English, keywords in those languages should be supplied—with a link to a translation program such as the one offered by AltaVista.

Content for Kids

Most parents want their children to be comfortable on the Internet, and most parents want to feel comfortable themselves when they see their kids exploring cyberspace. So when adults look at the library's Web page, they want to see that the library is guiding children to good sites. What does "good" mean? Educational, safe, and fun. Parents know that their children will be more likely to use the Internet wisely if interesting sites are immediately accessed. Children who are successfully engaged in positive Internet action are less prone to be bored and frustrated—and tempted to go to an inappropriate site.

Because so much of the Internet is geared to adult interests and reading levels, it is helpful if elementary school librarians display a short list of "Try These First" URLs. Specific sites might be highlighted. Megasites linking to other URLs can be a rich supply of online sources. In fact, librarians may develop a menu screen that links to desired pages but inhibits free-roaming URL typing. The Yahoo! site offers a search directory called Yahooligans, which is specifically geared toward children. Many library systems these days, both in public and school settings, have such pages, which makes it easy for the Web-challenged librarian to provide access. Academic institutions sometimes see access to youth sites as part of their mission. One such site is <http://sunsite.berkeley.edu/KidsClick!>. The American Library Association (ALA) also has a fine list available at <http://www.ala.org/parents/index.html>.

The library Web page can also link to unit-specific Web sites. With the advent of more resource-based and collaborative learning, Internet sources offer options for students of different reading levels and learning styles. As classroom teachers work with school librarians to design meaningful activities, relevant URLs can be found—and noted on the library's Web page. A new feature of the Internet is Web-based lessons. For example, WebQuests, designed in collaboration with Pacific Bell, offers simulations that incorporate online sources. Students can work on these projects at home with the library providing instant remote access. The library can also link to teacher's individual pages, which might include homework assignments or class readings.

Another possible feature of library Web pages is an online homework

> Most parents want their children to be comfortable on the Internet, and most parents want to feel comfortable themselves when they see their kids exploring cyberspace. So when adults look at the library's Web page, they want to see that the library is guiding children to good sites.

help option. The American Association of School Librarians (AASL) offers the successful KidsConnect link <http://www.ala.org/ICONN/AskKC.html>, which permits students to ask real librarians for academic help. Volunteers usually answer students' questions within 24 hours, suggesting research strategies or likely sources. Depending on time commitments, the local school librarian can offer the same service via e-mail, if the address is hot-linked on the Library Web page.

Thus, by using the library Web page as the opening screen page when the Internet is accessed at home, parents can feel more comfortable as they divide their time between supervising the family and doing evening chores.

Content for Parents

Parents need their own information, be it about technology, the school, or parenting issues. Information to parents about the Internet is becoming more common. Again, the ALA's site for parents provides a good introduction to features of the Net as well as guidelines for effective family use. Another site that helps ease parents' minds and offers good suggestions is <http://www.safekids.com>. Parents may want to do more than peer over their children's shoulders, though—they may want to experience the Internet first hand. The AASL's ICONnet service includes a series of online "courses" on Internet basics at <http://www.ala.org/ICONN/index.html>. These high-quality programs may be accessed gratis by parents as well as librarians. Several university libraries provide online Internet tutorials as well, such as <http://multiweb.lib.calpoly.edu/infocomp/modules/index.html> and <http://library.jmu.edu/library/gold/modules/htm>. Professional organizations offer online guidance for teachers, but parents can also take advantage of these programs at <http://www.iste.org>, <http://www.cue.org>, and other sites. Naturally, technology companies provide online guidance too (e.g., <http://www.apple.com> and <http://www.ibm.com>).

Parents may also use the Internet to further their own education in raising children. The National Parent Information Network facilitates the exchange of parenting information at <http://ericps.edu/uiuc.edu/npin/npinhome.html>. Parenthood Web, <http://www.parenthood-web.com>, provides practical advice. For health issues, parents can connect to <http://kidshealth.org/contents.html>. There are also sites for specific kinds of family needs (e.g., <http://www.parentswithoutpartners.org>, <http://www.mommytimes.com>, <http://www.fostercare.org/FPHP>, and <http://www.missingkids.org/index.html>). The Southwest Educational Development Laboratory site <http://www.sedl.org:80/hscp/welcome.html> suggests ways for parents and educators to collaborate. Not surprisingly, the U.S. Department of Education has a site, <http://www.edu.gov/PFIE/index.html>, with a similar mission.

Filling the Need

To best serve parents' needs and address their interests, school librarians do well to talk with PTA and Friends of the Library groups about ways that the library can serve them. Librarians gain credibility as they listen and respond to school community ideas, and the people they consult may even recommend valuable sites to include on the library's Web page. Who knows; the library may even get donations for Web development software or a Web server! And students gain more educated parents who feel more in control of the Net—for themselves and their children.

> Librarians gain credibility as they listen and respond to school community ideas, and the people they consult may even recommend valuable sites to include on the library's Web page.

Lesley S. J. Farmer is an Associate Professor at California State University, Long Beach, California.

By Jacqueline Seewald

Advocacy for School Libraries

ADVOCACY
Building Influence at the Grass Roots Level: Closing the School Year With Positive Public Relations

Media specialists may be out of jobs and funding for their programs if awareness of the need for advocacy and grass roots public relations goes unrecognized.

Essentially, advocacy is a two-headed coin: one side offers the big picture, the other an engraving in miniature. Each side is equally important. Gary N. Hartzell, an educator himself, deals with both aspects very well. He is, among other things, the author of *Building Influence for the School Librarian* (Linworth, 1994). He advocates: first, consciously striving to build influence where you work. In an ALA speech entitled "Power Is Not a Dirty Word," he urges media specialists to build power and influence with the building principal since he/she controls needed resources. Secondly, Hartzell urges writing articles and making presentations for educators other than librarians. Third, he suggests becoming active in state and national school library associations (we might add local organizations as well). Lobbying legislators and letting them know that librarians are politically involved people can only help our situation.

What can we do to build influence at the basic-grass roots level, namely in our own school and community? The answer is "quite a good deal!"

As we approach the close of the school year, it would be very easy to forget that public relations is still important. Keep in mind our priorities; we have to remember that our program is our promotion; likewise, our promotion is our program. The key word here is involvement, and it is something that requires vigilance; it can never wind down or end. What follows are practical suggestions that will help you create a significant sphere of influence.

Spring Ordering and Inclusion of Staff
Make up a form to place in every faculty member's mailbox. This form will explain that ordering of new books and materials for the next year is in progress and ask staff for their input. This lets everyone know that their ideas are valued. Who better to tell you what is needed in the collection than those people who use it? Also, it puts the faculty on notice that it is the time to state their needs.

List of New Materials
Bring out a list of any new materials. Hold back some materials so that something new will appear in June.

Internet Resources
If you have the Internet available in your media center, provide a list of Web addresses next to each computer. It can be especially geared to each month. (For June, job opportunities are good). Or, if time does not allow this, subscribe to one of the many magazines that offer Web addresses. For example, Central Jersey Library Cooperative offers *Tom's Quick Guide to the Internet*, which is updated monthly.

Also, consider setting up your own Web page. This too can be wonderful PR—a way of letting the community know you exist.

Bookmarks
Don't forget to provide new bookmarks. Students enjoy seeing these each month. It gives them the idea that books are important, and establishes good PR with teachers and students alike. Offering a little something extra, like attractive bookmarks, does not go unappreciated or unnoticed by students. It also tells them that this is a place where they are welcome. If you welcome them, they will come. And a full house is the best public relations program of all.

Networking
Don't forget networking even as you are closing down. Call the media specialists at the other schools in your district and offer to co-ordinate services with them. Keep an articulation going. It helps prevent isolation since a media specialist is typically the one and only in a given school.

Also, do not forget to contact the local librarians of the public libraries in your feeder districts. Remind them who you are and ask to assist in any way regarding students' summer reading programs.

Establishing Rapport with Students
When I see students reading a book, I ask them about it. When they take out a book I've read, I comment about it. Then I ask them to let me know what they thought of the book when they return it. This is just another way of making students feel welcome and letting them know that the media center staff is interested in them and what they think.

Encouraging the Return of Materials
One way to encourage return of books and materials early on is to send a special thank-you note to homeroom teachers who get their students to fully return their obligations. Sometimes that extra bit of recognition makes a difference in the amount of cooperation given.

The situation with staff members is different. Here, the administration makes our policy. My supervisor wants accountability. I keep a careful list of those who do not return equipment and materials. I cannot sign off their final paycheck if anything is missing. However, my supervisor will sign off as long as he is given some form of explanation. What I always do is send out reminders at the beginning of June to staff as to what each individual owes the media center. After that, I give a friendly, personal reminder. I think of it as "sugarcoated nagging." Almost everything is returned and no one can say that they weren't reminded.

THE TECHNOLOGY CONNECTION: BUILDING A SUCCESSFUL LIBRARY MEDIA PROGRAM

CHAPTER 6
THE OPEN HOUSE: LIBRARY MEDIA SPECIALIST AS HOST/HOSTESS

Media Center as Study Area during Final Exams

During exam week, students are usually discouraged from attending school other than their exam periods to keep the building as quiet and controlled as possible.

However, there are students who have to be in the building for some exam periods because of bus schedules and inability to obtain other means of transportation. Suggesting that students use the media center for quiet studying during exam week can be indispensable to our clients and is the best kind of public relations.

Graduation

Attending the graduation ceremony is important. Our staff is very much involved in the graduation process each year. We prepare senior envelopes, diplomas, and graduation programs. One of the nicest things is having the seniors come to us at the end of the school year and say things like: "Thank you for all the help you've given me these past four years," or "The media center has been my favorite place in the school."

At the graduation ceremony, don't be too shy to talk to parents, board of education members, and administrators. Shake some hands and schmooze a little. Let your school superintendent and principal know you're around and that you care. A little politicking never hurt. What you're doing is reminding folks that you are a member of the team. However, in the long run, what you want to do is create a sphere of influence. It is important that the media center be valued, and as media specialists, we symbolize the school media center.

Attending Board of Education Meetings:

You do not have to go to all of them! But once or twice a year when you might have some praise to give won't hurt. Like chicken soup for colds, it can only help. Perhaps the Booster Club made a donation or some students decorated the media center for a holiday. Did one of the soon-to-be graduates do something special for the media center? Perhaps you have an outstanding volunteer who is graduating? Let the board know you exist and that you're a positive force in the school community. You may get a payday in unexpected funding for those needed computers.

Media Specialist as Information Officer

You are an important resource for the school. As information officer, encourage your staff to use you as a source of information. When asked a question I can't answer, I tell people I'll find out, and then I make certain to do so. After all, I am the reference librarian for the school, just as you are. I'm often asked who a particular faculty member is. I seem to know everyone to some extent as I have contact with the entire faculty. We can provide information when it is called for. But how do we get this across to staff? I'm certain you've heard of the old expression "it pays to advertise."

Create your own billboards. You can make a poster using poster paper or buy ready-made materials from ALA. Hang up posters that are brightly colored and have short, snappy messages. They should say things like: "The Media Center Has The Answers. Bring Us Your Questions."

One way to be available to faculty is to eat in the teacher's room during regular lunch periods. I try to sit with a variety of people. I also rotate lunch periods. Of course, this is easy to do since I work with different classes and must continually vary my schedule. Regardless, it is important to keep lunch periods and break time flexible. During the school year, I've had lunch or break time with almost everyone on the faculty including administrators. Everyone is more relaxed at this time and many different things are discussed that I might not otherwise know about.

Lunch periods are also a good time to talk over possible lessons with teachers who might otherwise feel uncomfortable about asking for team planning. Fitting in is so important. It's too easy for teachers to look upon media specialists as "other." They have to realize that we are not just support staff but fellow teachers who are also professional librarians. We have a lot to offer throughout the school year and we can do a lot for them as well as the students. Otherwise, at crunch time, like during exams when they are busy grading and we are not, there may be some resentment.

> Lobbying legislators and letting them know that librarians are politically involved people can only help our situation.

Running a Summer Reading Book Exchange

During the last weeks of school, sponsor a summer book exchange program. I put in a daily announcement that faculty and students were to bring books for summer reading that they could exchange. Bring a book, take a book, etc. I put books in one box for students and another box for teachers to get things started. Soon, by word of mouth, books were being brought in for exchange by both staff and students. There was no cost to anyone but a good variety of books were exchanged for summer reading. This proved to be a good public relations promotion.

All though the year, I try to demonstrate courtesy and respect for the entire school staff. I treat others in a professional manner, the way I wish to be treated myself. Abiding by the golden rule is the heart of any media center public relations program. If you care, others will too. Your program will prosper as will your influence at the grass roots level, which in turn strengthens your power as a media center advocate.

Jacqueline Seewald is an Educational Media Specialist at Red Bank Regional High School in Little Silver, New Jersey.

www.ingramcontent.com/pod-product-compliance
Lightning Source LLC
Chambersburg PA
CBHW080409300426
44113CB00015B/2454